DATE DUE

Social Withdrawal, Inhibition, and Shyness in Childhood

Social Withdrawal, Inhibition, and Shyness in Childhood

Edited by
Kenneth H. Rubin
University of Waterloo, Canada
Jens B. Asendorpf
Max-Planck-Institute for Psychological Research, Germany

 LAWRENCE ERLBAUM ASSOCIATES, PUBLISHERS
1993   Hillsdale, New Jersey   Hove and London

Lawrence Erlbaum Associates, Inc., Publishers
365 Broadway
Hillsdale, New Jersey 07642

Library of Congress Cataloging in Publication Data

Social withdrawal, inhibition, and shyness in childhood / edited by
    Kenneth H. Rubin, Jens Asendorpf.
        p.   cm.
    Includes bibliographical references and indexes.
    ISBN 0-8058-1219-9 (cloth.)--ISBN 0-8058-1220-2 (paper)
    1. Solitude in children--Congresses.   2. Bashfulness in children-
-Congresses.   3. Inhibition in children--Congresses.   I. Rubin.
Kenneth H.   II. Asendorpf, Jens.
    [DNLM: 1. Inhibition (Psychology)--in infancy & childhood.
2. Shyness--in infancy & childhood.   3. Social Behavior--in infancy
& childhood.   WS 105.5.S6 S6784]
BF723.S624S63   1992
155.4'18232--dc20
DNLM/DLC
for Library of Congress   92-14379
                                                              CIP

Books published by Lawrence Erlbaum Associates are printed
on acid-free paper, and their bindings are chosen for strength
and durability.

Printed in the United States of America
10 9 8 7 6 5 4 3 2 1

Contents

Preface

Social withdrawal, social inhibition, shyness, reticence, and social isolation are terms that conjur up an image of an individual who spends time in solitude, alone, not interacting with others. Oft-times, some of these terms carry with them additional images — social anxiety, felt insecurity, fearfulness, wariness, loneliness. Yet, despite some shared meaning, a cursory reading of the literature suggests that the underlying causal mechanisms and developmental origins of each of these terms may vary. The primary purpose of this book, therefore, is to provide a state-of-the-art perspective on the origins, correlates, and consequences of social solitude in childhood.

Psychologists of varying theoretical persuasions have long held that social experiences are critical to normal developmental trajectories and that the lack of such experiences are worthy of compensatory attention. Surprisingly, however, little empirical attention has been directed to the study of the psychological significance of social solitude for children; as such, the publication of this volume is timely. The timeliness of publication is underscored by the common fact that *social withdrawal, inhibition,* and *shyness,* the terms that share the title of this volume, are often used interchangeably. This has led, no doubt, to a good deal of confusion in the developmental and clinical literatures. Thus, it is thought by some that solitude (howsoever defined) is not a developmental risk factor. One purpose of this volume is to present the reader with an understanding of how both halves of the previous statement can be true — that is, some forms of solitude may reflect maladaptation, others may not; some forms of solitude may predict negative outcomes, others may not.

In an effort to shed new light on the meanings and developmental course of social solitude in childhood, a group of esteemed scholars from Europe and North America was invited to share and exchange information in a lovely, isolated retreat in Doon, Ontario. The three day meeting took place in the summer of 1990; an international audience of researchers actively involved in the study of social withdrawal, social inhibition, or shyness in childhood was led in discussion by those scholars whose chapters are published herein. All but one discussion leader was able to submit a final draft by our final deadline. The product of their efforts is published in this multi-faceted volume.

The intellectually stimulating three-day meeting of scholars and the publication of this book would not have been possible without the financial support of the MacArthur Foundation (USA) and the Social Sciences and Humanities Research Council of Canada. We gratefully acknowledge their generous assistance. Special thanks are extended also to the assistants and secretaries at the University of Waterloo who devoted their precious time to the organizational matters required to bring together, in a rather remote setting, scientists from many countries: Latha Ramasubramanian, the workshop coordinator; Denise Mueller and Christine Schwendinger, Psychology Department secretaries; and Alice Bast, Psychology Department Administrative Assistant contributed enormously to the success of this symposium.

We hope that you, the reader, find the contents of this volume sufficiently stimulating to join us in our quest to better understand the developmental meanings, causes, and courses of social withdrawal, inhibition, and shyness in childhood.

Kenneth H. Rubin
Waterloo, Ontario

Jens B. Asendorpf
Munich, Germany

I

CONCEPTUAL AND METHODOLOGICAL ISSUES: AN OVERVIEW

1 Social Withdrawal, Inhibition, and Shyness in Childhood: Conceptual and Definitional Issues

Kenneth H. Rubin
University of Waterloo

Jens B. Asendorpf
Max-Planck-Institute for the Study of Psychology

What is meant by the terms "social withdrawal," "social inhibition," and "shyness?" Can these terms be used interchangeably? Are they used interchangeably when, for good reason, they should not? Do each of these terms, themselves, carry with them a variety of meanings?

These definitional questions are addressed in this chapter. Furthermore, conceptual, theoretical, developmental, and applied issues are discussed. But, to begin with, it is necessary to provide a rationale for the publication of this volume. From a personal perspective, the most facile way of doing so is to examine portions of two letters I received several years ago. These letters arrived in my office shortly after a description of the *Waterloo Longitudinal Project* (see Chapter 14) was carried in newspapers by the North American wire services.

The first letter provides the reader with a hint about the issues involved in the study of the development of social withdrawal, inhibition, and shyness—issues of biological disposition (Chapters 2, 3, 4, 5, 9), parental attributions and beliefs (Chapter 7), parent-child relationships (Chapters 4, 5, 6, 7), and extra-familial relationships (Chapters 8, 10, 11, 12, 13, 14, 15).

I am a former elementary school teacher and I am very aware of the importance of a child's readiness in all areas—social as well as academic, physical, and emotional.

My daughter and I have never been close. She was one who as a baby would stop crying when I set her on the floor instead of cuddling her. I gave up my career to do special things with her and we oftentimes clash. She prefers doing things alone instead of playing cards with me or other game-like involvement.

We had her repeat kindergarten for social reasons only. She would oftentimes say things like "Susie isn't nice to me." Last March on her own she told me she did not want to go to first grade. She is very passive at school, does not want group attention, prefers to play alone but likes to watch others play (she looks like she wants to be a part of the group but doesn't know how).

I feel that Julie was born this way. This is not because I don't want to blame myself. But this all started when she was a toddler. She was very independent around both of us. My husband is a very close participating member of the family. I know this is hard for you to give any suggestions without knowing our family but we are very close knit and happy. We have real need to help our daughter Julie because I feel it will get much worse for her when she's in school in the fall the whole day.

The second letter concerns outcomes of social withdrawal. It provides the reader and researcher with an urgent sense for the necessity of longitudinal data (Chapters 4, 5, 6, 13, 14, and 15).

I am taking the liberty of writing to you regarding an article in the newspaper last evening entitled "Socially-Withdrawn Child Studied."

I am now 51-years-of-age but definitely can identify with the article which appeared. I just wish—oh how I wish that in-depth studies were done regarding the severity of the problem in my formative years.

I have been employed for 27 years in the same position (stenographer) but my personality problem has been a detriment to me in my adult years.

I recall one instance in my third year of grade school and my teacher approached me after recess with the enquiry "have you no one to play with— I have noticed you standing by yourself at recess for several days now." I recall replying and *LYING*—"yes I've friends." The teacher was observant and I give her credit for this, however, I wish, oh how I wish, something had been done about my isolation at the tender age of 7 or 8. It has been a long, lonely road.

Again my apologies for taking the liberty of writing but am so happy, so very, very happy, that help is in store for the self-isolated child.

Thank you for listening to me.

Taken together these letters, and (a) the belief that social solitude is something that concerns and worries parents (Chapter 7), and (b) that it is perceived as deviant by age-mates (Chapter 11) mark the *lack* of socially interactive behavior for special attention. In the section that follows, we examine the phenomena of social withdrawal and shyness. A conceptual introduction to research on inhibition may be found in Chapter 2.

SOCIAL WITHDRAWAL: CONCEPTUAL AND THEORETICAL UNDERPINNINGS

Normal Developmental Perspectives. From our point of view, much of the *developmental* research extant concerning social withdrawal has its origins, not so much centered on the significance of behavioral solitude or a lack of social interaction in childhood, but rather on the importance of social exchange for normal growth and development. Thus, the conceptual underpinnings for much of the research on social withdrawal are drawn from the writings of Piaget and Sullivan concerning the significance of social *interaction* in human development.

Piaget (1970), for example, believed that the acquisition of knowledge stemmed from the product of an interaction between the subject (ostensibly the child) and the object of his or her attention. When the object of attention is another human, the child's thoughts, beliefs, or ideas are referred to as *social*-cognitions. In Piaget's earliest writings (Piaget, 1926, 1932), the preoperational child's social thoughts, ideas, and beliefs were portrayed as being highly biased in an egocentered direction. Other people were thought to think and feel about the world, and literally to see the world, in ways identical, if not highly similar to the young, preoperational child. In strictly Piagetian terms, the functional invariant of assimilation was considered to take primacy over accommodation. Traditional interpretations of Piaget's early work have suggested that suddenly and discontinuously, at some point in mid-childhood, the child becomes capable of sociocentered thought (Piaget, 1967): "At about the age of seven, the child becomes capable of cooperation because he no longer confuses his own point of view with that of others" (p. 39).

Although European and North American psychologists have long debated the age at which childhood egocentrism wanes, and although there are stage-type models of perspective-taking that suggest the phenomenon need not be considered either entirely present or absent (Selman, 1980), researchers in the 1960s and 1970s used the construct of egocentrism to explain why it was that young, preschool-aged children appeared more aggressive, less altruistic, and less cooperative than their early elementary school-aged counterparts (see Shantz, 1983 for a review). Indeed, to this day, psychologists infer that individual differences in social behavior can be accounted for by deficiencies or competencies in the abilities to (a) understand the thoughts, feelings, and intentions of others and (b) to consider the consequences of one's social behaviors for the self and for others (Dodge, 1986; Rubin & Krasnor, 1986; Selman, 1985; Shantz, 1983).

If perspective-taking in particular, and social cognition in general, does account for the expression of competent social behavior, how then does social cognition itself develop? The answer to this question is addressed in the following quotations:

1. Piaget (1928) believes that the major vehicle for the developmental decline of . . . cognitive egocentrism is social interaction, especially with peers. Conflicts, arguments, and other dissonant interpersonal experiences gradually compel the child to pay attention to perspective differences, and thereby eventually to generate some conceptions and information gathering skills regarding human psychological processes (Flavell, 1970, p. 1027).
2. The individual's cognitive coordinations may be actualized by social coordinations. This means that the individual must coordinate his actions with those of others as a first step towards mastering individualized systems of coordination (Doise, 1985, p. 297).
3. Social interaction may not be necessary for the emergence of some intelligent behaviors . . . but a sine qua non for others (e.g., organizing resources for problem solving utilizing the other people in one's surround) (Hartup, 1985, p. 73).

In short, there are strongly held theoretically driven beliefs that social interaction, and particularly peer interaction, serves as an impetus for the development of mature social thinking. In turn, it is posited that mature, sociocentered thinking provides an essential basis for the production of adaptive social behavior.

These beliefs found empirical support during the 1970s; during this decade, numerous researchers attempted to forge an empirical link between peer interaction, perspective-taking skills, and the development of socially adaptive and maladaptive behavior. For example, evidence for the relation between peer interaction and the development of social-cognition was derived from experimental demonstrations that peer exchange, conversations, and interactions produced *intrapersonal* cognitive conflict and a subsequent decline of egocentered thinking (e.g., Damon, 1977; Doise, Mugny, & Perret-Clermont, 1975). Evidence for an association between the *inability* to perspective-take and the demonstration of *maladaptive* social behavior and the experience of qualitatively poor peer relationshipswas also drawn from experimental work published in the 1970s (e.g., Chandler, 1973). Furthermore, research in the same decade demonstrated that perspective taking skills could be improved through peer interactive experiences, particularly those experiences that involved role-play or sociodramatic play. In turn, such improvement led to increases in prosocial behavior (Iannotti, 1978) and to decreases in aggressive behavior (Chandler, 1973).

From the statements offered earlier, it may be concluded that peer interaction is a significant force in the development of social cognition and, ultimately, in the development and display of adaptive social behavior. Social interaction, by drawing the child into peer groups, allows him or her to understand the rules and norms for these peer subcultures. It is this understanding of norms and of normative performance levels engenders, in the child, an ability to evaluate his or her own competency levels against the perceived standards of the peer group. Thus, in addition to facilitating the development of social-cognition, peer interaction enables the child to make self-appraisals and to understand the self in relation to significant others.

This view is not new; George Herbert Mead (1934) addressed this issue of self definition and identity almost sixty years ago (see also Chapter 12). He suggested that exchanges among peers, whether experienced in the arenas of cooperation or competition, conflict or friendly discussion, allowed the child to gain an understanding of the self as both a subject and an object. Understanding that the self could be an object of others' perspectives gradually evolved into the conceptualization of a "generalized other" or an organized and coordinated perspective of the "social" group. In turn, recognition of the generalized other led to the emergence of an organized sense of self.

From the theoretical perspectives outlined briefly here, it seems clear that peer interactive experiences are essential for normal social-cognitive and social behavioral development. Data supportive of these theoretical premises have led to the conclusion that peer interaction is a highly significant developmental force (see Hartup, 1983; Rubin & Coplan, in press; Schneider, Rubin, & Ledingham, 1985 for reviews). The study of *social solitude or withdrawal* is implicated in this conclusion when one asks about the consequences that befall children who do not interact with peers as often as is the norm for their age group. *Regardless* of the reasons for non-social behavior, whether it is voluntary or involuntary (see Asendorpf, 1990, and Chapter 13), whether it is associated with a biological disposition (Chapters 2, 3, 4, 5, 6, 9) or with felt insecurity derived from a poor parent-child relationship (Chapters 5, 6, 7, 14), those who propose that peer interaction plays a causal role in normal growth and development would likely express concern for the child who fails to interact, at a normal rate, with peers. In summary, one conceptual basis for the study of social withdrawal stems from the theory and data of those who propose that peer interactive experiences are critical for *normal* development.

Abnormal Developmental Perspectives.   A second impetus for studying social withdrawal stems from those concerned with *abnormal development*. The term "social withdrawal" can be found in almost every textbook on abnormal or clinical child psychology (e.g., Achenbach, 1982; Quay & Werry, 1986; Rosenberg, Wilson, Maheady, & Sindelar, 1991; Wicks-Nelson & Israel, 1989). It can also be found on most standardized assessments of abnormal socio-emotional development (e.g., Achenbach & Edelbrock, 1983). The phenomenon is cited consistently as evidence for an "overcontrolled disorder" (e.g., Lewis & Miller, 1990) or an internalizing problem (Achenbach & Edelbrock, 1981). In source after source, social withdrawal is contrasted with aggression as one of the two most consistently identified major dimensions of disturbed behavior in childhood (e.g., Moscowitz, Schwartzman, & Ledingham, 1985; Parker & Asher, 1987). Indeed, the lack of social interaction has been implicated in several DSM-III-R categories of psychopathology (e.g., adjustment disorder with withdrawal; avoidant personality disorder).

Given the seriousness with which social withdrawal in childhood is viewed by clinicians, it is not surprising that a multitude of treatment programs have been developed to help ameliorate the "problem" or to help prevent the negative consequences of the phenomenon (e.g., Furman, Rahe, & Hartup, 1979; Rubin, Hymel, Mills, & Rose-Krasnor, 1991; Strain & Kerr, 1981). Thus, many practitioners view social withdrawal as a problem in-and-of itself, and perhaps with a mind's eye on developmental theory, they believe the phenomenon is a potential cause or reflection of associated difficulties such as poor perspective-taking skills, negative self-esteem, loneliness, or depression.

Yet, despite these clinically derived concerns, it is the case that many clinical researchers have concluded that social withdrawal is *not* a risk factor in childhood (e.g., Kohlberg, LaCrosse, & Ricks, 1972; Robins, 1966). It is important to note, however, that this conclusion has been drawn generally from methodologically and conceptually weak data bases (see Chapter 14 for further discussion). Moreover, it has been unclear whether social withdrawal, as assessed in these early clinical investigations, remotely resembled the measurement or conceptualization of social withdrawal in more recent research. Indeed, it is now known that social withdrawal has a multitude of "faces," some of which may be more symptomatic or predictive of negative psychological outcomes than others (Rubin & Mills, 1988). It is this latter difficulty of definition that has led, in no small part, to our efforts in publishing the present volume.

In summary, it would appear safe to conclude that the study of social withdrawal gains its impetus from (a) theory and research concerning the significance of peer interaction for normal development, and (b) clinical beliefs that the phenomenon reflects disturbance that is worthy of prevention and treatment. It would also appear reasonable to conclude that the term "social withdrawal" conjurs up a wide variety of meanings to researchers; the result of this multitude of meanings may be that, in some disciplines or sub-disciplines, social withdrawal is viewed as an inconsequential force in human development.

DEFINING SOCIAL WITHDRAWAL

Thus far, we have used the term "social withdrawal" to the exclusion of the terms that share with it the title of this volume—"inhibition" and "shyness." It is our belief that these three constructs are intertwined and yet carry with them rather different meanings. The common thread that runs through these constructs is the behavioral expression of solitude. A thorough and extended discussion of the meaning of behavioral inhibition follows in Chapter 2. In this section, a brief historical and conceptual treatment of definitional issues pertaining to social withdrawal and shyness is presented.

What is meant by social withdrawal? Perhaps the most accurate response is "It depends on who one asks." A brief survey of the literature reveals that the following terms have been used interchangeably—social withdrawal, social isolation, sociometric neglect, sociometric rejection, shyness, inhibition, and social reticence.

In the hopes of establishing what social withdrawal is, it seems reasonable to begin by circuitously clarifying what it is *not!* Thus, we commence with reference to the literature on children's peer relationships, particularly manuscripts published in the 1970s concerning peer acceptance and rejection. Definitional confusion abounds in this work; consequently, it is not surprising that the same term may conjur up a multitude of meanings to a given audience.

For example, in the 1970s, a large number of researchers became interested in children's peer relationships and in how children acquired sociometrically assessed acceptance or popularity. One label that sociometricians applied to those who were unpopular amongst or unaccepted by their peers was "the socially isolated child." Oden and Asher (1977) were exemplary in this regard when they began their oft-cited manuscript concerning a social skills intervention program for *unpopular* children by writing, "Children who are socially isolated from their peers have limited opportunities for social learning" (Oden & Asher, 1977, p. 495). They concluded their manuscript by noting that their "coaching procedure was effective in increasing *isolated* children's peer acceptance."

These "isolated children" were unpopular, but were they also socially withdrawn? Did they play alone more often than their less isolated age-mates? And if they were alone more often than their more popular counterparts, was it because they were isolated *by* the peer group or because they isolated themselves *from* the group to begin with? Interestingly, and at the same time confusingly, sociometricians argued that the isolated child was *not* one who had a low frequency of interaction with peers (e.g., Asher, Markell, & Hymel, 1982). Thus, it was proposed that being isolated *by* peers (i.e., unaccepted) was conceptually distinct from socially withdrawing *from* peers. This was an important, but subtle, distinction, and it is one that has gained credence and acceptance in the contemporary literature on children's peer relationships (e.g., Asher & Coie, 1990). However, during the 1980s, this distinction between being isolated by peers and withdrawing in the face of peers led only to controversy and confusion. The confusion was caused, in part, by the sub-classification of different groups of sociometrically isolated children.

In the early 1980s, sociometricians distinguished between children who were actively disliked by their peers and those who received few, if any, positive *and* negative nominations as a best friend or playmate by their classmates (e.g., Coie & Dodge, 1983). The former group was identified as "rejected," the latter as "neglected." Both groups represented sub-classifications of earlier identified "isolated children."

Subsequently, in a series of papers, researchers attempted to examine the "causes" of peer acceptance and rejection. Dodge, Murphy, and Buchsbaum (1984) concluded from their own research that "children who respond with *withdrawal* [in peer situations] have a high probability of achieving *neglected* status among peers" and "that the characteristic behavior of [sociometrically] neglected children is withdrawal" (p. 171). From these statements, one would be led to assume that some children identified in the 1970s as "isolated" were also "withdrawn," despite the aforementioned conclusion reached earlier by Asher and colleagues (1982) that rate of interaction was unrelated to sociometric isolation. The new classification system, however, allowed sociometric isolation to be construed as either active (rejection = many negative nominations) or passive (neglect = few nominations of any sort). From data produced in the early 1980s, passive isolation or sociometric neglect was equated with social withdrawal. The most forceful statement concerning the relation between sociometric status and social withdrawal emanated from the writings of Coie and Kupersmidt (1983).

> These two facts about neglected boys — that they rarely offend others and that they seem to be able to become socially outgoing in new, small-group situations — may account for the evidence that they are not a group that is at long-term risk because of their social adjustment. In a follow-up study of socially withdrawn and isolated children who had originally been referred to the Dallas Child Guidance Clinic but not treated, Morris, Soroker, and Burns (1954) found that these children were not significantly at risk for psychiatric disorder. (p. 1415)

This statement, and others like it, led many researchers to infer an equivalence between sociometric classifications and behavioral prototypes. Sociometrically rejected or disliked children were assumed to be aggressive, sociometrically neglected children were withdrawn. This equation of socio-metric neglect and behavioral withdrawal, when taken in tandem with the consistent finding that sociometrically neglected children rarely differed from their "average" counterparts on measures of psychological maladap-tation (see Rubin & Coplan, in press for a review) gave added strength to the traditional clinical assumption that socially withdrawn children did not represent a group "at risk" for later difficulty.

Two comments are worth making at this juncture. First, there is actually very little empirical research to support the view that children who interact rarely with peers are sociometrically neglected. Indeed, there is growing evidence to suggest that with increasing age, children described as passive, sedentary loners are more likely to be actively disliked rather than passively neglected by peers (see Chapters 11 and 14). Second, the way social withdrawal is generally construed has little to do with peer reputation. Instead, *social withdrawal refers to the act of being alone,* of not interacting with others.

The bottom line is that social withdrawal is a behavioral term that should not be confused with *any* sociometric classification. Furthermore, social withdrawal should not be confused with the term social isolation. One may isolate oneself from the peer group and one may be isolated by the peer group. The former phenomenon is nicely illustrated by the item on Masten, Morison, and Pellegrini's (1985) Revised Class Play, "Someone who would rather play alone." The latter phenomenon is illustrated by the item "Someone who is often left out," which we take as a rejection item. It is entirely possible that there are some children who prefer to play alone and whose play while alone becomes salient and negatively perceived by the peer group. In this case the withdrawn child may become isolated by the peer group. Nevertheless, it is important to distinguish between withdrawal and isolation. Withdrawal has something to do with staying away from the peer group; isolation has something to do with the peer group's staying away from someone (see also Younger & Daniels, in press, for empirical support of this distinction).

Empirically, we have found that indices of withdrawal *from* the peer group are significantly associated with indices of isolation *by* the peer group, especially in late childhood (e.g., Hymel & Rubin, 1985; Rubin, Hymel, & Chen, in press; Rubin & Mills, 1988). But assessments and observations of aggression are likewise significantly associated with isola-tion by peers (Coie & Kupersmidt, 1983; Dodge et al., 1984; Rubin et al., in press). The upshot of these findings is that it would serve us well to distinguish conceptually between terms used in the language of sociometry and terms associated with behavioral observation and assessment.

In summary, it can safely be concluded that *social withdrawal is neither sociometric neglect, nor sociometric rejection, nor social isolation.* What then does this leave us with? For purposes of this volume, social withdrawal refers to a behavior best described as *solitude*. Although this clarifies the meaning of social withdrawal for the reader, it does little to explain the components or factors that may lead to its demonstration. These latter factors allow the distinction between different forms of social withdrawal — namely, passive withdrawal, inhibition, and shyness.

DIFFERENT FACES OF SOLITUDE

For several years, a number of researchers have suggested that solitary behavior can be displayed in many different ways and for many different reasons (e.g., Asendorpf, 1990, and Chapter 13; Rubin, 1982; Rubin & Mills, 1988). For example, drawing from earlier work by Moore, Evertson, and Brophy (1974), Rubin (1982) distinguished between solitary activity that was (a) immature, sensorimotor, and repetitious (functional play), (b) constructive, (c) dramatic, and (d) exploratory. In addition, children could be alone but unoccupied or watching others (onlooker behavior). During the preschool years, or from ages 3 to 5 years, solitary-constructive play was described as adaptive; indeed it was just the sort of activity that preschool teachers nurtured (Rubin, 1982). Solitary-functional and -dramatic play, on the other hand, were characterized as immature and somewhat disruptive. These latter forms of solitude were associated with indices of maladaptation and peer rejection (Rubin, 1982). Onlooker and unoccupied behavior were found to be associated with anxiety and wariness (Asendorpf, 1990).

During the mid-to-late years of childhood, the "faces" (or phenotype) of solitude remain the same, but their meanings (or genotypes) appear to change. For example, at ages 7 and 9 years, solitary-constructive and -exploratory behavior, as observed during free play periods in the peer group, are associated with markers of anxiety, negative self-appraisals of social competence, and lack of peer acceptance (Rubin, Hymel, LeMare, & Rowden, 1990; Rubin & Mills, 1988; Chapter 14). Thus, behavior that appeared to reflect adaptation and competence in early childhood carries with it a different meaning in middle and late childhood.

The frequent display of solitary-sensorimotor and -dramatic play is found to correlate positively with indices of impulsivity and aggression during mid-to-late childhood (Rubin & Mills, 1988). These data may be somewhat surprising to those who believe that dramatic play in childhood represents the pinnacle of ludic activity. However, as early as 4 years, approximately 70% of pretense, *when observed in a group setting,* is carried out cooperatively with others (Rubin, Fein, & Vandenberg, 1983). Solitary-pretense thus stands out like the veritable "sore thumb," especially when manifested frequently in the company of peers.

In summary, children's solitary behavior, when observed in group settings, appears to have a number of different "faces" as well as a multitude of meanings. The faces were described earlier; the meanings are discussed in the following section.

Different Meanings of Solitude. According to Asendorpf (1990, 1991, Chapter 13), the underlying "causes" of different types of solitary behavior are derived from approach and avoidance motivational mechanisms. For example, Asendorpf suggests that there are some children for whom solitude is preferred to social activity. These children may be more object- than people-oriented (Rubin, Maioni, & Hornung, 1976) and thus may prefer to be alone with toys or books. Asendorpf characterizes these children as having a low social approach motive but not necessarily a high social avoidance motive. Interestingly, this particular explanation for solitary behavior is rarely discussed in the developmental literature; when it is discussed, however, the focus is on *young,* preschool age children.

The behavioral manifestation of low social approach motivation seems best captured, *in early childhood,* by solitary-constructive and exploratory activity (Rubin, 1982). Rubin and colleagues refer to this type of play as *passive withdrawal* and during early childhood it is not contemporaneously associated with psychological maladaptation. As noted above, however, this same behavioral phenomenon *does* carry with it negative "baggage" in the middle and late years of childhood (e.g., Rubin & Mills, 1988; Chapter 14). As such, a low social approach motivation may lead developmentally, in some circumstances, to a high social avoidance motive. For example, family relationships difficulties (Chapters 4, 7), ecological hardship (Chapter 14), and peer rejection (Chapters 12, 13, 14, 15) each may contribute to the development of a high social avoidance motive in children whose solitude was originally "driven" by a low social approach motive.

A second type of withdrawn child is one who would like to engage others in interaction but for some reason is compelled to avoid them, *especially in novel settings.* This approach-avoidance conflict may lead to behavioral compromises such as observing others from afar or hovering along the margins of ongoing play groups. Thus, the solitary behavior of these internally conflicted children is not characterized by passive disinterest and solitary-constructiveness, but rather by social wariness. It is this group of children who may be representative of those described in the literature as behaviorally inhibited to the unfamiliar or shy (see Chapters 2, 3, 4, 5, 6, 9, and 13). The root cause of social inhibition, shyness, or wariness may be in the biological make-up of the child (Kagan, 1989, see also Chapter 2). Nevertheless, because these children spend much of their time away from the peer group, they may be described by some as socially withdrawn, but *primarily in novel situations.* It may be that the initial *interactive* experiences of *some* of these children prove negative (e.g., they may be bullied or teased, Chapter 15) or that their initial social wariness is reinforced by over-directive and overly-protective parents (Chapters 4, 5, and 8). As such, what might initially be described as biologically-driven behavioral inhibition to novel social settings may evolve, under some circumstances, into a more general, cross-situational form of social withdrawal (Chapters 4, 14).

It is important to note that shyness or wariness in the face of social novelty may also result from the expectation of negative, or insufficiently positive, evaluation (e.g., being ignored or rejected by others during social interaction, Asendorpf, 1991, Chapter 13; Buss, 1986). The non-social behaviors of these social-evaluatively shy children are probably similar to those of the behaviorally inhibited group described above; however, their onlooking and hovering activities may be less a function of temperamentally (biologically) driven causes than of a fear of being negatively evaluated not only by strangers, but also by members of personally significant reference groups (Chapters 10 and 13).

Finally, there may also be a third group of withdrawn children — those who have high social approach and *low* social avoidance motives! Interestingly, this mix of motives has not been discussed in the literature on social withdrawal. Yet, although these motivational underpinnings would suggest that these children would be rather sociable, it may be that their production of social behavior is incompetent. As a consequence of their social incompetence, these children may be isolated *by* their peers rather than isolated *from* them (Rubin et al., 1990). Rubin and colleagues have observed that these children are the most likely to display solitary-sensorimotor, solitary-dramatic, and aggressive behaviors in the peer group. As such, it may be that their immaturity and aggressiveness leads to rejection and ultimately to their social isolation.

SUMMARY

In summary, *social withdrawal* is an "umbrella" term subsuming all forms of behavioral solitude. It is a highly complex phenomenon that carries with it many "faces" and potential causes. *Shyness* is one form of social withdrawal that is motivated by social evaluative concerns, primarily in novel settings. *Inhibition* is a form of withdrawal characterized by social aloneness or withdrawal in novel settings. The bases for inhibition are conflictual approach-avoidance motives. *Passive-withdrawal,* or quiescent, passive play with objects may have as its original basis a low approach motivation. However, this behavior, if compounded by peer domination (Chapters 14, 15) and rejection (Chapter 11) may lead to negative self perceptions of social competence (Chapter 12). Thus, with time, passive withdrawal may have a dual motivational underpinning—low approach plus high avoidance.

The many faces and mechanisms underlying social withdrawal are described in the present volume. This state-of-the-art perspective on the phenotypes and genotypes of social withdrawal will provide the reader with an appreciation for why it is that the phenomenon has proved so "slippery" to developmental, social, and clinical psychologists. Indeed, although different "faces" of social withdrawal or solitude are described herein, it will be clear to the reader, upon completion of this volume, that there remains a critical need to examine whether different forms of solitude are equally benign or malignant vis-à-vis their association with or prediction of adaptive or maladaptive behavior. As such, this volume is intended to stimulate rather than satiate the researcher who is interested in the topics presented in this volume.

REFERENCES

Achenbach, T. M. (1982). *Developmental psychopathology.* New York: Wiley.

Achenbach, T. M., & Edelbrock, C. S. (1981). Behavioral problems and competencies reported by parents of normal and disturbed children aged four through sixteen. *Monographs of the Society for Research in Child Development, 46,* (1, Serial No. 188), 1–82.

Asendorpf, J. (1990). Development of inhibition in childhood: Evidence for situational specificity and a two factor model. *Developmental Psychology, 26,* 721–730.

Asendorpf, J. (1991). Development of inhibited children's coping with unfamiliarity. *Child Development, 62,* 1460–1474.

Asher, S. R., & Coie, J. (1990). *Peer rejection in childhood.* New York: Cambridge.

Asher, S. R., Markell, R., & Hymel, S. (1981). Identifying children at risk in peer relations: A critique of the rate of interaction approach to assessment. *Child Development, 52,* 1239–1245.

Buss, A. H. (1986). A theory of shyness. In W. H. Jones, J. M. Cheek, & S. R. Briggs (Eds.), *Shyness: Perspectives on research and treatment* (pp. 39–46). New York: Plenum Press.

Chandler, M. (1973). Egocentrism and anti-social behavior: The assessment and training of social perspective-taking skills. *Developmental Psychology, 9,* 326–332.

Coie, J. D., & Dodge, K. A. (1983). Continuities and changes in children's social status: A five year longitudinal study. *Merrill-Palmer Quarterly, 29,* 261–282.

Coie, J. D., & Kupersmidt, J. (1983). A behavioral analysis of emerging social status in boys' groups. *Child Development, 54,* 1400–1416.

Damon, W. (1977). *The social world of the child.* San Francisco: Jossey-Bass.

Dodge, K. A. (1986). A social information processing model of social competence in children. In M. Perlmutter (Ed.), *Minnesota Symposium on Child Psychology* (Vol. 18, pp. 77–125). Hillsdale, NJ: Lawrence Erlbaum Associates.

Dodge, K. A., Murphy, R. R., & Buchsbaum, K. (1984). The assessment of intention-cue detection skills in children: Implications for developmental psychopathology. *Child Development, 55,* 163–173.

Doise, W. (1985). Social regulations in cognitive development. In R. A. Hinde, A. N. Perret-Clermont, & J. Stevenson-Hinde (Eds.), *Social relationships and cognitive development.* (pp. 294–308). Oxford, UK: Clarendon Press.

Doise, W., Mugny, G., & Perret-Clermont, A. (1975). Social interaction and the development of cognitive operations. *European Journal of Social Psychology, 5*, 367-383.

Flavell, J. H. (1970). Concept development. In P. H. Mussen (Ed.), *Carmichael's manual of child psychology, Vol. 1*. (pp. 983-1060). New York: Wiley.

Furman, W., Rahe, D., & Hartup, W. W. (1979). Rehabilitation of socially withdrawn preschool children through mixed-age and same-age socialization. *Child Development, 50*, 915-922.

Hartup, W. W. (1983). Peer relations. In E. M. Hetherington (Ed.), *Handbook of child psychology: Vol. 4. Socialization, personality and social development* (4th edition, pp. 103-196). New York: Wiley.

Hartup, W. W. (1985). Relationships and their significance in cognitive development. In R. A. Hinde, A. Perret-Clermont, & J. Stevenson-Hinde (Eds.), *Social relationships and cognitive development* (pp. 66-82). Oxford, UK: Clarendon Press.

Hymel, S., & Rubin, K. H. (1985). Children with peer relationship and social skills problems: Conceptual, methodological, and developmental issues. In G. J. Whitehurst (Ed.), *Annals of Child Development, Vol. 2*. Greenwich, CT: JAI Press.

Iannotti, R. (1978). Effects of role-taking experiences on role-taking, empathy, altruism, and aggression. *Developmental Psychology, 14*, 19-124.

Kagan, J. (1989). Temperamental contributions to social behavior. *American Psychology, 44*, 668-674.

Kohlberg, L., LaCrosse, J., & Ricks, D. (1972). The predictability of adult mental health from childhood behavior. In B. B. Wolman (Ed.), *Manual of child psychopathology* (pp. 1217-1284). New York: McGraw-Hill.

Lewis, M., & Miller, S. M. (1990). *Handbook of developmental psychopathology*. New York: Plenum.

Masten, A. S., Morison, P., & Pellegrini, D. S. (1985). A Revised Class Play method of peer assessment. *Developmental Psychology, 3*, 523-533.

Mead, G. H. (1934). *Mind, self, and society*. Chicago: University of Chicago Press.

Moore, N. V., Evertson, C. M., & Brophy, J. (1974). Solitary play: Some functional reconsiderations. *Developmental Psychology, 10*, 830-834.

Morris, D. P., Soroker, E., & Burruss, G. (1954). Follow-up studies of shy, withdrawn, children − I: Evaluation of later adjustment. *American Journal of Orthopsychiatry, 24*, 743-754.

Moskowitz, D. S., Schwartzman, A. E., & Ledingham, J. E. (1985). Stability and change in aggression and withdrawal in middle childhood and early adolescence. *Journal of Abnormal Psychology, 94*, 30-41.

Oden, S., & Asher, S. R. (1977). Coaching children in social skills for friendship making. *Child Development, 48*, 495-506.

Parker, J. G., & Asher, S. R. (1987). Peer relations and later personal adjustment: Are low-accepted children at risk? *Psychological Bulletin, 102*, 357-389.

Piaget, J. (1926). *The language and thought of the child*. London: Routlege and Kegan Paul.

Piaget, J. (1928). *Judgment and reasoning in the child*. London: Routlege and Kegan Paul.

Piaget, J. (1932). *Six psychological studies*. New York: Random House.

Piaget, J. (1967). *The language and thought of the child*. London: Routlege and Kegan Paul.

Piaget, J. (1970). Piaget's theory. In P. H. Mussen (Ed.), *Carmichael's manual of child psychology, Vol. 1*. (pp. 703-732). New York: Wiley.

Quay, H., & Werry, J. (1986). *Psychopathological disorders of childhood*. New York: Wiley.

Robins, L. N. (1966). *Deviant children grown up*. Baltimore, MD: Williams & Wilkins.

Rosenberg, M. S., Wilson, R., Maheady, L., & Sindelar, P. (1992). *Educating students with behavior disorders*. Boston: Allyn & Bacon.

Rubin, K. H. (1982). Non-social play in preschoolers: Necessary evil? *Child Development, 53*, 651-657.

Rubin, K. H., & Coplan, R. (in press). Peer relationships in childhood. In M. Bornstein & M. Lamb (Eds.), *Developmental psychology: An advanced textbook* (3rd Ed.), Hillsdale, NJ: Lawrence Erlbaum Associates.

Rubin, K. H., Fein, G., & Vandenberg, B. (1983). Play. In E. M. Hetherington (Ed.), *Handbook of child psychology: Socialization, personality and social development.* New York: Wiley.

Rubin, K. H., Hymel, S., & Chen, X. (in press). Socio-emotional characteristics of aggressive and withdrawn children. *Merrill-Palmer Quarterly.*

Rubin, K. H., Hymel, S., LeMare, L. J., & Rowden, L. (1989). Children experiencing social difficulties: Sociometric neglect reconsidered. *Canadian Journal of Behavioral Science, 21,* 94–111.

Rubin, K. H., Hymel, S., Mills, R. S. L., & Rose-Krasnor, L. (1991). Conceptualizing different pathways to and from social isolation in childhood. In D. Cicchetti & S. Toth (Eds.), *The Rochester Symposium on Developmental Psychopathology, Vol. 2, Internalizing and externalizing expressions of dysfunction.* Hillsdale, NJ: Lawrence Erlbaum Associates.

Rubin, K. H., & Krasnor, L. R. (1986). Social-cognitive and social behavioral perspectives on problem solving. In M. Perlmutter (Ed.), *Cognitive perspectives on children's social and behavioral development* (pp. 1–68). The Minnesota Symposia on Child Psychology (vol. 18). Hillsdale, NJ: Lawrence Erlbaum Associates.

Rubin, K. H., Maioni, T. L., & Hornung, M. (1976). Free play behaviors in middle and lower class preschoolers: Parten and Piaget revisited. *Child Development, 47,* 414–419.

Rubin, K. H., & Mills, R. S. L., (1988). The many faces of social isolation in childhood. *Journal of Consulting and Clinical Psychology, 6,* 916–924.

Schneider, B., Rubin, K. H., & Ledingham, J. (1985). *Children's peer relations: Issues in assessment and intervention.* New York: Springer-Verlag.

Selman, R. L. (1980). *The growth of interpersonal understanding.* New York: Cambridge University Press.

Selman, R. L. (1985). The use of interpersonal negotiation strategies and communicative competences: A clinical-developmental exploration in a pair of troubled early adolescents. In R. A. Hinde, A. Perret-Clermont, & J. Stevenson-Hinde (Eds.), *Social relationships and cognitive development* (pp. 208–232). Oxford: Clarendon.

Shantz, C. U. (1983). Social cognition. In J. Flavell & E. Markman (Eds.), *Handbook of child psychology: Vol. 3. Cognitive development* (4th edition, pp. 495–555). New York: Wiley.

Strain, P., & Kerr, M. (1981). Modifying children's social withdrawal: Issues in assessment and clinical intervention. In M. Herson, R. Eisler, & P. Miller (Eds.), *Progress in behavior modification, Vol. 2* (pp. 203–248). New York: Academic Press.

Sullivan, H. S. (1953). *The interpersonal theory of psychiatry.* New York: Norton.

Wicks-Nelson, R., & Israel, A. (1991). *Behavior disorders of childhood.* Englewood Cliffs, NJ: Prentice Hall.

Younger, A., & Daniels, T. (in press). Children's reasons for nominating their peers as withdrawn: Passive withdrawal vs. active isolation? *Developmental Psychology.*

2 On the Temperamental Categories of Inhibited and Uninhibited Children

Jerome Kagan, Nancy Snidman, and Doreen Arcus
Harvard University

Two quiet revolutions gaining momentum in developmental laboratories are marked by an increased interest in the social as compared with the cognitive processes of children, and temperamental as compared with experiential factors. The different cohorts of scientists participating in these two revolutions occasionally encounter each other in studies of the extraordinary variation in social behavior that is so obvious among young children.

The renascence of temperamental constructs is due to many factors, especially to the writings of Thomas and Chess (1977), heightened awareness of intraspecific variation in closely related strains of animals (Pradhan, Arunasmitha, & Udaya, 1990; Scott & Fuller, 1965), and, finally, dramatic advances in the neurosciences that are providing new and surprising facts permitting us for the first time to entertain reasonable hypotheses relating physiology to behavior. For example, few scientists working before the Second World War would have been bold enough to suggest that an imbalance in neurotransmitters was related to serious depression, or that arrested growth of neurons in the limbic area during the prenatal months might be a major cause of autism. Both of these ideas have become popular because their empirical bases provided a scaffolding for possible explanations of very complex behaviors. Scientists are appropriately conservative and resist an explanation that does not rest on a rationale built on facts arranged in a logical argument. The environmental explanation of why a child was fearful, which was popular in the 1940s and 50s, was so familiar and reasonable, most scholars were reluctant to give it up until another equally logical one was provided. Neuroscientists are now supplying new facts that make it possible to suggest interpretations of excessive fearfulness that involve inherited variation in neurochemistry and neurophysiology.

THE NATURE OF THE BIOLOGICAL INFLUENCE

When we shift from a parent's verbal description of the child as the source of evidence to data from the physiological laboratory, we are forced to invent a different set of concepts. The categories that summarize a patient's complaints about chills, cramps, and nausea are different from those that are based on bacterial counts and MRI scans.

As we have written elsewhere (e.g., Kagan, 1989), one class of temperamental categories containing a large number of specific behavioral profiles might be defined by inherited physiological processes that predispose small proportions of children to display particular emotions and behaviors. The features of this class of temperaments are particular combinations of neurochemicals in the cerebrospinal fluid and neurotransmitter tracts, as well as receptor densities for these chemical substances. There are over 150 known chemicals in the brain, including amino acids, monoamines, peptides, and hormones, which, along with their receptors, determine the thresholds of responsiveness in specific parts of the central nervous system. It is believed that the concentrations of many of these chemicals, as well as the densities of their receptors, are under partial genetic control (Oxenstierna, Edman, Iselius, Oreland, Ross, & Sedvall, 1986). The variation in chemistry should be correlated with stable variation in the reactivity of brain sites that influence behavior, emotional reactivity, and chronic mood, especially in the limbic system, basal ganglia, and frontal cortex. Thus, it is likely that the stable differences in behavior and physiology observed among related strains of monkeys, cats, and dogs are due, in part, to the variation in neurochemistry (Blanchard, Flannelly, & Blanchard, 1986; Scott & Fuller, 1965; Suomi, 1987). Even the genetically homogeneous strain of Sprague Dawley rats display variation in behavior in unfamiliar environments, with the less emotional animals possessing lower concentrations of dopamine and its metabolites in parts of the brain compared with highly emotional rats (Pradhan et al., 1990).

The hypothesis that physiological criteria are components of the definition of temperament does not require a reductionistic bias. This view suggests only that some infants are born with a physiology that biases them initially to be more or less likely to develop one rather than another behavioral surface given certain environments. Each child's changing behavioral profile is a historical product of particular, genetically based reactions accommodating to equally particular sequences of experience. A useful metaphor represents each person's psychological qualities as a pale grey fabric composed of many thin black and white threads—symbolic of biology and experience — so tightly woven it is simply not possible to discern any distinctive black or white fibers.

Differential excitability in limbic sites, especially the amygdala and its multiple projections, could be a function of a wide variety of neurochemical profiles, including norepinephrine, corticotropin releasing hormone, glucocorticoids, GABA, and the opioids. It is not possible at the present time to point to any one of these as the critical molecule. We will have to wait for a reduction in uncertainty.

Meanwhile, scientists can make advances in understanding the behavioral components of the definition of temperament. Research in our own laboratory, as well as in the laboratories of others, has determined that about 15% of healthy, Caucasian, one to two year old children are extremely and consistently shy, timid, and fearful when they encounter unfamiliar situations. These children, when faced with unfamiliar people, tend to become quiet and restrained until their anxiety is reduced, timid in the face of challenge or unfamiliar objects, and avoidant of unfamiliar situations. Thus, the term *inhibited* refers not only to a shy demeanor when with unfamiliar children or adults, but also includes restraint, avoidance, and distress in confronting unfamiliar events that are not social. About one-half of these children, whom we call inhibited, retain their phenotype through the eighth year of life. The remaining half develop a normative profile with respect to shyness, restraint, and fear to unfamiliarity. But few become as bold and emotionally spontaneous as a larger group of children, about 30%, who are consistently sociable, spontaneous, and relatively fearless in the second year. These children approach unfamiliar peers and adults, are likely to enter unfamiliar situations with a short latency and are not perturbed by challenge.

Over three-fourths of this group, whom we call uninhibited, retain their style through the eighth year of life. A larger number of the uninhibited children retain their profile because this style is not subject to negative sanctions and is regarded as adaptive by both the child and his or her family. Thus, temperamental qualities are not immutable. A temperamental category simply reflects a slight bias for a certain set of behaviors. The physiology affects the probabilities that certain behaviors will occur, given particular rearing environments. There is always the opportunity for the child to learn to control the urge to withdraw to a stranger or to a large dog. Indeed, the role of the environment is more substantial in helping the child to overcome the tendency to withdraw than in making the child timid in the first place.

THE PHYSIOLOGY OF INHIBITED AND UNINHIBITED CHILDREN

The two temperamental groups differ in peripheral, physiological characteristics in ways that imply differences in the threshold of excitability of the amygdala and its projections to the cortex, hypothalamus, sympathetic nervous system, corpus striatum, and central grey. For example, inhibited and uninhibited children differ in the magnitude of cardiac acceleration and pupillary dilation to mild stress, tension in the skeletal muscles, and magnitude of rise in diastolic blood pressure when their posture changes from sitting to standing. In addition, they tend to differ in salivary cortisol levels in the early morning, with uninhibited children showing significantly lower levels than inhibited children.

It is not unimportant that Suomi and his colleagues have found that a small group of rhesus monkeys who are timid and fearful to the unfamiliar also display physiological characteristics, such as high levels of cortisol and a high heart rate, that resemble the profile of inhibited children (Suomi, 1987). It is likely that continued study of this primate model will provide eventually a deeper understanding of the neurophysiology of inhibited and uninhibited children.

Further, the characteristics of inhibited and uninhibited children show good evidence of heritability. A major research project at the Institute of Behavioral Genetics at the University of Colorado comparing monozygotic and dizygotic twins is finding heritabilities of about .40 for children seen at 14, 20, and 24 months of age. For example, 100 monozygotic and 100 dizygotic, same sex twin pairs were seen in the laboratory at 14 and 20 months of age. Latencies to leave the mother and approach toys in an unfamiliar environment, as well as latency to approach a stranger and a discrepant object were the variables used to index inhibition. In addition, the total proportion of time the child spent proximal to the mother was quantified during a free play period, and during encounter with a stranger and an unfamiliar object. These variables were combined to create an aggregate index of inhibition. Both inhibited and uninhibited behavior showed significant heritability ($h^2 = 0.4$) (Robinson, Kagan, Reznick, & Corley, unpublished).

PREDICTION FROM INFANCY

One important question concerns the qualities of young infants that might be predictive of inhibited and uninhibited behavior in the second year. If these two temperamental categories are influenced by inherited physiological processes, it should be possible to detect early signs of the two categories in the opening months of life.

Clues to the processes one might examine come from two sources. One clue comes from work on animals suggesting that the amygdala, which receives sensory information from all modalities, is the origin of important efferent circuits that monitor variation in motor activity and crying to unfamiliar stimulus events (Adamec & Stark-Adamec, 1986; Dunn & Everitt, 1988; Mishkin & Aggleton, 1981). One circuit originates in the basolateral area of the amygdala which projects to the ventromedial striatum and thence to the skeletal motor system. When this circuit is activated, infants should show an increase in motor activity, primarily in the form of flexing and extending of the limbs. Two other circuits involve the central nucleus of the amygdala (which receives information from the basolateral area) which projects to the cingulate cortex and central grey. Activation of these circuits can produce motor spasticity and arching of the back, and can mediate the distress calls of mammals (Jurgens, 1982). Hence, it is likely that these circuits participate in the distress cry of the human infant. Because high levels of both motor activity and crying to unfamiliar stimuli could be mediated by low thresholds in the amygdala and its projections, it follows that study of these two behaviors might supply early predictors of inhibited and uninhibited behavior.

A second clue comes from the work of Lagasse, Gruber, and Lipsitt (1989) who reported that infants who increase their sucking rate when the water they are ingesting suddenly turns sweet are likely to become inhibited in the second year while infants who show a minimal increase in sucking rate are more likely to become uninhibited. The entire corpus of evidence implies that a combination of high motor activity and frequent crying to novel stimulation might predict the later display of inhibited behavior. The complementary profile should predict uninhibited behavior.

We are studying longitudinally two large cohorts of children who were administered at four months of age a 40 minute battery involving presentation of auditory and visual stimuli. About 20–25% of these infants show frequent and vigorous motor activity—flexing and extending of the limbs, spasticity of the arms and legs, and spontaneous arches of the back—and frequent crying. These infants are called high reactive. About 40% of the infants show low levels of motor activity and rarely cry; these are called low reactive infants.

We have evaluated these infants at 14 months of age. Of the 17 episodes presented to the child at 14 months, the four that were most likely to produce a fearful reaction in the child were:

1. an unfamiliar woman opened the cabinet in the playroom revealing a metal robot and after remaining quiet for a minute, invited the child to approach and play with the robot; failure to approach was coded as fear;
2. small puppets appeared on the left or right side of the child's visual field accompanied by a taped female voice speaking a nonsense phrase in either a happy or emotional tone; crying to any of the ten trials was coded as fear;

3. the female examiner uncovered a rotating toy and spoke a nonsense phrase in an angry tone with a frown on her face; crying to this event was coded as fear;
4. if the child cried and refused to accept in his or her mouth a dropper containing liquid, that response was coded as fearful.

The data indicate that 62% of the high reactive infants were highly fearful (4 or more fears) while only 10% were minimally fearful (0 or 1 fear) when they confronted the battery of unfamiliar people, situations, and objects. By contrast, 59% of the low reactive infants were minimally fearful and only 12% highly fearful in the same contexts (see Table 2.1).

Physiological Reactivity. The infants who were both high reactive at four months and also highly fearful at 14 months differed from the low reactive-low fear children in ways that are in accord with some of the differences found for the older inhibited and uninhibited children (Kagan, Reznick, & Snidman, 1988). For example, the high reactive-high fear children showed large increases in heart rate to a drop of lemon juice, and were likely to have a cooler right than left side of the face to mild stress (based on analysis of thermography images). Further, high reactive infants had higher fetal heart rates and higher heart rates during sleep at two weeks of age while being held in an erect posture. These data suggest that the high reactive infants, many of whom become inhibited children, are under higher sympathetic tone than the low reactive infants (Snidman & Kagan, unpublished).

CATEGORIES VERSUS CONTINUA

It is important to note that we regard inhibited and uninhibited children, as well as high and low reactive infants, as belonging to two distinct qualitative categories. We do not regard the difference between inhibited and uninhibited children or high and low reactive infants as a continuous dimension.

TABLE 2.1
Proportion of High and Low Reactive Infants From Two Independent Cohorts Showing Low (0-1), Moderate (2-3) or High (4 or more) Fear at Fourteen Months (Total N = 430 from both cohorts)

Category	N	Low Fear	Moderate Fear	High Fear
High Reactive	93	10	28	62
Low Reactive	167	59	29	12

chi square = 84.3, 2df, $p < .00001$

American psychologists are prejudiced against positing categories of people, preferring to place individuals on a series of continuous psychological or biological dimensions. We believe that motor activity and irritability to unfamiliar stimuli in four month old infants are derived from different physiological processes; therefore, it seems unwise to sum the two behaviors to produce a derived variable called arousal or reactivity. We make this claim because a child with high motor activity who does not cry is qualitatively different from one who shows high motor activity and cries a great deal. The former child is less fearful and shows more positive affect in the second year. Moreover, the fears of the low motor-high cry child were more often characterized by timidity and reluctance to approach unfamiliar events rather than distress cries, while the fears of the high reactive child were characterized by both distress cries and reluctance to approach the unfamiliar.

Biologists do not base their categories of species on the addition of values on continuous traits like mass, length, or life span. A factor analysis of a dozen continuous characteristics of vertebrates would not reveal the current accepted taxonomy of fish, reptiles, birds, and mammals because it is a profile of characteristics, some of which are discontinuous (for example, internal or external fertilization), that defines a species.

One reason for the continued reliance on continua is the absence of theory to guide the parsing of persons into types. It took us several years to discover the infant reactive types and we would not have generated these categories by thought alone. Empirical measures that produce continuous distributions are easy to obtain; hence, it is prudent to rely on these continua during a pretheoretical era. But as insights occur in separate domains of inquiry, positing types will, on occasion, be useful and I submit will be helpful to theory. In a recent collaboration with Hal Stern and Don Rubin of the Department of Statistics at Harvard University, we compared a linear regression model that assumed motor activity and crying to be additive in a linear fashion in predicting fear in the second year, with a latent class analysis that assumed qualitative categories. The latter analysis was more predictive of the fear score at 14 months; infants who showed high motor activity and infrequent crying were less fearful than a linear regression analysis would predict, while low motor-frequent cry infants were more fearful than the regression model predicted.

There are many illustrations of the principle that as the values of one parameter change quantitatively the constellation of forces affecting a phenomenon can change qualitatively and create unique states. Moreover, related strains of macaques cannot be placed on a continuum of fearfulness or central nervous system arousal because each strain shows a unique profile of behavioral and physiological responses to an imposed stress (Clarke, Mason, & Moberg, 1988). That is why no scientist would combine rhesus and fasicularis monkeys in the study of the effects of a drug on fearful behavior.

Only a small proportion of infants — about 10% — show a combination of high motor activity and frequent crying at four months, high fear in the second year, and large cardiac accelerations to psychological stress. These variables are not positively correlated in a large unselected sample, only in a small group of individuals who inherit a particular temperamental profile. Stated more formally: (1) If each of n dependent variables has more than one origin, and (2) these origins are dependent, (3) but one origin is common to all dependent variables for a small proportion of the sample, then (4) the correlations among the dependent variables will be low, even though there is a category of individuals who is high or low on all of the variables.

The physicist Pierre Duhem in an essay entitled "Quantity and Quality" (1954) noted that most scientists strive to describe their data in mathematical form. Because mathematicians assume continuous magnitudes as a primary axiom, psychologists have preferred to classify all phenomena in terms of continuous dimensions. They also are friendly to the additional assumption that every psychological outcome can be understood eventually as a result of the addition of these magnitudes. But Duhem adds that nature also consists of qualities that cannot be formed simply by adding quantities.

Magnusson and Allen (1983) are also friendly to this point of view, for they believe that delinquent and conduct disorder children are best detected with a profile of biological and behavioral characteristics. This position has always been popular in clinical settings. Even though the I.Q. scores of ten Downs and 90 normal children fall on a continuum, psychologists agree that the two groups are qualitatively different because of the distinctive genetic origin of the former group.

An important implication of this work is a sensitivity to two different members of the family of affects we usually call anxiety. The inhibited child is vulnerable to anxiety generated by unfamiliar people, settings, and challenges. We might call this affect "anxiety to novelty." A distinctively different affect, which might be called "anxiety over one's personal qualities," is acquired as a result of identification with one's parents, class, or ethnic group. Questionnaire scales that are presumed to measure adult anxiety contain heterogeneous groups because an individual can attain a high score for different reasons.

Finally, it should be noted that acknowledging temperamental variation among children and adults has the potential of changing the interpretation each of us imposes on the behavior of others. Almost every modern theory of personality assumes that provocation of motives, conflicts, and standards, acquired over a lifetime, can produce physiological reactions characteristic of strong emotions. But most believe that the primary source of these physiological reactions is in what the mind has learned. Thus, it is assumed that a child develops a school phobia only because of past experiences.

However, let us turn the penny upside down and entertain the possibility that for some children, on some occasions, the brain generates a state that provokes the mind to invent some basis for the change in feeling tone. Under these conditions, a learned fear of abandonment may not be the root cause of a school phobia. Rather, for a small group of children temperamental characteristics could produce a spontaneous discharge of limbic circuits and the sudden generation of a conscious state of uncertainty that required an interpretation. Because school is a place where stressful events occur, the child could conclude that he is afraid of school. With this child the origin of the phobia may not be primarily a derivative of past experiences in the home.

One consequence of this point of view is that some of us may become too tolerant of extreme emotional reactions in others because most citizens of Western cultures believe that psychological characteristics originating in biology are less subject to personal will than are those that originate only in past experience. Although that assumption is probably invalid most of the time, it is still easier to be persuaded that each person's will can monitor moods and behaviors more effectively if they were learned than if they were influenced in part by the person's inherent temperament. Although this belief is neither logical nor empirically valid, it represents a potential danger to which we should remain alert as temperamental constructs increase in favor in the years ahead.

ACKNOWLEDGMENTS

This research was supported by a grant by the John D. and Catherine T. MacArthur Foundation and the Leon Lowenstein Foundation.

REFERENCES

Adamec, R. E., & Stark-Adamec, C. (1986). Limbic hyperfunction, limbic epilepsy, and interictal behavior. In B. K. Doane & K. E. Livingston (Eds.), *The Limbic System* (pp. 129–145). New York: Raven.

Blanchard, R. T., Flannelly, K. J., & Blanchard, D. C. (1986). Defensive behaviors of laboratory and wild Rattus Norvegicus, *Journal of Comparative Psychology, 100,* 101–107.

Clarke, A. S., Mason, W. A., & Moberg, G. P. (1988). Differential behavioral and adrenocortical responses to stress among three macaque species. *American Journal of Primatology, 14,* 37–52.

Dunn, L. T., & Everitt, B. J. (1988). Double dissociations of the effects of amygdala and insular cortex lesions on condition taste aversion, passive avoidance and neophobia in the rat using the excitotoxin ibotenic acid. *Behavioral Neuroscience, 102,* 3–9.

Jurgens, U. (1982). Amygdalar vocalization pathways in the squirrel monkey. *Brain Research, 241,* 189–196.

Kagan, J., Reznick, J. S., & Snidman, N. (1988). Biological bases of childhood shyness. *Science, 240,* 167–171.

Kagan, J. (1989). Temperamental contributions to social behavior. *American Psychologist, 44,* 668–674.

LaGasse, L., Gruber, C., & Lipsitt, L. P. (1989). The infantile expression of avidity in relation to later assessments. In J. S. Reznick (Ed.), *Perspectives on Behavioral Inhibition.* Chicago: University of Chicago Press.

Magnusson, D., Allen, V. I. (1983). *Human Development: An Interactional Perspective,* New York: Academic Press.

Oxenstierna, G., Edman, G., Iselius, C., Oreland, L., Ross, S. B., & Sedvall, G. (1986). Concentrations of monoamine metabolites in the cebrospinal fluid of twins and unrelated individuals, *Journal of Psychiatric Research, 20,* 19–29.

Pradhan, N. Arunasmitha, S., & Udaya, H. B. (1990). Behavioral and neurochemical differences in an inbred strain of rats. *Physiology and Behavior, 47,* 705–708.

Scott, J. P., & Fuller, J. L. (1965). *Genetics and the social behavior of the dog,* University of Chicago Press (reprinted as *Dog Behavior: A Genetic Basis,* University of Chicago Press, 1974).

Suomi, S. J. (1987). Genetic and maternal contributions to individual differences in rhesus monkey biobehavioral development. In N. A. Krasnegor, E. M. Blass, M. A. Hofer, & W. P. Smotherman (Eds.), *Prenatal Development: A Psychobiological Perspective* (pp. 397–420). New York: Academic Press.

Thomas, A., & Chess, S. (1977). *Temperament and Development,* New York: Brunner/Mazel.

II

BIOLOGICAL AND FAMILIAL FACTORS: INDEPENDENT AND INTERDEPENDENT CONTRIBUTIONS

3 Childhood Temperament and Cerebral Asymmetry: A Neurobiological Substrate of Behavioral Inhibition

Richard J. Davidson
University of Wisconsin-Madison

The idea that individual differences in temperamental qualities are sub-served by stable biological characteristics has a long history. Most observers within the past century who have written on the subject of temperament have speculated that such individual differences are "biologically based" (e.g., Thomas & Chess, 1977). Unfortunately, the ascription of a biological basis to a trait adds little to its understanding for several reasons. First, it is unclear whether a heritable cause is implied when a biological basis is proposed. Second, from a psychobiological perspective, any difference in behavior must be biologically based because the brain is the organ that underlies behavioral operations. In this sense, temperamental differences are no different from any other trait-like difference among people. So, we must ask the question whether temperamental characteristics enjoy any special status among traits with respect to their underlying biological substrates. I believe the answer to this question must be affirmative. At least some temperamental characteristics refer to differences among individuals in basic or elemental processes such as propensity to approach or withdraw in the face of novelty. Such differences in basic biobehavioral processes are more likely to have *direct* links with underlying biological processes than more complex traits such as obedience to authority or religious values. While such differences must also be biologically based in the trivial sense (i.e., the proximal cause of any behavior must be a particular underlying pattern of biological events), they are likely to depend upon an incredibly complex pattern of biological activity in many different systems.

   This chapter focuses on one particular substrate — frontal lobe asymmetry — of one specific temperamental quality — behavioral inhibition. It is likely that other biological systems will be more relevant to different temperamental qualities. It is also surely to be the case that frontal asymmetry is but one component of a limbic-cortical circuit that regulates individual differences in behavioral inhibition. More is said about this latter issue in a later section. The electrophysiological methods my laboratory has developed to study these brain systems is first described. I then present a brief overview of studies we have conducted that illustrate the effects of phasically arousing certain approach and withdrawal-related emotions on measures of frontal activation asymmetry. These studies provide the foundation for a series of studies on individual differences in baseline measures of frontal activation asymmetry. I describe the nature of such individual differences and underscore their relevance to understanding affective style. Finally, I apply these procedures and theoretical concepts to the understanding of behavioral inhibition and present data supporting an association between individual differences in frontal activation asymmetry and wariness to novelty in young children.

ELECTROPHYSIOLOGICAL MEASURES OF HEMISPHERIC ACTIVATION

Several important considerations apply in the choice of methods to study regional brain activity that underlies emotion and affective style. Many of the core phenomena of emotion are brief and therefore require measures that have a very fast time resolution. Moreover, periods of peak emotional intensity are unpredictable. They can occur at different points in time for different subjects in response to the same emotional stimulus. For example, some facial expressions of emotion are present for as little as 1–2 seconds. An ideal method should resolve activity as brief as the behavioral manifestations of emotion. It is also important to be able to record physiological activity over much longer time intervals. This is needed when subjects are presented with affect elicitors that last several minutes, requiring physiology to be integrated over the entire period of the eliciting stimulus. In addition, as I describe in detail below, one of the most exciting new areas in psychophysiological research on emotion is the study of the biological bases of individual differences in emotional reactivity. Such studies often require baseline physiology to be integrated over several minutes in order to obtain a reliable estimate of an individual's characteristic pattern. Thus, with respect to time resolution, the ideal measure would range from sub-second intervals to several minutes.

Another important consideration is related to the first. Data must be stored in a form that permits post-hoc extraction of epochs of varying durations. The capacity for post-hoc data extraction is required so that physiology coincident with overt behavioral measures of emotional state (e.g., facial expression) can be extracted. In some of the research described below, brain activity that is coincident with the display of spontaneous facial expressions of emotion is extracted for analysis. Other measures of emotional state might also be utilized in a similar fashion, including vocal indices and on-line self-report. This requirement presupposes the accurate synchronization of the behavioral and physiological data streams. Modern computer and video technology allow for this possibility.

Another essential requirement of any measure of regional brain activity used in the study of emotion is that it be relatively non-invasive. There are three major reasons for this. First, the more intrusive a method, the greater the interference with the elicitation of actual emotion. For example, certain types of PET scan protocols are highly intrusive and it is difficult to override the anxiety that is an inherent side effect of the procedure. It would likely be very difficult to elicit strong positive affect in many subjects undergoing a PET scan. The second important reason for limiting measures of regional brain activation to those that are relatively non-invasive is the need to study individuals over time as they undergo several different emotional states. It is crucial that psychophysiological studies of emotion compare among at least two different emotions and a baseline period (see Davidson, Ekman, Saron, Senulis, & Friesen, 1990, for a complete discussion of methodological desiderata in psychophysiological studies of emotion). Such comparisons enable the investigator to determine if the physiological pattern observed during the emotion period differs from baseline, and if the pattern is simply characteristic of emotion per se (in which case the pattern associated with each of the two different emotions will not differ) or is emotion-specific. The third reason for preferring relatively non-invasive procedures is the possibility of using them with infants and young children. These age groups are particularly important to study in research on the biological bases of emotion and temperament and the methods used must be appropriate for this population.

In light of these considerations, we have been using scalp-recorded brain electrical activity to make inferences about regional brain activation during the experimental arousal of acute emotions and emotion-related patterns of brain activity during resting baselines. The electroencephalogram (EEG) meets all of the requirements noted above. It is non-invasive, has a fast time resolution, and can be effectively synchronized with a behavioral data stream that permits extraction of data based upon post-hoc specification of periods of intense behavioral signs of emotion.

We have used recordings of brain electrical activity to make inferences about regional brain activation both during baseline periods as well as in response to a variety of emotion elicitors in adults, toddlers, and infants. We can examine brain activity during very brief epochs of emotion (e.g., on the order of one second), provided that periods of the same emotion type occur sufficiently frequently within an individual. To obtain stable estimates of spectral power from which measures of activation are derived, one needs a minimum of approximately 10–15 seconds of activity. The individual epochs themselves can be as brief as one second, but when aggregated together, their sum must exceed approximately 10 seconds in length (Davidson, 1988; Tomarken, Davidson, Wheeler, & Kinney, in press). Movement and muscle activity frequently accompany the generation of emotion. Moreover, temperamental differences among children may be associated with tonic differences in background muscle tension. We have developed procedures to statistically partial out the contributions of the muscle activity from the EEG (see Davidson, 1988, for a description of the method, and Henriques & Davidson, 1990, for the application of the method in an actual experiment). Finally, we use an electrode cap for EEG recording (Blom & Anneveldt, 1982). Such a cap permits accurate and rapid placement of electrodes and is particularly useful in studies with infants and children, where rapid application of electrodes is essential.

The principal measure extracted from the EEG in the studies I present in this chapter is power in the alpha band, which in adults represents activity between 8 and 13 Hz. A wealth of evidence indicates that power in this frequency band is inversely related to activation in adults (e.g., Shagass, 1972). In the studies I describe on infants and toddlers, we have used power in a lower frequency band as our dependent measure because this represents the functional equivalent of adult alpha activity (see e.g., Davidson & Fox, 1989; Davidson & Tomarken, 1989). Our measures of band power are computed from the output of a Fast Fourier Transform (FFT), which decomposes the brain activity into its underlying sine wave components.

In the following section I briefly review the findings from several recent studies performed in our laboratory where we examined brain activity during the experience/expression of experimentally aroused positive and negative emotion.

ANTERIOR ASYMMETRIES DURING THE EXPERIMENTAL AROUSAL OF POSITIVE AND NEGATIVE EMOTION IN ADULTS AND INFANTS

On the basis of an extensive body of literature, we have proposed that the left frontal region subserves a major approach system in the brain, while the homologous right frontal region is implicated in a withdrawal system. Emotions that are predominantly accompanied by approach-related action should therefore be associated with relative left-sided frontal activation, while those accompanied by withdrawal-related action should be associated with relative right-sided frontal activation (see Davidson, 1984; Davidson & Tomarken, 1989; Davidson, in press, for reviews). In a study with adults (Davidson, Ekman, Saron, Senulis, & Friesen, 1990), we tested this hypothesis by exposing subjects to short film clips designed to elicit approach-related positive emotion and withdrawal-related negative emotion (see Sobotka, Davidson, & Senulis, in press, for another example of this basic effect using reward and punishment contingencies). Happiness and amusement were the positive emotions and disgust was the negative emotion. Subjects were presented with two positive and two negative film clips, matched in intensity, in a darkened room while we videotaped their facial behavior unobtrusively. We also recorded brain electrical activity from the left and right frontal, central, anterior temporal, and parietal regions.

The video record of each subject was coded with Ekman and Friesen's (1978) *Facial Action Coding System* (FACS). FACS scoring of the facial data from this experiment revealed that the two most frequently occurring expressions were happy expressions in response to the positive film clips and disgust expressions in response to the negative film clips. For each subject, the onset and offset of each of these two expression types was entered into the computer so that brain electrical activity coincident with these expressions could be extracted.

Following removal of all periods associated with artifact, the EEG during happy and disgust facial expressions was Fourier transformed and power in different frequency bands was computed. As we predicted, the happy periods were associated with more left frontal activation than the disgust periods, while the latter were associated with more right-sided frontal activation than the happy periods. This same basic pattern was also found in the anterior temporal leads. No reliable differentiation between emotion conditions was found in the central and parietal scalp regions.

When we examined frontal asymmetry on an individual subject basis, we found that every subject showed more relative right-sided activation in the disgust compared with the happy condition. We also found that there were large differences among individuals in their average asymmetry scores (across emotion conditions). The difference between happy and disgust conditions appears to be superimposed upon subjects' basal levels of asymmetry. In the next part of this chapter, I underscore the importance of such individual differences by illustrating their relation to measures of affective reactivity and temperament.

In a series of collaborative studies with Nathan Fox, we have found similar asymmetries in frontal brain activity during the experimental arousal of emotions in infants. These studies were designed to determine whether the cerebral asymmetries that we found to be associated with emotion in adults are present during the first year of life. In our first infant study (Davidson & Fox, 1982), we presented 10-month-old infants with a videotape of an actress displaying laughter and distress while EEG was recorded from the left and right frontal and parietal regions. We found that the positive condition elicited more left-sided frontal activation than the negative condition. This finding was obtained in two separate samples of infants. In another study, we (Fox & Davidson, 1986) tested newborn infants to determine whether this asymmetry was present at birth. Neonates were presented with tastes that differed in hedonic valence while brain electrical activity was recorded. We found that tastes producing facial signs of disgust were associated with more right-sided frontal activation compared with tastes producing a more positive facial expression (sucrose).

In more recent work with Fox (Fox & Davidson, 1988), we studied brain electrical activity during the expression of different facial signs of emotion in 10-month-old infants. Emotion was elicited via the approach of the mother and a stranger. Of prime interest to us was a comparison between two types of smiles. One of these involves activity in both the zygomatic muscle (cheek) *and* orbicularis oculi (around the eye) while the other involves activity only in the zygomatic region. The difference between these two smile types was first described by the French anatomist Duchenne (1862/1990). Duchenne's work figured heavily in Darwin's (1872) book *The Expression of the Emotions in Man and Animals.* According to Darwin's discussion, Duchenne suggested that the emotion of "frank joy" is accompanied by activity in both the zygomatic and orbicularis oculi muscles, while smiles not associated with felt happiness are accompanied only by activity in the zygomatic region. Ekman and Friesen (1982) provided the first modern empirical support for this proposal by showing that smiles involving activity in both of these facial regions were much more highly correlated with self-reports of happiness than smiles produced by activity in the zygomatic region only. In light of this evidence, we were intrigued by the possibility that these two types of smiles could be discriminated electrophysiologically.

Artifact-free EEG data were obtained on 19 infants, all born of right-handed parents. EEG was recorded from the left and right frontal and parietal regions and quantified in the same manner as described earlier for the studies with adults. Infants were exposed to episodes of both mother approach and stranger approach. Facial behavior and EEG were recorded in response to each episode. Facial behavior was coded with Ekman and Friesen's (1984) EM-FACS system, which is a streamlined version of FACS designed explicitly for the coding of facial behavior related only to emotion.

We first computed the incidence of each of the two smile types in response to both stranger and mother approach. Seventy-five percent of the infants displayed smiles without orbicularis oculi activity to the stranger, while in response to mother approach, 78% of the infants displayed smiles with orbicularis oculi activity. The difference in the frequency of occurrence of these two smile types is highly significant ($p < .005$). In other words, smiles indicative of felt happiness were more likely to occur in the situation in which genuine positive affect would be expected (mother approach), while a potentially threatening situation (stranger approach) was more likely to elicit the other type of smile. We also coded the duration of the two smile types since Darwin (1872) suggested that the more "genuine" smiles (i.e., those with orbicularis activity) were longer in duration compared with the other type of smile. Our results confirmed Darwin's (1872) suggestion: the mean duration of smiles with orbicularis activity was 2.39 sec., while the mean duration of smiles without orbicularis activity was 1.49 sec. ($p < .01$). The central question posed in this study was whether the two smiles types could be discriminated on the basis of frontal brain electrical asymmetry. We specifically predicted that smiles with orbicularis activity would be accompanied by more relative left-sided frontal activation compared with the other smiles. As shown in Fig. 3.1, the data strongly supported this hypothesis. Consistent with the majority of our previous findings, regional specificity was once again indicated by the absence of significant differences in the parietal region (see Fig. 3.1).

We have recently examined EEG asymmetry during these two types of smiles in adults (Ekman, Davidson, & Friesen, 1990). In this study, we were also able to examine the relation between the duration of these smile types and self-reports of emotion. We found that higher intensities of self-

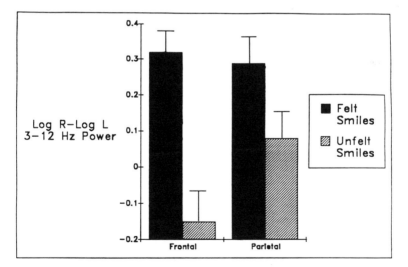

FIG. 3.1. Mean frontal (F3 and F4) and parietal (P3 and P4) asymmetry scores (log right minus log left power) for "felt" and "unfelt" smiles in response to mother and stranger approach in 10-month-old infants. Higher numbers on this laterality metric denote greater relative left-sided activation (From Fox & Davidson, 1988).

reported amusement were associated with increased duration of smiles with eye muscle involvement ($r = .70$) while the duration of smiles without eye muscle activity were not associated with self-reports of amusement ($r = .14$). Most importantly, smiles with orbicularis activity were associated with significantly more left anterior activation than smiles lacking orbicularis activity. This pattern of anterior asymmetry is precisely the same found to discriminate between these two smile types in infants.

INDIVIDUAL DIFFERENCES IN ANTERIOR ASYMMETRY: RELATION TO AFFECTIVE STYLE AND TEMPERAMENT

In the study of EEG during happy and disgust facial expressions that was described in a previous section, I noted that although all of the subjects showed more relative right-sided frontal activation during disgust compared with happy emotions, these state effects were superimposed upon widely varying individual differences in the absolute direction and magnitude of frontal asymmetry. A number of investigators in the area of lateralization have underscored the importance of individual differences in measures assumed to reflect asymmetrical arousal of portions of the cerebral hemispheres (e.g., Hellige, 1990; Levy, 1983). Recently, in a large N study in adults, we established that individual differences in electrophysiological measures of anterior asymmetry are stable over time (Tomarken, Davidson, Wheeler, & Kinney, in press), with test-retest correlations ranging between 0.66 and 0.73 for different measures of anterior activation asymmetry. Over the past several years, we performed a number of studies with subjects of varying ages that have examined relations between individual differences in anterior asymmetry and other psychological and biological measures sensitive to dispositional mood, affective reactivity, and temperament. In the following, I selectively review several components of this research effort, with an emphasis on studies of early differences in emotional reactivity and temperament.

Prior to discussing our findings from studies with infants and toddlers, I briefly review the results from several recent studies with adults that provide an important foundation for the developmental investigations. In three studies in normal adults (Tomarken, Davidson, & Henriques, 1990; Wheeler, Davidson, & Tomarken, in press), we examined whether individual differences in baseline measures of frontal activation asymmetry predicted reactivity to brief positive and negative emotional film clips. We specifically hypothesized that subjects with greater relative right-sided frontal activation at rest would respond more intensely to stimuli designed to elicit withdrawal-related emotions such as fear and disgust. Subjects with accentuated relative left-sided frontal activation were hypothesized to respond with more intense positive affect to film clip stimuli designed to elicit happiness and amusement. The first prediction was confirmed in all studies. The greater the relative right-sided frontal activation, the more intense was the subjects' report of fear and disgust in response to film clip stimuli designed to elicit these emotions. Although the magnitude of left-sided frontal activation was positively correlated with intensity of positive affect reported in response to the positive film clips, this relation was significant in only the third study (Wheeler et al., in press), where more stringent criteria were used to estimate individual differences in frontal asymmetry. In each of these studies we evaluated whether frontal asymmetry accounted for significant variance in reported emotion in response to the film clips after the variance accounted for by baseline measures of mood were partialled out. All of the significant effects remained equally significant when the effects of baseline mood were statistically removed.

In other research with adults, we have found that subjects with greater right-sided frontal activation report themselves to differ in their dispositional mood state from subjects with left-sided frontal activation. Those with extreme right-sided activation report more negative and less positive mood than their left-activated counterparts (Tomarken, Davidson, Wheeler, & Doss, 1992). In addition to differences on self-report measures, we have also found extreme right and left frontally activated subjects to differ on biological measures that have been related to individual differences in emotional responding in other research. In one study (Kang, Davidson, Coe, Wheeler, Tomarken, & Ershler, 1991), we compared extreme right and left frontally activated subjects on measures of immune function. We found that the right frontal subjects showed significantly less natural killer (NK) cell activity. Whether or not these differences in NK activity are associated with differences in health status must await longitudinal research.

The theoretical model of anterior asymmetry that we have proposed suggests that the left and right frontal regions of the human brain subserve approach and withdrawal systems respectively. Moreover, individual differences in the magnitude of activation of these regions should be associated with differences in approach and withdrawal-related functions. I have described some of the associations we have found for adults. The domain of early childhood temperament represents a natural and ideal context in which to explore this association in more detail. Behavioral inhibition is a temperamental construct specifically linked to approach and withdrawal tendencies. Behaviorally inhibited children have been described as those who either do not approach or actively withdraw in the face of novelty. Behaviorally uninhibited children are characterized by their explicit tendency to approach in the presence of novel and/or unfamiliar objects or persons. Because such individual differences are frankly expressed and rather pronounced in young children, the study of relations between this temperamental dimension and anterior cerebral asymmetry represents a fruitful domain in which to extend this line of research.

An important starting point for our current studies of temperament and cerebral function was a collaborative study with Fox (Davidson & Fox, 1989) that examined relations between early manifestations of individual differences in emotional reactivity and frontal activation asymmetry. Among 10-month-old infants, there is substantial heterogeneity in the response to maternal separation. Some infants become distressed immediately and will cry as soon as their mother has departed. Other infants will show a very different pattern of response and evince relatively few signs of negative affect. We (Davidson & Fox, 1989) divided 10-month-old infants into two groups based on whether or not they cried in response to a brief episode of maternal separation lasting approximately 60 sec. We found that about half of our group cried within this time period and half did not. We recorded baseline measures of frontal and parietal activation from the two hemispheres approximately 30 minutes prior to subjecting the infants to the episode of maternal separation. We then examined EEG measures of frontal activation asymmetry during this preceding baseline period, separately for the group of infants who subsequently cried and those who did not cry. We found a large difference in frontal asymmetry that predicted which infants would cry and which would not cry. The criers had greater right-sided and less left-sided frontal activation during the preceding baseline period compared with the non-criers. Parietal asymmetry from the same points in time failed to differentiate between the groups. To establish that the emotional states of the two groups of infants during the baseline period itself (when measures of brain activity were obtained) were comparable, we coded the facial behavior of the infants during this period. There were no differences between the infants who subsequently cried in response to maternal separation and those who did not in the frequency or duration of any facial signs of emotion during the baseline period. This suggests that our measures of regional brain activity were not reflecting phasic state differences between criers and non-criers. These data were the first to show that in infants, individual differences in frontal asymmetry predict affective reactivity. The direction of the relation is identical to that observed in our studies with adults. Subjects who show greater relative right-sided frontal activation at rest are likely to express more intense negative affect in response to a stressful event compared with their more left-frontally activated counterparts.

The findings in both adults and infants provided the foundation for a current study in our laboratory on relations between temperament and frontal asymmetry (Davidson, Finman, Straus, & Kagan, 1992). Kagan and his colleagues (e.g., Kagan, Reznick, & Snidman, 1988) have been studying the temperamental construct of behavioral inhibition for the past 10 years. Behavioral inhibition refers to the young child's tendency to withdraw and/or freeze in situations of novelty or unfamiliarity. Behaviorally inhibited children at 2½ years of age would likely withdraw in response to a novel object, such as a robot. Such a child would also be unlikely to approach a stranger, to climb through a toy tunnel and to interact with a same sex peer. In a novel peer play situation, behaviorally inhibited children spend the majority of their time in close proximity to their mothers, without playing or interacting in any way. While Kagan and his colleagues have studied autonomic differences between inhibited and uninhibited children, there have been no studies on central nervous system differences between these groups. We therefore embarked upon a longitudinal study whose principal aims were to determine if inhibited children showed greater relative right-sided frontal activation compared with uninhibited children, and to examine relations between frontal asymmetry and measures of behavioral inhibition over time.

To select groups of inhibited and uninhibited children, we adopted the procedures that Kagan and his colleagues had developed (Kagan et al., 1988). At 31 months of age, we tested 386 children in a peer play session. The children were randomly selected from birth announcements in the newspaper. Two unfamiliar same-sex peers came to the laboratory with their mothers and were escorted to a large play room. The mothers were instructed to sit on chairs and fill out an extensive series of questionnaires. They were instructed not to interact with their children. There were age-appropriate toys on the floor in the play room, including a toy tunnel through which the children could crawl. At minute 10 of the play session, the experimenter brought a remote-controlled robot into the room. The robot began to speak and walk toward each of the children. It was controlled by an experimenter behind a one-way mirror. After remaining in the room for 3 minutes, the robot said that it was tired and had to go home to take a nap. The experimenter then entered the room and removed the robot. At minute 20, a stranger entered the room who was not seen before by either child. The stranger was holding a tray on which were placed several very attractive toys. The stranger invited the children to play with the toys. After 3 minutes, the stranger left the tray of toys on the floor for the children to play with and then departed. The play session ended at minute 25.

During the entire play session, two observers were positioned behind a one-way mirror to code the behavior of each child. The major measures coded included the total time the child was proximal to mother (within arm's length) and not interacting, the latency to touch the first toy, the latency to speak the first utterance, the latency to approach the robot, the latency to approach the stranger, and the latency to enter the tunnel. On the basis of these measures, we selected three groups of children for our longitudinal study. The criteria we used were based on the work of Kagan et al. (1988), but were more stringent. The inhibited children were those who spent more than 9.5 minutes (out of a total of 25 minutes) proximal to mother and also met four of the following five additional criteria: (a) latency of ≥ 3 minutes to touch their first toy; (b) latency of ≥ 3 minutes to speak their first utterance; (c) no approach to the robot; (d) no approach to the stranger; and (e) latency of ≥ 10 minutes to enter the tunnel. The criteria for the uninhibited children were all of the following: (a) total duration of time proximal to mother ≤ 30 seconds; (b) latency of ≤ 30 seconds to touch their first toy; (c) latency of ≤ 60 seconds to speak their first utterance; (d) latency of ≤ 60 seconds to approach the robot; (e) latency of ≤ 60 seconds to approach the stranger; (f) latency of ≤ 60 seconds to take a toy from the stranger; and (g) enter the tunnel at some point during the session.

In addition to selecting groups of inhibited and uninhibited children, we also selected a group of middle children who had values in the mid-range for all of the measures described earlier. We selected approximately 28 subjects in each of the three groups, balanced evenly by sex. The average duration of time spent proximal to mother among children in the inhibited and uninhibited groups underscores the magnitude of the difference between the two extreme groups. The inhibited children remained proximal to their mothers for an average of 1171 seconds (of a total of 1500 seconds – 25 minutes – representing 78% of the total time) while the uninhibited children were proximal to their mothers for an average of 9 seconds (representing less than 1% of the total time).

We tested the longitudinal cohort at 38 months of age in a session during which we recorded brain electrical activity at rest and in response to several tasks. To date, we have only analyzed the data for the resting baselines. Our major prediction was that inhibited children would show greater relative right-sided frontal activation compared with their uninhibited counterparts. Middle children were hypothesized to fall in-between. Figure 3.2 presents the frontal asymmetry data for the three groups. Frontal asymmetry scores were computed by subtracting log left power in the 7–10 Hz frequency band (the functional analog of alpha activity in the adult) from log right alpha power. Thus, positive numbers on this score denote left-sided activation while negative numbers denote right-sided activation. As can be seen from this figure, inhibited children show right frontal activation, while the uninhibited children show the opposite pattern. The middle children fall predictably in between the two extreme groups.

For theoretical reasons, it is important to ascertain how the two hemispheres are contributing to this group difference in asymmetry. If the primary difference among the groups is in the withdrawal-related component, we would expect the inhibited children to show *more* right frontal

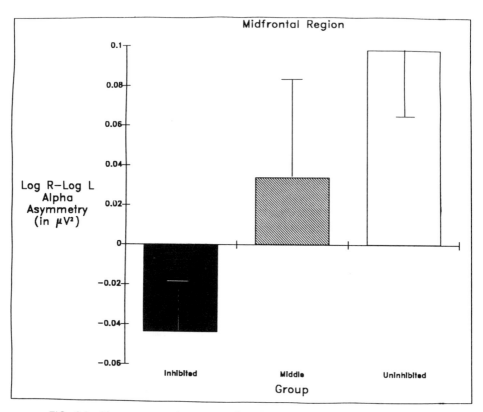

FIG. 3.2 Mean asymmetry scores (log right minus log left power in the 7-10 Hz band—the toddler alpha frequency range) for the mid-frontal electrodes for inhibited, middle, and uninhibited children. Higher numbers on this metric denote greater relative left-sided activation (From Davidson, Finman, Straus, & Kagan, 1992).

activation compared with the uninhibited children. However, if the fundamental difference between the groups is in the approach-related component, we would expect the inhibited children to show *less* left frontal activation compared with their uninhibited counterparts. This latter pattern would suggest that inhibited children show deficits in approach-related behavior and emotion, rather than accentuated withdrawal-related behavior. Most accounts of behavioral inhibition have implied a strong linkage to fear and anxiety. On this view, the difference among groups should be most pronounced in the right frontal region. Figure 3.3 presents the frontal EEG data for each of the three groups, separately by hemisphere. The Group × Hemisphere interaction was highly significant ($p = .0003$). As can be seen from this figure, the difference among the groups is clearly more pronounced in the left hemisphere, with the inhibited children showing more

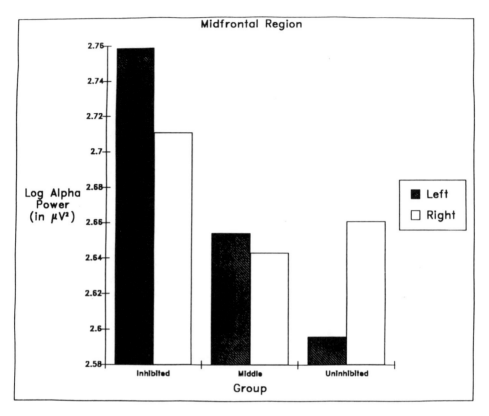

FIG. 3.3   Mean log-transformed power in the 7–10 Hz band in the left and right mid-frontal region for inhibited, middle, and uninhibited children (From Davidson, Finman, Straus, & Kagan, 1992).

power (i.e., less activation) in this region compared with the other two groups. These data indicate that the group difference is much more pronounced in the approach-related system and suggest that it would be most appropriate to characterize the inhibited children as showing deficits in a frontal approach system, rather than hyper-activation in a frontal withdrawal system. It is important to underscore the fact that these differences were observed in a relatively unstressed baseline situation and are therefore unlikely to be a function of group differences in phasic emotional response to the situation.

It is instructive to consider the possibility that our sample of inhibited children is more extreme than samples that have been studied previously by Kagan's group. Certainly, the magnitude of the difference between our extreme groups on the play session variables (e.g., time proximal to mother) is greater than Kagan observed in his sample. It is also possible that there are different sub-types of inhibition, with one sub-type characterized by approach-related deficits and the other characterized by accentuated withdrawal tendencies. Our grouping procedures may have inadvertently selected for subjects in the former category. A testable prediction that follows from our initial finding is that our sample of inhibited children should not differ from uninhibited children in their propensity to display withdrawal-related negative affect in response to appropriate elicitors. Rather, they should be more prone to sadness and depression-like reactions following situational elicitors of these emotions. We intend to examine these predictions in the course of our future longitudinal work.

The pattern of decreased left frontal activation we found among our inhibited children is similar to the pattern we have reported in depressives (see e.g., Henriques & Davidson, 1990; Henriques & Davidson, 1991; Schaffer, Davidson, & Saron, 1983). It is important to emphasize that this pattern is viewed as a marker of *vulnerability* to emotion and behavior that is associated with deficits in the approach system. Such vulnerability will become expressed as psychopathology only in response to relatively extreme life stresses. Thus, only a small percentage of affected individuals (i.e., those with the marker) would be expected to actually develop an affective disorder. However, a larger percentage might be expected to have subclinical characteristics such as dysthymic mood, shyness, and decreased dispositional positive affect. It will be of interest to examine these children as they confront increasingly more complex life challenges (e.g., entry into school) to help define what the environmental circumstances are that predispose individuals with decreased left frontal activation to exhibit depression-related symptomatology.

It will be equally of interest to study the children at the opposite extreme. It is not clear whether the uninhibited children are likely to be display impulsive behavior and show an over-sensitivity to reward contingencies. We are currently testing some of these hypotheses in our assessment of the children at 4½ years of age.

SUMMARY AND CONCLUSIONS

This chapter presented an overview of our program of research on anterior asymmetries associated with emotion and affective style. I proposed that the anterior regions of the left and right cerebral hemispheres are specialized for approach and withdrawal processes, respectively. Using electrophysiological measures of regional cortical activation, data were presented that demonstrated that in both adults and infants, the experimental arousal of approach-related positive affect was associated with selective left anterior activation, while arousal of withdrawal-related negative affect was associated with selective right anterior activation. In the second half of the chapter, evidence was presented that indicated that individual differences in patterns of anterior asymmetry are stable over time and predict important features of affective style, including early childhood temperament. At 38 months of age, children who were classified as behaviorally inhibited when they were 2½ years exhibited less left frontal activation than their behaviorally uninhibited peers.

Among the most important unanswered questions in this line of research is the degree to which these individual differences are modifiable through experience. For example, a certain portion of the extremely inhibited children will become less inhibited as a function of encouragement and nurturing from their parents. Will frontal asymmetry parallel behavioral changes in the propensity to exhibit wariness in novel situations? We will address this question as part of the longitudinal follow-up of the original cohort of children. A related question concerns the variability in frontal asymmetry within our groups. For example, not all children with decreased left frontal activation are inhibited. Are the children who show decreased left frontal activation but are not currently inhibited more likely to *become* inhibited with development? Or, can we identify anything in the home environments of children with decreased left frontal activation who are not inhibited that may have buffered them from the expression of behavioral inhibition? These are some of the many important questions that longitudinal study of these children can begin to answer.

From the data already available, it is clear that asymmetry in the anterior cortical regions is significantly associated with emotion and emotional reactivity. It will be important for future research to characterize both the proximal and distal causes of this asymmetry. The study of proximal causes will necessarily require the examination of subcortical and neurochemical contributions. By combining the administration of certain pharmacological agents with simultaneous measurement of brain electrical activity, new insights about the possible underlying neurochemical systems that mediate asymmetrical brain electrical activity might emerge. For example, in recent research with rhesus monkeys (Davidson, Kalin, & Shelton, in press), we found that the administration of diazepam significantly increased left frontal activation in restrained infants compared with administration of vehicle. The lateralized effect of diazepam raises an important question about possible lateralization in the distribution of benzodiazepine receptors or endogenous benzodiazepines. These questions can now be approached with human subjects using positron emission tomography and a labeled benzodiazepine receptor antagonist (Persson et al., 1985).

The distal causes of the individual differences in anterior asymmetry that have been described are likely to be some combination of heritable and early environmental factors. The available evidence on these distal causes is meager, although it is likely that new insights will emerge over the next decade as the appropriate research is performed. It is clear that frontal asymmetry is a central biological marker of childhood temperament. This association has raised many more questions than it has answered, but hopefully this program of research will stimulate others to explore this problem in the future.

ACKNOWLEDGMENTS

The research described in this article was supported in part by an NIMH Research Scientist Development Award MH00875, NIMH grants MH40747 and MH43454 and by a grant from the John D. and Catherine T. MacArthur Foundation. Portions of this chapter were adapted from Davidson (in press).

REFERENCES

Blom, J. L., & Anneveldt, M. (1982). An electrode cap tested. *Electroencephalography and Clinical Neurophysiology, 54,* 591–594.

Darwin, C. (1872/1965). *The expression of the emotions in man and animals.* Chicago: University of Chicago Press.

Davidson, R. J. (1984). Affect, cognition and hemispheric specialization. In C. E. Izard, J. Kagan, & R. Zajonc (Eds.), *Emotion, Cognition and Behavior.* New York: Cambridge University Press.

Davidson, R. J. (1988). EEG measures of cerebral asymmetry: Conceptual and methodological issues. *International Journal of Neuroscience, 39,* 71–89.

Davidson, R. J. (in press). Anterior cerebral asymmetry and the nature of emotion. *Brain and Cognition.*

Davidson, R. J., Ekman, P., Saron, C. D., Senulis, J. A., & Friesen, W. V. (1990). Approach/withdrawal and cerebral asymmetry: Emotional expression and brain physiology I. *Journal of Personality and Social Psychology, 58,* 330–341.

Davidson, R. J., Finman, R., Straus, A., & Kagan, J. (1992). Childhood temperament and frontal lobe activity: Patterns of asymmetry differentiate between wary and outgoing children. Submitted for publication.

Davidson, R. J., & Fox, N. A. (1982). Asymmetrical brain activity discriminates between positive versus negative affective stimuli in human infants. *Science, 218,* 1235–1237.

Davidson, R. J., & Fox, N. A. (1989). Frontal brain asymmetry predicts infants' response to maternal separation. *Journal of Abnormal Psychology, 98,* 127–131.

Davidson, R. J., Kalin, N. H., & Shelton, S. E. (in press). Lateralized effects of diazepam on frontal brain electrical asymmetries in rhesus monkeys. *Biological Psychiatry.*

Davidson, R. J., & Tomarken, A. J. (1989). Laterality and emotion: An electrophysiological approach. In F. Boller & J. Grafman (Eds.), *Handbook of Neuropsychology, Vol. 3* (pp. 419–441). Amsterdam: Elsevier.

Duchenne, B. (1862/1990). *Mechanisme de la physionomie humaine ou analyse electrophysiologique de l'expression des passions.* Paris: Bailliere. Reprinted by Cambridge University Press.

Ekman, P., Davidson, R. J., & Friesen, W. V. (1990). Duchenne's Smile: Emotional expression and brain physiology, II. *Journal of Personality and Social Psychology, 58,* 342–353.

Ekman, P., & Friesen, W. V. (1978). *The Facial Action Coding System: A Technique for the Measurement of Facial Movement.* Palo Alto, CA: Consulting Psychologists Press.

Ekman, P., & Friesen, W. V. (1982). Felt, false and miserable smiles. *Journal of Non-verbal Behavior, 6,* 238–252.

Ekman, P., & Friesen, W. V. (1984). *Emotion Facial Action Coding System (EM-FACS).* San Francisco: University of California, San Francisco.

Fox, N. A., & Davidson, R. J. (1986). Taste-elicited changes in facial signs of emotion and the asymmetry of brain electrical activity in human newborns. *Neuropsychologia, 24,* 417–422.

Fox, N. A., & Davidson, R. J. (1988). Patterns of brain electrical activity during facial signs of emotion in ten month old infants. *Developmental Psychology, 24,* 230–236.

Hellige, J. B. (1990). Hemispheric asymmetry. *Annual Review of Psychology, 41,* 55–80.

Henriques, J. B., & Davidson, R. J. (1990). Regional brain electrical asymmetries discriminate between previously depressed and healthy control subjects. *Journal of Abnormal Psychology, 99,* 22–31.

Henriques, J. B., & Davidson, R. J. (1991). Left frontal hypoactivation in depression. *Journal of Abnormal Psychology, 100,* 535–545.

Kagan, J., Reznick, J. S., & Snidman, N. (1988). Biological bases of childhood shyness. *Science, 240,* 167–171.

Kang, D. H., Davidson, R. J., Coe, C. L., Wheeler, R. E., Tomarken, A. J., & Ershler, W. B. (1991). Frontal brain asymmetry and immune function. *Behavioral Neuroscience, 105,* 860–869.

Levy, J. (1983). Individual differences in cerebral asymmetry: Theoretical issues and experimental considerations. In J. B. Hellige (Ed.), *Cerebral hemisphere asymmetry: Method, theory and application* (pp. 465–515). New York: Praeger.

Persson, A., Ehrin, E., Eriksson, L., Farde, L., Hedstrom, C. G., Litton, J. E., Mindus, P., & Sedvall, G. (1985). Imaging of [^{11}C]-labelled RO-15-1788 binding to benzodiazepine receptors in the human brain by positron emission tomography. *Journal of Psychiatric Research, 19,* 609–622.

Schaffer, C. E., Davidson, R. J., & Saron, C. (1983). Frontal and parietal EEG asymmetries in depressed and non-depressed subjects. *Biological Psychiatry, 18,* 753–762.

Shagass, C. (1972). Electrical activity of the brain. In N. S. Greenfield & R. A. Sternbach (Eds.), *Handbook of Psychophysiology* (pp. 263–328). New York: Holt, Rinehart and Winston.

Sobotka, S. S., Davidson, R. J., & Senulis, J. A. (in press). Anterior brain electrical asymmetries in response to reward and punishment. *Electroencephalography and Clinical Neurophysiology.*

Thomas, A., & Chess, S. (1977). *Temperament and development.* New York: Brunner/Mazel.

Tomarken, A. J., Davidson, R. J., & Henriques, J. B. (1990). Resting frontal brain asymmetry predicts affective responses to films. *Journal of Personality and Social Psychology, 59,* 791–801.

Tomarken, A. J., Davidson, R. J., Wheeler, R. W., & Kinney, L. (in press). Psychometric properties of resting anterior EEG asymmetry: Temporal stability and internal consistency. *Psychophysiology.*

Tomarken, A. J., Davidson, R. J., Wheeler, R. W., & Doss, R. (1992). Relations between individual differences in anterior brain asymmetry and fundamental dimensions of emotion. *Journal of Personality and Social Psychology, 62,* 676–687.

Wheeler, R. W., Davidson, R. J., & Tomarken, A. J. (in press). Frontal brain asymmetry and emotional reactivity: A biological substrate of affective style. *Psychophysiology.*

4

Antecedents and Consequences of Shyness in Boys and Girls: A 6-year Longitudinal Study

Anette Engfer
State Institute for Early Education and Family Research West Germany

Several chapters of this volume paint a rather grey picture of the antecedents and consequences of social withdrawal, inhibition, and shyness. Each of these characteristics appears to be more or less clinically relevant, being the outcome of or forecasting impaired social relationships.

But shyness is not necessarily maladaptive. As a transient fear of the unfamiliar, it may have a protective function as it activates attachment behavior (see Stevenson-Hinde, this volume). Shyness as bashful expressive behavior is not only accepted as "feminine" (see Stevenson-Hinde, 1988), but may even assume flirtative qualities. Therefore, shyness may have quite different qualities in different social contexts, for different people (boys and girls in particular), and in different phases of development.

In our longitudinal study of 39 German children in their families, shyness has not been the primary focus; rather, it has been more of a "by-product" of our investigation. Therefore, we have not systematically inquired into the early antecedents of shyness. Yet, some of our results may contribute to a better understanding of the differential meanings of this construct, since we have extensive data, collected over the first six years after the birth of these children.

We have examined two components or core aspects of shyness. First, we studied *fear of the unfamiliar,* strange people in particular. This is usually a transient reaction being observable in children after the second half of the first year, but it may also persist in older children. We observed this transient reaction at two points in time, namely at 33 months and 6.3 years. Second, this fear of strangers may develop into a rather consistent and stable pattern when relating to unfamiliar peers and adults. As such, it adopts *trait-like* qualities because it describes rather stable interindividual differences. This fear of unfamiliar people is not a handicap in relationships with familiar people, nor is it generally linked to a lack of social competence (see Asendorpf, this volume). In our research, trait-like shyness was assessed by use of a 7-item scale filled out by the mothers at 43 months. At 6.3 years, the same scale was used to assess the trait-shyness of the children in our sample from the perspective of fathers, mothers, and preschool teachers.

A third component of shyness may be *social withdrawal.* In this case, some children, even in familiar contexts, stay remote from peers. It appears as if these children have difficulties making friends and may be rejected by their agemates. Rubin, Younger, Hymel, Asendorpf, and others (in this volume) have depicted the serious consequences that eventually may evolve for these children in terms of impaired self-confidence, sadness, loneliness, and depression. Such components or correlates of shyness, namely difficulties in making friends, oversensitivity and sadness, and lack of social attractiveness were rated by fathers, mothers, and preschool teachers at 6.3 years.

Compared to some of the other studies presented in this volume, our data base is limited in a number of ways. First, the sample is relatively small. Second, shyness was originally not the focus of our study. Third, our data were comprised of rating-scales rather than behavioral or physiological observations. As such, our study must be considered as exploratory and most of our findings definitely need to be replicated in other samples.

Two main questions will be explored in this chapter: (1) *What is the developmental path into shyness?* Most theories about the origin of shyness assume that the phenomenon is preceded by high levels of emotional arousal in infancy. Buss and Plomin (1986) view shyness as the intersection of two genetically preprogrammed characteristics, namely of emotionality and lack of sociability, with the greater impact derived from emotionality. In a similar vein, Kagan, Reznick, and Snidman (1986), and Fox and Calkins (this volume), as well as others, have demonstrated that the early antecedents of subsequent inhibition may be high distress to frustration, irritability, and higher physiological excitability at exposure to visual and acoustic stimuli. Rubin, LeMare, and Lollis (1990) have suggested a developmental path into social withdrawal where infants with a lower threshold for arousal are thought to react intensively to novelty, to be difficult to soothe, and in conjunction with insensitive caretaking may develop into insecure, dependent, anxious, and withdrawn children.

Although shyness, social withdrawal, and inhibition are somewhat different theoretical constructs (see Rubin, Asendorpf, and Kagan, this volume), they share these basic assumptions about early infant excitability as a precursor of later problems. Therefore, in this chapter, I examine whether this developmental path from initial infant excitability into later shyness can be substantiated. One factor that is lacking in all these assumptions about the origins of shyness is the *gender-specific* perspective. Stevenson-Hinde and Hinde (1986, 1988) depict the differential meanings of shyness in boys and girls in a developmental perspective. Specifically, they have found that shyness in girls is associated with positive aspects of the mother-child relationship, whereas shyness in boys is not; mothers of boys expressed some dissatisfaction with the fact that their sons had not outgrown their "childish" shyness by 50 months. Similar findings have been reported by Radke-Yarrow, Richters, and Wilson (1988), who found that shyness in girls was associated with tender and affectionate mother-daughter relationships whereas mothers of shy boys were less pleased with and less accepting of their sons. Therefore, it appears as if shyness in girls may be more acceptable to parents than shyness in boys. Consequently, one should expect that shyness in boys would be actively discouraged while shyness in girls would not only be accepted, but also implicitly rewarded by parents, thus leading to a greater temporal continuity of shy behavior in girls. Likewise, it seems possible that the family conditions associated with shyness may differ for boys and girls. In this chapter, developmental paths leading to shyness in boys and girls are differentiated.

(2) *Which conditions may explain growth or decline in shyness?* Correlations mainly reflect the temporal stability of interindividual differences; they hardly reveal causal mechanisms (see Hinde, 1988). These mechanisms can be uncovered, however, if we look for the conditions associated with the change of the characteristics under study. Therefore, in the study reported herein, I examined those family variables that were associated with observed changes in child shyness. Specifically, subgroups of children who shifted in the amount of observable shyness were compared to subgroups of children exhibiting rather stable patterns of shyness over the course of time. These comparisons shed some light on the conditions effecting growth or decline in shyness.

METHOD

The data presented here come from a larger longitudinal study on the development of distressed mother-child relationships. The sample consisted of 39 families living in Munich, Germany and its surroundings. At delivery, the mothers were between 23 and 43 years of age with a median of 30 years. The families were mainly middle and lower middle class. At 6.3 years there were 25 boys and 14 girls in our sample, 11 boys and 8 girls being first-born, the rest being second or later-born children. Three girls and 7 boys of these first-born children grew up without siblings.

Assessments were made at eight points in time (for an overview see Table 4.1). All scales used in this study were constructed according to the criteria of classical test construction. Therefore only items with sufficient item validities were included, the internal consistencies of these scales were — with a few exceptions — at least in the magnitude of $\alpha = .80$. Since there were so many variables assessed in this study, I describe only the most important ones in detail:[1]

Time 1: On the maternity ward (0–10 days), *maternal sensitivity* and child characteristics were observed and judged by medical doctors (for a detailed description of these scales see Engfer & Gavranidou, 1987).

Time 2: Four months after delivery the following variables were assessed by questionnaires: (a) Maternal *child-care attitudes* and child-related feelings were assessed with several scales of a new questionnaire that was pre-tested on 170 mothers (see Codreanu, 1984; for a detailed description of these scales see Engfer & Gavranidou, 1987). One group of scales (i.e., Punishment and Rigidity) assessed a dogmatic, power assertive approach to childrearing. Another group of scales (i.e., Aggravation, Frustration, and Nervous Exhaustion) assessed maternal feelings of overload and aggravation in caring for the child. The Overprotection-Scale measured an almost irrational fear that something may happen to the child. (b) Perceived *child characteristics:* Adapting from Broussard and Hartner (1970), we used 5-point rating scales of behavioral problems babies may present to their mothers. Perceived child difficultness included frequent crying, restlessness, and lack of soothability (for details see Engfer, 1986a). Lack of Adaptability described the difficulties in establishing regular feeding and sleeping routines.

(c) Maternal *personality characteristics* were assessed with six scales of a well-known German Personality Inventory (FPI, see Fahrenberg, Selg, & Hampel, 1978). We used the scales of Nervousness, Depressiveness, Irritability, Neuroticism, Shy Inhibition, and Composure. Eighteen months after delivery (t_4), we used the same inventory again. At 6.3 years (t_7), we assessed both maternal and paternal personality characteristics with a reduced set of personality scales (i.e., Depressiveness, Irritability, and Composure). Mainly for economic reasons we dropped the Shy Inhibition Scale from our battery of tests. Therefore, we could not test the empirical relations between this parental personality characteristic and children's shyness. This omission proved to be very unfortunate for the present evaluation of our data, because we found such strong empirical relations between maternal Shy Inhibition as assessed initially and subsequent shyness both in boys and girls.

---

[1]A detailed description of all instruments used in this study can be provided on request by the author.

TABLE 4.1

Variables, Procedures, and Times of Measurement in the Longitudinal Study
on the Development of Distressed Mother-Child Relationships

Variables	Procedures	Times of measurement							
Demographic Characteristics of the Family	Interview		t_2					t_7	
Personality Characteristics of									
- Mothers	Freiburg Personality Questionnaire		t_2		t_4			t_7	
- Fathers	Freiburg Personality Questionnaire							t_7	
Marital Relationship of									
- Mothers	Relationship Inventory		t_2				t_6	t_7	
- Fathers	Relationship Inventory						t_6	t_7	
Mother Perceived Behavior Problems of the Child	Broussard-Scale		t_2		t_4				
	ICQ-Scales (Bates et al. 1979)				t_4		t_6		
	Child Behavior Questionnaire						t_6	t_7	
Father Perceived Behavior Problems of the Child	ICQ-Scales (Bates et al. 1979)						t_6		
	Child Behavior Questionnaire							t_7	
Parent Perceived Child *Shyness*	Questionnaire						t_6	t_7	
Pre-School Teacher Perceived Child *Shyness*	Questionnaire							t_7	
Maternal Childcare Attitudes and Child Related Feelings	Questionnaire		t_2		t_4			t_7	
Paternal Childcare Attitudes and Child-Related Feelings	Questionnaire						t_6	t_7	
Observed Maternal Behavior	Rating Scales	t_1		t_3		t_5			
Observed Child Characteristics	Rating Scales	t_1		t_3		t_5		t_7	t_8
Observed Child *Shyness*	Rating Scales					t_5		t_7	t_8
Child Self-Concept	Pictorial Scale (Harter & Pike, 1983)							t_7	t_8
Child Cognitive Competence	Hamburg Wechsler Intelligence Scale								t_8

Time 3: Eight months after delivery, three independent observers rated maternal sensitivity and child characteristics in a free play situation of half an hour duration in the homes of the families. *Maternal sensitivity* included sensitivity to the signals of the baby, responsiveness, quality of physical contact, etc. (for methodological details see Engfer, 1986b). The following aspects of *child behavior* were rated: *Infant Moodiness, Activity,* and *Infant Social Responsiveness* (for methodological details see Kalden, Müller-Osten, & Engfer, 1987).

Time 4: Eighteen months after delivery we used the same instruments as at four months after delivery to assess: (a) Maternal *child-care attitudes* and child-related feelings; (b) maternal *personality characteristics;* and (c) mother-perceived *child characteristics.* In addition to the modified version of the Broussard and Hartner Scale (1970), which was used again at this point in time, we assessed mother-perceived child characteristics with selected items of the Infant Characteristics Questionnaire (ICQ) developed by Bates, Freeland, and Lounsbury (1979). Among others, the following aspects of child behavior were measured by these new scales: *Moodiness* (3 items), and *Forceful Demand of Attention* (4 items; for details see Engfer, 1986a).

Time 5: At 33 months we assessed the children in their homes. At this time, two female psychology students served as research assistants who did not know anything about the children and the families, whom they met for the first time. This also marked the first time that child *shyness* was explicitly observed and rated by use of three 5-point rating scales. These included: (a) initial shyness of the child in the mildly stressful situation when we entered the family as strangers to the child; (b) the extent to which the child remained dependent on and close to the mother; and (c) how frequently the child turned to the mother in times of need or unhappiness. In a similar way the *cooperativeness* of the child was assessed (4 items). Maternal behavior was rated for *Dominance* (3 items) including frequent attempts to control the behavior of the child.

Time 6: At 43 months the following variables were included in our assessment: (a) Perceived *child characteristics:* Child *Moodiness* and *Forceful Demand of Attention* were again assessed with the Infant Characteristics Questionnaire from the perspectives of both fathers and mothers. In addition, the mothers completed a more comprehensive questionnaire about behavioral characteristics and problems typical of children in this age group (Child Behavior Questionnaire, see Gavranidou, Heinig, & Engfer, 1987) such as *Shyness, Aggressiveness, Compliance,* and *Lack of Persistence.* Perceived *Child Shyness* (7 items) included diverse aspects of shy behavior such as shyness towards strange adults, shyness towards unknown peers, taking time in making friends, being easily embarrassed and insecure, etc. Perceived *Child Moodiness* and *Sensitivity* (6 items) describes a child being fearful, easily worried, oversensitive, crying easily etc. Perceived *Social Competence* (7 items) describes an uninhibited, sociable, self-confident child. The *Shyness* scale correlated significantly with the *Moodiness* scale ($r = .67, p < .001$) and the *Social Competence* scale ($r = -.47, p < .001$). (b) The quality of the *marital relationship* was assessed with a well-known German Relationship Inventory (Partnerschaftsfragebogen, PFB, see Hahlweg, 1979) including the dimensions of marital *Conflict, Communication,* and *Affection* (for details see Engfer, 1988). This Relationship Inventory was completed by both spouses.

Time 7: At 6.3 years the following variables were included in our assessment: (a) *Child-care attitudes* and child related feelings were measured again with a slightly modified version of the questionnaire we used 4 and 18 months after delivery. This time both fathers and mothers filled out this questionnaire. (b) Parental *personality characteristics* were measured with a reduced set of the same personality scales (FPI, see Fahrenberg et al., 1978) we had used with the mothers 4 and 18 months after delivery. This time both parents completed the questionnaire. (c) Perceived *characteristics of the child* were assessed by an extended and slightly modified version of the 43–months Child Behavior Questionnaire. This questionnaire was completed by mothers, fathers, and preschool teachers. We added other aspects of perceived child characteristics (such as *Cognitive Competence;* 5 items) particularly relevant in this age group. Perceived *Child Shyness* (8 items), *Moodiness* (4 items), and *Social Competence* (7 items), *Aggressiveness* (10 items), and *Lack of Persistence* (7 items) were assessed in a similar way as at t_6. At this point in time, the sample size for the children being judged by their preschool teachers was reduced to 11 girls and 22 boys because six children had entered school. (d) Corresponding to these perceived characteristics of children, we assessed the *self-concept* of these 6.3-year-old children with a German adaptation of the Pictorial Scale of Perceived Competence and Social Acceptance for Young Children by Harter and Pike (1983).

(e) The most central aspect of child behavior related to the present evaluation of shyness was the observation and rating of *children's shy behavior* during our assessment in the home of the family. These ratings were done by a new female research psychologist who was a stranger to the children. This researcher was blind to the prior behavior and history of these children and their families.

Initially we intended to rate children's shyness by using only two items, namely "shyness in the initial phase of contact" and "reluctance to talk during the assessment." But these two items were so highly correlated with other aspects of child behavior that we incorporated these other aspects into the compound scale of shyness as well. These other aspects of child behavior were "lack of self-confidence," "dejected mood," "timidity," "reticence," "worry," and "unhappiness." This last rating of shyness was much more complex than our 33-month assessment of shyness and was much closer to the description of unhappy, socially withdrawn behavior. Other aspects of child behavior rated in a similar way were *Lack of Cooperativeness* (9 items), and *Competence* (5 items).

(f) Dimensions of the *marital relationship* were reassessed with the Relationship Inventory ("Partnerschaftsfragebogen") by Hahlweg (1979). In addition, we used a *Resignation* Scale (see Engfer & Schneewind, 1978) to assess general feelings of discontent and unhappiness.

Time 8: At 6.8 years the *cognitive competence* of the children was assessed by the use of two subtests (i.e., Vocabulary and Block-Design Test) of the German Hamburg Wechsler Intelligence Test for Children (HAWIK, see Hardesty & Priester, 1966). Again, the *self concept* of the children was assessed with the German adaptation of the Pictorial Scale of Perceived Competence and Social Acceptance.

We used mainly Spearman rank correlations and *t*-tests to examine the results. The small number of boys and girls made it unlikely that significant differences between these correlations would be found. The gender differences in correlations reported in the next section should therefore be regarded with caution.

RESULTS

1. Is Infant Excitability and/or Lack of Adaptability a Precursor of Shyness?

For the sample as a whole, we did not find any significant relations substantiating the assumption that infant excitability could predict later shyness as observed at 33 months. A somewhat different picture emerged, however, if these relations were examined for boys and girls separately. The observed shyness of the 33-month old girls was positively related to mother-perceived adaptability, $r = .41$, $p < .05$, at 4 months. In other words, girls who were observed as reacting shyly and as staying close to their mothers did not have any difficulties in establishing sleeping and eating routines in early infancy. During our 8-month assessment, subsequently shy girls were observed as being more active, $r = .45$, $p < .05$, and responsive, $r = .46$, $p < .05$, in interaction with their mothers; that is, they appeared to be socially competent and alert babies.

For boys these relations were quite different. The shy behavior of 33-month old boys was positively related to different aspects of child "difficultness" as rated by their mothers at 18 months. Boys who were observed as being shy were said to be less adaptable to sleeping and eating routines, $r = -.57$, $p < .01$, to be more moody and whiny, $r = .41$, $p < .05$, and to be more clingy, dependent, and forcefully demanding maternal attention, $r = .49$, $p < .01$, at 18 months.

Therefore, our findings support the notion that child excitability and lack of adaptability was a predictor of shyness, but only for boys. In 33-month old girls, shy behavior was preceded by infant adaptability (t_2), alertness and social responsiveness (t_3).

A somewhat different picture emerged, however, if the antecedents of observed *shyness at 6.3 years* were examined. Although there were still some differences between boys and girls in terms of the variables being related to subsequent shyness, the pattern and signs of correlations had become equivalent for both sexes. Observed shyness of 6.3 year old girls was found to be significantly related to early indicators of intense and unstable mood, that is, to mother-perceived lack of soothability, $r = .68$, $p < .01$, and crying/restlessness at four months, $r = .56$, $p < .01$; to observed moodiness, $r = .76$, $p < .001$, and lack of responsiveness, $r = .52$, $p < .01$, at eight months; and to mother-perceived child difficultness, that is, to crying, restlessness, and sleeping problems, $r = .54$, $p < .05$, at 18 months. At 43 months, subsequently shy girls were described by their mothers as being less socially competent, $r = -.47$, $p < .05$.

Although in the early phase of infancy, mother-perceived child characteristics were found to be unrelated to the shyness of boys six years later, as early as 8 months several predictive relations emerged. Subsequently shy boys were observed as being more moody, $r = .33$, $p < .05$, and less responsive, $r = -.31$, $p < .05$, in interaction with their mothers. At eighteen months they were perceived as being slightly more moody, $r = .34$, $p < .05$. At 43 months, they were perceived by both parents as being more moody (mothers: $r = .47$, $p < .01$; fathers: $r = .44$, $p < .01$) and by their mothers as being more shy, $r = .33$, $p < .05$.

Therefore, our findings substantiate the notion that shyness may be predicted by child characteristics related to higher levels of emotionality. But these empirical relations differed according to the sex of the child and to the point in time when shyness was observed. At 33 months, boys' shyness was preceded by different aspects of mother-perceived child difficultness while at this age the shyness of girls was preceded by child characteristics indicative of infant adaptability and socially responsive, alert behavior. At 6.3 years, the observed relations between early child characteristics and subsequent shyness had become roughly equivalent for both sexes with infant moodiness being a precursor of shyness both in boys and girls. However, the observed relations between these early infant characteristics and shyness at 6.3 years were stronger for girls than for boys. The

6.3 year shyness of boys was only moderately related to their infant moodiness, and parent perceived moodiness became a significant predictor of their subsequent shyness only after the age of 43 months.

2. Which Other Child Characteristics Predict Shyness?

If we examine the child characteristics being predictively associated with observed shyness, again different relations emerged for boys and girls (see Table 4.2).

Boys who at 33 months displayed considerable fear of strangers and stayed close to their mothers were described in unfavorable terms at 43 months and at 6.3 years both by their mothers and fathers. At 43 months, they were described by their mothers as being more shy, more moody and oversensitive, and less self-confident, happy, and socially competent. This view was basically shared by their fathers who also saw them as more moody.

At 6.3 years, boys who at 33 months appeared to be fearful of strangers and rather dependent of their mother's presence were still seen as significantly more shy and less cognitively and socially competent by their mothers. Their fathers described them as being slightly more shy, more aggressive, and less socially competent. Their preschool teachers judged them as being less cognitively competent. In addition, the 33-month shyness of boys predicted significantly a lower self-confidence concerning perceived social acceptance by peers (t_7; t_8) and perceived cognitive competence and athletic skills (t_8; see Table 4.2) in the Pictorial Scale of Perceived Competence and Social Acceptance.

In contrast to these unfavorable characteristics associated with the 33-month shyness of boys, the shyness of 33-month old girls was found to be predictively related to a variety of *positive* characteristics both at 43 months and 6.3 years. Girls who were rated as shy and staying close to their mothers at 33 months were perceived as being more compliant and less demanding of attention by their mothers, and less moody by their fathers at 43 months. At 6.3 years they were described as being more cognitively competent by their mothers, and as less aggressive, less moody, and far more cognitively and socially competent by their fathers. In addition, the 33-month shyness of girls predicted a better self-confidence in terms of perceived social acceptance by peers and by their mothers at t_8 (see Table 4.2).

At 6.3 years, the observed relations between shyness and other characteristics had become equivalent for boys and girls (see Table 4.3). In spite of some differences in the patterns and magnitude of correlations between our assessment of shyness and the characteristics ascribed to boys and girls by

TABLE 4.2

Spearman Rank Correlation Between Child Characteristics and Observed Shyness at 33 Months in Boys ($N = 25$) and Girls ($N = 14$)

Variables	boys	girls
t_6: 43 months after delivery		
Mother Perceived Child Characteristics:		
- Compliance	.10	.40*
- Social Competence	−.53**	−.02
- Shyness	.50**	−.05
- Moodiness	.56***	−.35+
- Forceful Demand for Attention	−.09	−.41*
Father Perceived Child Characteristics:		
- Moodiness	.43*	−.53*
t_7: 6.3 years after delivery		
Mother Perceived Child Characteristics:		
- Moodiness	.32*	−.24
- Shyness	.62***	−.09
- Cognitive Competence	−.56**	.50*
- Social Competence	−.42*	.22
Father Perceived Child Characteristics:		
- Moodiness	.10	−.47*
- Shyness	.39*	−.27
- Aggressiveness	.35*	−.49*
- Social Competence	−.43*	.82***
- Cognitive Competence	−.27	.60**
Pre-School Teacher Perceived Child Characteristics:		
- Cognitive Competence	−.40*	.24
t_7: 6.3 years after delivery		
Self Concept Child:		
- Perceived Acceptance Peers	−.40*	.11
t_8: 6.8 years after delivery		
Self Concept Child:		
- Perceived Cognitive Competence	−.52**	.02
- Perceived Acceptance Peers	−.62***	.46*
- Perceived Athletic Skills	−.38*	.16
- Perceived Acceptance Mother	−.16	.36+

$+p < .10$; $*p < .05$; $**p < .01$; $***p < .001$

other people, these observed relations substantiate the validity of this 6.3 year assessment of shyness.

Girls and boys who were observed as being shy at 6.3 years were judged by their mothers as being more shy, more moody and less socially competent. Fathers perceived them as being more shy, more aggressive, more moody, and far less socially competent. Although our observation of shy behavior in boys yielded only one very moderate relation to the way

TABLE 4.3

Spearman Rank Correlation Between Child Characteristics and Observed Shyness at 6.3 Years in Boys (N = 25) and Girls (N = 14)

Variables	boys	girls
t₇: 6.3 years after delivery		
Mother Perceived Child Characteristics:		
- Aggressiveness	.17	.51*
- Patience/Persistence	.09	− .52*
- Social Competence	− .37*	− .86***
- *Shyness*	.53**	.67**
- Moodiness	.40**	.45 +
Father Perceived Child Characteristics:		
- Aggressiveness	.57**	.53*
- Patience/Persistence	.09	− .40+
- Social Competence	− .65**	− .63**
- *Shyness*	.47**	.67**
- Cognitive Competence	− .77***	− .25
- Moodiness	.33*	.46 +
Preschool Teacher Perceived Child Characteristics:		
- Aggressiveness	− .17	.73**
- Patience/Persistence	− .10	− .74**
- Social Competence	− .26	− .75**
- *Shyness*	.30*	.62*
- Moodiness	− .12	.74**
Self Concept Child:		
Perceived Athletic Skills	− .49**	.02
t₈: 6.8 years after delivery		
Self Concept Child:		
- Perceived Cognitive Competence	− .45**	− .59**
- Perceived Peer Acceptance	− .50**	− .29
- Perceived Athletic Skills	− .41**	− .00
- Perceived Acceptance Mother	− .44**	− .56**

+p < .10; *p < .05; **p < .01; ***p < .001

these boys were judged by their preschool teachers ($r = .30, p < .05$ for shyness), girls who were observed as being shy were consistently rated in more negative terms by their preschool teachers. They were perceived as being more shy, more aggressive, more moody, less patient and persistent, and socially less competent.

While we found only one significant relation between the observed shyness of 6.3 year old boys and their concurrently assessed self-perceived athletic skills ($r = -.49, p < .01$) in the Pictorial Scale of Perceived Competence and Social Acceptance, more predictive relations emerged half a year later for both boys and girls. Boys who were observed as being shy and withdrawn at t_7 were significantly less self-confident in terms of their perceived cognitive competence, athletic skills, and their perceived acceptance by peers and their mothers at t_8. Girls' shyness at 6.3 years was significantly related to their more negative appraisal of their own cognitive competence and their acceptance by their mothers at t_8 (see Table 4.3).

These negative relations between our observations of shy behavior and the impaired self-confidence of children at this later point in time underscore the validity of our rating scales for the assessment of shy and withdrawn behavior. We do not know why these empirical relations became more significant over time. This finding may be related to the greater cognitive maturity of the children, to their familiarity with the procedure when it was used this second time, or to experiences during the last year of preschool that enhanced processes of growing self-awareness (see also below).[2]

The negative correlations between observed shyness in boys and their self-perceived athletic skills underscore the significance of motoric skills for feelings of self-confidence in boys of this age group. This finding is in harmony with the observations reported by Hymel and colleagues in this volume. That we did not find comparable relations in girls may have to do with the pictorial items of these self concept scales, which depict mainly outdoor and playground activities to assess athletic skills and peer acceptance.

3. Is Insensitive Maternal Care an Antecedent of Shyness?

The developmental path into shyness proposed by Rubin and colleagues (Rubin & Lollis, 1988; Rubin et al., 1990) considered insensitive mothering as an essential factor that in conjunction with child excitability may lead to insecure-resistant attachment relationships and subsequent problems in peer relationships. Because we did not assess the quality of attachment in our longitudinal study, we could not directly test the proposed relations between insensitive mothering, insecure-resistent attachment, and subsequent shy/withdrawn behavior. But we were able to examine the empirical relations between maternal sensitivity and subsequent child shyness. Maternal sensitivity was rated twice over the course of the early mother-child relationship, namely on the maternity ward (t_1) and eight months after delivery (t_3). At 33 months (t_5), maternal dominance in interaction with the child was observed and rated.

For our 33-month assessment, the only relation between maternal sensitivity in the neonatal period and the shyness of 33-month shyness of girls was positive, but short of significance, $r = .42$, $p < .10$. However,

---

[2]The reliability of the Pictorial Scales remained basically unchanged, except for the Scale of Perceived Maternal Acceptance which showed an improvement from $\alpha = .58$ (at t_7) to $\alpha = .71$ (at t_8).

mothers of shy girls were contemporaneously observed as being somewhat less dominant and controlling, $r = -.49, p < .05$; no such relations could be found for boys. Thus, the initial shyness of girls apparently was embedded into a more harmonious mother-daughter relationship.

A somewhat different picture emerged, when the maternal antecedents of 6.3-year shy behavior were examined. Although the first assessment of maternal sensitivity did not predict subsequent child shyness, as early as eight months after delivery these empirical relations emerged and tended to be stronger for girls, $r = -.68, p < .01$, than for boys, $r = -.30, p < .10$. Therefore, our data corroborate the notion that shy/withdrawn behavior may be linked to insensitive mothering, but these relations apply mainly to the shyness of 6.3-year-old girls.

4. Which Other Maternal Factors Predicted the Development of Shyness?

Although the empirical relations between insensitive mothering and child shyness were few and of moderate magnitude only, other findings reveal the role of maternal factors in the development of shyness. Their impact seemed to depend, however, on the sex of the child and on the age at which shyness was observed.

At 33 months, only one predictive relation was found for boys. Their shy behavior at 33 months was significantly related to mother's Shyness and Inhibition as assessed 4 months after delivery, $r = .54, p < .01$. For girls, 33-month shy behavior was predicted by maternal characteristics indicative of psychological well-being and emotional stability as assessed four months after delivery. Shyness was *negatively* related to maternal Depressiveness, $r = -.54, p < .05$; Nervousness, $r = -.46, p < .05$; Irritability, $r = -.47$, $p < .05$; Neuroticism, $r = -.57, p < .01$, and Shyness-Inhibition, $r = -.47, p < .05$. Girls' shyness was positively related to maternal Composure, $r = .48, p < .05$. Comparable empirical relations emerged for the same maternal personality characteristics as assessed 18 months after delivery.

Girls' shy behavior at 6.3 years, however, was *positively* and highly significantly related to the same psychological characteristics of their mothers as assessed 4 and 18 months after delivery. Corresponding to these maternal personality characteristics indicative of depressiveness and irritability were the child-care attitudes and child related feelings assessed at 4 and 18 months as well as at 6.3 years. Mothers of subsequently shy girls scored higher on scales measuring angry impatience, anxious overprotectiveness, and power assertive attitudes in relationship with their daughters (see Table 4.4).

Summing up, these empirical relations suggest that shyness in girls is

TABLE 4.4
Spearman Rank Correlation Between Maternal Factors and Observed Shyness
at 6.3 Years in Boys (N = 25) and Girls (N = 14)

Variables	boys	girls
t$_2$: 4 months after delivery		
Maternal Childcare Attitudes and Feelings:		
- Rigidity	.17	.57**
- Aggravation	.06	−.72**
- Overprotectiveness	−.04	.60**
- Nervous Exhaustion	.22	.75***
Maternal Personality:		
- Nervousness	.14	.58**
- Depressiveness	.21	.58**
- Irritability	.01	.45*
- Neuroticism	.08	.48*
- Shy Inhibition	.15	.81***
t$_4$: 18 months after delivery		
Maternal Childcare Attitudes and Feelings:		
- Aggravation	.20	.53*
- Overprotectiveness	−.13	.68**
- Nervous Exhaustion	.26	.46*
Maternal Personality:		
- Nervousness	.28	.63**
- Depressiveness	.20	.49**
- Neuroticism	−.01	.36+
- Shy Inhibition	.26	.70***
t$_7$: 6.3 years after delivery		
Maternal Childcare Attitudes and Feelings:		
- Rigidity	−.23	.56*
- Aggravation	.17	.76***
- Overprotection	−.10	.61**
- Nervous Exhaustion	.35*	.80***
- Punishment	.21	.62**
Maternal Personality:		
- Depressiveness	−.06	.58**

*p < .05; **p < .01; ***p < .001

much more closely linked to maternal characteristics than shyness in boys. The quality of this association apparently depends on the age when shy behavior of girls was observed. Their 33-month shyness appears to be related to maternal well-being, patience, and emotional stability, while their 6.3 year shyness was predictable from maternal characteristics associated with irritability and nervous exhaustion, and child related feelings and attitudes indicative of a hostile, impatient, and distressed mother-daughter relationship. These data suggest that shyness may carry with it a different meaning for younger than for older children, especially in girls. I discuss this possibility in the following.

In summary, the data reported herein suggest different models of the development of shyness for boys and girls.

For boys (see Fig. 4.1) we found a *continuous chaining of characteristics* starting from mother-perceived child characteristics at 4 and 18 months and leading directly up to observed shy behavior at 33 months. The 33-month assessment of shyness for boys predicted maternal perceived shyness and concomitant problems in social relations at 43 months. These problems appeared to be relatively stable as the correlations ($r = .50$ to $r = .67, p < .001$) with the corresponding 6.3 year assessments indicate. The contemporaneous correlations between mother-perceived shyness, our observational assessment of shyness, and the negative self concept of these boys underscore the validity of this assessment.

Thus, shyness in boys predicts a rather stable family reputation of impaired social competence that subsequently is even reflected in the self concept of these children. Here it is interesting to note that fathers and mothers judged the shyness of their sons at 6.3 years rather similarly ($r = .73, p < .001$). Compared to the girls' data, however, few characteristics of the early mother-son relationship were directly linked to the observed shyness of boys at 6.3 years.

For girls (see Figure 4.2) the developmental path into shyness differed in two important ways:

1. The 33-month observation of shyness was *not* a continuous link in the chain, but rather a turning point of the path into shyness.

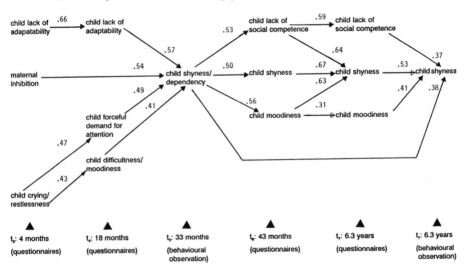

Note: All coefficients are Spearman rank coefficients

FIG. 4.1   The developmental path of shyness in boys ($N = 25$).

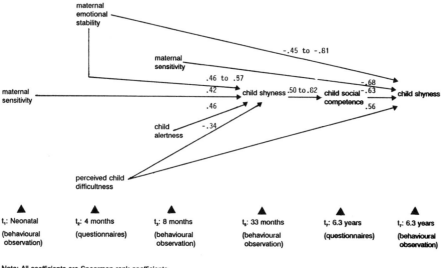

Note: All coefficients are Spearman rank coefficients

FIG. 4.2   The developmental path of shyness in girls (N = 14).

2. Very early characteristics of the mother-daughter relationship were significantly and directly related to the subsequent shyness at 6.3 years. Such direct relations could hardly be found in the developmental path of boys.

These empirical relations suggest a number of interpretations. First, shyness as observed at 33 months may mean quite different things in boys and girls. While in girls it was found to be related to a harmonious mother-daughter relationship, this was not the case for boys. Considering the findings that the 33-month shyness in girls was related to the emotional stability and sensitivity of the mother, to various positive child characteristics ascribed to them prior and subsequent to this assessment, and to a more positive self concept at age 6.8, it looks as if the apparent shyness of girls was, in reality, a proxy for *secure base* behavior.

Shyness in 33-month old boys may have a quite different meaning, however, coming much closer to what traditionally has been described as "dependent" behavior (see Maccoby & Masters, 1970). The syndrome of behavioral difficulties in which it was embedded underscores the notion of clingyness and immaturity as the high correlations with forceful demand of attention, moodiness, and lack of adaptability indicate. Therefore, it looks as if observed shyness in 33-month old boys was preceded and followed by child characteristics depicting a rather dependent, unhappy, and socially less competent child.

These findings are in harmony with the results of other studies where shyness of girls was found to be embedded in positive mother-child relationships, while shyness in boys was not (see Stevenson-Hinde, 1988; Radke-Yarrow et al., 1988). However, these gender-specific correlates of shyness applied only to our 33-month assessment of shyness; they did not pertain to the shyness as assessed at 6.3 years.

While for boys there was a small, albeit significant correlation, $r = .38$, $p < .05$, between the 33-month and 6.3 year assessment of shyness, we did not find this predictive relation for girls. Consequently, our data do not substantiate the notion that shyness in girls might show greater continuity or temporal stability than shyness in boys, as one would expect if one was to assume that shyness in girls is more accepted and thus possibly reinforced by parents.

The most impressive difference between boys' and girls' shyness is that boys' shyness seemed to emerge rather independent of what the mothers felt or did. Likewise, we could not find any empirical relations between boys' shy behavior and any of the paternal characteristics that were assessed over the course of our study (i.e., childcare attitudes and child related feelings at t_6 and t_7, paternal personality characteristics at t_7). Thus, our data cannot identify the sources of shyness for boys. Perhaps shyness in boys is genetically preprogrammed, and temperamental factors unfold their influence over time. The only strong correlation that was found for maternal factors was the relation between maternal Shy Inhibition and boys' shyness at 33 months. This correlation could be interpreted as support for such a genetic hypothesis.

While shyness of boys appeared rather unrelated to maternal feelings and actions, this was not the case in girls. The data strongly supported the notion that maternal feelings and actions, as assessed at all points in time, were highly and significantly related to the 6.3-year shyness of their daughters. Specifically, we found that shyness of girls at 6.3 years was embedded in a mother-daughter relationship showing many symptoms of distress. It was found to be related to insensitive mothering, maternal feelings of angry impatience, hostility and power assertion, and diverse aspects of child difficultness as assessed in the early phase of infant development.

These characteristics correspond to the developmental path Rubin and colleagues (Rubin et al., 1990; Rubin & Lollis, 1988) have suggested as being typical of subsequently rejected children. This developmental path describes a difficult child being mothered insensitively thereby leading to insecure avoidant attachment relationships. In conjunction with an authoritarian style of parenting, these children subsequently will be rejected by their agemates mainly because of their hostile and aggressive behavior.

Although we did not assess directly the quality of the attachment relationship, some of our findings neatly support this hypothesis. As early as 4 months after delivery, subsequently shy girls were perceived as being less soothable and far more difficult by their mothers. Four months later, their relationship looked anything but harmonious as these mothers lacked sensitivity and their babies displayed unhappy mood and disinterest in their social environment. The feelings and childcare attitudes that these mothers displayed at all times fit the description of an "authoritarian" style of parenting, as they were a mixture of power assertion, impatience, and hostility. From the perspective of their 6.8 year old daughters, these mothers were more remote and less caring.

In harmony with the assumptions of the developmental path suggested by Rubin and colleagues, our observation of girls' shy behavior was significantly related to the aggressiveness-ratings of their parents and their preschool teachers. Thus, the behavioral manifestations of shyness apparently depend on contextual conditions. When we entered the family home as strange adults, the girls behaved shyly, while in other social contexts, such as in relationship with parents or peers, aggressive tendencies could show more easily.

Consequently, our assessment of 6.3-year shyness in girls may have been an indicator for a whole host of behavioral difficulties these shy girls exhibit in other social contexts, including unhappiness, oversensitiveness, and shyness as internalizing problems and aggressiveness as externalizing problems. Therefore, these girls' emotional problems may become manifest in both (e.g., internalizing and externalizing) ways and as such may be empirically unseparable. This syndrome of both withdrawn *and* aggressive behavior has been described by Asendorpf (1990) and by Ledingham and Schwartzman (1984). According to the findings of the latter, the developmental prognosis is particularly poor for children exhibiting this syndrome of both withdrawal and aggression.

Last, but not least, we cannot exclude the possibility that these high correlations between maternal factors and the emotional problems of their daughters were effected by genetic similarity between mothers and daughters. Then these relations could be interpreted as implying that emotionally unstable, hostile, and unsensitive mothers had daughters in which the same emotional problems became manifest in terms of shy, withdrawn, and aggressive behavior at 6.3 years. Because comparable similarities were not found between mothers and sons or between fathers, daughters, and sons, such a genetic influence must be sex-specific (e.g., linked to the X-chromosome).

Alternatively, our data fit the notion frequently proposed by feministic and/or psychoanalytic authors, namely that maternal influences are mirrored in the daughters (positive and negative characteristics alike) due to the almost symbiotic closeness of the mother-daughter relationship. In contrast, boys are forced into a greater greater autonomy and dissimilarity from their mothers because over the course of their development they have to change their object of identification and move away from the maternal to the paternal model of sex-role development (see Huston, 1983). Because we did not find any correlations between paternal characteristics and shyness in sons, we can only speculate whether the sons' move towards the paternal model of sex-role development had not yet taken place, whether the relevant characteristics reflecting such a move were not included in our study, or whether these assumptions about the sex-role development of boys are empirically invalid.

CHANGES IN SHYNESS

In the last section of this chapter I examine the conditions associated with observed *changes* in shyness. Specifically, subgroups of children who shifted in the degree of observable shyness are compared with children exhibiting rather stable patterns of shyness over time. To define these groups, the distributions of shyness scores both at 33 months and 6.3 years were roughly trichotomized. Due to a slightly uneven distribution of these scores, with more children receiving scores at the lower end of these shyness-scales, we had the largest group of children ($N = 10$) scoring low in shyness at both times and a fairly small group of children ($N = 4$) scoring high at both times. The two groups of children showing marked changes in shyness were of the same size, with six children in each the "High-to-Low" and the "Low-to-High" shyness group. To define these groups, we included only those children who exhibited changes from the lower third to the higher third of the distribution and vice-versa, and excluded children shifting from intermediate levels into high or low shyness.

For these comparisons of subgroups of children exhibiting stable or variable patterns of shyness, we combined the data of girls and boys. This was done because the subsample of girls was too small to allow for further differentiations in terms of stable and unstable subgroups, and because at 6.3 years the observed relations between shyness and other characteristics had become roughly equivalent for both sexes.

According to the findings described earlier, we nevertheless expected gender-specific differences in the developmental patterns of shyness. It will be recalled that the observed shyness of 33-month old girls was embedded in various positive characteristics of the mother-child relationship, while the girls' shyness at 6.3 years was related to many unfavorable maternal factors. Therefore, it appears as if the "healthier" developmental path for girls consisted in a change from initially higher to subsequently lower shyness. Consequently, we expected to find more girls than boys in the group of children shifting from high-shy to low-shy behavior between 33 months and 6.3 years and that mainly maternal factors would account for this "positive" shift away from shyness. The observed greater temporal stability of shyness in boys would lead to an over-respresentation of boys in the consistently high or consistently low shy groups.

The characteristics distinguishing the group of consistently high-shy children from children shifting from high to low shyness, are displayed in Table 4.5.

In harmony with our assumptions, more girls ($N = 4$) than boys ($N = 2$) belonged to the group changing from high to low shyness, while the stable high-shy group contained only boys. In other words: Approximately 1/3 of all girls in our sample belonged to this group shifting from high to low shyness, while a comparable change was observable for less than 10% of the boys (2 out of 25).

Concerning our second hypothesis that mainly maternal factors would account for the differences between these two groups, the results were not quite as straightforward. The mothers of children in the consistently shy group were significantly older than those in the unstable "High-to-Low" shyness group. In addition, mothers of the consistently shy children were more depressed (t_2; t_7) and they expressed greater acknowledgment of the use of high power assertive strategies to deal with their children (t_2; t_4; t_7). These mothers also appeared less sensitive (t_3) and more aggravated and frustrated (t_4) than those of unstable shy children.

The fathers of consistently shy children also suggested more power assertive strategies to socialize their children (t_7). Interestingly, mothers of stable shy children characterized them as more difficult (t_4), noncompliant (t_6; t_7), and aggressive (t_6; t_7). Fathers characterized their stable shy children as more moody (t_6; t_7), aggressive (t_7), shy (t_7), and as less cognitively competent (t_7) than those of unstable shy children. These parental perceptions were substantiated by our own behavioral observations where children in the "High-Shy" group appeared more moody and unhappy (t_3) and less cooperative (t_5) than children in the "High-to-Low" shy group. Therefore, we cannot completely dismiss the notion that children in the "High-Shy" group were, in fact, somewhat different and more difficult to care for than the children in the "High-to-Low" shy group.

Another set of variables distinguishing these two groups were marital data. Compared to the "High-to-Low" shy group, the parents of the stable "High-Shy" group described their marital relationship as more distressed at 43 months. Mothers assessed their relationship as significantly lower in mutual disclosure and communication; they described their husbands as being less affectionate. Husbands described their wives as being more

TABLE 4.5
Group Comparison of Children Scoring High-high in Shyness (N = 4) Versus High-low in Shyness (N = 6) Between 33 Months and 6.3 Years

Variables	Groups	x	SD	t-Value	df	p
t_2: 4 months after delivery						
Age Mother	HH	33.50	5.44	2.53	8	.05
	HL	26.83	2.99			
Maternal Childcare Attitudes and Feelings:						
- Punishment	HH	28.75	1.50	9.45	7	.001
	HL	18.60	1.67			
Maternal Personality:						
- Depressiveness	HH	6.57	3.50	3.10	3.28	.05
	HL	1.20	.84			
t_3: 8 months after delivery						
- Observed Maternal	HH	33.50	3.44	− 3.15	8	.01
Sensitivity	HL	43.41	5.56			
- Observed Child	HH	3.26	.61			
Moodiness	HL	2.42	.40	2.67	8	.01
t_4: 18 months after delivery						
Maternal Childcare Attitudes and Feelings:						
- Rigidity	HH	28.00	4.69	2.66	7	.05
	HL	20.40	3.91			
- Aggravation	HH	27.00	8.98	2.76	7	.01
	HL	14.80	3.96			
- Frustration	HH	33.50	6.60	2.53	7	.05
	HL	21.80	7.12			
- Punishment	HH	33.00	4.24	4.74	7	.001
	HL	22.20	2.58			
t_4: 18 months after delivery						
Mother Perceived Child Characteristics:						
- Child Difficultness	HH	9.25	1.70	2.69	7	.05
(= crying/restless)	HL	6.00	1.80			
t_5: 33 months after delivery						
Observed Lack of	HH	15.66	2.51	2.34	7	.05
Cooperativeness Child	HL	10.66	3.20			
t_6: 43 months after delivery						
Mother Perceived Child Characteristics:						
- Aggressiveness	HH	14.75	3.59	4.07	7	.01
	HL	7.60	1.51			
- Non-Compliance	HH	18.50	3.10	3.33	7	.01
	HL	12.20	2.58			

TABLE 4.5 (*Continued*)

Variables	Groups	x	SD	t-Value	df	p
Father Perceived Child						
- Moodiness	HH	18.75	3.59	3.30	5	.01
	HL	11.33	1.52			
Marital Relationship:						
Mother perceived						
- Communication	HH	12.00	2.64	− 4.46	5	.01
	HL	24.25	4.10			
- Affection	HH	13.33	4.50	− 2.64	5	.04
	HL	20.00	2.16			
t_6: 43 months after delivery						
Marital Relationship:						
Father perceived						
- Conflict	HH	10.33	3.21	4.60	2.13	.04
	HL	1.66	.57			
t_7: 6.3 years after delivery						
Maternal Childcare Attitudes and Feelings:						
- Punishment	HH	28.25	2.98	3.20	8	.01
	HL	19.66	4.72			
Paternal Childcare Attitudes and Feelings:						
- Punishment	HH	26.33	2.08	3.79	6	.01
	HL	17.60	3.57			
Mother Perceived Child Characteristics:						
- Aggressiveness	HH	26.50	6.60	2.31	8	.05
	HL	17.50	5.68			
t_7: 6.3 years after delivery						
Father Perceived Child Characteristics:						
- Aggressiveness	HH	27.00	2.64	3.04	6	.02
	HL	15.80	5.89			
- *Shyness*	HH	18.66	1.52	3.50	6	.01
	HL	12.60	2.70			
- Cognitive Competence	HH	15.00	2.00	− 2.69	6	.03
	HL	18.00	1.22			
- Moodiness	HH	10.00	1.00	3.66	6	.01
	HL	5.80	1.78			
Marital Relationship:						
Father Perceived						
- Resignation	HH	12.33	1.52	4.07	6	.01
	HL	3.80	4.07			
Observed Child Characteristics:						
- Lack of Cooperativeness	HH	28.00	11.57	2.21	8	.05
	HL	16.66	4.50			

quarrelsome. At 6.3 years, these negative accounts of the marital relationship remained, albeit only from the perspective of fathers. These fathers were generally less satisfied with their marriage, as indicated by their higher scores on the Resignation Scale.

Summarizing these findings, a shift away from shyness was more typical of girls than of boys. In comparison to the "High-Shy" group, the "High-to-Low" shy group displayed many characteristics indicative of a very harmonious mother-child and marital relationship. The positive characteristics associated with the shift away from shyness were not limited to any particular developmental phase within which this shift occurred, but were present throughout the whole course of the mother-child relationship.

Another comparison was that between those children who remained un-shy at both assessments ($N = 10$) and those who changed from "Low-to-High" shyness between 33 months and 6.3 years ($N = 6$).

The former comparison of children shifting away from shyness with children remaining very shy demonstrated that these groups differed from the very beginning in the course of their mother-child relationship. If we compare the group of consistently un-shy children with children shifting into shyness, very few such differences in the early period become evident, and these relate mainly to child characteristics (see Table 4.6).

Children who became more shy over the course of time were perceived by their mothers as being more difficult during infancy because they were less soothable (t_2) and had more problems with sleeping through and adjusting to sleeping and eating routines (t_4). At eight months these children were observed as being more moody and unhappy, at 43 months mothers perceived them as socially less competent.

The most pronounced differences between these groups emerged at 6.3 years, however. At this point in time children in the "Low-to-High" shy group were described as being more shy, less persistent and less socially competent from the perspective of mothers, fathers, and preschool teachers alike. These differences were highly significant on almost all scales used to assess child characteristics from the perspective of these adults relating to the children at home and at preschool.

Summarizing these results, the following observations appear worthy of note. Children who shifted into shyness apparently were already somewhat more sensitive and vulnerable in their infancy as they were more difficult to soothe, had more sleeping problems, and greater difficulties in establishing sleeping and eating routines. But their main problems seemed to emerge at some time within the span between 43 months and 6.3 years, that is, the time when all children had entered kindergarten. Here it seems of interest to note that the children shifting into shyness were judged in less favorable terms on all dimensions of child characteristics assessed from the perspective of preschool teachers.

Trying to unravel the possible causes or correlates of this shift into shyness, we first examined family variables distinguishing the "Low-to-High" from the stable "Low" shy group. Neither the ordinal position of the child nor the fact that children were dethroned by the birth of a sibling appeared to be relevant, because none of these conditions distinguished these groups. The only finding pointing to more family stress was the fact that at 6.3 years both parents expressed some more dissatisfaction with their marital relationship, but these differences were short of significance.

Although we used identical scales to assess child related feelings and attitudes as well as personality characteristics both in mothers and in fathers, the results of our group comparison indicated that this family stress was mainly experienced by the mothers; at 6.3 years they felt more aggravated and exhausted in their relationships with their children (see Table 4.6). We do not know where these maternal feelings came from, whether they resulted from the problems in the marital relationship, or from an increased awareness of the problems their children had in relationship with other people, or were influenced by third factors not included in our study.

In addition, we found other conditions that may have explained the shift into shyness. The first condition that distinguished the two comparison groups was the number of children who changed kindergarten shortly before our assessment. Four children (66%) of the group shifting into shyness had experienced such a change, compared to only two children (20%) belonging to the consistently low shy group (see Asendorpf, in press, for a similar finding). In the sample as a whole, we found nine children who had experienced a similar change due to the fact that the parents had moved or changed their working routines so that a change in child-care arrangements was necessary. All these children were judged by their preschool teachers in less favorable terms; according to their view, they exhibited higher moodiness, aggressiveness, and lack of persistence. Children entering a new preschool group may show these initial reactions in their attempts to gain social attention (Schmidt-Denter, 1988), or they simply may be judged differently by their preschool teachers (Hinde & Tobin, 1986).

But children shifting into shyness were also perceived as being cognitively less competent by their preschool teachers. Since they were judged in a similar way by their fathers and by us as outside observers at our 6.3 year assessment (see Table 4.6), we examined whether these children received lower scores in our assessment of their cognitive competence half a year later. Here we found that children showing the shift into shyness as compared to consistently low-shy children scored lower on the Vocabulary, but not on the Block-Design Test of the Hamburg Wechsler Intelligence Scales. Therefore, it looks as if children with limited abilities of expressing

TABLE 4.6
Group Comparison of Children Scoring Low-low in Shyness (N = 10) Versus
Low-high in Shyness (N = 6) Between 33 Months and 6.3 Years

Variables	Groups	x	SD	t-Value	df	p
t_2: 4 months after delivery Mother Perceived Child Characteristics:						
- Lack of Soothability	LL	1.40	.51	−2.43	14	.01
	LH	2.16	.75			
t_3: 8 months after delivery Observed Child Moodiness	LL	2.66	.48	−2.00	12	.05
Moodiness	LH	3.14	.35			
t_4: 18 months after delivery Mother Perceived Child Characteristics:						
- Sleeping Problems	LL	2.00	.75	−2.27	12	.05
	LH	3.16	1.69			
- Lack of Adaptability	LL	1.25	.46	−2.05	12	.05
	LH	2.00	.89			
t_6: 43 months after delivery Mother Perceived Child Characteristics:						
- Social Competence	LL	23.60	1.95	2.44	14	.02
	LH	21.66	2.87			
t_7: 6.3 years after delivery Maternal Childcare Atti- tudes and Feelings:						
- Aggravation	LL	16.00	2.77	−2.69	12	.02
	LH	21.00	4.19			
- Exhaustion	LL	7.88	1.53	−2.90	6.09	.02
	LH	12.66	3.83			
t_7: 6.3 years after delivery Mother Perceived Child Characteristics:						
- Lack of Patience/	LL	14.44	1.85	−3.30	13	.006
Persistence	LH	20.83	4.83			
- Social Competence	LL	24.22	3.27	3.76	13	.002
	LH	16.66	4.54			
- *Shyness*	LL	10.66	2.87	−2.72	6.15	.03
	LH	18.83	6.96			
- Moodiness	LL	7.00	1.85	−3.43	12	.005
	LH	11.00	2.53			

TABLE 4.6 (Continued)

Variables	Groups	x	SD	t-Value	df	p
Father Perceived Child Characteristics:						
- Lack of Patience/	LL	14.44	3.00	− 2.42	13	.03
Persistence	LH	18.16	2.78			
- Aggressiveness	LL	19.50	3.02	− 2.21	12	.04
	LH	23.16	3.12			
- Social Competence	LL	24.50	2.50	4.18	12	.001
	LH	19.16	2.13			
- Shyness	LL	11.77	3.66	− 2.50	13	.03
	LH	18.33	6.53			
- Cognitive Competence	LL	18.73	1.68	4.62	11	.001
	LH	13.00	2.55			
t_7: 6.3 years after delivery Preschool Teacher Perceived Child Characteristics:						
- Lack of Patience/	LL	11.71	3.54	− 2.52	11	.02
Persistence	LH	18.00	5.40			
- Social Competence	LL	24.16	2.13	2.84	8	.02
	LH	19.25	3.40			
- Shyness	LL	13.00	4.93	− 2.14	11	.05
	LH	19.33	5.75			
- Cognitive Competence	LL	17.00	1.58	2.98	8	.01
	LH	13.00	2.55			
Observed Child Characteristics:						
- Cognitive Competence	LL	20.60	3.80	4.14	14	.001
	LH	12.00	4.38			
t_8: 6,8 years after delivery Cognitive Competence Child:						
- Hamburg-Wechsler	LL	17.80	2.53	2.32	6.79	.03
Vocabulary Score	LH	13.66	4.67			
Self Concept Child:						
- Cognitive Competence	LL	21.30	1.25	2.44	5.95	.05
	LH	18.00	3.16			
- Perceived Acceptance	LL	17.10	2.68	3.09	14	.01
Mother	LH	13.33	1.63			

75

themselves may be at a disadvantage in social relationships. Although this finding about the impaired verbal abilities of the shy children differed from the results of Asendorpf (1989) who found shyness and cognitive competence to be unrelated, it corresponds to the general observation of Rubin et al. (1990) about the relative ineptitude of shy children to verbally express their needs to agemates. It also is in harmony with the data of Evans presented in this volume. In the light of her findings, we should not only note that lack of verbal expressiveness reduces the chances of shy children to assert themselves in relationships with agemates, we should also consider the possibility that the shyness of these children inhibited them in their performance during our assessment of their verbal abilities and therefore made them look less competent than they really were.

While we did not find any differences between the consistently low shy and the low-high shy children in their self-concept at 6.3 years, such significant differences emerged half a year later. At this time, children who had shifted into shyness between 33 months and 6.3 years scored significantly lower on the scales of self-perceived cognitive competence and of perceived acceptance by their mothers. Therefore, it looks as if processes of growing self-awareness or events specific to this last year of preschool effected this change, enlarging the differences between stably un-shy and increasingly shy children.

Summarizing these results, it looks as if children who were already somewhat more sensitive and vulnerable in early childhood showed this shift into shyness because during their preschool years they experienced the cumulative impact of deteriorating family relationships as well as a change in their peer-group environment. Because these children were more poorly equipped to verbally assert their needs, they must have developed a growing sense of their own incompetence, as the corresponding change in their self-concept indicated.

Asendorpf (this volume) has suggested, with reference to his results, that the peculiarities of the German preschool system may partially account for these findings. In German preschools, children usually stay together as a group for about three to four years. Each year the oldest children leave the group as they enter school, but they are replaced by the youngest children entering kindergarten around the age of three. Consequently, older children enjoy almost automatically a higher social status due to their age and due to their "seniority" within the same group.

Children who change their preschool class may be at some disadvantage. They cannot rely on naturally grown peer-relationships in this setting; in addition, they may not enjoy as automatically, the privileges of being the "older" ones, that is, being well known to and admired by the younger children in their group. On top of these disadvantages, an increasing number of cognitive tasks are introduced in the last year of preschool to prepare children for the transition to school. Children who do not perform as well as their agemates on these verbal tasks may then develop a certain sense of failure at this early age. Their anticipation of failure may make them look less cooperative and more shy during assessments resembling such tasks, and our assessments around their age of six presumably shared some of these characteristics, evoking feelings of ambivalence and insecurity in these children.

SUMMARY AND CONCLUSIONS

In this chapter, I described data collected over the course of more than six years to examine the development of shyness in early childhood. Perhaps the most interesting results of the study were as follows:

1. The developmental paths into shyness apparently differed for boys and girls: While boys' shyness was found to be rather independent of family characteristics, the shyness of girls appeared to be closely linked to maternal characteristics.

2. Contrary to our assumptions, the shyness of boys showed a more continuous and stable developmental path than the shyness of girls. While the 33-month shyness of boys allowed prediction of their 6.3-year shyness, this was not the case for girls.

3. Shyness was not a unitary concept, but had quite different meanings depending on the sex of the child and the age at which it was assessed. While the observed shyness of 33 month old girls was embedded in a very harmonious mother-child relationship and, thus, was preceded and followed by many positive characteristics ascribed to shy girls, shyness in same-aged boys had much more negative implications, coming close to what could best be described as immature and dependent behavior. At 6.3 years the observed shyness of boys and girls embodied equivalent qualities as it corresponded to a syndrome of sadness, over-sensitiveness, and lack of social and verbal competence.

4. The analysis of the characteristics associated with marked shifts in shyness showed that shifts away from shyness were more typical of girls than of boys and were related to positive characteristics observed over the whole course of the mother-child relationship. In contrast, the conditions associated with marked shifts into shyness revealed that children who as infants were already somewhat more sensitive and vulnerable showed a marked increase in shyness under the cumulative impact of deteriorating family relationships and an abrupt change in the peer-group environment. Both changes were located in the preschool years of childhood. Therefore, different developmental phases have to be considered if marked changes away from or into shyness are to be accounted for.

ACKNOWLEDGMENTS

This research project was supported by a grant from the German Research Council. I would like to thank Lind Heinig, Maria Gavranidou, and Mechthild Gödde for their help in conducting this study. Likewise, I want to thank Ken Rubin and Jens Asendorpf for their constructive comments on an earlier version of this paper and for their help in writing proper English.

REFERENCES

Asendorpf, J. B. (1989). *Soziale Gehemmtheit und ihre Entwicklung* (Social inhibition and its development). Heidelberg/New York/London: Springer.

Asendorpf, J. B. (1990). Beyond social withdrawal: Shyness, unsociability, and peer avoidance. *Human Development, 33,* 250–259.

Asendorpf, J. B. (in press). Beyond stability: Predicting interindividual differences in intraindividual change. *European Journal of Psychology.*

Bates, J. E., Freeland, C. A. B., & Lounsbury, M. L. (1979). *Measurement of infant difficultness. Child Development, 50,* 794–803.

Broussard, E. R., & Hartner, M. S. S. (1970). Maternal perception of the neonate as related to development. *Child Psychiatry and Human Development, 1,* 16–25.

Buss, A. H., & Plomin, R. (1986). The EAS approach to temperament. In R. Plomin, & J. Dunn (Eds.), *The study of temperament: Changes, continuities and challenges* (pp. 67–79). Hillsdale, N.J.: Lawrence Erlbaum Associates.

Codreanu, N. (1984). *Kindbezogene Einstellungen von Müttern mit Kleinkindern* (Child-care attitudes of mothers of infants). Munich University: Unpublished Masters Thesis.

Engfer, A. (1986a). Antecedents of behaviour problems in infancy. In G. A. Kohnstamm, (Ed.), *Temperament discussed: Temperament and development in infancy and childhood* (pp. 165–180). Lisse: Swets & Zeitlinger.

Engfer, A. (1986b). *Intergenerational influences on the mother-child relationship.* Paper presented at the 11th International Congress of the International Association for Child and Adolescent Psychiatry and Allied Professions, Paris, July 21–25, 1986.

Engfer, A. (1988). The interrelatedness of marriage and the mother-child relationship. In R. A. Hinde, & J. Stevenson-Hinde (Eds.), *Relationships within families: Mutual influences* (pp. 104–118). Oxford: Clarendon Press.

Engfer, A., & Gavranidou, M. (1987). Antecedents and consequences of maternal sensitivity. In H. Rauh, & H.-C. Steinhausen (Eds.), *Psychobiology and early development* (pp. 71–99). North-Holland: Elsevier.

Engfer, A., & Schneewind, K. A. (1978). *Der Ehefragebogen. Arbeitsbericht 21 aus dem Projekt Eltern-Kind-Beziehungen an der Universität München.* (The marriage-questionnaire. Research report no. 21 of the research project "parent-child-relationships" at the Munich University). Munich University: Unpublished Research Report.

Fahrenberg, J., Selg, H., & Hampel, R. (1978). *Freiburger Persönlichkeitsinventar. F-P-I.* (Freiburg Personality Inventory, F-P-I). Göttingen: Hogrefe.

Gavranidou, M., Heinig, L., & Engfer, A. (1987). *Dokumentation der zu t_6 eingesetzten Erhebungsinstrumente. Arbeitsbericht Nr. 7 aus dem Forschungsprojektzur "Entwicklung punitiver Mutter-Kind-Interaktionen im sozioökologischen Kontext"* (Documentation of the instruments used at t_6. Research report no. 7 of the research project about the "development of punitive mother-child interactions in socioecological context"). Munich: Unpublished Research Report.

Hahlweg, K. (1979). *Konstruktion und Validierung des Partnerschaftsfragebogens (PFB)* (Construction and validation of the relationship questionnaire). *Zeitschrift für Klinische Psychologie, 8,* 17–40.

Hardesty, F. P., & Priester, H. J. (1966). *Hamburg-Wechsler-Intelligenztest für Kinder* (Hamburg-Wechsler-intelligence-test for children). Bern: Huber 1966.

Harter, S., & Pike, R. (1983). *The Pictorial Scale of Perceived Competence and Social Acceptance for Young Children.* University of Denver.

Hinde, R. A. (1988). Continuities and discontinuities: conceptual issues and methodological considerations. In M. Rutter (Ed.), *Studies of psychosocial risk: The power of longitudinal data* (pp. 367–383). Cambridge: Cambridge University Press.

Hinde, R. A., & Tobin, C. (1986). Temperament at home and behaviour at preschool. In G. A. Kohnstamm (Ed.), *Temperament discussed: Temperament and development in infancy and childhood* (pp. 123–132). Lisse: Swets & Zeitlinger.

Huston, A. C. (1983). Sex-typing. In P. H. Mussen (Ed.), *Handbook of child psychology. Fourth edition. Vol. IV. Socialization, personality, and social development* (pp. 387–467). New York: Wiley.

Kagan, J., Reznick, S. J., & Snidman, N. (1986). Temperamental inhibition in early childhood. In R. Plomin & J. Dunn (Eds.), *The study of temperament: Changes, continuities and challenges* (pp. 53–65). Hillsdale, N.J.: Lawrence Erlbaum Associates.

Kalden, M., Müller-Osten, U., & Engfer, A. (1987). *Neudefinition, Erprobung und Validierung der Skalen zum angemessenen Elternverhalten im ersten Lebensjahr. Arbeitsbericht 5 aus dem Forschungsprojekt zur "Entwicklung punitiver Mutter-Kind-Interaktionen im sozioökologischen Kontext"* (Definition, application, and validation of the scales measuring adequate parental behaviour during the first year of life. Research report no. 5 of the research project about the "development of punitive mother-child interaction in socioecological context"). Munich: Unpublished Research Report.

Ledingham, J. E., & Schwartzman, A. E. (1984). A 3-year follow-up of aggressive and withdrawn behavior in childhood: Preliminary findings. *Journal of Abnormal Child Psychology, 12,* 157–168.

Maccoby, E. E., & Masters, J. C. (1970). Attachment and dependency. In P. H. Mussen (Ed.), *Carmichael's manual of child psychology. Third edition* (Vol. II, pp. 73–157). New York: Wiley.

Radke-Yarrow, M., Richters, J., & Wilson, W. E. (1988). Child development in a network of relationships. In R. A. Hinde & J. Stevenson-Hinde (Eds.), *Relationships within families: Mutual influences* (pp. 48–67). Oxford: Clarendon Press.

Rubin, K. H., LeMare, L., & Lollis, S. P. (1990). Social withdrawal in childhood: Developmental pathways to peer rejection. In S. R. Asher, & S. Lollis (Eds.), *Children's status in the peer group.* New York: Cambridge University Press.

Rubin, K. H., & Lollis, S. P. (1988). Origins and consequences of social withdrawal. In J. Belsky, & T. Nezworski (Eds.), *Clinical implications of attachment* (pp. 219–252). Hillsdale, N.J.: Lawrence Erlbaum Associates.

Schmidt-Denter, U. (1988). *Soziale Entwicklung: Ein Lehrbuch über soziale Beziehungen im Laufe des menschlichen Lebens* (Social development. A textbook about social relationships over the life-course). München-Weinheim: Psychologische Verlags Union.

Stevenson-Hinde, J. (1988). Individuals in relationships. In R. A. Hinde, & J. Stevenson-Hinde (Eds.), *Relationships within families: Mutual influences* (pp. 68–80). Oxford: Clarendon Press.

Stevenson-Hinde, J., & Hinde, R. A. (1986). Changes in associations between characteristics and interactions. In R. Plomin, & J. Dunn (Eds.), *The study of temperament: Changes, continuities, and challenges* (pp. 115–129). Hillsdale, N.J.: Lawrence Erlbaum Associates.

Pathways to Aggression and Social Withdrawal: Interactions Among Temperament, Attachment, and Regulation

Nathan A. Fox
Susan D. Calkins
University of Maryland

THEORETICAL BACKGROUND

Two independent research areas in developmental psychology have recently found spheres of important intersection. The two areas, research on infant and child temperament and work on shyness and rejection and early childhood, have had separate, and in general, non-overlapping paths. Research in both areas has been concerned with measurement and definitional issues. For quite some time, temperament researchers relied on maternal report/questionnaire data for the measurement of individual differences. These data were used to develop notions regarding the stability and composition of temperamental factors. In addition, questionnaire data were factor analyzed to define traits or dispositions which constituted temperament (Goldsmith, Buss, Plomin, Rothbart, Thomas, Chess, Hinde, & McCall, 1987). The temperament research area has undergone a great deal of change since Thomas, Chess, and Birch (1968) first outlined seven basic traits and the notion of goodness-of-fit. The change has been in the direction of more laboratory or home based observation of infant behavior and the use of behavioral measures to derive conceptually driven factors describing individual differences in infant personality (Matheny & Wilson, 1981; Rothbart, 1981; Rothbart & Derryberry, 1981).

Research on shyness and social isolation has undergone a similar revision in both its methodological and conceptual domains. The dominant method for examining social isolation was (and in much research still is) sociometric analysis. Children are asked to nominate peers who they would least like to play with, who are least popular, and who are most aggressive. From this work emerged important notions about who socially isolated children were, and how they fit into the social milieu. In addition, conceptual distinctions between isolation and rejection were developed (Asher & Wheeler, 1985; Rubin, LeMare, & Lollis, 1990). Here too, the impetus for change has been through the use of observational data and the clustering of certain behaviors into conceptually relevant categories reflecting peer interaction (Rubin, 1985).

Two significant developments have promoted the intersection of temperament research and work on peer rejection. In the early 1980's, Jerome Kagan and his colleagues at Harvard began to investigate groups of preschool children selected for their extreme responses to novel or mildly stressful events (Garcia-Coll, Kagan, & Reznick, 1984). These children actively withdrew from social situations and exhibited fearful responses to novelty. Kagan and colleagues found that there was significant stability in behavior over time among these extremely fearful children. In addition, there was a unique and stable pattern of psychophysiological responses that characterized these children, reflecting increased sympathetic activation (Kagan, Reznick, & Gibbons, 1989; Kagan, Reznick & Snidman, 1987). Inhibited toddlers displayed elevated heart rates, higher basal cortisol readings, and greater pupil dilation. When these young children were followed into the elementary school grades, Kagan found that, in general, their behavioral and physiological profiles remained stable. Fearful, inhibited toddlers became shy, isolated elementary school age children (Kagan, Reznick, Snidman, Gibbons, & Johnson, 1988).

Kagan's research on this temperamental pattern, which he has called behavioral inhibition, is notably different from prior research on infant temperament in a number of ways. First, it almost exclusively used behavioral observation and laboratory measures of response as opposed to questionnaires to identify and measure the phenomenon. Second, Kagan argued that the trait he had isolated and identified reflected a categorical rather than continuous dimension of infant temperament. Thus, it was necessary to select individuals from the extremes of the population. Indeed, subsequent research demonstrated that the stability and prediction from infancy to early childhood is only evident with selected extreme samples (Kagan, Reznick, & Gibbons, 1989). Third, the strength of Kagan's data and his arguments for categorical analysis rest on the strong correspondence between psychological behavior and psychophysiological response. There seem to be stable physiological patterns that corresponded to the behavioral profiles of inhibition that he identified. And, these profiles are remarkable only within the extremes of the population and not within the general sample.

Around the time that the Harvard group was describing the behavioral and psychophysiological profiles of behaviorally-inhibited children, Rubin and colleagues were completing studies on social isolation and rejection in school age children (Rubin, 1982; 1985; Rubin et al., 1990; Rubin, Daniels-Bierness, & Bream, 1983). Rubin studied the play and peer inter-actions of elementary school children and found that there were subtle but important distinctions to be made between those children who were isolated from the peer group and those who were likely to be rejected because of their play behavior. And, he found important differences in social and clinical outcome depending upon the manner in which social isolation or rejection was expressed. Rubin's work in this area was notable for a number of reasons: First, although derived from a sociometric background, this new work relied heavily on detailed behavioral observation of children; second, these observations occurred not only in the laboratory but in the school setting as well so that there was important corroborative information on the generalization of these isolated or maladaptive social behaviors beyond the laboratory. A third notable aspect of Rubin's work was his attempt to link theoretically these behaviors, observed in school-age children, to their manifestations in early infancy, in particular with early attachment patterns. Rubin's notion was that particular patterns of infant temperament might, given certain configurations of maternal response, lead to secure or insecure attachment relationships. These relationships may in turn produce maladaptive behaviors with peers. For example, certain patterns of insecurity might predispose a child to social isolation and rejection by peers.

It seems obvious that these two research efforts, work on behavioral inhibition and work on social isolation, should inform, and perhaps, assist one another in understanding the etiology and pathways by which certain temperamental behaviors are transformed into socially-maladaptive re-sponses in children. However, for this to occur a number of missing pieces to the puzzle needed to be articulated, investigated, and their data put into the perspective of these two research areas. Three pieces of the puzzle for which there were preciously little data are obvious. First, Kagan and colleagues had begun their work with two-year-old children on behavioral inhibition. Little was known about the patterns of infant behavior, that might be related to inhibited behavior in toddlerhood (but see Kagan & Snidman, 1991). What temperamental profile, both behaviorally and physiologically, predicted inhibition in the toddler? What types of early mother-infant interaction contributed to the development of inhibition?

A second issue that arose from the paths that Rubin and colleagues described is how these early temperamental profiles might influence devel-oping attachment relationships (Rubin et al., 1990). Specifically, could particular attachment relationships develop as a function of the tempera-ment of the infant, and how might this process contribute to the develop-ment of inhibited behavior? (Calkins & Fox, in press). Finally, if these temperament/attachment/inhibition relations can be identified, what processes would then lead to the transformation of the behaviorally inhibited toddler to the socially isolated or rejected child? The missing pieces, then, involved careful description of the particular types of infant temperament that might contribute to subsequent social behaviors and the processes by which these transformations take place.

Filling in the missing pieces of the inhibition/social isolation puzzle clearly required a longitudinal perspective examining both individual difference phenomena and socio-emotional development in infancy. Such a perspective is provided by a study that began in our laboratory several years ago. We have conducted a longitudinal study exploring the relations among behavioral and physiological reactivity, temperament, and socio-emotional behaviors in the first years of life. Using data collected during assessments at several different ages, we constructed a model that may be used to predict inhibited versus uninhibited behavior in toddlerhood, and that we believe may be useful in identifying socially isolated and rejected school-age children. The study we present assessed temperament using multiple measures at ages 2 days, 5 months, 14 months, and 2 years (Calkins & Fox, in press; Fox, 1989; Stifter & Fox, 1990). In addition, attachment and inhibition were assessed at 14 and 24 months respectively. The numerous measures collected in this effort present a complex picture of the relations among temperament, attachment, and inhibition, and offer a unique opportunity to observe the development of particular patterns of isolated behavior in early childhood. In order to fully explicate the model, it would be helpful to chart the path taken from its earliest formulations.

PSYCHOPHYSIOLOGICAL AND BEHAVIORAL INDICES OF REACTIVITY IN INFANCY

The aim of the early phase of our longitudinal study was to examine patterns of reactivity and regulation, both physiological and behavioral, that could characterize certain types of infant temperament. The concepts of reactivity and regulation have been central to the work of Rothbart, whose model of infant temperament we adopted for this study (Rothbart, 1989; Rothbart & Derryberry, 1981; Rothbart & Posner, 1985). The goal of the research was to provide links between behavioral and physiological reactivity and specify regulatory mechanisms that might be involved in the modulation of reactivity. Central to this paradigm has been the idea that reactivity may be indexed or measured both behaviorally and physiologically. We have used measures of heart rate variability, or vagal tone, to index physiological reactivity (see Fox, 1989, for a discussion of this measure). And, we have measured latency, duration, and intensity of emotional displays as well as motor activity to reflect behavioral reactivity.

Table 5.1 presents an outline of the study, the ages at which infants were observed, the assessments used, and the measures derived from these assessments to examine both physiological and behavioral reactivity.

The first important hint that there were important individual differences in infant reactivity came from our examination of the relations between newborn and 5-month assessments. During the newborn assessment, heart rate was recorded during active and quiet sleep, and infant responsivity to the removal of a pacifier was observed. At five months, heart rate was again recorded, and the infant's responses to arm restraint, a procedure designed to elicit anger, were noted. The infants also played peek-a-boo with their mothers and with a stranger. Another procedure, in which infants were shown a series of novel visual stimuli, was administered to elicit response to novelty. Finally, mothers completed a temperament questionnaire, the Infant Behavior Questionnaire (IBQ, Rothbart, 1981).

Examination of the relations between newborn and five-month measures (Stifter & Fox, 1990) revealed two distinct patterns of reaction and behavior/physiology correspondence. The first pattern described infants

TABLE 5.1

Procedures and Measures of Temperament and Attachment at 2 Days, 5 Months, 14 Months, and 24 Months

Age at Assessment	Procedures	Measures
2 days	Pacifier withdrawal	Cry/No cry, latency to cry
	EKG recording	Heart period, vagal tone
5 Months	Arm restraint	Cry/No cry, latency to cry
	Novel slide stimuli	Cry/No cry, frequency of crying
	Peek-a-boo	Motor activity
	IBQ	6 Scales
	EKG Recording	Heart period, vagal tone
14 Months	Free play/Stranger approach/ Novel object.	Behavioral Inhibition score
	Ainsworth-Wittig Strange Situation	Attachment classification Cry Frequency, Latency to cry
	Toddler Behavior Assessment Questionnaire	5 Scales
	EKG Recording	Heart period, vagal tone
24 Months	Modified Strange Situation. Free play. Stranger approach. Presentation of novel object, robot. Clown approach.	Behavioral Inhibition score
	Toddler Behavior Assessment Questionnaire	5 Scales
	EKG recording	Heart period, vagal tone

who cried to pacifier withdrawal at two days of age, cried to arm restraint at five months of age, and were rated by their mothers as being active, highly distressed when frustrated but not fearful. These infants displayed high vagal tone, reflecting, perhaps, a degree of organization and maturity of the autonomic nervous system that would allow for adaptive responses to a novel and interesting environment. The second pattern of response characterized infants who were in fact "non-responders" to the frustrating events: they did not cry to pacifier withdrawal at two days of age, they did not cry to arm restraint at five months, but they were likely to cry to mild stress and novelty at five months. Mothers rated these infants as highly active but also fearful of novelty. These infants displayed a pattern of low vagal tone reflecting, through a less mature and less well organized autonomic response, the inability to respond adaptively to changes in the environment. These infants were also more likely to be characterized as fussy and irritable, while the former type of infant, though negative in its affect to frustration, was more positive overall in its emotional tone.

The conclusions drawn from this first phase of the longitudinal study were that (1) vagal tone may be a physiological indicator of individual differences in infant reactivity, and (2) negative reactivity to one kind of event (frustration) may be distinct from negative responses to other kinds of events (novelty). These two patterns of response may represent different temperamental patterns present early in the first months of life.

RELATIONS BETWEEN BEHAVIORAL AND PHYSIOLOGICAL REACTIVITY AND SOCIAL DEVELOPMENT

The notion that reactivity may be elicited in a variety of contexts and may be differentially related to affective responses drove the data analyses over the next phase of the longitudinal research. At 14 months of age, 52 infants and their mothers returned to the laboratory for an assessment designed to elicit behaviors indicative of the child's socio-emotional development. Several minutes of the child's heart rate were recorded during both baseline and challenge situations. The child was then observed in a playroom setting designed to elicit response to novelty. First, the child played with a set of toys for 5 min while the mother sat nearby. Following free play, a stranger entered the room and sat with her head bowed for three minutes. If the child did not approach within three minutes, the stranger raised her head and began playing with the toy she had brought into the room with her. If the child was still reluctant to approach, the stranger then attempted to engage the child with the toy. The stranger then removed from its hiding place a small battery-powered robot that made high pitched sounds and moved around the room. The child was encouraged, for a period of not more than two minutes, to touch the robot. The stranger then left the room and the mother and infant were then observed in the Ainsworth-Wittig Strange Situation (Ainsworth, Blehar, Waters, & Wall, 1978). During this visit, the mothers also completed the Toddler Behavior Assessment Questionnaire (TBAQ, Goldsmith, 1987).

The pattern of findings from the newborn and five-month data had alerted us to the role that vagal tone might have as an index of temperamental or affective reactivity. We examined this more carefully at 14 months by isolating those subjects who consistently, across different measurement conditions, displayed high or low vagal tone. We knew from the newborn and five-month data that high vagal tone was associated with high reactivity particularly to frustration and that low vagal tone was associated with irritability and negative affect in response to novelty. Examination of the data at 14 months (Fox, 1989) indicated that infants in the high vagal tone group were more positive in their affect during social interaction than infants in the low vagal tone group. Infants in the high vagal tone group displayed, at 14 months, positive approach behaviors toward the stranger and the robot. They were more positive in their affective tone across the measurement conditions. Thus, infants who were reactive negatively at 5 months to frustration (arm restraint) were more sociable at 14 months. The context of their negative emotion at 5 months is critical in understanding this outcome. Recall that, in addition to displaying negative affect to arm restraint, the reactive infants also displayed positive affect during peek-a-boo, and were rated by their mothers as being less distressed to novelty. These infants were thus not fussy across all contexts and in fact were not considered irritable or difficult infants by maternal report.

The implications of the finding regarding the approach tendencies of infants who were frustrated and reactive at 5 months are several. First, these data suggest a link between early temperament and subsequent social responding. Infant reactivity to various types of events plays a role in the infant's interactions with others. Second, it confirms a link between certain measures of autonomic organization and a temperamental dimension of reactivity. And third, it underscores the importance of defining the context in which reactivity or any other temperamental factor is measured.

Infant reactivity, of course, appears within the context of the caregiving environment. Parental response to an infant who is highly active and reactive to frustration may mediate the manner in which these tendencies are transformed with development. Parents may value the child who is eager to explore and who is highly active and thus, they may choose not to restrict the actions of the child. These parental behaviors would reduce the incidence of negative reactions and confrontations between parent and child. On the other hand, it is obviously critical for parents to impose, at each developmental level, limitations on the freedom and movement of their child. The manner in which these limitations are imposed, particularly on a child who does not easily tolerate setting of limits, may affect the manner in which that child ultimately deals with the social world. It is clear then that parental strategies and responsivity with the highly active, highly reactive-to-frustration child may lead to different outcomes in social responding.

A similar set of descriptions might also apply for the infant who is highly reactive to novelty, who is irritable and fussy. Parents may decide to minimize the frequency of presentation of new and differentiated environments to such a child in order to lessen the incidence of negative affect. Alternatively, parents may decide to ignore the negative affect responses of the child and reduce the degree of responsivity to the child's bids for comfort. Either situation would result in distinct outcomes of social responding by the child at later developmental periods.

The best method for investigating these different situations is to observe directly the manner in which parents interact with their child. In addition, it would obviously be important to have some idea about the type of child temperament, preferably obtained from independent laboratory measurement. An alternative, which we employed in our study, was to examine the quality of the attachment relationship between mother and child. This approach would allow us to infer the degree and manner of responsivity that the mother provided the child during the first year of the child's life.

RELATIONS BETWEEN TEMPERAMENT AND ATTACHMENT

The analyses we performed allowed examination of possible differences among the three major attachment groups (Avoidant/Secure/Resistant) in any of the measures of infant temperament that we had collected. We first looked at the measures of response to pacifier withdrawal procedure at 2 days of age. A significant difference was found between the secure group and the insecure (avoidant and resistant combined) groups in terms of the tendency to cry to pacifier withdrawal (see Table 5.2). The infants who would later develop avoidant/insecure and resistant/insecure attachments were more likely to have cried when their pacifier was removed at 2 days of age than were the infants who later developed secure attachment relations (Calkins & Fox, in press).

It is interesting that although the nature of their insecure attachments were different, avoidant and resistant infants demonstrated similar patterns of reactivity shortly after birth. Further analyses of the five-month temper-

TABLE 5.2
14-Month Attachment by Response to Pacifier Withdrawal at 2 Days

		Attachment Classification	
Response to Pacifier Withdrawal		Insecure (A & C)	Secure (B)
	Cry	11	16
	No Cry	3	19

X2 = 4.36, $p < .03$

ament data were performed specifically examining infant response on the arm restraint and novel slide stimuli procedures at five months. The frequencies, by attachment group, for crying to these events are presented in Table 5.3. Although in some instances differences did not reach conventional levels of significance, it was apparent that more avoidant infants cried to arm restraint (designed to measure reactivity to frustration) but did not cry to novel stimuli (designed to elicit reactivity to novelty). Conversely, resistant infants were more likely to cry to novel stimuli, but not to arm restraint (Calkins & Fox, in press).

In addition to displaying negative affect to a frustrating event, avoidant infants were rated significantly higher on motor activity during the peek-a-boo session, and mothers of avoidant infants rated them significantly higher on activity level compared to either infants classified as resistant or securely attached infants. Thus, while these two insecure groups displayed greater negative reactivity at birth, they seem, by 5 months of age, to display different patterns of response that may play a role in the development of their insecure attachment relationships at 14 months. Avoidant and resistant infants cries to different elicitors; they differed on motor reactivity and on maternal ratings of activity level. These different constellations of behavioral reactivity thus differentiated the two groups of infants who at 14 months were classified as either avoidant or resistant.

TABLE 5.3
14-Month Attachment by Response to Arm Restraint and Novel Stimuli at 5 Months

		Attachment Classification		
Reactivity to Arm restraint		Avoidant (A)	Secure (B)	Resistant (C)
	Cry	4	13	2
	No Cry	3	21	5
Reactivity to Novel stimuli		Avoidant (A)	Secure (B)	Resistant (C)
	Cry	2	18	6
	No Cry	5	16	3

It is well accepted that infant individuality will influence behavior in the Strange Situation. There are now a number of studies using both observational and questionnaire methods for recording infant temperament that have found relations between infant characteristics and behavior in the Strange Situation. Perhaps most acknowledged is the role of temperament in predicting the degree of distress to separation. A review and meta-analysis by Goldsmith and Alansky (1987) clearly demonstrated evidence across studies for a temperamental predisposition to react negatively to mild stress like separation. What is less clear is the role of infant temperament in determining the quality of the attachment relationship (secure or insecure). Attachment theorists, while acknowledging the role of temperament in influencing infant behavior, have insisted that the quality of the bond is still the result of the interactional pattern between caregiver and child. However, even here the evidence is not unanimous. For example, Fox, Kimmerly, and Schafer (1991) reviewed 11 studies and reported a high degree of concordance of attachment classification and sub-classifications between an infant and its mother and father. This pattern also seems to hold for the concordance of classification to mother or to primary caregiver (Fox et al, 1991). The most parsimonious explanation for the results of this meta-analysis is that the quality of the bond as measured in the Strange Situation is affected by the infant's temperament characteristics. Infants with a propensity to cry to mild stress and novelty may be more likely to be classified as resistant while those who have a propensity to respond negatively to frustration and limitations may in fact be more likely categorized as avoidant.

The data from our longitudinal study suggest these relations among temperament and attachment quality as well. Infants who are reactive to novelty at five months are more likely to be classified as C (insecure/resistant), while those who are more reactive to frustration (arm restraint) are more likely classified as A (insecure/avoidant) (Calkins & Fox, in press).

FROM BIRTH TO 2 YEARS: TEMPERAMENT, ATTACHMENT AND BEHAVIORAL INHIBITION

The next step in our investigation was to determine if the patterns of infant behavior that we identified during the first five months of life and that were related to infant attachment behavior were also related to the infant's social behaviors during the second year of life. To this end, we were interested in examining the relations between what Kagan and colleagues have called behavioral inhibition and infant temperament and attachment.

When the children were 24 months old, they returned to the laboratory with their mothers and were observed in a series of procedures designed to assess their responses to novelty. First, the child was observed in 10 min of free play and a brief (3 min or less) separation and a reunion (5 min) episode. Following this modified Strange Situation, an unfamiliar adult entered the room and sat silently in a chair opposite the mother for 30 sec. The stranger then spoke to the mother for 30 sec, but did not attempt to interact with the child. After the 30 sec period, the stranger uncovered a battery operated robot that moved in a circular fashion and made high pitched sounds. The child was invited to touch the robot, and was given one minute in which to do so. The child was then presented with a tunnel large enough for the child to enter, and invited by the stranger to do so. This epoch lasted for 2 min, after which the stranger left the room. Two minutes later, an adult clown, first knocked and opened the playroom door, then entered and stood silently for 30 sec. The clown then attempted to interact with the child, and invited the child to touch her (the clown's) nose. In addition, heart rate was recorded, and mothers completed the TBAQ. At 24 months, we computed an index of behavioral inhibition comprised of the following standardized and summed variables: latency to vocalize during free play; proximity to mother during free play, stranger, robot, tunnel, and clown sequences; latency to approach during these episodes; and latency to cry to these events. High frequencies of proximity to mother, long latencies to approach and vocalize to the stranger, clown, and objects, and short latencies to cry to these episodes were associated with high scores on the index.

A number of important relations, some of them surprising, emerged from the longitudinal data set that suggest that both infant temperament and quality of attachment are influential in the development of inhibited behavior. We attempt to sort through these findings in the following section by addressing several issues that may help us to link the temperament and shyness literatures.

INFANT TEMPERAMENT AND ATTACHMENT AS LINKS TO INHIBITION

The first surprise in our data was that there were few, if any, significant relations between measures of infant reactivity at the newborn or five-month period and behavioral inhibition at 24 months. Although laboratory behavior revealed little in the way of prediction to inhibition, maternal report of infant behavior across the 24-month period provided a clear and consistent picture. Several of these maternal ratings of temperament were correlated with inhibited behavior in toddlerhood. Maternal assessments of their infant's smiling (positive affect) and activity level at 5 months were negatively correlated with inhibition. Infants whose mothers rated them low on the smiling and activity subscales displayed more inhibited behaviors in the laboratory at 24 months. Maternal ratings of temperament at 14 months indicated that behavioral inhibition was negatively correlated with the pleasure subscale, and positively correlated with social fear. Twenty-four-month maternal ratings of infant temperament again provided corroboration of the earlier pattern. There was a negative correlation between inhibition and activity level, and a positive correlation between inhibition and maternal rating of social fear. Thus, across the three ages on which maternal assessment data was available, there seemed to be a relation between uninhibited behavior in toddlerhood and the child's tendency to display high amounts of activity and pleasure in infancy, and a relation between inhibited behavior and maternal ratings of social fear in early toddlerhood (Calkins & Fox, in press).

Why should infant behavior, as observed in the laboratory, do so poorly in predicting inhibition at 24 months while maternal report, relatively speaking, does so well? One possible answer to this question is that the link between infant temperament and behavioral inhibition at 24 months may not be a direct one. That is, the dimensions of reactivity measured at the earlier ages may alone not directly map onto inhibited responses at 24 months. These temperamental patterns may be modified and transformed by their interaction with the environment, in this case the manner in which caregivers respond to them. Maternal perception of infant behavior, on the other hand, would more likely remain stable over time. Indeed, its stability may be a clue into how mothers respond to their infants' reactive responses. If this conclusion is correct, then while infant temperamental variables should not present strong direct relations with inhibition, measures which more strongly reflect the interaction between temperament and environment (for example, attachment quality) should present strong associations with behavioral inhibition.

To examine this possibility, we examined the scores on the index of inhibition with respect to attachment classification (avoidant/insecure versus resistant/insecure versus secure). The mean inhibition scores for these three attachment groups are presented in Figure 5.1. An ANOVA comparing the three groups revealed a significant difference among them: Infants classified as resistant/insecure obtained lower scores on the index of behavioral inhibition than did infants classified as avoidant/insecure. Infants whose attachments to their mothers were categorized as resistant tended to display long latencies to approach novel objects and people, they cried more quickly to these events, and they spent much time in proximity to their mothers during these episodes. Infants whose attachments were classified as avoidant tended to approach novel objects and people quickly, they did not cry to these events, and they spent little time in proximity to their mother during these episodes (Calkins & Fox, in press).

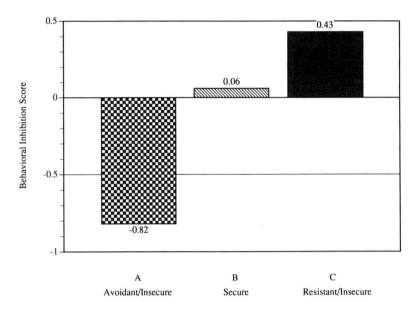

FIG. 5.1. Mean Behavioral Inhibition Score By Attachment Group (ABC) (from Calkins & Fox, in press)

Given that the infant's temperament may be playing a role in the development of subsequent attachment relationships, and that the three attachment groups displayed different patterns of inhibited versus uninhibited behavior in toddlerhood, we set out to examine whether temperament and attachment may interact in some way to produce inhibition. We looked at the independent and interactive contributions of fearful reactivity (crying to novel stimuli), attachment classification, and frustrated reactivity (crying to arm restraint) in terms of behavioral inhibition. We found that there was a significant interaction between responses to frustration and attachment classification in predicting behavioral inhibition. Infants who had not cried to arm restraint and who were classified as resistant in terms of attachment had the highest scores on the index of inhibition. Infants who had cried to arm restraint and were classified as avoidant in terms of attachment had mean inhibition scores that placed them on the uninhibited end of the spectrum (Calkins & Fox, in press).

These findings suggest that while behavioral inhibition is not directly related to infant temperament (at least as we measured it in the laboratory at 2 days and 5 months), it was a function of the interaction of attachment classification and temperament. The fact that infant reactivity was not directly related to behavioral inhibition suggests that the path is an indirect one in which temperamental traits are mediated by the quality of relationships within the family, and perhaps by maternal responsivity.

THE INTERACTION OF TEMPERAMENT AND ATTACHMENT

The literature on the role of temperament in developing attachment relationships suggests that infant irritability may be related to insecure attachments (Crockenberg, 1981; Goldsmith & Alansky, 1987; Miyake, Chen, & Campos, 1985). In general, these studies have been unable to find temperamental correlates that specifically relate to either avoidant or resistant insecure attachments. Rather, these studies distinguish between secure and insecure infants based upon infant temperamental variables or predict along the continua of A1-B2 or B3-C2 (Belsky & Rovine, 1987). However, our current approach may help clarify some of the confusion surrounding these issues. By making distinctions between types of reactivity in infancy, we have been able to find relations among different temperamental patterns and the two different types of insecure classification. Infants high in reactivity to frustration were more likely to be classified as insecure/avoidant while those high in reactivity to novel events were more likely classified as resistant/insecure.

Different styles of infant reactivity are likely to interact with maternal responsivity to produce different attachment patterns. Infants who are easily frustrated by limitations may be difficult to control and may elicit negative responses from parents. An infant who is unwilling to be constrained will likely not be distressed when left alone by the parent and may avoid proximity to a parent who, from the child's perspective, is likely to attempt to control his or her behavior. Alternatively, an infant who is easily distressed and fearful may prove burdensome in his or her constant need for comfort. The sheer volume of requests for soothing suggests that the parent may not always respond contingently. The consequent uncertainty of the parent's response may exacerbate the stress of a separation, and, moreover, may produce an infant who is angry and ambivalent toward an unpredictable caretaker. Reactivity, in the form of either frustration or fear, may interact with parental responsivity to produce specific attachment relationships.

Our data on attachment/inhibition confirm the relations described here. Infants classified as avoidant who had presented with a temperamental pattern of reactivity to frustration displayed uninhibited behaviors at 24 months. Infants classified as resistant who had presented with a temperament pattern of reactivity to novelty displayed inhibited behaviors when faced with the same stimuli. Avoidant infants were quick to approach the stranger, the clown, the tunnel, and the robot; they did not cry or fret to these events, and they did not spend much time in proximity to their mothers when given the opportunity to play freely in the room, or when they were faced with novelty. Indeed, they displayed approach behaviors and an eagerness to explore the unknown. Resistant infants tended to fuss to the novel events, were unlikely to approach the stranger, the clown, the tunnel, and the robot, and they spent a lot of time clinging to their mothers. Avoidant infants have developed a repertoire of exploratory behaviors that may be unhindered by parental interference; indeed parents may restrict movements such that the child may evade proximity in order to lessen the risk of having freedom of movement hindered. Resistant infants, on the other hand, may be especially sensitive, or reactive to novelty, and have developed strategies for coping with this stress that include avoiding its proximity while maintaining caregiver proximity.

FROM INHIBITION/EXTROVERSION TO SOCIAL ISOLATION/REJECTION: THE ROLE OF SELF-REGULATION

The longitudinal data we have presented suggest that there may be diverging paths of early reactivity that interact with maternal caretaking style to produce inhibited versus uninhibited behavior. There is, however, yet another element that must be raised in order to understand the complex multiple pathways through which early personality is formed. We have clearly shown that there are individual differences in reactivity. There are, in addition, individual differences in the degree to which infants regulate that reactivity (Fox, 1989; Fox & Stifter, 1989; Rothbart & Derryberry, 1981). The ability to regulate affective responses is multiply determined. There are clear individual differences early on in the infant's own abilities and skills at regulating its arousal (Tronick, 1982). In addition, parents often are able to provide their infant with the strategies to cope with arousal (giving an infant a pacifier is one clear way in which parents help infants deal with their arousal). Thus, it is important to investigate the multiple means by which infants develop, learn, and utilize different coping strategies in the service of affect regulation.

Infants who are easily frustrated may try to cope with their reactions by removing the thing that is blocking their goal and continuing their high degree of exploration and activity. Parents may respond by providing an independent environment in which they set few limits on the infant's behaviors. Or they may view the infant's frustrated, angry responses as a sign of difficulty. Fearful infants, on the other hand, may cope with their reactivity through withdrawal. Parents may provide a protective environment for that child, or they may view their infant's fear as evidence of irritability and difficulty.

In extreme instances, infants may not receive adequate maternal intervention. Or, the pattern of interaction may result in excessive reliance on maternal support. In both instances the result may be the imbalance between autonomy and exploration. The result of such an imbalance between maternal support and autonomy would have consequences for the development of regulatory abilities.

Figure 5.2 provides a hypothetical scheme for the outcomes of the interaction between highly reactive infants and styles of regulation. Frustrated, uninhibited infants may not experience sufficient maternal control and limit-setting, nor possess their own internal resources for regulating activity, either of which would enable them to develop strategies for modulating approach and exploratory behaviors for appropriate individuals and contexts. They may develop aggressive, confrontational behaviors that are difficult to manage in a peer setting. Infants who are easily frustrated but who have the internal resources to cope with their arousal, or who have caregivers who are willing to set limits and provide strategies to deal with their reactivity will emerge as extroverted and highly social children. Fox (1989), for example, found that 5-month-old infants who were highly reactive to restraint were, in general, highly social at 14 months of age. These infants could have had their own resources to deal with their activity or parents who provided the coping mechanisms to deal appropriately with their frustration.

Fearful, inhibited infants may develop the opposite pattern. Because they rarely exhibit autonomous behavior, fail to approach novelty, and lack

		Regulation	
		High	**Low**
Reactivity	**Frustrated**	Extroverted (social)	Uninhibited (aggressive)
	Fearful	Anxious (neurotic)	Inhibited (withdrawn)

FIG. 5.2 Hypothetical Outcomes of the Interaction of Regulation and Reactivity

exploratory skills, they may become isolated and socially withdrawn children in the face of peer interaction. Negotiating interactions with peers may be difficult for these children, because they are unable to begin that interaction with the necessary approach behaviors. They will tend to exist on the periphery of activity, and become isolated from the play of their peers. And, parents may not provide the contexts to assist these children in coping with their fear. Infants who are fearful need not, however, develop withdrawn or inhibited patterns of behavior. Parents might attempt to shelter these children from exposure to situations of novelty and stress. Or the child might develop his or her own means for dealing with their fear of novel situations. In these instances, it is possible that the emergent pattern would be one of anxious or neurotic behavior—of a child worried about events and situations, but still able to function appropriately in the social world.

At least two pieces of data lend support to our speculations regarding the path from inhibition-insecurity to social isolation and rejection. Sroufe and colleagues (Renken, Egeland, Marvinney, Mangelsdorf, & Sroufe, 1989) identified a number of predictor variables associated with passive-withdrawal and aggression in elementary school. Among the factors that appeared to contribute to these behaviors was avoidant attachments (aggression) and resistant attachments (passive-withdrawal). Second, Gersten (1989), in analyzing a subset of the inhibited children from Kagan's longitudinal research, found that children who were isolated in kindergarten had been inhibited at 21 months of age.

It would seem that the repertoire of the child's own resources for regulation of affective states, coupled with a lack of maternal support for the development of appropriate self-regulatory strategies, might influence subsequent peer interactions. Children who lack the ability to control their affective responses and activity level may be viewed by peers as intrusive and aggressive, and may be subject to rejection by those peers. Children who are unable to approach unfamiliar peers to play a game or share a toy may withdraw from, and, eventually, be rejected by, their peers. These peer experiences are at least one consequence of temperamental reactivity interacting with caretaking style in the process of the development of self-regulatory skills.

SUMMARY AND CONCLUSIONS

We have used data from a longitudinal study of a sample of infants from birth through 2 years to describe a model of early socio-emotional development. This model includes a description of the possible paths from two types of early reactivity to social behavior in early childhood. The paths we have identified suggest that individual differences in reactivity to different types of events influence the development of primary attachment relationships. Furthermore, the interactions with the caretaker will influence the child's developing repertoire of social skills. This repertoire represents the regulatory skills the child will bring to bear in a variety of interactions with new people and events, including interactions in peer settings.

The two types of infants identified in our sample have been referred to as avoidant/uninhibited and resistant/inhibited. Avoidant/uninhibited infants tend to be easily frustrated by limits imposed on them by others. By the beginning of the second year, they display approach behaviors toward novel people, objects, and events. Observations of their relations with their mothers indicate that they tend not to need a lot of proximity or support in new situations, display little distress when separated, and do not desire much contact upon reunion. By the second year of life, these children exhibit a considerable amount of exploratory behavior in new situations and are quick and eager to approach new objects and people. They may, as a consequence of relying very little on their mothers, fail to develop strategies for modulating their approach behaviors, and in interactions with peers, may seem aggressive.

In contrast to this type of infant is the resistant/inhibited infant. These infants tend not to be frustrated by limits, but they are distressed by novelty. Given the frequent encounters with novelty in early infancy, these infants may become burdensome in their frequent bids for attention, and may rely excessively on parents for support. Both the highly aggressive child, the product of an avoidant/insecure early relationship and a lack of clear limit setting, and the highly inhibited child, whose history includes rejection and an ambivalent early relationship with an insensitive parent, are at-risk for subsequent behavioral problems. Our current work has been a first attempt to elucidate the early factors and processes that contribute to these problems, which become social issues during the school years.

ACKNOWLEDGMENTS

The research presented in this chapter was supported by a grant from The National Institutes of Health (HD 17899) to Nathan A. Fox.

REFERENCES

Ainsworth, M. D., Blehar, M. C., Waters, E., & Wall, S. (1978). *Patterns of attachment.* Hillsdale, NJ: Lawrence Erlbaum Associates.

Asher, S. R., & Wheeler, V. A. (1985). Children's loneliness: A comparison of rejected and neglected peer status. *Journal of Consulting and Clinical Psychology, 53,* 500–505.

Belsky, J., & Rovine, M. (1987). Temperament and attachment security in the strange situation: An empirical rapprochement. *Child Development, 58,* 787–795.

Calkins, S. D., & Fox, N. A. (in press). The relations among infant temperament, security of attachment and behavioral inhibition at 24 months. *Child Development.*

Crockenberg, S. B. (1981). Infant irritability, mother responsiveness, and social support influences on the security of mother infant attachment. *Child Development, 52,* 857–868.

Fox, N. (1989). Psychophysiological correlates of emotional reactivity during the first year of life. *Developmental Psychology, 25,* 364–372.

Fox, N., Kimmerly, N., & Schafer, W. (1991). Attachment to mother/attachment to father: A meta-analysis. *Child Development, 62,* 210–225.

Fox, N. A., & Stifter, C. A. (1989). Biological and behavioral differences in infant reactivity. In G. A. Kohnstamm, J. Bates, & M. K. Rothbart (Eds.), *Temperament in Childhood* (pp. 169–181). New York: Wiley.

Garcia-Coll, C., Kagan, J., & Reznick, J. S. (1984). Behavioral inhibition in young children. *Child Development, 55,* 1005–1019.

Gersten, M. (1989). Behavioral inhibition in the classroom. In S. Reznick (Ed.), *Perspectives on behavioral inhibition.* Chicago: University of Chicago Press.

Goldsmith, H. H. (1987). *The Toddler Assessment Questionnaire: A preliminary manual.* Unpublished, Department of Psychology, University of Oregon.

Goldsmith, H. H., & Alansky, J. A. (1987). Maternal and infant temperamental predictors of attachment: A meta-analytic review. *Journal of Consulting and Clinical Psychology, 55,* 805–816.

Goldsmith, H. H., Buss, A. H., Plomin, R., Rothbart, M. K., Thomas, A., Chess, S., Hinde, R., & McCall, R. B. (1987). What is temperament? Four approaches. *Child Development, 58,* 505–529.

Kagan, J., & Snidman, N. (1991). Infant predictors of inhibited and uninhibited profiles. *Psychological Science, 2,* 40–44.

Kagan, J., Reznick, J. S., & Gibbons, J. (1989). Inhibited and uninhibited types of children. *Child Development, 60,* 838–845.

Kagan, J., Reznick, J. S., & Snidman, N. (1987). Physiology and psychology of behavioral inhibition. *Child Development, 58,* 459–1473.

Kagan, J., Reznick, J. S., Snidman, N., Gibbons, J., & Johnson, M. O. (1988). Childhood derivatives of inhibition and lack of inhibition toward the unfamiliar. *Child Development, 59,* 1580–1589.

Matheny, A., & Wilson, R. (1981). Developmental tasks and rating scales for the laboratory assessment of temperament. *JSAS catalog of selected documents in psychology, 11,* 81–82.

Miyake, K., Chen, S., & Campos, J. J. (1985). Infant temperament, mother's mode of interaction, and attachment in Japan: An interim report. In I. Bretherton & E. Waters (Eds.), *Growing points in attachment theory and research: Society for Research in Child Development Monographs.* Serial No. 209. (pp. 276–291). Chicago: Society for Research in Child Development.

Renken, B., Egeland, B., Marvinney, D., Manglesdorf, S., & Sroufe, A. (1989). Early childhood aggression and passive withdrawal in early elementary school. *Journal of Personality, 57,* 257–281.

Rothbart, M. K. (1981). Measurement of temperament in infancy. *Child Development, 52,* 569–578.

Rothbart, M. K. (1989a). Biological processes in temperament. In G. A. Kohnstamm, J. Bates & M. K. Rothbart (Eds.), *Temperament in childhood* (pp. 169–181). New York: Wiley.

Rothbart, M. K., & Derryberry, D. (1981). Development of individual differences in temperament. In M. E. Lamb & A. L. Brown (Eds.), *Advances in developmental psychology* (Vol. 1, pp. 37–86). Hillsdale, NJ: Lawrence Erlbaum Associates.

Rothbart, M. K., & Posner, M. I. (1985). Temperament and the development of self regulation. In L. C. Hartlage & C. F. Telzrow (Eds.), *The neuropsychology of individual differences: A developmental perspective* (pp. 93–123). New York: Plenum.

Rubin, K. (1982). Non-social play in preschoolers: Necessary evil? *Child Development, 53,* 651–657.

Rubin, K. (1985). Socially withdrawn children: An "at-risk" population? In B. H. Schneider, K. H. Rubin, & J. E. Ledingham (Eds.) Children's peer relations: Issues in assessment and intervention (pp. 125–139). New York: Springer-Verlag.

Rubin, K., Daniels-Bierness, T., & Bream, L. (1983). Social isolation and social problem solving: A longitudinal study. *Journal of Consulting and Clinical Psychology, 52,* 17–25.

Rubin, K. H., LeMare, L., & Lollis, S. P. (1990). Social withdrawal in childhood: Developmental pathways to peer rejection. In S. R. Asher & J. D. Coie (Eds.), *Children's status in the peer group.* New York: Cambridge University Press.

Rubin, K. H., & Lollis, S. P. (1988). Origins and consequences of social withdrawal. In J. Belsky & T. Nezworski (Eds.), *Clinical implications of attachment* (pp. 219–253). Hillsdale, NJ: Lawrence Erlbaum Associates.

Stifter, C. A., & Fox, N. A. (1990). Infant reactivity: Physiological correlates of newborn and five-month temperament. *Developmental Psychology, 26,* 582–588.

Thomas, A., Chess, S., & Birch, H. (1968). *Temperament and behavior disorders in children.* New York: New York University Press.

Tronick, E. Z. (1982). *Social interchange in infancy: Affect cognition and communication.* Baltimore: University Park Press.

6 Wariness to Strangers: A Behavior Systems Perspective Revisited

Joan Stevenson-Hinde
Anne Shouldice
University of Cambridge

This chapter uses a behavior systems approach to shed light on developmental changes in wariness in young children. Firstly, we describe how the approach has clarified both short-term and long-term changes in responsiveness to a constant stimulus situation. Secondly, we use the concept of a "behavior system" to identify features which both an individual construct (wariness/fear) and a relational construct (attachment) have in common. Finally, we illustrate with our own data how such thinking may be applied to the issue of stability and change in wariness in children aged 2.5 to 4.5 years.

What characterizes a systems approach? In general, a system is an abstraction, anchored to precisely defined criteria, including external events as well as actions. "In brief, the approach is to evaluate *relative* system isolation within a dynamic and multilevelled framework" (Fentress, 1991, p. 99). Following conventional usage, the term "behavior system" refers to a distinct motivational system, which nevertheless interacts with other systems. Here, no particular physiological mechanisms are implied, for such a term "is a 'software' one, comparable to a computer program that performs a particular job irrespective of whether the computer into which it is fed employs valves, transistors, or integrated circuits" (Hinde, 1982, pp. 63–64; see also Hinde, 1966/70, Ch. 8). A "systems approach emphasizes the patterning or organization of behaviors, both within and between individual behavioral systems" (Greenberg & Marvin, 1982, p. 481; see also Bischof, 1975; Bowlby, 1969/82).

This is best summed up by Fentress (1991), who is concerned not solely with behavior, but with synthesizing across different levels of analysis: "In the study of behaviour as well as neuroscience the investigator must typically deal with interlocking *networks* of organisational processes, rather than being satisfied with simple linear conceptualisations . . . the theme of interactive/self-organising systems . . . exhibits often surprising parallels across problems of neurobehavioural integration and its development" (p. 78).

SHORT-TERM AND LONG-TERM CHANGES IN RESPONSIVENESS

With a behavior systems approach, "Differences in responsiveness of one individual at different times can be understood on the basis of variations in the balance between different motivational systems" (Baerends, 1976, p. 733). In an exemplary set of field experiments, Baerends has postulated behavior systems to describe changes in behavior of incubating herring gulls. For example, when given a choice of two egg models on the rim of a nest, an incubating herring gull normally retrieves the larger one first. However, when accompanying behavior suggests a relatively high tendency to escape (escape system) compared with the tendency to incubate (incubation system), the smaller egg is retrieved first (Baerends & Kruijt, 1973). Turning to children, Bretherton and Ainsworth (1974) described the behavior of one-year-olds in a strange situation in terms of the organization of four behavior systems: wary/fear, attachment, exploratory, and sociable.

Over a longer period, the concept of a behavior system is a useful way of organizing developmental data. In their analysis of the many and varied responses of preschool children aged 2, 3, and 4 years in an Ainsworth Strange Situation (Ainsworth, Blehar, Waters, & Wall, 1978), Greenberg and Marvin (1982) achieved an elegant simplicity by assigning functionally equivalent responses to the above four behavior systems. "Since behaviors are often interchangeable both within and between behavior systems, the assignment often depended on the social and behavioral context" (p. 483). With their coding system, behavior systems could occur simultaneously or in sequence. In practice, not all possible combinations of the four behavior systems occurred. For example, after the stranger entered the room, but before she began interacting with the child, only five combinations were observed. Furthermore, whereas most two-year-olds showed a combination of wary and attachment behavior, sometimes followed by exploration near mother, most three- and four-year-olds showed exploration (i.e., watched the stranger enter, but continued to play, occasionally glancing at the stranger).

COMMON ASPECTS OF BEHAVIOR SYSTEMS WITH REFERENCE TO WARY/FEARFUL BEHAVIOR AND ATTACHMENT BEHAVIOR

In general, wary/fearful behavior has been taken to index a temperamental construct (e.g., Goldsmith et al., 1987), whereas attachment behavior has been taken to index a relational construct (e.g., Hinde, 1982). This in turn has led to some territorial disputes (e.g., Sroufe, 1985; Kagan, 1989). The following points are intended to be "territorial-free."

Outcome

In the sense of having a predictable outcome, both wary and attachment behavior may be viewed as "goal-directed" (Hinde & Stevenson, 1969). A predictable goal of attachment behavior is gaining and/or maintaining proximity or communication with an attachment figure (e.g., Ainsworth et al., 1978; Bowlby, 1969/82; Bowlby, 1991). Such proximity may decrease arousal. In human infants, heart rate may accelerate upon separation from mother and decrease once proximity is regained (Sroufe & Waters, 1977).

The outcome of fearful behavior is to decrease or avoid proximity to and/or interaction with the feared object, either through alerting a caregiver to intervene or directly through the child's own behavior. This need not involve increasing *physical* distance from the fear-eliciting stimulus. *Psychological* avoidance of a fear-eliciting stimulus has been likened to "cut-off" behavior (e.g., Chance, 1962; Tinbergen, 1959). Again, arousal may be decreased. For example, gaze aversion to a stranger occurred when heart rate acceleration was near its peak, and the infant again looked at the stranger when the rate neared basal level (Sroufe & Waters, 1977).

Function

In evolutionary terms, a common function of both a fear and an attachment system is thought to be protection from harm (Ainsworth et al., 1978; Bowlby, 1969/82; Sroufe, 1977). Fear of both the unfamiliar and being left alone would have been essential for survival in the environment in which we evolved. Interestingly, children's "irrational" fears such as fear of the dark, fear of water, and fear of snakes are more ubiquitous in children than are fears more appropriate to the present day, such as fear of cars or guns (Marks, 1987). Thus, our propensities both to fear certain situations and to maintain proximity with mothers may have been guided by natural selection, with the common function of protection from harm.

Context

With a behavior systems approach, the *context* in which a behavior pattern occurs is crucial for further analysis and interpretation (Fentress, 1991; Stevenson-Hinde, 1989). Particular stimuli that elicit attachment behavior may be internal (e.g., illness, fatigue) or external (e.g., separation from the attachment figure). However, *context* will determine whether or not attachment behavior occurs to these stimuli. For example, if an infant is at home and used to mother coming and going from one room to another, attachment behavior may not be activated when she leaves the room. On the other hand, attachment behavior is likely to be activated if the infant is in a strange situation and the mother leaves (e.g., Ainsworth et al., 1978).

Similarly, the occurrence of wary behavior depends crucially on context, as well as on aspects of a stimulus that is novel and/or perceived to be potentially harmful. As with attachment behavior, wary behavior is more likely to occur in the context of a strange situation than at home, and with increased distance from mother (e.g., Skarin, 1977; Sroufe, Waters, & Matas, 1974).

Alternative Behavior

"Inhibited behavior" refers to initial withdrawal to unfamiliar or challenging events (e.g., Kagan, 1989), and "attachment behavior" involves gaining and/or maintaining proximity with an attachment figure (e.g., Bowlby, 1988). In neither case is any particular item of behavior specified. Indeed, alternative behaviors may be employed by *different* children in the *same* context or by the *same* child in *different* contexts.

In contexts where an inferred goal is gaining and/or maintaining proximity with an attachment figure, a human infant may cry, cling, suck, or even smile (e.g., Ainsworth et al., 1978; Bowlby, 1969/82). To the extent that different children have different preferred ways of responding, correlations between different types of behavior within a particular context will be low. Furthermore, to the extent that a given child shows different behavior in different contexts (e.g., crying on separation but smiling on reunion), correlations involving a particular type of behavior across contexts, or cross-situational consistency, will be low. Nevertheless, each child may be behaving entirely predictably.

With wary behavior, one child may have a high latency to approach but show few other indications, while another may approach right away but show wary behavior in various ways while doing so. Indeed, in our study of 2.5-year-olds meeting an adult female stranger, the correlation between *latency* to approach and *ratings* of wary behavior (involving facial expression, posture, and movement) was far from perfect ($r = .44$, $N = 82$;

Stevenson-Hinde & Shouldice, 1990). Similar levels of intercorrelations among indices of inhibition occur in other studies (e.g., Reznick, 1989). Furthermore, a given child might show different levels of wariness in different contexts (e.g., wary with an adult stranger but not on entering a strange room). Again, this is reflected in our data with 2.5-year-olds, where the correlation between an index of wariness (latency + ratings) in the two contexts was only .24 (Stevenson-Hinde & Shouldice, 1990). Thus, for both attachment and wariness, behavior directed towards a particular outcome may vary, depending on the individual and the context.

Developmental Aspects

Early-Appearance. Behavior patterns such as clinging, smiling, or crying, which can all serve as attachment behavior, are present from birth. Similarly, components of fearful behavior, such as crying or startle responses, are present from birth. However, in the above sense of goal-directedness, both an attachment and a wary behavior system may properly be inferred only over the last half of the first year of life. For example, the onset of negative responses to a stranger, such as a frown or gaze aversion, occurs during the second half of the first year (e.g., Schaffer, Greenwood, & Parry, 1972; Waters, Matas, & Sroufe, 1975). Over a similar age range, attachment behavior becomes more organized (e.g., Ainsworth et al., 1978; Bowlby, 1969/82). Both coincide with a developmental shift in the expression of emotionality (Emde, Gaensbauer, & Harmon, 1976).

Changes in Expression. Age-appropriate behavior is observed in relation to both systems. For example, while an infant may cry when mother leaves, an older child may follow mother, or still later ask her where she is going. Similar developmental changes occur with fearful behavior. Whereas an infant might cry on meeting a stranger, a toddler might withdraw and/or have a wary expression, and an older child might look down and have a relatively long latency to speak to the stranger. Such changes need not imply instability, but rather they may reflect "heterotypic continuity" (Kagan, 1971).

Narrowing the Range of Objects of Attachment or Fear. An infant's attachment behavior initially occurs in an undirected manner, then is undiscriminatingly directed to any available person, and finally to preferred figures. Preferences do not emerge until about four months of age (Ainsworth et al., 1978; Bowlby, 1969/82).

Similarly, stimuli that elicit fear are initially wide-ranging, and then become narrowed. A particularly good example of tuning a fear response, and of the importance of interactions with others for doing this, is provided by Seyfarth and Cheney's (1986) observations of vervet monkeys. The adults of this species respond with a different alarm call to each of three types of predators: snakes, mammalian predators, and birds of prey. Young vervets initially respond to a wide range of objects. They may give a response appropriate to a bird of prey to a falling leaf. However, they come to give an alarm call appropriate to each type of predator, and not to falling leaves, through observing adults, especially their mothers. With humans, some infants are particularly prone to the acquisition of learned fears (Bronson & Pankey, 1977).

Changes in Objects of Attachment or Fear.   In addition to the range of appropriate stimuli narrowing during development, the nature of appropriate stimuli changes as well. With attachment behavior, whereas parental figures are preferred early on, humans turn to peers in adolescence and adulthood. This does not mean that early attachments disappear, just that new ones are preferred. Parents may still be turned to when all else fails, and their loss mourned (Ainsworth, 1991; Weiss, 1982).

Similarly with wary behavior, while a strange adult is an appropriate stimulus early on, a more potent stimulus by about four years is an unfamiliar peer(s) (Kagan, Reznick, & Snidman, 1987). Still later, a situation that involves being evaluated may produce behavior indicating "fear of negative evaluation" (e.g., Asendorpf, 1986), something not observed at earlier ages.

Social Influences

Social influences on wary behavior may be inferred from studies involving comparisons between boys and girls in terms of what social interactions were associated with the behavior in question. Take for example shyness, rated from maternal interview questions about initial approach/withdrawal to strange people and places (for details, see Simpson & Stevenson-Hinde, 1985). Individuals were consistent from 42 to 50 months (Spearman $r = .61$, $N = 41$, $p < .001$, two-tailed). For girls at 50 months, shyness was significantly positively correlated with: mother sensitive to child, mother enjoys child, joint activities with mother and with father, a positive relationship with the older sibling, and conversational questions to mother. On the other hand, shyness was negatively correlated with: child actively hostile to mother, child passive (i.e., not engaged) with mother, mother/child activity changes (implying that they did not do one thing for long), child reactively hostile to peers in nursery school, and both peers and adults disconfirming the child. For 50-month-old boys, each set of correlations went in the opposite direction (Stevenson-Hinde & Hinde, 1986).

Similar associations have been found by Radke-Yarrow and her colleagues in their research on families with and without a history of
psychiatric disorder. They found that "Mothers seemed not to be pleased
with shyness in boys. Boys' shyness was associated with less joyfulness in
their mothers. Mothers' interactions with shy girls, in contrast, were
characterized by tenderness, affection, and sadness" (Radke-Yarrow, Richters, & Wilson, 1988, p. 58).

During the interviews in our own study, some mothers complained that
their sons should have grown out of their shyness, having been in nursery
school for a year, while others commented with pleasure that their
daughters preferred being at home with them. Thus, mothers (and fathers)
may have different attitudes towards shyness in boys and shyness in girls,
with shyness in boys becoming less acceptable as they get older. This agrees
with the finding by Kagan et al. (1987), that, of children selected as being
inhibited or uninhibited at 21 months, more boys than girls had changed
from inhibited to uninhibited at 5.5 years. On the other hand, "A much
smaller group of originally uninhibited children, about 10% and typically
girls from working-class families, became more inhibited at later ages. The
interviews with these mothers suggested they wanted a more cautious child
and encouraged such a profile" (p. 1462). Mills & Rubin (1990) found that
although mothers and fathers reported stronger responses to problematic
social behavior (including aggression) of daughters than of sons, mothers
were less likely to report intervening to modify social withdrawal if they
viewed it as a trait, rather than as a temporary state (e.g., due to age or
environmental influences). Negative life events were also associated with
maternal reports of nonresponsiveness to social withdrawal.

Social influences on attachment behavior are best inferred from measures
of its quality and patterning, as well as intensity (Ainsworth et al., 1978). In
addition to Ainsworth's classic research, the Grossmanns' longitudinal
studies have related maternal sensitivity—reflected in affectionate holding,
appropriate reactions to crying, and frequent responses to vocalizations,
often with a tender-warm voice quality—to a secure classification of
attachment to mother in the Strange Situation (Grossmann, Grossmann,
Spangler, Suess, & Unzner, 1985; Grossmann & Grossmann, 1991). Insecure patterns are viewed as strategies developed by the child in the course of
interacting with an attachment figure who does not show the above
characteristics of sensitivity. Thus, an Insecure-Avoidant pattern upon
reunion may reflect an emphasis on maintaining neutrality with a rejecting
mother (Main & Weston, 1982), while an Insecure-Ambivalent pattern may
reflect an emphasis on dependence to an unpredictable mother (Egeland &
Farber, 1984), and an Insecure-Controlling pattern may reflect a child who
has had to take charge with a mother who is emotionally unavailable, due

to problems of her own, such as depression or lack of resolution of mourning (Ainsworth & Eichberg, 1991; Main & Hesse, 1990; Radke-Yarrow, 1991).

Individual Differences

The above mention of strategies is not unrelated to individual differences, in the sense of measuring a characteristic that might endure, across situations and across time. Given stable family circumstances, such individual differences in the quality of attachment to mother have been shown to be stable over the first six years (reviewed in Bowlby, 1991).

With wary behavior, individual differences are also consistent from infancy to childhood (e.g., Rothbart, 1989). In a sample of extreme children, selected at 21 months as being either inhibited or uninhibited, indices of behavioral inhibition were significantly correlated over the years, with $r = .67$ ($p < .001$) from 21 months to 7.5 years (Kagan, Reznick, Snidman, Gibbons, & Johnson, 1988). When extremes were not selected, the correlations were lower, but still significant. Thus, in a normative sample indices of inhibition were significantly correlated over the years, from 14 to 20 months ($r = .51$), 14 to 32 months ($r = .44$), and 20 to 32 months ($r = .25$) (Reznick, Gibbons, Johnson, & McDonough, 1989, Table 3).

WARINESS OF STRANGERS AND PATTERNS OF ATTACHMENT FROM 2.5 TO 4.5 YEARS

Thus, both wary and attachment behavior systems may be inferred from birth, with unfamiliar situations activating both over the first few years of life. Given the close relation between attachment and wary behavior, the above attachment strategies might be associated with the expression of wary behavior in particular ways. For example, children emphasizing dependence might be expected to be observed as most wary, while those with controlling strategies should hide their wariness as much as possible in order to remain in charge. The most secure children should be least fearful (e.g., Bowlby, 1969/82), although if frightened, they should be able to express their feelings freely to a sensitively responsive mother (e.g., Grossmann & Grossmann, 1991).

Furthermore, because "there appears to be a decreased developmental coupling of the attachment and wary systems" (Greenberg & Marvin, 1982, p. 489), one would predict that the above associations might not hold by the time a child is about four years old. It should be noted that our measures, reported later, differed from those of Greenberg and Marvin. Whereas they considered the *co-occurrence or not* of two degrees of wariness (mild and strong) and three other behavior systems (attachment, exploratory, and sociable), we assessed wariness along a *continuum,* and then, *in a later episode,* we assessed attachment behavior in terms of the *pattern* of attachment shown upon reunion.

We now report results from a sample of 82 (41 of each sex) 2.5-year-olds, followed up at 4.5 years ($N = 78$).

Wariness Ratings

At each age, only a few minutes after mother and child had been in an observation room, (a) a female stranger entered, (b) sat down and chatted with mother for 30 sec, and (c) offered the child a small puzzle (if need be, making up to four successive offers, spaced by 15 sec). Then (d) once the child approached, or upon the fourth offer, the stranger sat on the floor and attempted to engage the child in play. Four separate ratings (for a, b, c, and d) were made from video-tapes. Each rating, based on a checklist covering facial expression, movements of hands and mouth, avoidance of stranger, and body tension, was made on a four-point scale from (0) no wariness, as if stranger was a familiar adult to (3) high wariness, a persistent expression or more than one major expression. The four ratings were then summed, to give a possible range of 0–12. (See Stevenson-Hinde & Shouldice, 1990, for details. Another index of wariness of stranger, latency to approach, is not discussed here, because at 4.5 years 54 of the 78 children approached the stranger immediately on the first offer.)

At 2.5 years, the mean wariness rating over the whole sample was 4.7, with a standard deviation of 2.9 and a range from 0–12. This did not differ significantly from 4.5 years when the mean was 4.3, with a standard deviation of 2.4 and a range from 1–11. Consistency in the ratings over the two years was significant ($r = .33$, $N = 78$, $p < .001$, one-tailed).

Attachment Classifications

At each age, attachment classifications were based solely upon the child's behavior during the first three minutes of reunion with mother. At 2.5 years, the usual Ainsworth Strange Situation procedure was used, with two reunions (see Stevenson-Hinde & Shouldice, 1990, for details). This procedure was no longer appropriate for 4.5-year-olds, when only one reunion occurred following a separation of about 12 min, which included the administration of the Separation Anxiety Test (see Shouldice & Stevenson-Hinde, 1992, for details). At each age, coding followed the guidelines developed by Cassidy and Marvin (1989). Four secure classifications (Very Secure, Secure-Reserved, Secure-Ambivalent, and Secure-Controlling) and three insecure classifications (Avoidant, Ambivalent, and Controlling) are considered here. Children classed as Disorganized or Insecure-Other were "forced" into one of the above patterns, but this could not be done with children classed as Secure-Other, who were therefore not used in the present analyses. This left 78 children in the above seven classifications at 2.5 years, and 68 at 4.5 years. Over the two years, 29 out of 68 children remained in the same one of the seven classifications. When children were forced into the conventional three classes — Avoidant, Secure, or Ambivalent — stability was 72% (N = 78).

Relations Between Wariness and Attachment at Each Age

At 2.5 years, wariness ratings varied significantly with attachment classification (one-way ANOVA, $F(6) = 3.59$, $p < .004$). The least wary with a stranger were those children classified as Very Secure ($n = 12$) or Secure-Controlling ($n = 6$) with mother (see Fig. 6.1). In particular, children in either classification were significantly less wary than those classed as Secure-Reserved ($n = 17$), Secure-Ambivalent ($n = 5$), Avoidant ($n = 17$), or Ambivalent ($n = 15$) [between-group contrasts tested by the t-statistic (SPSS, 1986): 8 significant at $p < .01$]. As predicted, the Ambivalent children were the most wary ($M = .56$).

Yet for the same children at 4.5 years, the relation between wariness and attachment classification was non-significant (one-way ANOVA, $F(6) = 1.34$, $p = .25$). This parallels the findings that wary and attachment behavior occurred simultaneously in 1-year olds (Bretherton & Ainsworth, 1974) and 2-year-olds but not in 3- and 4-year-olds (Greenberg & Marvin, 1982). A likely interpretation of these two sets of results is that the coupling between wary and attachment behavior systems becomes looser with age (Greenberg & Marvin, 1982).

Another interpretation could be that our index of wariness of strangers or of attachment at 4.5 years was somehow less good than at 2.5 years. For example, Kagan, Reznick, & Snidman (1987) suggest that by about 4 years, unfamiliar peers are a more potent stimulus than an unfamiliar adult. Offsetting this is Asendorf's (1989) suggestion that by 4.5 years fear of negative evaluation might be relevant as well any initial fear of a strange person. With the present wariness ratings, we have seen that the mean, standard deviation, and range was similar from 2.5 to 4.5 years, and that consistency over time was significant. Furthermore, the laboratory ratings were significantly correlated with maternal ratings based on behavior to strangers outside the laboratory (see Stevenson-Hinde & Shouldice, 1990 for details), although the correlation was lower at 4.5 ($r = .24$, $N = 78$) than at 2.5 years ($r = .44$, $N = 82$).

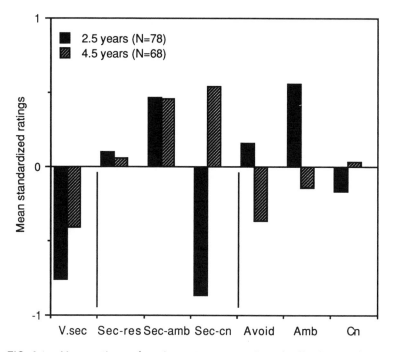

FIG. 6.1. Mean ratings of wariness to stranger (standardized at each age), according to classifications of attachment based upon reunion with mother: Very Secure, Secure-Reserved, Secure-Ambivalent, Secure-Controlling, and Avoidant, Ambivalent, and Controlling. Ratings and classifications were made on the same children at each age.

Similarly, the attachment classifications at 4.5 years were predictable from 2.5 years (see above) and significantly associated with other behavior. For example, significant associations occurred between these classifications and children's responses on the Separation Anxiety Test. Compared with children who were Insecure on reunion, more Secure children gave appropriate negative responses, while fewer Secure children gave persistent denials, over-positive responses, interruptions, or incoherent responses (Shouldice & Stevenson-Hinde, 1992). In addition, direct observations were made on a subsample of the present sample, during freeplay in playgroups, when they were 4.0 to 4.5 years old. Compared with children classed at 4.5 years as Ambivalent ($n = 11$), children classed as Secure ($n = 24$) showed significantly *less* seeking attention, seeking approval, showing-off, plotting, and hostile teasing, and *more* laughing, inquiring, and including others. On sociometric assessment, secure children were rejected less and accepted more. With adults in the playgroups, secure children showed significantly *less* seeking help, seeking attention, ignoring, and negative behavior, and *more* agreement and positive behavior (Turner,

1989). Because of the smaller sample size, comparisons involving Avoidant or Controlling children were not possible. However, an overall analysis of Secure versus Insecure boys and girls showed not only a significant main effect for attachment classification, but also a significant interaction effect between attachment and sex of child (Turner, 1991). Thus, with the present sample, attachment classifications at 4.5 years did relate to other behavior in predictable ways.

Changes in Wariness with Attachment Status Held Constant

We have already seen that, over the whole sample, wariness ratings were consistent and did not change significantly with age. However, in view of the significant relation at 2.5 years but not at 4.5 years between wariness and classifications of attachment (Fig. 6.1), we may ask how wariness ratings changed over time, given a constant attachment status. For each of the four *Secure* classifications, six boys and six girls remained in the same one (Very Secure: $n = 3$; Secure-Reserved: $n = 3$; Secure-Ambivalent: $n = 1$; and Secure-Controlling: $n = 5$). Their wariness ratings *increased* significantly from a mean of 2.9 at 2.5 years to 5.4 at 4.5 years ($t(11) = -3.87$, $p = .003$, two-tailed). Note that their mean of 2.9 at 2.5 years was extremely low, compared to the mean over the whole sample of 4.7 ($N = 82$); and at 4.5 years, a mean of 5.4 out of a possible 12 is not high.

For each of the three *Insecure* classifications, nine girls and eight boys remained in the same one (Avoidant: $n = 5$; Ambivalent: $n = 11$; and Controlling: $n = 1$). Their wariness ratings *decreased* significantly from a mean of 5.2 at 2.5 years to 3.7 at 4.5 years ($t(16) = 2.61$, $p < .02$, two-tailed). This decrease occurred for both the Avoidant group (from a mean of $- .09$ at 2.5 years, to $- .70$ at 4.5 years) and the Ambivalent group (from a mean of .44 at 2.5 years to $- .05$ at 4.5 years).

Thus, while the stably secure children went from showing very little wariness to moderate wariness, the stably insecure children did the reverse. This raises the question of the meaning of the ratings at the two different ages. From a systems point of view, ratings of behavior to an adult female stranger may provide a less pure index of a wary behavior system at 4.5 years than at 2.5 years. For example, it is possible that children (not necessarily those who are wary or fearful), through experience of meeting people (as by going to playgroup), learn to evaluate a stranger before approaching. Indeed, this may be a competent strategy in dealing with unfamiliarity, and one that might be expected of secure children (see above). On the other hand, Avoidant children might have developed ways of concealing any fearfulness, while Ambivalent children might come to show dependent behavior to adults, as an extension of their dependent strategy with mother. Indeed, when the present Ambivalent children were observed in playgroup, they showed a higher relative frequency of seeking help and seeking attention from adults than did Secure children (Turner, 1989). The development of such strategies would detract from the between-group differences observed at 2.5 years (Fig. 6.1).

CONCLUSION

There is no reason to assert that a wary behavior system is any more biological or constitutional or primary than an attachment behavior system. Both share common properties, in terms of the relevance of context, outcome, and function. In addition, both are early appearing, change during development, and are influenced by social interactions. Finally, both show consistent individual differences from infancy to early childhood, and probably beyond.

In early childhood, unfamiliar situations activate both systems, many times over (e.g., Greenberg & Marvin, 1982). In our own longitudinal study, indices of wariness and attachment were significantly related in 2.5-year-olds, with children classified as Very Secure and Secure-Controlling showing least wariness to a stranger and children classed as Ambivalent and Secure-Ambivalent most wary. However, the significant relation between wariness and attachment classification disappeared when the children reached 4.5 years. As in Greenberg and Marvin's (1982) study, a looser coupling of the two systems with age is suggested.

Over the whole sample, wariness ratings showed no significant change with age. However, changes in wariness were revealed when attachment status was held constant. That is, considering only those children who remained in the same attachment classification at both ages, children who remained in the same secure attachment classification (Very Secure, Secure-Reserved, Secure-Ambivalent, or Secure-Controlling) became more wary with age, while the other consistent children (Avoidant, Ambivalent, or Controlling) became less wary.

In accordance with previous findings with secure children, our secure 4.5-year-olds expressed their feelings more clearly on the Separation Anxiety Test and were observed to get on better than insecure children with peers and adults in a playgroup setting. This suggests that those secure children who at 4.5 years held back more than they had done at 2.5 when meeting a stranger may in fact be showing competent behavior (e.g., appraising the situation) characteristic of secure children. Thus, at 4.5 years, the ratings may reflect evaluation of the stranger as well as wariness, with the two constructs intertwined when applied to unfamiliar situations.

ACKNOWLEDGMENTS

We are grateful to R. A. Hinde and R. S. Marvin for their constructive comments on the manuscript. This research was supported by the Medical Research Council, London. In addition, participation in the Attachment Working Group of the John D. & Catherine T. MacArthur Foundation Network on Early Childhood Transitions enabled the attachment classifications to be made and checked for reliability. We are especially grateful to R. S. Marvin who gave advice and did the reliability coding as well.

REFERENCES

Ainsworth, M. D. S. (1991). Attachment and other affectional bonds across the life cycle. In C. M. Parkes, J. Stevenson-Hinde, & P. Marris (Eds.), *Attachment across the life cycle* (pp. 33–51). New York: Routledge.

Ainsworth, M. D. S., Blehar, M. C., Waters, E., & Wall, S. (1978). *Patterns of attachment.* Hillsdale, NJ: Lawrence Erlbaum Associates.

Ainsworth, M. D. S., & Eichberg, C. G. (1991). Effects on infant-mother attachment of mother's unresolved loss of an attachment figure, or other traumatic experience. In C. M. Parkes, J. Stevenson-Hinde, & P. Marris (Eds.), *Attachment across the life cycle* (pp. 160–183). New York: Routledge.

Asendorpf, J. (1986). Shyness in middle and late childhood. In W. H. Jones, J. M. Cheek, & S. R. Briggs (Eds.), *Shyness: Perspectives on research and treatment* (pp. 91–103). New York: Plenum.

Asendorpf, J. (1989). Shyness as a final common pathway for two different kinds of inhibition. *Journal of Personality and Social Psychology, 57,* 481–492.

Baerends, G. P. (1976). The functional organization of behaviour. *Animal Behaviour, 24,* 726–738.

Baerends, G. P., & Kruijt, J. P. (1973). Stimulus selection. In R. A. Hinde & J. Stevenson-Hinde (Eds.), *Constraints on learning* (pp. 23–50). New York: Academic Press.

Bischof, N. (1975). A systems approach toward the functional connections of fear and attachment. *Child Development, 46,* 801–817.

Bowlby, J. (1969/82). *Attachment and loss, Vol. 1: Attachment.* London: Hogarth.

Bowlby, J. (1988). *A secure base: Clinical applications of attachment theory.* London: Hogarth.

Bowlby, J. (1991). Ethological light on psychoanalytical problems. In P. Bateson (Ed.), *The development and integration of behaviour* (pp. 301–313). Cambridge: Cambridge University Press.

Bretherton, I., & Ainsworth, M. D. S. (1974). Responses of one-year-olds to a stranger in a strange situation. In M. Lewis & L. A. Rosenblum (Eds.), *The origins of fear* (pp. 131–164). New York: Wiley.

Bronson, G. W., & Pankey, W. B. (1977). On the distinction between fear and wariness. *Child Development, 48,* 1167–1183.

Cassidy, J., & Marvin, R. S. (1989). *Attachment organization in preschool children: Coding guidelines.* Seattle: MacArthur Working Group on Attachment.

Chance, M. R. A. (1962). An interpretation of some agonistic postures: The role of 'cut-off' acts and postures. *Symposium Zoological Society of London, 8,* 71–89.

Egeland, B., & Farber, E. A. (1984). Infant-mother attachment: Factors related to its development and changes over time. *Child Development, 55,* 753–771.

Emde, R. N., Gaensbauer, T., & Harmon, R. (1976). Emotional expression in infancy: A biobehavioral study. *Psychological Issues, Mon. 37.* New York: International Universities Press.

Fentress, J. C. (1991). Analytical ethology and synthetic neuroscience. In P. Bateson (Ed.), *The development and integration of behaviour* (pp. 77–120). Cambridge: Cambridge University Press.

Goldsmith, H., Buss, A. H., Plomin, R., Rothbart, M. K., Thomas, A., Chess, S., Hinde, R. A., & McCall, R. B. (1987). What is temperament? Four approaches. *Child Development, 58,* 505–529.

Greenberg, M. T., & Marvin, R. S. (1982). Reactions of preschool children to an adult stranger: A behavioral systems approach. *Child Development, 53,* 481–490.

Grossmann, K. E., & Grossmann, K. (1991). Attachment quality as an organizer of emotional and behavioral responses in a longitudinal perspective. In C. M. Parkes, J. Stevenson-Hinde, & P. Marris (Eds.), *Attachment across the life cycle* (pp. 93–114). New York: Routledge.

Grossmann, K., Grossmann, K. E., Spangler, G., Suess, G., & Unzner, L. (1985). Maternal sensitivity and newborn's orientation responses as related to quality of attachment in northern Germany. In I. Bretherton & E. Waters (Eds.), *Growing points of attachment theory and research* (pp. 233–256). *Monographs of the Society for Research in Child Development,* Serial No. 209, *50*(1–2).

Hinde, R. A. (1966/70). *Animal Behaviour: A synthesis of ethology and comparative psychology,* 2nd ed. New York: McGraw-Hill.

Hinde, R. A. (1982). Attachment: Some conceptual and biological issues. In C. M. Parkes & J. Stevenson-Hinde (Eds.), *The place of attachment in human behavior* (pp. 60–76). New York: Basic Books.

Hinde, R. A., & Stevenson, J. G. (1969). Goals and response control. In L. R. Aronson et al. (Eds.), *Development and evolution of behavior* (pp. 216–237). New York: Freeman.

Kagan, J. (1971). *Change and continuity in infancy.* New York: Wiley.

Kagan, J. (1989). The concept of behavioral inhibition to the unfamiliar. In J. S. Reznick (Ed.), *Perspectives on behavioral inhibition* (pp. 1–23). Chicago: University of Chicago Press.

Kagan, J., Reznick, J. S., & Snidman, N. (1987). The physiology and psychology of behavioral inhibition in children. *Child Development, 58,* 1459–1473.

Kagan, J., Reznick, J. S., Snidman, N., Gibbons, J., & Johnson, M. O. (1988). Childhood derivatives of inhibition and lack of inhibition to the unfamiliar. *Child Development, 59,* 1580–1589.

Main, M., & Hesse, E. (1990). Lack of resolution of mourning in adulthood and its relationship to infant disorganization: Some speculations regarding causal mechanisms. In M. T. Greenberg, D. Cicchetti, & E. M. Cummings (Eds.), *Attachment in the preschool years: Theory, research and intervention* (pp. 162–182). Chicago: University of Chicago Press.

Main, M., & Weston, D. (1982). Avoidance of the attachment figure in infancy: Descriptions and interpretations. In C. M. Parkes & J. Stevenson-Hinde (Eds.), *The place of attachment in human behavior* (pp. 31–59). New York: Basic Books.

Marks, I. M. (1987). *Fears, phobias and rituals.* Oxford: Oxford University Press.

Mills, R. S. L., & Rubin, K. H. (1990). Parental beliefs about problematic social behaviors in early childhood. *Child Development, 61,* 138–151.

Radke-Yarrow, M. (1991). Attachment patterns in children of depressed mothers. In C. M. Parkes, J. Stevenson-Hinde, & P. Marris (Eds.), *Attachment across the life cycle* (pp. 115–126). New York: Routledge.

Radke-Yarrow, M., Richters, J., & Wilson, W. E. (1988). Child development in a network of relationships. In R. A. Hinde & J. Stevenson-Hinde (Eds.), *Relationships within families: Mutual influences* (pp. 48–67). Oxford: Claredon Press.

Reznick, J. S. (Ed.) (1989). *Perspectives on behavioral inhibition.* Chicago: University of Chicago Press.

Reznick, J. S., Gibbons, J. L., Johnson, M. O., & McDonough, P. M. (1989). Behavioral inhibition in a normative sample. In J. S. Reznick (Ed.), *Perspectives on behavioral inhibition* (pp. 25–49). Chicago: University of Chicago Press.

Rothbart, M. K. (1989). Behavioral approach and inhibition. In J. S. Reznick (Ed.), *Perspectives on behavioral inhibition* (pp. 139–157). Chicago: University of Chicago Press.

Schaffer, H., Greenwood, A., & Parry, M. (1972). The onset of wariness. *Child Development, 43,* 164–175.

Seyfarth, R., & Cheney, D. (1986). Vocal development in vervet monkeys. *Animal Behaviour, 34,* 1640–1658.

Shouldice, A. E., & Stevenson-Hinde, J. (1992). Coping with security distress: The Separation Anxiety Test and attachment classification at 4.5 years. *Journal of Child Psychology & Psychiatry, 33,* 331–348.

Simpson, A. E., & Stevenson-Hinde, J. (1985). Temperamental characteristics of three- to four-year-old boys and girls and child-family interactions. *Journal of Child Psychology & Psychiatry, 26,* 43–53.

Skarin, K. (1977). Cognitive and contextual determinants of stranger fear in six- and eleven-month-old infants. *Child Development, 48,* 537–544.

Sroufe, L. A. (1977). Wariness of strangers and the study of infant development. *Child Development, 48,* 731–746.

Sroufe, L. A. (1985). Attachment classification from the perspective of infant-caregiver relationships and infant temperament. *Child Development, 56,* 1–14.

Sroufe, L. A., & Waters, E. (1977). Heart rate as a convergent measure in clinical and developmental research. *Merrill-Palmer Quarterly, 23,* 3–25.

Sroufe, L. A., Waters, E., & Matas, L. (1974). Contextual determinants of infant affective response. In M. Lewis & L. Rosenblum (Eds.), *The origins of fear* (pp. 49–72). New York: Wiley.

Stevenson-Hinde, J. (1989). Behavioral inhibition: Issues of context. In J. S. Reznick (Ed.), *Perspectives on behavioral inhibition* (pp. 125–138). Chicago: University of Chicago Press.

Stevenson-Hinde, J., & Hinde, R. A. (1986). Changes in associations between characteristics and interactions. In R. Plomin & J. Dunn (Eds.), *The Study of temperament: Changes, continuities and challenges.* (pp. 115–129). Hillsdale, NJ: Lawrence Erlbaum Associates.

Stevenson-Hinde, J., & Shouldice, A. (1990). Fear and attachment in 2.5-year-olds. *British Journal of Developmental Psychology, 8,* 319–333.

Tinbergen, N. (1959). The functions of territory. *Bird Study, 4,* 14–27.

Turner, P. J. (1989). Relationships in playgroup: An attachment perspective. (Doctoral dissertation, Cambridge University, 1989). *Dissertation Abstracts International, 50.*

Turner, P. J. (1991). Relations between attachment, gender and behavior with peers in preschool. *Child Development, 62,* 1475–1488.

Waters, E., Matas, L., & Sroufe, L. A. (1975). Infants' reactions to an approaching stranger: Description, validation, and functional significance of wariness. *Child Development, 46,* 348–356.

Weiss, R. S. (1982). Attachment in adult life. In C. M. Parkes & J. Stevenson-Hinde (Eds.), *The place of attachment in human behavior* (pp. 171–184). New York: Basic Books.

7 Socialization Factors in the Development of Social Withdrawal

Rosemary S. L. Mills
Kenneth H. Rubin
University of Waterloo

The study of social withdrawal in childhood is predicated on the assumption that having opportunities to play and interact with other children is important for socioemotional development. This assumption has received broad support from all theories of child development that give consideration to the significance of peer interaction (e.g., Hartup, 1983; Mead, 1934; Piaget, 1926; Sullivan, 1953). More recently, there has been growing empirical support for it as well, provided by studies demonstrating that children who are extremely withdrawn relative to their age-mates tend to remain withdrawn and increasingly tend to manifest socioemotional difficulties as they grow older (Rubin, Hymel, & Mills, 1989; Rubin & Mills, 1988).

These difficulties appear to be of an internalizing nature, including anxiety, negative self-perceptions, and feelings of depression (e.g., Rubin et al., 1989; Rubin & Mills, 1988). This link between social withdrawal and internalizing difficulties is not surprising, given the fact that social withdrawal is considered to be the paradigmatic symptom of psychological overcontrol or internalizing problems in childhood (Achenbach & Edelbrock, 1981; Altmann & Gotlib, 1988). As such, this link has guided our efforts to address the prime question of why some children isolate themselves from the social milieu and subsequently begin to evidence internalizing problems.

To enable us to study the origins and course of extreme social withdrawal in childhood, we have described a developmental model in which we suggest that socioemotional adjustment is a product of transactions between inborn characteristics in the child (especially temperamental dispositions), socialization experiences within and outside the family (especially with parents), and certain setting conditions that affect parents (particularly their childrearing beliefs and values, stressful life circumstances, and psychosocial resources) (Rubin, LeMare, & Lollis, 1990; Rubin & Lollis, 1988; Rubin & Mills, 1991). It is postulated that children who are most likely to withdraw from social interaction with peers are those who are temperamentally prone to fearfulness and inhibition in new situations, *and* whose parents are unable to respond to them with sensitivity because they hold childrearing beliefs, attitudes, or values that are not conducive to sensitive responsiveness (see also Fox & Calkins, this volume). These individual and relationships "sources" of withdrawal are hypothesized to have their greatest impact under conditions of familial stress, and/or the lack of intra- and/or interpersonal resources for parental coping. The resultant quality of the parent-child relationship is likely to lead to the development of a sense of felt insecurity in the child, which derives from the child's experience of the parent as someone who is unavailable and unresponsive (Rubin et al., 1990; Fox & Calkins, this volume). In turn, we suggest that this sense of insecurity generalizes to all subsequent relationships, and produces a complementary belief that the self is unworthy and incompetent. These "internal working models" or cognitive representations of self and others contribute to the child's anxiety, inhibition, and withdrawal in new social situations.

Essentially, then, we suggest that social withdrawal is a joint product of characteristics in the child and certain setting conditions that influence parental sensitivity to the child: parental cognitions and beliefs, stressful external conditions, and psychosocial resources. In this chapter we focus on the setting factors posited in the model. We briefly discuss their significance, and then describe our efforts to evaluate their role in the development of social withdrawal.

THE ROLE OF PARENTAL SENSITIVITY IN THE DEVELOPMENT OF SOCIAL COMPETENCE

Most theories of child development consider patterns of interaction in the family, particularly between parent and child, to be an important factor in social development. In our model of the development of social withdrawal, we have drawn predominantly upon attachment theory in suggesting that the development of social competence requires the establishment of an emotionally secure parent-child relationship (e.g., Ainsworth, Blehar, Waters, & Wall, 1978; Bowlby, 1969). Such a relationship provides the child with support that facilitates social exploration, a model of responsiveness that generalizes to other interpersonal relationships, and a sense of personal effectance that facilitates the learning of social skills. According to attachment theorists, the development of a secure relationship depends, in turn, on the parent's ability to respond to the child in a sensitive manner, that is, contingently, consistently, and appropriately. When parents respond sensitively, they are seen as providing the child with a sense of control over the environment and as teaching the child that the parent is available, predictable, and responsive.

In keeping with these tenets of attachment theory, variations in the quality of mother-child attachment in early childhood are related to variations in indices of maternal sensitivity (Egeland & Farber, 1984; Lyons-Ruth, Connell, Grunebaum, Botein, & Zoll, 1984; Spieker & Booth, 1988). Moreover, patterns of attachment are concurrently and predictively related to variations in social competence in early and middle childhood (e.g., Cohn, 1990; Jacobson & Wille, 1986; Sroufe & Fleeson, 1986).

Evidence has been hard to come by, however, with regard to the patterns of parental insensitivity associated with social withdrawal (Hetherington & Martin, 1986; Maccoby & Martin, 1983; Martin, 1975). Socially competent children appear to have parents who set clear expectations, exert control rationally, communicate openly, and provide warmth and support (Baumrind, 1967; Maccoby & Martin, 1983). Aggressive and undercontrolled children, in contrast, have parents who model and inadvertently reinforce aggressive and impulsive behavior, and who are harsh and rejecting toward their children (Becker, 1964; Huesmann, Eron, Lefkowitz, & Walder, 1984; Loeber & Dishion, 1983; Olweus, 1980; Patterson, 1982). The parents of socially withdrawn children have been described in conflicting ways, as authoritarian (rigid and punitive), overprotective (dominating and intrusive), underinvolved, overinvolved, demanding, infantilizing, detached, and rejecting (Baumrind, 1967; Hetherington & Martin, 1986; Levy, 1943; Martin, 1975; Wahler & Dumas, 1987).

The fact that contradictory parenting patterns have been implicated in social withdrawal may be a consequence of conceptual and methodological problems associated with the construct of social withdrawal. Socially withdrawn children undoubtedly form a heterogeneous group whose behavior reflects different psychological underpinnings. In our work, we have suggested, for example, that children can be isolated from their peers either because they have been ostracized *by* the peer group or because they have chosen to withdraw themselves *from* the peer group (Rubin, Hymel, Mills, & Rose-Krasnor, 1991; Rubin & Mills, 1988). Rejection by the peer group may be precipitated by any number of factors (Hartup, 1983). Similarly, voluntary withdrawal may be associated with different underlying motives. For example, Asendorpf (1986, 1989, 1990) has distinguished between withdrawal caused by a wish to avoid social interaction, withdrawal caused by disinterest in social interaction, and withdrawal caused by conflict concerning social interaction. In our model, we have suggested that an important subtype of voluntary social withdrawal is comprised of children for whom withdrawal reflects anxiety associated with felt insecurity.

While one would expect different subtypes of social withdrawal to be associated with different socialization experiences, the failure to make distinctions between different types of withdrawal has meant that in studies of the socialization correlates of social withdrawal, different subtypes have been aggregated. The heterogeneity of the samples may account for the confusing picture that has emerged from these studies.

Methodological shortcomings in the assessment of child and parental behavior have also mitigated against forming a clear picture of parents whose children are socially withdrawn. Socially withdrawn children have generally been identified using procedures of undetermined reliability and validity (Rubin et al., 1990). Similarly, parents have been studied using unproven or questionable procedures. There are virtually no observational data regarding how parents of socially withdrawn children actually interact with their children. Rather, parental behavior has typically been assessed using indices derived from interviews with parents or questionnaires filled out by parents, or using ratings made by observers (e.g., Baumrind, 1967). These measures typically have poor or unknown reliability and validity (Holden & Edwards, 1989). Moreover, they usually provide information about general characteristics only. While it is important to identify patterns of behavior that are consistent across different situations, there is also a need to identify how such general patterns are reflected in specific situations.

In view of the conceptual and methodological flaws in the current literature, it is not surprising that the patterns of parenting associated with social withdrawal remain unclear. In our research, we have sought to identify patterns of parenting associated with a specific subtype of withdrawal, namely, social withdrawal associated with felt insecurity. We suggest that such insecurity is rooted in the quality of parent-child interaction, and that it may originate from transactions between a hyper-reactive temperament in the child and a lack of sensitive responsiveness in parents. We believe further that this insensitivity is a joint product of three setting conditions that affect parents: parental cognitions and beliefs, stressful socioecological conditions existing external to the parent, and the parent's psychosocial resources for coping with stress.

THE ROLE OF PARENTAL COGNITIONS IN PARENTAL SENSITIVITY

We have suggested that parental sensitivity is, to some extent, determined by parental cognitions, that is, the ideas and beliefs parents have about child behavior and development (Rubin & Mills, 1992; Rubin, Mills, & Rose-Krasnor, 1989). There is no doubt that parents' behaviors are guided, in part, by their values (Emmerich, 1969; Kohn, 1977; Stolz, 1967); by their beliefs about how children develop and how quickly they develop (e.g., Dix & Grusec, 1985; Goodnow, Knight, & Cashmore, 1985); by the methods they believe will promote optimal development (e.g., Maccoby & Martin, 1983); and by their ideas about the causes of their children's behavior (e.g., Bugental & Shennum, 1984; Dix, Ruble, & Zambarano, 1989; Grusec & Kuczynski, 1980). Thus, patterns of parental thinking and feeling may indirectly affect children's social development by guiding parental behaviors. These behaviors include not only the anticipatory or *proactive* strategies parents use to promote competent social behavior in their children, but also the *reactive* strategies they use to modify or eliminate unskilled and unacceptable behaviors that occur.

If the way parents think affects their sensitivity, and if their sensitivity contributes to children's socioemotional development, then it is quite possible that parents of socially withdrawn children differ from other parents in their patterns of cognition. The study of these patterns may provide clues about this contribution. Toward this end, we began by studying normative parental cognitions. More specifically, we studied four types of cognitive variables that might be relevant to the development of social withdrawal: parents' beliefs about how children learn socially competent behavior; the reactive strategies they choose for modifying unskilled social behaviors; the attributions they make about the causes of unskilled social behaviors; and their emotional appraisals of unskilled social behaviors.

Normative Parental Cognitions.   If lack of parental sensitivity is an important factor in the development of social withdrawal, then it is important to know what parents typically believe about children's *modes of learning* social skills. There is evidence that some level of parental involvement in organizing and managing children's social contacts is associated with positive peer relations (e.g., Finnie & Russell, 1988; Ladd & Golter, 1988; Parke, MacDonald, Beitel, & Bhavnagri, 1988; Russell & Finnie, 1990). Moreover, the more mothers value and feel responsible for their children's sociability, the more they tend to become involved in promoting their children's peer relationships (Cohen, 1989). The importance parents place on their own direct involvement may be an important area of individual difference between parents, given the suggestion in the literature that parents of socially withdrawn children may be overcontrolling and/or overinvolved. In our research we wanted to know how important parents think it is for them to play a directive role in promoting their child's social skills, and what other influences they might consider important besides their own. This would provide us with norms against which to compare the parents of socially withdrawn children.

For the same reason, we also considered it important to know what *reactive strategies* parents normally choose for influencing common forms of unskilled social behavior. By middle childhood, if not sooner, parents regard both aggression and social withdrawal as problematic behaviors (Bacon & Ashmore, 1985). We know very little, however, about the kinds of strategies parents generally choose for dealing with these behaviors, other than the fact that they suggest the use of more force with antisocial acts than with other types of behavior (Grusec, Dix, & Mills, 1982; Grusec & Kuczynski, 1980).

Another type of cognition that may have implications for the development of social withdrawal is the *attributions* parents make about the causes of unskilled social behaviors. Researchers have suggested that parents' causal attributions may influence their emotional and behavioral reactions to children's social behaviors (e.g., Dix & Grusec, 1985; Weiner & Graham, 1984). For example, the more parents hold their children responsible for negative behaviors, the more they favor power-assertive discipline (Dix, Ruble, & Zambarano, 1989). If parents of socially withdrawn children are overcontrolling, it may be partly because they tend to blame unskilled social behaviors on traits in their children. In order to obtain normative information to use as a basis against which to compare the parents of socially withdrawn children, we examined parents' causal attributions about their children's displays of aggression and social withdrawal.

Finally, we also investigated parents' *affective reactions* to their children's unskilled social behaviors. As with causal beliefs, it is likely that parents' emotions affect their choices of influence strategies. For example, it has been found that parents' negative mood states cause them to discipline their children more sternly (Dix, Reinhold, & Zambarano, 1990), while in depressed mothers these mood states can be associated with either more coerciveness or more nonresponsiveness (Kochanska, Kuczynski, & Maguire, 1989). There is some evidence that both aggressive and socially withdrawn behavior elicit negative affect in parents (Bugental, Blue, & Lewis, 1990; Bugental & Shennum, 1984; Dix, Ruble, & Zambarano, 1989; Grusec, Dix, & Mills, 1982). If parents of socially withdrawn children are overcontrolling, it may be partly because they have strong negative reactions of one kind or another to their children's unskilled behaviors. Since little is known about the constellation of affective reactions that particular types of unskilled social behaviors elicit in parents, we sought to obtain normative information about parents' affective reactions to their children's displays of aggression and social withdrawal.

Our first objective, then, was to establish a set of norms for these four types of parental cognition.

Normative Age-Related Changes in Parental Cognitions. We also sought to establish norms developmentally. In keeping with the transactional nature of the parent-child relationship, changes in children should be associated with changes in parents. Parents change at least some of their childrearing attitudes and practices as their children grow older (McNally, Eisenberg, & Harris, 1991; Miller, 1988; Roberts, Block, & Block, 1984). There is some reason to believe that this occurs at least partly because parents have beliefs about developmental change. Because of these beliefs, they think differently about some behaviors as their children grow older. Given the developmental nature of children's social behavior, age-related changes probably occur in parental ideas and beliefs about their children's social behaviors. These changes may well, in turn, lead to changes in the way parents respond to these behaviors.

For example, it has been established that parents have beliefs about the age at which particular skills emerge (e.g., Goodnow, Cashmore, Cotton, & Knight, 1984; Hess, Kashigawi, Azuma, Price, & Dickson, 1980). Dix and Grusec (1985) proposed that these beliefs are associated with changes in parental attributions about the causes of specific child behaviors as children grow older. With age, parents expect and/or observe developmental advances in children's knowledge and skills, and this causes them to adjust the standards by which they judge child behaviors. In accordance with attribution principles, behaviors that are very discrepant from standards tend to be attributed to internal dispositions (e.g., "personality"). These attributions, in turn, influence parental perceptions. Consistent with this analysis, mothers consider negative behaviors more intentional and dispositional in older children than in younger children, and the more intentional and dispositional they believe them to be, the more upset they feel about them (Dix, Ruble, Grusec, & Nixon, 1986; Dix, Ruble, & Zambarano, 1989).

Since children become less aggressive and more sociable as they move from early to middle childhood (Parke & Slaby, 1983; Rubin, Watson, & Jambor, 1978), it is quite likely that parents adjust their expectations about these behaviors during this period of time, and that aggressive and withdrawn behaviors become increasingly discrepant from their standards. When such behaviors occur in middle childhood, parents may begin to attribute them to traits in their child and may have stronger negative affective reactions to them than they did in early childhood. One purpose of the present study, therefore, was to assess the possibility of change in parental attributions about and affective reactions to their children's displays of aggression and social withdrawal.

Given the links that have been established between these cognitions and the choice of power-assertive strategies (Dix, Ruble, & Zambarano, 1989; Dix, Reinhold, & Zambarano, 1990), parents may also begin to choose more power-assertive strategies when aggressive and withdrawn behaviors occur in middle childhood. However, Dix et al. (1989) found that attributions about the child's competence were a less important predictor of discipline strategies with older than with younger children. This finding suggests that changes in strategy choices may depend less on age-related beliefs about the *causes* of unskilled behaviors than they do on other age-related beliefs. Beliefs about *how development occurs* are likely to be important. It has been established, in the cognitive domain at least, that parents' beliefs about how children acquire knowledge bear some relation to their teaching strategies (Miller, 1988). For example, parents who believe that children actively construct their knowledge tend to use teaching strategies that allow active construction (Sigel, 1982; Sigel & McGillicuddy-DeLisi, 1984).

Moreover, as children's capabilities develop, parents may adjust their strategies to their child's current capability (Bruner, 1985; Wertsch, 1984; Wood, 1980). Such "scaffolding" entails providing more support when children demonstrate difficulty performing tasks and less support as they demonstrate independent performance. As development occurs, then, it is likely that parents expect their children to be more self-regulating and that they adjust their teaching strategies accordingly. They may believe that learning is more self-directed in older children and that guidance and instruction is less important. When unskilled behaviors like aggression and withdrawal occur, they may increasingly expect their children to engage in problem-solving. For example, with older children parents may be more inclined to ask questions and less inclined to tell them what to do (Elias & Ubriaco, 1986). A number of studies provide evidence that scaffolding does indeed occur, but that it is less likely to occur in parents who lack sensitivity to their children (Pratt, Kerig, Cowan, & Cowan, 1988; Wertsch, 1984; Wood, 1980). Thus, it may be that parents of socially withdrawn children do not make the same age-related adjustments in their cognitions as other parents. If they tend to be authoritarian and therefore more rigid in their beliefs, for example, then their cognitions may show less change than those of other parents. In order to obtain normative information to use as a basis against which to compare the parents of socially withdrawn children, we examined age-related changes in parents' beliefs about modes of learning social skills and in their appraisals of their children's displays of aggression and social withdrawal.

Our second objective, then, was to assess longitudinal changes in mothers' choices of strategies for dealing with aggression and social withdrawal. Since these changes may result partly from changes in mothers' beliefs about how children learn social skills, we also examined changes in mothers' beliefs about how their children learn social skills and assessed the contribution of these beliefs to the prediction of mothers' strategy choices for dealing with unskilled social behaviors.

THE IMPACT OF SOCIOECOLOGICAL AND PSYCHOSOCIAL FACTORS ON PARENTAL SENSITIVITY

Parental sensitivity depends not only on parents' cognitions and beliefs about children and development but also on their ability to cope with problems *external to* the parent-child relationship. Their ability to cope with such problems depends, in turn, on (a) the amount of stress they are under due to external conditions that strain their resources, and (b) the adequacy of their psychosocial resources for coping with stress.

According to most models, stress is a reaction to events or conditions that are perceived as challenging to resources (e.g., Hobfoll, 1988; Lazarus & Folkman, 1984). Adverse environmental conditions (e.g., poverty, unemployment, poor housing), the accumulation of multiple problems, and being exposed to adversity over a prolonged period of time, all are conditions that most people would consider threatening to their resources and hence as stressful. Appraising events as stressful may produce negative psychological states (e.g., feelings of helplessness, low self-esteem) that interfere with effective coping (Cohen & Wills, 1985; Lazarus & Folkman, 1984). When this occurs, parents are likely to be less able to cope effectively with the needs of a child (e.g., Belsky, 1984). Indeed, there is growing evidence that stressful conditions are associated either with parental irritability and the use of overdirective or punitive control techniques, or with withdrawal from interaction and neglect of the child (Crnic & Greenberg, 1990; Patterson, 1983; Wahler & Dumas, 1987).

Drawing upon these models of stress, we suggest that stress interferes with parental sensitivity by leading to dysfunctional cognitive appraisal of situations (Cohen & Wills, 1985; Lazarus & Folkman, 1984). Thus, parents exposed to prolonged or severe adversity, or who suffer an accumulation of crises, may deviate from the norm in their ideas and beliefs about children and childrearing. For example, parents who are burdened by many demands may appraise their children negatively, or they may be so preoccupied that they simply tune them out. In order to test this hypothesis, we sought to determine whether relations exist between parents' cognitions and their socioecological circumstances.

Another objective of our research was to examine the role that parents' psychological and social resources may play in counteracting these stress effects. Inner psychological qualities and interpersonal conditions are considered to be sources of resistance to stress effects (Cohen & Wills, 1985;

Kessler & McLeod, 1985). Whether psychosocial resources actually prevent the appraisal of conditions as *stressful* is an issue that has not yet been settled, but there is some evidence that they may at least facilitate efforts to cope with the experience of stress itself, by preventing or altering the negative psychological states that tend to accompany stress appraisal. Evidence is accumulating that suggests that psychosocial factors such as the psychological maturity of the parents, the socioemotional functioning of the parents, the quality of the marital relationship, and the availability of a supportive social network, help to "buffer" parents against stress effects on their ability to respond sensitively to their children. We know, for example, that older mothers interact more sensitively with their infants than younger mothers (Ragozin, Basham, Crnic, Greenberg, & Robinson, 1982); that infants' attachment relationships with the mother may prove to be insecure when she is or has been depressed (Radke-Yarrow, Cummings, Kuczynski, & Chapman, 1985; Spieker & Booth, 1988) or has insecure representations of attachment relationships (e.g., Bretherton, 1985, 1990; Main, Kaplan, & Cassidy, 1985); that mothers who experience affectionate and relatively conflict-free marital relationships feel competent in their parenting roles and are observed to be sensitive, affectionate parents (Engfer, 1988); and that mothers who have a sense of support from relatives, friends, and spouse are less restrictive and punitive (e.g., Colletta, 1979). In order to assess whether psychosocial resources aid stress-resistance by influencing cognitive processes, we sought to determine whether the relations between parents' cognitions and their socioecological circumstances are moderated by psychosocial factors.

In summary, the purpose of our initial studies (Mills & Rubin, 1990, 1992; Rubin & Mills, 1992; Rubin, Mills, & Rose-Krasnor, 1989) was to assess normative parental beliefs and cognitions about children's social behaviors and skills, and normative age-related changes that might occur in these beliefs and cognitions as children move from early to middle childhood. Another purpose was to examine the relations between parents' beliefs and cognitions and their socioecological conditions and psychosocial resources. Toward these ends, we studied a sample of mothers, each of whom had a four-year-old child. We re-contacted as many of these mothers as we could two years later, when their children had reached the age of six. In both phases of the study, mothers completed a set of (mailed) questionnaires. Their beliefs about modes of learning social skills were assessed by asking them to indicate the importance of various influences on the development of several social competencies. Their attributions, affective reactions, and strategy choices were assessed by asking them to read descriptions of hypothetical incidents of peer-directed aggression and withdrawal and answer several questions. We also gathered information about mothers' socioeconomic status (indexed by the occupational status of the mother or father, whichever was higher), their recent experience of negative life events, and their supportive social contacts.

STUDY 1: MOTHERS' IDEAS AND BELIEFS ABOUT SOCIAL BEHAVIORS

In the first phase of our normative study, the participants included 122 mothers, each with a 4-year-old child attending daycare or preschool. We were able to contact 100 of these mothers two years later when their children were 6 years old; of these 100, 45 agreed to participate in a second phase of data collection. Although the attrition rate was high, the longitudinal sample was quite representative of the original sample in terms of demographic characteristics. Mothers ranged widely in age, occupational status, and level of education. Mothers completed the same set of questionnaires in both phases of the study.

Beliefs about Modes of Learning Social Skills.   We gathered information about mothers' beliefs about how children learn social skills by giving them short descriptions of four social skills (getting acquainted with someone new; resolving peer conflicts; getting accepted into an ongoing play group of unfamiliar peers; persuading other children to do what one wants) and asking them to judge the relative importance of four general modes of learning: (1) *directive teaching* (being rewarded for appropriate behavior and punished for inappropriate behavior; being told exactly how to act); (2) *observation* (observing what other children do; observing what adults do); (3) the child's *personal experiences* (experiencing interactions with others; experiencing the feelings that arise when being with someone); and (4) *explanations* offered by adults (being taught and encouraged at school; being told why one should act in a certain way) (see Elias & Ubriaco, 1986).

Data analyses indicated that, when their children were four years of age, mothers considered personal experience to be the most important way for their children to acquire social skills. Observational learning was secondary, and being taught by adults through explanation and directive teaching were considered least important. Mothers' judgments did not change over the two years, with the exception that they placed more importance on observational learning at age six than they had at age four. Judging from this normative sample, then, mothers believe social competence develops mostly through self-mediated learning, and that their own direct teaching efforts are not an important strategy for them to use, at least proactively.

Reactive Strategies, Attributions, and Emotions.   We gathered information about mothers' cognitions concerning unskilled social behaviors by presenting them with stories describing hypothetical incidents in which their own child behaved aggressively or in a socially withdrawn way in a peer-group situation. Two of the scenarios depicted their children behaving consistently in an aggressive manner; two scenarios described their children behaving consistently in an anxious-withdrawn manner. Following each story, mothers were asked what *emotions* they would feel if their own child consistently acted this way, what *attributions* they would make about the causes of the behavior, and what *strategies* they thought they would use to modify the behavior.

With regard to reactive *strategies,* we found that at both ages four and six, mothers said they would most likely react to their child's aggression with moderately power assertive strategies (e.g., gentle instructions, reasoning) and to withdrawal with low-power techniques (e.g., redirecting the child), information-seeking (e.g., seeking help or advice), and planful strategies (e.g., arranging opportunities for peer play). As one might expect, mothers were more likely to advocate high- and moderate-power strategies in response to aggression than to withdrawal, and were more likely to suggest low-power strategies in reaction to withdrawal than to aggression. However, we also found changes over the two years; there was an increase in the extent to which low-power strategies (in particular, asking the child what is wrong) were reported in reaction to both withdrawal and aggression, a decrease in reported information-seeking in response to both withdrawal and aggression, and a decrease in choice of "no response" to displays of social withdrawal. In short, as their children got older, mothers were less likely to suggest that they would ignore their children's unskilled behaviors, more likely to suggest that they would deal with it first-hand, and more likely to indicate that they would deal with it through low-power strategies such as talking to their children about the reasons for their behavior.

As far as *causal attributions* were concerned, mothers did not view social withdrawal or aggression as particularly stable characteristics. At both ages four and six, they attributed these behaviors primarily to temporary internal states such as mood or fatigue. They also made some distinctions between these two types of behavior. They were more likely to attribute aggression than withdrawal to age-related factors such as immaturity; this was particularly true for mothers of *boys.* By the time their child was six, however, mothers were less likely to explain either type of behavior on the basis of age-related factors, and were slightly more likely (nonsignificant change) to attribute them to a trait in their child.

Finally, with regard to mothers' *affective reactions* to aggression and withdrawal, their predominant response to aggression and withdrawal at both times was *concern.* Next to concern, mothers were mostly angry and disappointed about aggression, and mostly puzzled about withdrawal. Not surprisingly, mothers indicated that they would be more angry, disappointed, and embarrassed about aggression than withdrawal, and more puzzled about withdrawal than aggression. Over time, mothers of girls became more negative about aggression and mothers of boys became less negative. No change occurred in mothers' affective reactions to social withdrawal.

It appears, then, that while mothers consider aggression and social withdrawal to be of equal concern in early childhood, their other reactions to these behaviors are quite different. Aggression elicits more negativity and a stronger inclination toward power-assertion than social withdrawal, which appears to be something of an enigma to them. It also appears that mothers' ideas and beliefs about their children's social behaviors show considerable continuity over time. As children moved from early to middle childhood, mothers continued to believe that personal experience and observational learning are the most important influences on the development of social skills. They also continued to choose the same strategies for reacting to unskilled social behaviors: mainly moderate-power strategies for aggressive behavior and low-power strategies for social withdrawal. Not only did mothers' cognitions and beliefs stay the same over the two-year interval, but there was considerable consistency between their earlier and later beliefs, and the same relation was found between negative affect and choice of power-assertive strategies at age six as had been found with the original sample at age four (Mills & Rubin, 1990). For example, mothers who favored power-assertive strategies when their child was four years old still favored these strategies when their child was six, and those who reported feeling more negative about aggression and social withdrawal continued to favor power-assertive strategies for dealing with these behaviors.

The few changes that were found in mothers' cognitions about aggressive and socially withdrawn behavior may be due to maternal "timetables" with respect to the acquisition of certain skills (e.g., Goodnow, Cashmore, Cotton, & Knight, 1984; Hess, Kashigawi, Azuma, Price, & Dickson, 1980). For example, these timetables may be responsible for the decrease in mothers' tendency to attribute aggression and social withdrawal to age-related factors. By the time children enter school, aggression and withdrawal may be less easily excused as reflecting immaturity or a passing phase. In keeping with the fact that parents not only have age-related expectations but also gender-related expectations (e.g., Atkinson & Endsley, 1976; Bacon & Ashmore, 1985; Lytton & Romney, 1991), affective reactions to aggression became more negative in mothers of girls and less negative in mothers of boys. As children grow older, aggressive behavior may become more discrepant from the accepted norm in girls and less discrepant in boys, with the result that mothers become more disapproving of it in girls and more inured to it in boys.

Changes in mothers' choices of strategies for dealing with unskilled social behaviors and in their beliefs about modes of learning social skills also seem best explained by age-related changes in expectations about developmental change. Mothers' reporting of more low-power influence strategies (e.g., asking their child to explain) and their assignment of more importance to observational learning of social skills over time may reflect their awareness of advances in their children's ability to reason and reflect and their recognition that older children require less "hands-on" direction and discipline (Clifford, 1959). These changes may also indicate that parents expect an increase in self-regulatory behavior with age; as such, they are suggestive of the significance of parents' perceptions of the zone of proximal development (e.g., Wertsch, 1984).

Relations Between Maternal Cognitions, Stress, and Psychosocial Resources.   We expected that mothers who experienced a good deal of stress and who had the weakest sense of social support would deviate most from the norm in their cognitions and beliefs. Indeed, at age four, we found that the lower the family's socioeconomic status, the more mothers tended to react to aggressive and withdrawn behaviors with negative emotions and the more they were inclined to choose power-assertive strategies for dealing with aggression. This was particularly true for mothers who had little sense of support and the behavior of concern was aggression. When the experience of socioeconomic stress was prolonged, that is, when low socioeconomic status persisted over the two-year time span of the study, mothers with little sense of social support were more inclined to attribute aggression to a trait in their children and more likely to choose power-assertive strategies for dealing with social withdrawal. Thus, there was some evidence that mothers under stress are more at risk of thinking in ways conducive to insensitive parental responding, and may continue to be at greater risk as long as their stress persists. The finding that perceived support moderated the effects of stress supports the notion that the tendency to appraise situations negatively may be offset by the availability of social resources.

Finally, we also found evidence that the relations between stress and maternal ideas and beliefs may be highly specific. While the accumulation of negative life events over time did not add significantly to the prediction of mothers' cognitions about unskilled social behaviors, it was negatively related to beliefs about the importance of self-mediated learning. It may be that mothers suffering repeated misfortune cannot afford to believe in processes they must leave to the control of their children.

With these findings as a normative standard, the next step in our program of research was to determine whether the mothers of socially withdrawn children would differ from those with average children with respect to any of the four types of maternal cognitions. Thus, *normally,* one would not expect mothers to consider directive teaching a very important proactive strategy for promoting social competence. Again, normally, one might expect mothers to be somewhat negative and moderately power assertive in dealing with aggressive behavior, but certainly not very negative or very directive in their responses to social withdrawal. Given these norms about maternal beliefs, we asked whether the mothers of socially withdrawn children were highly controlling, as the literature suggests. We asked also whether they believed more strongly than other mothers in the use of directive strategies to proactively teach social skills, and whether they reacted more negatively and suggested the use of high-power reactive strategies for dealing with socially withdrawn and aggressive behavior more often than the norm. We asked further whether the mothers of withdrawn children differed from the norm with respect to both socially withdrawn and aggressive behavior, or only with respect to one type of behavior, and whether they experienced more stress than other mothers. Finally, we asked whether they were more likely than mothers of normal children to lack a sense of support from others.

MATERNAL FACTORS ASSOCIATED WITH SOCIAL WITHDRAWAL IN EARLY CHILDHOOD

In order to determine whether mothers of socially withdrawn children differed from other mothers in their cognitions about social behaviors, their experiences of stress, or their psychosocial resources, we returned to our original sample of 122 preschoolers. First we identified small groups of mothers whose children were either extremely withdrawn or extremely aggressive, as well as a larger comparison group of mothers whose children were average in their socioemotional adjustment. Then we compared the mothers of these children with regard to their beliefs about how children learn social skills and their cognitions about aggressive and socially withdrawn behavior (Rubin & Mills, 1990).

Using both observations and teacher ratings, we identified three groups of children. *Withdrawn-Internalizing* children were defined as those who were high on observed socially withdrawn behavior and teacher-rated internalizing difficulties, but *not* high on observed negative/aggressive behavior or on teacher-rated externalizing difficulties. In contrast, we defined *Aggressive-Externalizing* children as high on observed negative/aggressive behavior and teacher rated externalizing difficulties, but *not* high on socially withdrawn behavior or on internalizing difficulties. Finally, we defined *Average* children as those who were below the cut-off points on all four criterion indices. We then compared the mothers of these three groups of children to see if they differed in any of their beliefs or cognitions.

First, we found a difference between the three target groups in the amount of importance mothers placed on their proactive socialization practices. The mothers of Withdrawn-Internalizing children placed significantly more importance on *directive teaching* than did the mothers of either of the other two groups, for all four social skills (getting acquainted with someone new, resolving peer conflicts, getting accepted into a new play group, persuading others to do what one wants).

Next, we compared the three target groups with respect to the extent to which they suggested each of several types of strategies for dealing with aggression and social withdrawal. On the basis of the normative data, we defined "high coercion" as the proportion of high-power strategies reported for dealing with aggressive behaviors and as the proportion of high-plus moderate-power strategies reported for dealing with socially withdrawn behaviors. "Low coercion" was defined as the proportion of low-plus moderate-power strategies reported for dealing with aggression and as the proportion of low-power strategies reported for dealing with social withdrawal. A third category, "indirect or no response," was comprised of strategies that did not involve an immediate reaction to the child's behavior, such as seeking information, arranging opportunities for peer experience, or simply choosing not to respond.

The analyses revealed that for *both* socially withdrawn and aggressive behavior, mothers of Withdrawn-Internalizing children were significantly more likely to report high-power strategies than the mothers of either of the other two groups of children. Conversely, the mothers of Withdrawn-Internalizing children were less likely to report indirect-no response strategies than were the mothers of either of the other two groups of children. Mothers of Aggressive-Externalizing children did not differ from mothers of Average children in the extent to which they reported high-power strategies, but they were more likely to report indirect-no response strategies than mothers of Average children. Mothers of Average children were more likely to report the use of low-power strategies than the mothers of either of the other two groups of children.

Our third set of data analyses revealed significant differences between the three target groups with respect to two types of causal attributions: attributions to a trait in the child and to age-related factors. Mothers of Withdrawn-Internalizing children were significantly more likely than mothers of Average children to attribute *both* aggression and withdrawal to a trait in the child. Mothers of Aggressive-Externalizing children did not differ from either of the other two target groups. Mothers of Withdrawn-Internalizing children and mothers of Average children were equally likely to attribute *aggression* to age-related factors, and more likely to do so than mothers of Aggressive-Externalizing children. There were nonsignificant differences between the three target groups in the extent to which mothers attributed *social withdrawal* to age-related factors.

Our fourth set of analyses indicated significant differences between the three target groups with respect to mothers' reported emotional reactions to socially withdrawn and aggressive behaviors. Not surprisingly, mothers of Average children were significantly more puzzled about displays of withdrawal and aggression than either of the other two groups of mothers. Mothers of both the Withdrawn-Internalizing children and the Aggressive-Externalizing children reported a stronger *anger* reaction to these behaviors than did the mothers of Average children. Lastly, mothers of Withdrawn-Internalizing children reported stronger feelings of disappointment, embarrassment, and guilt about displays of *both* withdrawal and aggression than the other two groups of mothers. For these three emotions, there were nonsignificant differences between the two latter groups.

Finally, to determine whether the mothers of socially withdrawn children also differ from other mothers either in external stressors or in their perceptions of support from others, we then compared the three target groups with respect to socioeconomic status, mothers' experience of negative life events, and mothers' perceptions of social support. We found that the groups differed in one respect: mothers of Withdrawn-Internalizing children were lower in *socioeconomic status* than those of Average children.

Summary.   Our findings indicate quite clearly that mothers' beliefs concerning the importance of attaining social skills and the means by which they would help their children become socially competent are associated with their children's social competence. They also paint a remarkably consistent picture of mothers whose children are socially withdrawn. The fact that these latter mothers placed greater importance on a directive approach to teaching social skills than did mothers of average children, and were more likely to choose controlling strategies for dealing with unskilled social behaviors, suggests that socially withdrawn preschoolers tend to have mothers who are highly controlling. The causal attributions and emotional reactions of these mothers are also indicative of overdirection, and taken together with the evidence concerning their external sources of stress, they provide some tentative insights about why these mothers are overcontrolling. Mothers of socially withdrawn children were not only less tolerant of unskilled social behaviors than the other mothers, but they also felt more angry, disappointed, guilty, and embarrassed about these behaviors, and they were more inclined to blame them on traits in their children. This constellation of emotions and attributions suggests that mothers of socially withdrawn children may be somewhat irritable and unable to moderate their affective reactions to problematic behaviors. These data, in fact, mesh well with recent reports that maternal affective disorders, specifically depression, are sometimes associated with displays of socially reticent behavior in young children (e.g., Kochanska, 1991; Rubin, Both, Zahn-Waxler, Cummings & Wilkinson, 1991).

While these data are consistent with the link often drawn between social withdrawal and parental overcontrol (e.g., Hetherington & Martin, 1986), they represent the first time, to our knowledge, that an empirical link has been established between indices of parental overcontrol and a specific form of social withdrawal, defined as reflecting anxiety associated with felt insecurity. Our findings left us with two important questions. First, do mothers of socially withdrawn children continue to evidence overcontrol in their ideas and beliefs as their children grow older? As our initial studies showed, mothers adjust some of their ideas about their children's social behaviors as their children reach school-age. In their strategy choices, for example, they begin to favor less power-assertive responses to their children's unskilled social behaviors. At the same time, mothers show a good deal of consistency in their thinking as their children move from early to middle childhood, for example, mothers who were more controlling at age four were also more controlling at age six. While consistency may be the rule for mothers whose children are average in social competence, it may *not* be for mothers confronted with problematic behaviors in their children. Such behaviors may cause parents to engage in problem-solving efforts that lead them to change their ideas and beliefs about their children's behaviors. As a result, the pattern of ideas and beliefs distinguishing mothers of socially withdrawn children from other mothers may differ across developmental levels.

It is also likely that parents evaluate behaviors not only by reference to generalized age norms but also by reference to what is normative behavior for their own child. The notion of adaptation level (Maccoby & Martin, 1983) suggests that over time parents become accustomed to certain characteristic behavior patterns in their children, develop more tolerant attitudes toward them, and establish a broader range for what behavior they consider acceptable. In line with this notion, Olweus (1980) found that mothers of aggressive adolescent boys became more permissive toward aggression over time. If parents evaluate their children by reference to individual rather than general norms, then it is possible that mothers of socially withdrawn children may react less to this type of behavior as their children grow older.

A second question raised by our initial findings concerns how the overcontrol that we found on the level of mothers' thinking is reflected in their patterns of behavior. Given the complexity of the connections between self-reported and actual behavior, and the possibility that asking hypothetical questions does not access the decision processes involved in actual parenting situations, it cannot be assumed that mothers of socially withdrawn children necessarily *behave* in a more controlling fashion than other mothers.

In our next study, therefore, we set out to address both these questions, by examining mothers' cognitions and behaviors developmentally.

STUDY 2: MATERNAL FACTORS ASSOCIATED WITH SOCIAL WITHDRAWAL IN MIDDLE CHILDHOOD

In this study, we examined the cognitions, the socioecological circumstances, the psychosocial resources, and the behaviors of mothers who had a 5- or a 9-year-old child who had been identified as withdrawn-internalizing, aggressive-externalizing, or average in social competence. Peer-nominations and teacher-ratings of children's social behaviors were used to identify these three groups of children. At age 5, peer assessments were obtained by asking kindergarten children to nominate up to three classmates who fit each of three behavioral descriptions (of an aggressive child, a socially withdrawn child, and a cooperative child). The number of nominations each child received from same-sex classmates for each description were totalled and then standardized within classroom and gender groups in order to adjust for variations in class size and numbers of boys and girls. At age 9 (grade 4), peer assessments were obtained by administering the *Revised Class Play* (Masten, Morison, & Pellegrini, 1985). Children were asked to nominate up to three classmates who best fit each of 30 behavioral descriptions. The number of nominations each child received from same-sex peers for each item was tallied and standardized, with the resulting scores then being summed to create two factor scores. One factor score was the Aggression-Disruption factor found by Masten et al. (1985). The second, labeled Passive Isolation, consisted of a sub-cluster of four items from Masten et al.'s Sensitivity/Isolation factor. This sub-cluster appears to describe the construct of anxious withdrawal and is both concurrently and predictively associated with internalizing difficulties (Rubin & Mills, 1988).

Teacher ratings for the 5-year-olds were obtained using the *Preschool Behavior Questionnaire* (Behar & Stringfield, 1974), a 30-item scale that best yields two factors (Moller & Rubin, 1988): an Internalizing factor consisting of items describing fearfulness, anxiety and solitude, and an Externalizing factor consisting of items describing hostile-aggressive and impulsive-distractible behaviors. At age 9 years, grade 4 teachers were requested to complete the *Teacher-Child Rating Scale* (Hightower, Work, Cowen, Lotyczewski, Spinell, Guare, & Rohrbeck, 1986), a measure of socioemotional development designed for use with elementary-school children. Factor scores for two of the six factors tapped by the scale were computed: Shyness-Anxiety and Acting-Out. These two factors were described by Hightower et al. (1986) as most similar to other broadband dimensions such as internalizing versus externalizing difficulties, as defined by Achenbach and Edelbrock (1981). Accordingly, we construed the Shyness-Anxiety and Acting-Out factor scores as measures of internalizing and externalizing difficulties, respectively.

Using both same-sex peer nominations and teacher ratings, we identified three groups of children in each grade. *Withdrawn-Internalizing* children were defined as those who were high (at least one full standard deviation above the mean for their grade and sex) on peer nominations of passive isolation *and* teacher-ratings of internalizing, but *not* high (at or below the mean) on peer nominations of aggression-disruption or on teacher-ratings of externalizing. In contrast, we defined *Aggressive-Externalizing* children as high on peer nominations of aggression-disruption *and* teacher-ratings of externalizing, but *not* high on peer nominations of passive isolation or on teacher-ratings of internalizing. Finally, we defined *Average* children as those who were not high (i.e., who were less than one standard deviation above the mean for their grade and sex) on any of the four criterion measures.

In order to observe their mothers interacting with them in a peer-interaction situation, we then formed pairs of mother-child dyads that would visit our laboratory at the same time. In each grade, each mother-child dyad was paired with a second dyad that consisted of an unfamiliar, same-sex Average child and mother. This procedure resulted in a target sample comprised, in kindergarten, of 11 Withdrawn-Internalizing children (7 girls, 4 boys), 12 Aggressive-Externalizing children (5 girls, 7 boys), and 43 Average children (24 girls, 19 boys), of whom 10 (6 girls, 4 boys) were randomly assigned to be the focus of the observation session; and in grade 4, of 11 Withdrawn-Internalizing children (6 girls, 5 boys), 14 Aggressive-Externalizing children (4 girls, 10 boys), and 39 Average children (20 girls, 19 boys) of whom 7 (5 girls, 2 boys) were randomly assigned to be focal.

These children and their mothers then visited our laboratory to be interviewed and administered a set of questionnaires, and to participate in an observation session in either a focal or a nonfocal capacity. At the time of this visit, the kindergarten children were close to 6 years of age ($M = 70.4$ mos., $SD = 3.7$ mos.) and the grade 4 children were close to 10 years of age ($M = 119.0$ mos., $SD = 5.1$ mos.). In the following, we report the results of comparisons between the Withdrawn-Internalizing and Average target groups.

Beliefs about Social Skills.   In an interview, mothers were asked a series of questions concerning their beliefs about the development of two social skills: (a) making friends, and (b) sharing possessions. For each skill, mothers were asked how early children evidence the skill, how important it is to attain, how stable a child's competence in that skill is (both for children who are good at it and for those who have difficulty), what causes stability, and how competent their own child is in that skill. One target-group difference was found, with respect to mothers' beliefs about the causes of stability in children who are good at making friends. Although mothers generally attributed stability primarily to critical periods, mothers of Withdrawn-Internalizing children in grade 4 were more likely than those of Average children to think that children who are good at making friends continue to be because of experience. It may be that, by the time their children reach late childhood, mothers of socially withdrawn children are acutely aware of the difference between the social experiences of children who are socially at ease and those who are not. An interesting asymmetry in our findings is that these mothers were *not* more likely than other mothers to attribute stable *difficulty* making friends to experience. This could reflect an attitude of "developmental optimism," in which experience is seen as facilitating but not as hindering social development (Goodnow, Knight, & Cashmore, 1985).

Next, mothers were asked the reasons why they thought children might succeed or why they might fail in attaining these social skills. For each *failure* attribution, mothers were asked to indicate how difficult it would be for parents to change that reason. Attributions were classified into one of three general categories: (a) *child-centered* (e.g., "just born that way," "too insecure,"); (b) *external-direct* (e.g., "was never taught how," "wasn't punished for hitting others"); (c) *external-indirect* (e.g., "never had a chance to play with others," "was allowed to make decisions on her own"). One difference was found between the target groups of mothers. In both kindergarten and grade 4, mothers of Withdrawn-Internalizing children considered it more difficult than did mothers of Average children for a parent to *change* the cause of a child's difficulty making friends.

Mothers were also asked to describe what parents should or should not do to help their children learn the two social skills, and to rate the importance of doing something to help. The strategies they suggested were coded as being either high, moderate, or low in power assertion, or as involving information-seeking or planning. Our analyses of these data yielded nonsignificant target-group differences.

Reactive Strategy Choices, Attributions, and Affective Reactions. The mothers in this second study were given the same stories described earlier, depicting hypothetical displays of aggression and withdrawal. In their *strategy choices,* we found that the Withdrawn-Internalizing and the Average target-group mothers *did not* differ in how they said they would deal with aggression, but they differed in how they said they would deal with social withdrawal. Specifically, mothers of Withdrawn-Internalizing children in *both* kindergarten and grade 4 were much less likely than mothers of Average children to say that they would respond, in any way at all, to displays of social withdrawal.

Our target-group comparisons with respect to mothers' *attributions* about the causes of aggressive and socially withdrawn behaviors indicated that, in both kindergarten and grade 4, mothers of Withdrawn-Internalizing children were more likely than mothers of Average children to attribute both these behaviors to traits in their children.

Finally, our analyses of mothers' *affective reactions* to the stories indicated that, in both kindergarten and grade 4, mothers of Withdrawn-Internalizing children had less pronounced reactions than mothers of Average children, that is, they felt *less* disappointed, disgusted, embarrassed, and sad about aggression, and *less* disappointed, sad, guilty, surprised, and puzzled about social withdrawal. In our earlier study of four-year-olds, the difference between mothers of Withdrawn-Internalizing and Average children was in the opposite direction.

Perceptions of Child.   We also examined mothers' perceptions of their children's adjustment, in order to determine whether mothers of socially withdrawn children recognized their children's behavioral tendencies and considered them problematic. Mothers were asked to rate their children's problem behaviors by completing the parent rating form of the Child Behavior Checklist (Achenbach & Edelbrock, 1981). Comparisons between the Withdrawn-Internalizing and Average target groups of mothers revealed that, in both kindergarten and grade 4, mothers of Withdrawn-Internalizing children perceived their children as being significantly more withdrawn and as having more internalizing difficulties than mothers of Average children.

Stress and Support.   We also compared the three target groups with respect to socioeconomic status, mothers' experience of negative life events, and mothers' perceptions of social support. We found that in neither grade did the groups differ in any of these factors.

Mothers' Behavior.   In order to observe patterns of maternal behavior, mothers were observed interacting with their children in a 35-minute session. This session consisted of six segments varying in their situational demands. In the first segment, in accordance with previous instructions, the mother asked her child to tidy up a mess left behind in the play room (Compliance Task). When this task was completed (or when five minutes had elapsed), an experimenter entered and told mother and child that they could play for about five minutes (Dyadic Free Play Segment). Next, the nonfocal dyad was introduced and the nonfocal child was given time to adjust to the situation before being left alone with the focal dyad. Following the departure of the nonfocal mother, there were three segments supervised by the focal mother: five minutes of Triadic Free Play, five minutes of Peer Conflict (sharing a special toy), and seven minutes of Peer Cooperation (building with Lego blocks).

Proactive behaviors directed by the focal mother to her own child were coded using a social problem-solving taxonomy focusing on the goals the mother had and the strategies she used to accomplish these goals (Booth, Rose-Krasnor, & Rubin, 1991; Rubin, Mills, & Rose-Krasnor, 1989). **Proactive goals** included *adult-oriented* objectives (initiating joint activities between focal and nonfocal child, initiating other activities involving the focal child, stopping joint activities, stopping other activities), *child-oriented* objectives (continuing joint activities, continuing other activities, monitoring feelings or activities, getting information), *teaching* values or information, and *initiating independent behavior.* **Proactive strategies** included *high power* strategies (direct commands, negative evaluations, and negative incentives), *moderate power* strategies (indirect requests, rules, explanations, and positive incentives); *support* (positive evaluations, physical or verbal comforting, verbal help, and physical help); and *questions.*

The majority of mothers' proactive goals were either *adult-centered* or *child-centered.* Our analyses of these goals revealed that mothers of Withdrawn-Internalizing children did not differ from mothers of Average children, in either kindergarten or grade 4, in the relative proportion of adult- vs. child-centered goals, either when they were alone with their children (Compliance and Dyadic Free Play segments) or when they were with their children in a social situation (Triadic Free Play, Peer Conflict, and Peer Cooperation segments). Our analyses of mothers' proactive strategies revealed that, compared to mothers of Average children in both grades, mothers of Withdrawn-Internalizing children were as likely to use *high power* strategies when they were alone with their children (Compliance and Dyadic Free Play segments), but were proportionately less likely to do so when they were with their children in a social situation (Triadic Free Play, Peer Conflict, and Peer Cooperation segments).

Summary.   The findings of our second study paint a rather different picture of mothers of socially withdrawn children. In contrast to the first study, mothers of socially withdrawn children in the second study did not appear to be under greater stress than other mothers. They were also quite tolerant of their children's behavioral tendencies, although they were well aware that their children were having difficulties. And in contrast to our first study, in which we found that mothers of socially withdrawn children favored an active approach to promoting their child's social behavior by choosing directive teaching strategies, in our second study mothers did not seem to be trying to change their child's behavior. Indeed, these mothers considered it much more difficult than did those of average children for a parent to influence the cause of a child's difficulty making friends. Congruent with this finding, they were more likely to say they would not respond to social withdrawal in their children, and in their actual behavior in a peer play context they were less likely to be directive in a proactive way.

CONCLUSIONS

In this chapter, we have described a program of research designed to demonstrate that social withdrawal is associated with disruptions in parental sensitivity that may result from stressful conditions and a lack of psychosocial resources for coping with stress. Our data, although correlational, were generally consistent with our premises, at least in *early* childhood. Mothers of withdrawn children were more likely than mothers of average children to believe that social skills should best be taught in a directive manner and that unskilled behaviors should be responded to in a directive or coercive fashion. These mothers were also more likely than mothers of average children to indicate that they would feel angry, disappointed, guilty, and embarrassed about unskilled behaviors, and were more inclined to attribute them to traits in their children. And finally, these mothers were under more socioeconomic strain than mothers of average children.

In our second study, however, a rather different set of maternal cognitions distinguished socially withdrawn from average children, and socioecological and psychosocial factors did not differentiate between the two groups. Mothers of socially withdrawn children in this study perceived themselves as having less influence on the cause of a child's difficulty making friends than mothers of average children, were more likely to say they would do nothing at all in response to withdrawn behavior, and appeared to be more tolerant of unskilled social behaviors. In short, they appeared to be, if anything, underreactive rather than overreactive.

It is important to note that collectively the data from the preschool, kindergarten, and grade four children are cross-sectional; in addition, they emanate from different studies and samples. Therefore, it is impossible to ascertain whether the discrepant findings reflect changes in mothers or differences between the samples. It is quite possible that they arise from sample differences. For example, the children in the preschool sample were drawn from a socioeconomically varied number of preschools and day care centers. Several of these preschools were governmentally administered and housed children from high risk backgrounds. The children in the elementary school study were generally of middle-class background. As such, the findings for the mothers of the withdrawn preschoolers versus withdrawn elementary schoolers may have reflected differences associated with social class as well as differences attributable to developmental change. It is known, for example, that mothers from lower socioeconomic backgrounds are more likely than middle-class mothers to use power assertive techniques when interacting with their children (e.g., Booth, Rose-Krasnor, & Rubin, 1991; Mills & Rubin, 1990).

In addition, variability in the results may be attributed to the different targeting strategies used in the two studies. Teacher ratings were used in conjunction with direct observation in the first study, and in conjunction with peer ratings in the second study. Since there appear to be different forms of social withdrawal (e.g., Asendorpf, 1989, 1990; Rubin & Mills, 1988), it is quite possible that the two samples differed in the *types* of socially withdrawn children that we studied.

Obviously, a longitudinal approach is needed to ascertain whether mothers of socially withdrawn children in fact change as their children grow older, and only an examination of the across-time relations between changes in mothers and changes in children would allow us to make inferences about the influence processes that occur between mothers and children. Do mothers reappraise their child's behavioral tendencies as they grow older, and is this reappraisal best predicted by factors in the child or by factors in the mother and the environment in which she is carrying out her parenting role? As socially withdrawn children grow older and it becomes obvious that their behavioral tendencies are persistent, mothers may gradually reappraise both their child and the strategies they have been using to influence their child, and come to think of their child's withdrawal as an unchangeable characteristic, or one which cannot be modified through directive teaching. This may, in turn, prompt them to scale down their expectations or decide that trying to change their child's behavior directly would be futile.

In addition to reappraising their child and the effectiveness of their teaching strategies, mothers may also modify their thinking in response to the consequences that social withdrawal has for their child. In this regard, social withdrawal may be a very different phenomenon for girls and boys. Although there is some evidence to suggest that social reticence has a higher incidence rate among girls than among boys (Kochanska, 1991; Reznick, Gibbons, Johnson, & McDonough, 1989; Rutter & Garmezy, 1983), it appears to have less devastating consequences for girls than for boys (Caspi,

Elder, & Bem, 1988; Olweus, 1991). This seems best explained by the fact that some of the features of social withdrawal (e.g., timidity, passivity) are more congruent with sex-role stereotypes for girls than for boys and therefore associated with less social rejection. Parents appear to apply these stereotypes even to very young children (e.g., Atkinson & Endsley, 1976), but it may not be until they observe in middle childhood the relatively benign consequences that social withdrawal has for girls that they begin to put less pressure on their daughters to change this behavior. Because girls constituted the majority of the withdrawn children in our kindergarten and grade 4 samples, the discrepant findings of the two studies could be accounted for by an increasing tolerance for social withdrawal in girls. To explore this interpretation, however, longitudinal changes will need to be examined as a function of the sex of the child.

The sex of the *parent* may be just as important a factor in the equation as the sex of the child, particularly in middle childhood. There is some evidence that fathers consider social withdrawal more of a problem for boys than for girls (e.g., Bacon & Ashmore, 1985), presumably because of the potential for boys to be branded a "sissy" by the peer group. If, as a result of their heightened sensitivity to feminine-stereotyped behavior, fathers discourage social withdrawal in their sons more actively than in their daughters, then older socially withdrawn boys may have quite different socialization experiences than girls. For older boys, the critical relationship processes may be occurring in interactions with father rather than with mother.

It could also be that mothers' appraisals of their child's socially withdrawn behavior change not only because this behavior carries a different meaning as children grow older but also because of other, external changes. Since our second study involved not simply older children but older *families,* changes in the stability of family relationships, in socioeconomic status, and in family size all may have contributed to changes in the mothers over time. These factors may be associated with a lessening of anxious overinvolvement in mothers as their children grow older. But again, only through longitudinal research will it be possible to determine whether these factors do in fact contribute to changes in mothers' beliefs and teaching strategies, and whether they prove to be protective factors in the long-term development of socially withdrawn children.

ACKNOWLEDGMENTS

The research described in this chapter was supported by grants from Health and Welfare Canada, The Social Sciences and Humanities Research Council of Canada, and The Ontario Mental Health Foundation. Author Mills received postdoctoral fellowship support from the Social Sciences and Humanities Research Council of Canada; author Rubin was supported by a Killam Research Fellowship (Canada Council). We gratefully acknowledge the participation of the children, parents, and teachers who have made this program of research possible. Thanks go also to our students and assistants Maria Costaki, Allison Langlois, Angela Lynch, Melanie Mann, Karen McEwan, Rebecca Mitchell, Latha Ramasubramanian, and Margo Rubin for their generous and productive collaborative participation.

REFERENCES

Achenbach, T. M., & Edelbrock, C. S. (1981). Behavioral problems and competencies reported by parents of normal and disturbed children aged four through sixteen. *Monographs of the Society for Research in Child Development, 46,* (1, Serial No. 188).

Ainsworth, M. D. S., Blehar, M., Waters, E., & Wall, S. (1978). *Patterns of attachment.* Hillsdale, NJ: Lawrence Erlbaum Associates.

Altmann, E. O., & Gotlib, I. H. (1988). The social behavior of depressed children: An observational study. *Journal of Abnormal Child Psychology, 16,* 29–44.

Asendorpf, J. B. (1986). Shyness in middle and late childhood. In W. H. Jones, J. M. Cheek, & S. R. Briggs (Eds.), *Shyness: Perspectives on research and treatment* (pp. 91–103). New York: Plenum Press.

Asendorpf, J. B. (1989). Shyness as a final common pathway for two different kinds of inhibition. *Journal of Personality and Social Psychology, 57,* 481–492.

Asendorpf, J. B. (1990). Beyond social withdrawal: Shyness, unsociability, and peer avoidance. *Human Development, 33,* 250–259.

Atkinson, J., & Endsley, R. C. (1976). Influence of sex of child and parent on parental reactions to hypothetical parent-child situations. *Genetic Psychology Monographs, 94,* 131–147.

Bacon, M. K., & Ashmore, R. D. (1985). How mothers and fathers categorize descriptions of social behavior attributed to daughters and sons. *Social Cognition, 3,* 193–217.

Baumrind, D. (1967). Child care practices anteceding three patterns of preschool behavior. *Genetic Psychology Monographs, 75,* 43–88.

Becker, W. C. (1964). Consequences of different kinds of parental discipline. In M. L. Hoffman & L. W. Hoffman (Eds.), *Review of child development research* (pp. 169–208). New York: Russell Sage Foundation.

Behar, L., & Stringfield, S. (1974). A behavior rating scale for the preschool child. *Developmental Psychology, 10,* 601–610.

Belsky, J. (1984). The determinants of parenting: A process model. *Child Development, 55,* 83–96.

Booth, C. L., Rose-Krasnor, L., & Rubin, K. H. (1991). Relating preschoolers' social competence and their mothers' parenting behaviors to early attachment security and high risk status. *Journal of Social and Personal Relationships, 8,* 363–382.

Bowlby, J. (1969). *Attachment and loss. Vol. 1.* New York: Basic Books.

Bretherton, I. (1985). Attachment theory: Retrospect and prospect. In I. Bretherton & E. Waters (Eds.), Growing points of attachment theory and research. *Monographs of the Society for Research in Child Development, 50* (1–2, Serial No. 209).

Bretherton, I. (1990). Open communication and internal working models: Their role in the development of attachment relationships. In R. A. Thompson (Vol. Ed.), *Nebraska Symposium on Motivation 1988,* Vol. 36, *Socioemotional development* (pp. 57–113). Lincoln, NB: University of Nebraska Press.

Bruner, J. (1985). Vygotsky: A historical and conceptual perspective. In J. Wertsch (Ed.), *Culture, communication, and cognition: Vygotskian perspectives* (pp. 21–34). Cambridge: Cambridge University Press.

Bugental, D. B., Blue, J., & Lewis, J. (1990). Caregiver beliefs and dysphoric affect directed to difficult children. *Developmental Psychology, 26,* 631–638.

Bugental, D. B., & Shennum, W. A. (1984). "Difficult" children as elicitors and targets of adult communication patterns: An attributional-behavioral transactional analysis. *Monographs of the Society for Research in Child Development, 49* (1, Serial No. 205).

Caspi, A., Elder, G. H., Jr., & Bem, D. J. (1988). Moving away from the world: Life-course patterns of shy children. *Developmental Psychology, 24,* 824–831.

Clifford, E. (1959). Discipline in the home: A controlled observational study of parental practices. *Journal of Genetic Psychology, 95,* 45–82.

Cohen, J. S. (1989). *Maternal involvement in children's peer relationships during middle childhood.* Unpublished doctoral dissertation, University of Waterloo.

Cohen, S., & Wills, T. A. (1985). Stress, social support, and the buffering hypothesis. *Psychological Bulletin, 98,* 310–357.

Cohn, D. A. (1990). Child-mother attachment of six-year-olds and social competence at school. *Child Development, 61,* 152–162.

Colletta, N. (1979). Support systems after divorce: Incidence and impact. *Journal of Marriage and the Family, 41,* 837–846.

Crnic, K. A., & Greenberg, M. G. (1990). Minor parenting stresses with young children. *Child Development, 61,* 1628–1637.

Dix, T. H., & Grusec, J. E. (1985). Parent attribution processes in the socialization of children. In I. E. Sigel (Ed.), *Parental belief systems: The psychological consequences for children* (pp. 201–233). Hillsdale, NJ: Lawrence Erlbaum Associates.

Dix, T., Reinhold, D. P., & Zambarano, R. J. (1990). Mothers' judgment in moments of anger. *Merrill-Palmer Quarterly, 36,* 465–486.

Dix, T. H., Ruble, D., Grusec, J. E., & Nixon, S. (1986). Social cognition in parents: Inferential and affective reactions to children of three age levels. *Child Development, 57,* 879–894.

Dix, T. H., Ruble, D. N., & Zambarano, R. J. (1989). Mothers' implicit theories of discipline: Child effects, parent effects, and the attribution process. *Child Development, 60,* 1373–1391.

Egeland, B., & Farber, E. A. (1984). Infant-toddler attachment: Factors related to its development and change over time. *Child Development, 55,* 753–771.

Elias, M., & Ubriaco, M. (1986). Linking parental beliefs to children's social competence: Toward a cognitive-behavioral assessment model. In R. Ashmore & D. Brodzinsky (Eds), *Thinking about the family: Views of parents and children* (pp. 147–179). Hillsdale, NJ: Lawrence Erlbaum Associates.

Emmerich, W. (1969). The parental role: A functional cognitive approach. *Monographs of the Society for Research in Child Development, 34,* (8, Serial No. 132).

Engfer, A. (1988). The interrelatedness of marriage and the mother-child relationship. In R. Hinde & J. Stevenson-Hinde (Eds.), *Relations between relationships within families* (pp. 104–118). Oxford, UK: Oxford University Press.

Finnie, V., & Russell, A. (1988). Preschool children's social status and their mothers' behavior and knowledge in the supervisory role. *Developmental Psychology, 24,* 789–801.

Goodnow, J. J., Cashmore, J., Cotton, S., & Knight, R. (1984). Mothers' developmental timetables in two cultural groups. *International Journal of Psychology, 19,* 193–205.

Goodnow, J. J., Knight, R., & Cashmore, J. (1985). Adult social cognition: Implications of parents' ideas for approaches to development. In M. Perlmutter (Vol. Ed.), *Cognitive perspectives on children's social and behavioral development. Vol. 18. The Minnesota Symposia on Child Psychology* (pp. 287–329). Hillsdale, NJ: Lawrence Erlbaum Associates.

Grusec, J. E., Dix, T., & Mills, R. (1982). The effects of type, severity, and victim of children's transgressions on maternal discipline. *Canadian Journal of Behavioural Science, 14,* 276–289.

Grusec, J. E., & Kuczynski, L. (1980). Direction of effect in socialization: A comparison of the parent vs. the child's behavior as determinants of disciplinary techniques. *Developmental Psychology, 16,* 1–9.

Hartup, W. W. (1983). The peer system. In E. M. Hetherington (Vol. Ed.), *Handbook of child psychology, Vol. 4. Socialization, personality, and social development* (pp. 103–196). New York: Wiley.

Hess, R. D., Kashiwagi, K., Azuma, H., Price, G. G., & Dickson, W. P. (1980). Maternal expectations for mastery of developmental tasks in Japan and the United States. *International Journal of Psychology, 15,* 259–271.

Hetherington, E. M., & Martin, B. (1986). Family factors and psychopathology in children. In H. C. Quay & J. S. Werry (Eds.), *Psychopathological disorders of childhood* (pp. 332–390). New York: Wiley. 3rd ed.

Hightower, A. D., Work, W. C., Cowen, E. L., Lotyczewski, B. S., Spinell, A. P., Guare, J. C., & Rohrbeck, C. A. (1986). The Teacher-Child Rating Scale: A brief objective measure of elementary children's school problem behaviors and competencies. *School Psychology Review, 15,* 393–409.

Hobfoll, S. E. (1988). *The ecology of stress.* Washington, DC: Hemisphere.

Holden, G. W., & Edwards, L. A. (1989). Parental attitudes toward child rearing: Instruments, issues, and implications. *Psychological Bulletin, 106,* 29–58.

Huesmann, L. R., Eron, L. D., Lefkowitz, M. M., & Walder, L. O. (1984). Stability of aggression over time and generations. *Developmental Psychology, 20,* 1120–1134.

Jacobson, J. L., & Wille, D. E. (1986). The influence of attachment pattern on developmental changes in peer interaction from the toddler to the preschool period. *Child Development, 1986, 57,* 338–347.

Kessler, R. C., & McLeod, J. D. (1985). Social support and mental health in community samples. In S. Cohen & S. L. Syme (Eds.), *Stress and anxiety* (pp. 219–240). New York: Academic.

Kochanska, G. (1991). Patterns of inhibition to the unfamiliar in children of normal and affectively ill mothers. *Child Development, 62,* 250–263.

Kochanska, G., Kuczynski, L., & Maguire, M. (1989). Impact of diagnosed depression and self-reported mood on mothers' control strategies: A longitudinal study. *Journal of Abnormal Child Psychology, 17,* 493–511.

Kohn, M. L. (1977). *Class and conformity: A study in values.* Chicago: University of Chicago Press. 2nd ed.

Ladd, G. W., & Golter, B. S. (1988). Parents' management of preschooler's peer relations: Is it related to children's social competence? *Developmental Psychology, 24,* 109–117.

Lazarus, R. S., & Folkman, S. (1984). *Stress, appraisal, and coping.* New York: Springer.

Levy, D. M. (1943). *Maternal overprotection.* New York: Columbia University Press.

Loeber, R., & Dishion, T. (1983). Early predictors of male delinquency: A review. *Psychological Bulletin, 94,* 69–99.

Lyons-Ruth, K., Connell, D., Grunebaum, H., Botein, M., & Zoll, D. (1984). Maternal family history, maternal caretaking, and infant attachment in multiproblem families. *Journal of Preventive Psychiatry, 2,* 403–425.

Lytton, H., & Romney, D. M. (1991). Parents' differential socialization of boys and girls: A meta-analysis. *Psychological Bulletin, 109,* 267–296.

Maccoby, E. E., & Martin, J. A. (1983). Socialization in the context of the family: Parent-child interaction. In E. M. Hetherington (Vol. Ed.), *Handbook of child psychology, Vol. 4. Socialization, personality, and social development* (pp. 1–102). New York: Wiley.

Main, M., Kaplan, N., & Cassidy, J. (1985). Security in infancy, childhood, and adulthood:

A move to the level of representation. In I. Bretherton & E. Waters (Eds.), Growing points of attachment theory and research. *Monographs of the Society for Research in Child Development, 50* (1-2, Serial No. 209).

Martin, B. (1975). Parent-child relations. In F. Horowitz (Ed.), *Review of child development research* (pp. 463-540). Chicago: University of Chicago Press.

Masten, A. S., Morison, P., & Pellegrini, D. (1985). A revised class play method of peer assessment. *Developmental Psychology, 21,* 523-533.

McNally, S., Eisenberg, N., & Harris, J. D. (1991). Consistency and change in maternal child-rearing practices and values: A longitudinal study. *Child Development, 62,* 190-198.

Mead, G. H. (1934). *Mind, self, and society.* Chicago, Ill.: University of Chicago Press.

Miller, S. A. (1988). Parents' beliefs about children's cognitive development. *Child Development, 59,* 259-285.

Mills, R. S. L., & Rubin, K. H. (1990). Parental beliefs about problematic social behaviors in early childhood. *Child Development, 61,* 138-151.

Mills, R. S. L., & Rubin, K. H. (1992). A longitudinal study of maternal beliefs about children's social behavior. *Merrill-Palmer Quarterly, 38,* 494-512.

Moller, L., & Rubin, K. H. (1988). A psychometric assessment of a two factor solution for the Preschool Behavior Questionnaire in mid-childhood. *Journal of Applied Developmental Psychology, 9,* 167-180.

Olweus, D. (1980). Familial and temperamental determinants of aggressive behavior in adolescents – A causal analysis. *Developmental Psychology, 16,* 644-660.

Olweus, D. (1991). Bully/victim problems among schoolchildren: Basic facts and effects of a school-based intervention program. In D. J. Pepler & K. H. Rubin (Eds.), *The development and treatment of childhood aggression* (pp. 411-448). Hillsdale, NJ: Lawrence Erlbaum Associates.

Parke, R. D., MacDonald, K. B., Beitel, A., & Bhavnagri, N. (1988). The role of the family in the development of peer relationships. In R. DeV. Peters & R. J. McMahan (Eds.), *Social learning systems approaches to marriage and the family* (pp. 17-44). New York: Brunner-Mazel.

Parke, R. D., & Slaby, R. G. (1983). The development of aggression. In E. M. Hetherington (Vol. Ed.) and P. H. Mussen (Series Ed.), *Handbook of child psychology: Vol. 4. Socialization, personality, and social development* (pp. 547-641). New York: Wiley.

Patterson, G. R. (1982). *Coercive family processes.* Eugene, OR: Castilia Press.

Patterson, G. R. (1983). Stress: A change agent for family process. In N. Garmezy & M. Rutter (Eds.), *Stress, coping, and development in children* (pp. 235-264). New York: McGraw-Hill.

Piaget, J. (1926). *The language and thought of the child.* London: Routlege and Kegan Paul.

Pratt, M. W., Kerig, P., Cowan, P. A., & Cowan, C. P. (1988). Mothers and fathers teaching 3-year-olds: Authoritative parenting and adult scaffolding of young children's learning. *Developmental Psychology, 24,* 832-839.

Radke-Yarrow, M., Cummings, E. M., Kuczynski, L., & Chapman, M. (1985). Patterns of attachment in two- and three-year-olds in normal families and families with parental depression. *Child Development, 56,* 884-893.

Ragozin, A. S., Basham, R. B., Crnic, K. A., Greenberg, M. T., & Robinson, N. M. (1982). Effects of maternal age on parenting role. *Developmental Psychology, 18,* 627-634.

Reznick, J. S., Gibbons, J. L., Johnson, M. O., & McDonough, P. M. (1989). Behavioral inhibition in a normative sample. In J. S. Reznick (Ed.), *Perspectives on behavioral inhibition* (pp. 25-49). Chicago: University of Chicago Press.

Roberts, G. C., Block, J. H., & Block, J. (1984). Continuity and change in parents' child-rearing practices. *Child Development, 55,* 586-597.

Rubin, K. H., Both, L., Zahn-Waxler, E. C., Cummings, M., & Wilkinson, M. (1991). Dyadic play behaviors of children of well and depressed mothers. *Development and Psychopathology, 3,* 243-251.

Rubin, K. H., Hymel, S., Mills, R. S. L., & Rose-Krasnor, L. (1991). Conceptualizing different pathways to and from social isolation in childhood. In D. Cicchetti & S. Toth (Eds.), *Internalizing and externalizing expressions of dysfunction: Rochester Symposium on Developmental Psychopathology, Vol. 2.* (pp. 91–122). Hillsdale, NJ: Lawrence Erlbaum Associates.

Rubin, K. H., Hymel, S., & Mills, R. S. L. (1989). Sociability and social withdrawal in childhood: Stability and outcomes. *Journal of Personality, 57,* 238–255.

Rubin, K. H., LeMare, L., & Lollis, S. (1990). Social withdrawal in childhood: Developmental pathways to rejection. In S. R. Asher & J. D. Coie (Eds.), *Peer rejection in childhood* (pp. 217–249). New York: Cambridge University Press.

Rubin, K. H., & Lollis, S. (1988). Origins and consequences of social withdrawal. In J. Belsky & T. Nezworski, (Eds.), *Clinical implications of attachment* (pp. 219–252). Hillsdale, NJ: Lawrence Erlbaum Associates.

Rubin, K. H., & Mills, R. S. L. (1988). The many faces of social isolation in childhood. *Journal of Consulting and Clinical Psychology, 56,* 916–924.

Rubin, K. H., & Mills, R. S. L. (1990). Maternal beliefs about adaptive and maladaptive social behaviors in normal, aggressive, and withdrawn preschoolers. *Journal of Abnormal Child Psychology, 18,* 419–435.

Rubin, K. H., & Mills, R. S. L. (1991). Conceptualizing developmental pathways to internalizing disorders in childhood. *Canadian Journal of Behavioural Science, 23,* 300–317.

Rubin, K. H., & Mills, R. S. L. (1992). Parents' thoughts about children's socially adaptive and maladaptive behaviors: Stability, change, and individual differences. In I. Sigel, J. Goodnow, & A. McGillicuddy-deLisi (Eds.), *Parental belief systems* (2nd ed., pp. 41–68). Hillsdale, NJ: Lawrence Erlbaum Associates.

Rubin, K. H., Mills, R. S. L., & Rose-Krasnor, L. (1989). Parental beliefs and children's social competence. In B. Schneider, G. Atilli, J. Nadel, & R. Weissberg (Eds.), *Social competence in developmental perspective* (pp. 313–331). Dordrecht, Netherlands: Kluwer.

Rubin, K. H., Watson, K., & Jambor, T. (1978). Free play behaviors in preschool and kindergarten children. *Child Development, 49,* 534–536.

Russell, A., & Finnie, V. (1990). Preschool children's social status and maternal instructions to assist group entry. *Developmental Psychology, 26,* 603–611.

Rutter, M., & Garmezy, N. (1983). Developmental psychopathology. In E. M. Hetherington (Vol. Ed.), *Handbook of child psychology, Vol. 4. Socialization, personality, and social development* (pp. 775–911). New York: Wiley.

Sigel, I. E. (1982). The relationship between parents' distancing strategies and the child's cognitive behavior. In L. M. Laosa & I. E. Sigel (Eds.), *Families as learning environments for children* (pp. 47–86). New York: Plenum.

Sigel, I. E., & McGillicuddy-DeLisi, A. V. (1984). Parents as teachers of their children: A distancing behavior model. In A. D. Pellegrini & T. D. Yawkey (Eds.), *The development of oral and written language in social contexts* (pp. 71–92). Norwood, NJ: Ablex.

Spieker, S. J., & Booth, C. L. (1988). Maternal antecedents of attachment quality. In J. Belsky & T. Nezworski (Eds.), *Clinical implications of attachment* (pp. 95–135). Hillsdale, NJ: Lawrence Erlbaum Associates.

Sroufe, L. A., & Fleeson, J. (1986). Attachment and the construction of relationships. In W. Hartup & Z. Rubin (Eds.), *The nature and development of relationships.* Hillsdale, NJ: Lawrence Erlbaum Associates.

Stolz, L. M. (1967). *Influences on parent behavior.* Stanford, CA: Stanford University Press.

Sullivan, H. S. (1953). *The interpersonal theory of psychiatry.* New York: Norton.

Wahler, R. G., & Dumas, J. E. (1987). Family factors in childhood psychology; toward a coercion-neglect model. In T. Jacob (Ed.), *Family interaction and psychopathology; theories, methods, and findings* (pp. 581–627). New York: Plenum.

Weiner, B., & Graham, S. (1984). An attributional approach to emotional development. In C. Izard, J. Kagan, & R. Zajonc (Eds.), *Emotions, cognitions, and behavior* (pp. 167–191). New York: Cambridge University Press.

Wertsch, J. V. (1984). The zone of proximal development: Some conceptual issues. In B. Rogoff & J. V. Wertsch (Eds.), *Children's learning in the "zone of proximal development."* San Francisco: Jossey-Bass.

Wood, D. (1980). Teaching the young child: Some relationships between social interaction, language, and thought. In D. Olson (Ed.), *The social foundations of language and thought* (pp. 280–296). Norton.

III SOCIAL BEHAVIORS, SKILLS, AND RELATIONSHIPS

8 Inhibition and Children's Experiences of Out-of-Home Care

Anders G. Broberg
University of Göteborg

INTRODUCTION

One distinctive feature of Swedes, according to foreigners, is our degree of shyness and introversion. The study reported in this chapter concerns inhibition in relation to experiences of out-of-home care among Swedish toddlers and pre-schoolers. Although the present study was not designed to assess cross-cultural differences in inhibition, it is important that this construct be studied in samples other than the ones reported thus far (i.e., middle-class, Caucasian, North American children). The study reported herein is part of *The Göteborg Child Care Project,* which began in 1982. The broader purpose of The Göteborg Child Care Project has been to examine the effects of daycare on young children's development, in the context of other formative factors, such as child, family, and child care characteristics.

In an earlier report, we have presented data regarding the stability and correlates of social inhibition in the Göteborg sample (Broberg, Lamb, & Hwang, 1990). The aims of this report were to corroborate and expand our earlier findings by constructing a broad, reliable measure of inhibition, and studying the stability and correlates of this measure. More specifically, inhibition was examined in relation to (a) children's capacity to play with peers, (b) their dependency on their mothers, (c) their adaptation to out-of-home care settings, and (d) mothers' and careproviders' descriptions of these children's emerging personality styles.

Inhibition and Social Withdrawal

Ever since Thomas, Chess and their colleagues began publishing data from the New York Longitudinal Study (Thomas, Chess, Birch, Herzig, & Korn,

1963), individual differences in temperament have been invoked to explain children's reactions to novel circumstances and people. When challenged with novelty, some young children become quiet, cease activity, or retreat to a familiar person. Other children of similar intellectual ability and social background do not change their ongoing behavior, and may even approach the unfamiliar object or person. Garcia-Coll, Kagan, and Reznick (1984) have described children who retreat from new situations and cease their activity as *inhibited* and children who seem unafraid of novelty as *uninhibited*. Other researchers have restricted their focus to infants' and toddlers' interactions with people, excluding reactions to inanimate social stimuli, and have used the term *sociability* to describe the cluster of behaviors under study (Beckwith, 1972; Bretherton, 1978; Clarke-Stewart, Umeh, Snow, & Pederson, 1980; Lamb, 1982; Thompson & Lamb, 1982). Researchers focusing on social behaviors in pre-schoolers and elementary school-aged children frequently discuss related behaviors using the terms *social withdrawal* (Gersten, Langner, Eisenberg, Simcha-Fagan, & McCarthy, 1976; Rubin, 1985; Rubin, & Lollis, 1988; Younger, Schwartzman, & Ledingham, 1986) or *shyness* (Asendorpf, 1989; Buss, 1986; Hinde, Stevenson-Hinde, & Tamplin, 1985). As Rubin, Hymel, and Mills (1988) have pointed out, researchers have used vastly different definitions and methodologies to study inhibition and withdrawal in childhood. An important aim of the present study, therefore, was to arrive at a coherent and clearly defined measure of *inhibition*.

Researchers have found inhibition to be an important dimension of temperament that is, at least partly, heritable (Daniels & Plomin, 1985; Plomin & Daniels, 1986; Plomin & Stocker, 1989), and stable over time (Bronson, 1966; Caspi, Elder, & Bem, 1988; Hinde, Stevenson-Hinde & Tamplin, 1985; Kagan, 1989; Kagan & Moss, 1962; Moskowitz, Schwartzman, & Ledingham, 1985; Rubin & Mills, 1988). In addition, the behavioral profile has physiological correlates (Kagan, Reznick, & Snidman, 1988; Rosenberg & Kagan, 1989), and comparative psychologists have suggested that similar behavioral patterns are heritable, stable over time, and predictive of a range of adaptive/maladaptive behaviors in other mammals (Stevenson-Hinde, Stillwell-Barnes, & Zunz, 1980; Suomi, 1987).

The tendency to be inhibited versus uninhibited has also been the focus of debate. Within the "sociability tradition," inhibited and uninhibited behaviors are generally seen as poles of a sociability continuum, whereas researchers in the "inhibition tradition" are more inclined to view the phenomenon as a dichotomous construct. According to Kagan and co-workers (Kagan, Reznick, & Snidman, 1987), around 10% of all children show marked inhibition in a variety of contexts between 2 and $5\frac{1}{2}$ years of age, and they differ from the rest of the population in ways indicative of a qualitative rather than quantitative difference (Kagan, 1989). Thus a second aim of the present study was to determine the temporal stability and the distributional characteristics of our measure of inhibition.

Kagan and Moss (1962) found inhibition to the unfamiliar to be the only one of 15 infantile behaviors to predict later behavior. Children who were extremely inhibited until age 3 were easily dominated by their peers and were likely to withdraw from social interaction between 3 and 6 years of age. Between ages 6 and 10, they were still socially timid and, if boys, they avoided sports and other "masculine" activities as adolescents. Rubin and Mills (1988) found "passive-anxious withdrawal" in contrast to "active-immature withdrawal" to be consistent over time and predictive of later internalizing problems, including anxiety, loneliness, and depression. Other researchers have suggested that inhibition is related to the introversion-extraversion dimension in adulthood and predictive of anxiety and panic disorders (Kagan, Reznick, & Snidman, 1990; Rosenbaum, Biederman, & Gersten, 1989). In keeping with these earlier reports, a third aim of the present study was to relate inhibition to children's early developing personality styles, in order to describe the possible early roots of later internalizing problems.

Is inhibition affected by out-of-home care experiences, and if so how? From a social learning point of view, one could argue that the increased contact with unfamiliar children and adults inherent in enrollment in out-of-home care will over time make children with such experiences less inhibited than their home-reared counterparts. If, on the other hand, the tendency to react with fear rather than with curiosity to novel stimuli is deeply rooted in some children, then one could argue that such children would probably either not change at all, or they would become more inhibited if placed in out-of-home care because they would have to learn how to avoid to be exposed to frightening stimuli by withdrawing from social interaction. This line of reasoning comes close to Kagan's (1989) argument why second-borns should be more inhibited than first-borns. Studying children's inhibition in daycare settings in addition to studying children at home also makes possible cross-situational comparisons. Unfortunately, only a few reports exist in which inhibition or sociability has been studied in relation to out-of-home care. Maccoby and Feldman (1972), Tizard and Tizard (1971), and Clarke-Stewart et al. (1980) all found sociability with strange adults to be negatively related to nonparental child care experiences, whereas Thompson and Lamb (1982) found no consistent associations between measures of nonparental care experience and sociability. Broberg, Lamb, and Hwang (1990) found inhibition, as measured at home, to be related to initial, but not later, adjustment to out-of-home care, and they reported no differences between children cared for exclusively at home, and children with two years of daycare experience, on their measures of inhibition. We explore these relations in greater depth by adding indicators of inhibition from the out-of-home care settings to our former measures of inhibition.

Finally, girls appear to be somewhat more sociable than boys (Clarke-Stewart et al., 1980; Thompson & Lamb, 1983), as well as more likely than boys to be inhibited (Reznick, Gibbons, Johnson, & McDonough, 1989; Rosenberg & Kagan, 1989). In a recent review, Marks (1987) concluded that girls respond earlier, more often, and with a more intense fear to strange adults than boys do. Overall, therefore, girls appear to be both more sociable and more fearful—a pattern of findings consistent with other evidence that girls are more emotionally responsive than boys are (Block, 1976).

In summary, the aims of the present study were: (a) to construct a coherent and clearly defined measure of inhibition; (b) to determine the temporal stability and the distributional characteristics of this measure; (c) to corroborate and expand earlier findings regarding the relation between inhibition and children's behaviors in play situations; and (d) to relate inhibition to children's early developing personality styles.

PROCEDURE

Subjects.   Names of children on the waiting lists for municipal childcare facilities were obtained from local authorities in all areas of the city from June 1982 to October 1983. Parents were individually contacted and invited to participate in the research. To be enrolled in the study, the child had to fulfill the following criteria: (i) be between twelve and twenty-four months old; (ii) be firstborn, or at least not living with siblings under twelve years of age; (iii) live with both parents, whether or not they were married.

In addition, the child must not have begun regular daycare, and must not have had more than a total of four weeks of out-of-home care prior to our first visit with the family.

Of the eligible families, approximately 75% agreed to participate. One-hundred-and-forty-six children (72 girls) were enrolled in the study. One group consisted of children receiving center-based daycare[1] ($N = 54$). Others were unable to get places in centers but were either offered care in municipal family daycare homes (8), or the parents themselves made arrangements with private daymothers (25)—they constituted a second, family daycare, group ($N = 33$). A final group of children did not enter either centers or family daycare facilities—they remained at home in the care of their parents ($N = 59$). Both mothers and fathers completed a Swedish translation of Block's (1965) 91–item Child Rearing Practises

---

[1]A description of Swedish day care is provided in Broberg & Hwang, 1991.

Report (CRPR); parents in the different care groups did not differ with respect to their general attitudes to child rearing (Broberg, Lamb, & Hwang, 1990).

Hollingshead (1975) scores showed that children came from a range of backgrounds. Maternal and paternal Hollingshead scores, and maternal and paternal age, did not differentiate the families with children in our home care and daycare center groups from two-parent families in the larger sample (Broberg & Hwang, 1986). However, the parents of children in our family daycare group had significantly higher overall Hollingshead scores and were on the average older than families from the larger sample (see Broberg, Lamb, & Hwang, 1990).

During the three years of the study reported here, ten families dropped out. Two families refused further participation, and eight families either had children who became severely ill or moved far away from the Göteborg area. The size of the sample reported here, therefore, comprised 136 children, their parents and careproviders.

Pre-Assessment (Phase I).   After agreeing to participate, all families were visited in their homes by a member of the research staff. The research assistant rated the child's reactions when the assistant, as a strange adult, made increasingly intimate overtures to the child during the first 5 minutes of her or his visit. The parents were given a copy of Rothbart's (1981) Infant Behavior Questionnaire (IBQ), and were instructed how to observe their child and fill out the questionnaire during the next two weeks. A second home-visit was then arranged. On this occasion, the research assistant also observed the child interacting with a peer of roughly the same age, selected by the parents.

Children in the daycare groups began out-of-home care within two weeks of the second home visit. Six weeks later their child care facilities were visited by a member of the research staff who interviewed the principal careprovider about the child's adjustment. Finally, we observed the child playing with agemates in the out-of-home care setting. Two weeks later, parents were asked to rate their children's adjustment to the out-of-home care setting using the same scales as had been used by the care providers.

One Year Follow-Up (Phase II).   Twelve months after the first interview, the families were visited again. During one visit, stranger sociability was again assessed, and parents were interviewed about child care arrangements. During a second visit, the child was observed playing alone during a short separation from the mother and, after a break for snacks and drinks, we observed the child interacting with a peer. The mother was also asked to describe her child's emerging personality style using Block and Block's (1979; 1980) 100–item California Child Q–sort (CCQ). On a subsequent visit to the child-care facility, a teacher who knew the child well was interviewed and asked to describe the child by using the CCQ, and the child was observed playing with agemates.

Two Year Follow-Up (Phase III). One year later, a third phase of assessments took place. During an initial visit to the child's home, the research assistant rated his or her sociability, and parents were questioned about their out-of-home care arrangements, and their child's adjustment to day care. On a second visit, children were observed playing with a peer, and mothers were asked to describe their children using the CCQ. A visit to the child care facility was then made to permit observation of the children playing in the daycare settings, and we interviewed the careproviders about their perceptions of the children's adjustment to daycare. Because of concerns raised by the careproviders in Phase II regarding the applicability of some of the CCQ-items in the daycare settings, careproviders were instead asked to describe the children's personality styles using Baumrind's (1971) 72–item Peer Behavior Q-sort (PBQ).

MEASURES[2]

Sociability with a Strange Adult. Sociability was assessed upon the observer/interviewer's arrival at the child's home using a procedure developed and more fully described by Stevenson and Lamb (1979) and Thompson and Lamb (1983). The child's responses, when the interviewer made increasingly intimate contact with the child, were rated on 5–point scales. In addition, the observer recorded overall impressions of the child's sociability on a 9-point scale. The ratings were then added to yield an overall measure of sociability.

Play with Peers. In each phase of the study, the children were observed interacting at home for 30 minutes with peers chosen by the parents. Although all peers were familiar to the subjects, the degree of familiarity varied greatly. Regardless of whether they were classified as inhibited or uninhibited, children were just as likely to interact with familiar peers as with less familiar ones.

The 30-minute episodes were divided into consecutive 15-second observation units, followed by 15-second breaks for recording the child's behavior. For each observation unit, the observer rated the quality of peer play using Howes' (1980) 6-point rating scale. *Noninvolvement in peer play* was accorded a score of 0. *High quality peer play* was defined as the sum of

---

[2]A detailed description of the measures is available from the author upon request.

units in which ratings of 3, 4, or 5 were assigned divided by the total number of units during which children had been involved in peer play. This measure was thus independent of the measure of non-involvement in peer play.

In addition to the Howes' rating scale, the observers also noted the incidence of a number of behaviors during the peer play session (23 in Phases I and II and 22 in Phase III). The standardized and summed incidence of nine different behaviors were summed to yield a composite score of *positive peer behaviors*. Also coded was the incidence of child standing/sitting *aimless*. The frequency of children's *interactions with adults* during the peer play session were also recorded. In Phase III, but not in Phases I and II, interaction with adult that was *initiated by the child* was separated from interaction with adult that was *initiated by the adult*. Children's vocalizations were also coded in all phases. The incidence of child vocalizations and the incidence of child crying were recorded. In Phase III, we were able to adjust the vocalization variable to the children's more advanced language development and therefore split the vocalization variable into *undirected vocalizations* (i.e., vocalizations not specifically directed to anyone), *positive or neutral vocalizations* (i.e., communicative vocalizations to a specific peer or group of peers), and *negative vocalizations* (i.e., verbally aggressive communication with a peer or group of peers).

Griffiths' Test of Mental Abilities.   The language subscale (C-scale) of the Swedish standardization (Alin-Åkerman & Norberg, 1980) of the Griffiths' (1954; 1970) test of mental abilities was given individually to each child in their home environment in order to measure children's language development (Phases II and III only).

Mothers' and Careproviders' Ratings.   Maternal ratings of inhibition in Phase I were based on the fear subscale of Rothbart's (1981) *Infant Behavior Questionnaire* (IBQ), a standardized parent-report measure of infant temperament. In Phases II and III, a rated composite of inhibition was constructed using the standardized scores of eight items (e.g., "is fearful and anxious"; "is inhibited and constricted"; "is shy and reserved, makes social contacts slowly") on Block and Block's (1979) *California Child Q-sort* (CCQ). The reliability of the composite scores (Cronbach's alphas) were .70 (maternal rating in Phase II), .79 (careprovider's ratings in Phase II), and .75 (maternal rating in Phase III) respectively. In Phase III a composite inhibition rating was also constructed using the standardized scores of seven of the items (e.g., "spectator"; "socially withdrawn"; "typically in the role of a listener") on Baumrind's (1971) *Peer Behavior Q-sort* (PBQ). The reliability of the composite score (Cronbach's α) was .84.

Inhibition. Previously, we have described in detail the development and stability of a composite measure of inhibition based on children's noninvolvement in peer play, and their degree of sociability when faced with a strange adult (Broberg, Lamb, & Hwang, 1990). In Phase I, when children averaged 16 months of age, that composite measure also took into account children's fearfulness, as measured by the fear subscale of Rothbart's IBQ. In order to obtain inhibition composites that utilized the same types of measures in all three phases, the inhibition rating scales based on CCQ- and PBQ-items described above (and outlined in detail in the appendix) were constructed. *Inhibition in the home setting* was defined as the sum of the standardized scores of (i) the observed lack of sociability towards a strange adult (i.e., the reversed total score of the Stevenson & Lamb, 1979, measure of sociability), (ii) noninvolvement in peer play (i.e., the number of "0-s" on Howes', 1980, rating scale) during a peer play observation at home, and, (iii) maternal ratings of fear (using the fear subscale of Rothbart's IBQ when children averaged 16 months of age) and maternal ratings of inhibition (when children averaged 28 and 40 months of age), using Block & Block's (1979) CCQ as described.

Inhibition in the day care setting was defined as the sum of the standardized scores of (i) noninvolvement in peer play (i.e., the number of "0-s" on the Howes', 1980, rating scale) during a peer play observation in the day care setting, and, (ii) careproviders' inhibition ratings, in Phases II and III (using Block & Block's, 1979, CCQ in Phase II and Baumrind's, 1971, PBQ in Phase III as described).

Mothers' and Careproviders' Ratings of Children's Emerging Personality Styles. Mothers' perceptions of their children were tapped using Block & Block's (1979) 100-item California Child Q-sort (CCQ) (Phases II and III). Careproviders also sorted the CCQ-items (Phase II), or Baumrind's (1971) 72-item Peer Behavior Q-sort (PBQ) (Phase III).

Adjustment to Childcare Arrangements. After some of the children had entered out-of-home care, careproviders were asked to rate the children's adjustment in relation to peers, to staff, and to parents on 5-point rating scales (ranging from 1 = much poorer adjustment than average to 5 = much easier adjustment than average). The three scales were then summed. Two months later parents made similar ratings, which were also summed to a total adjustment score. One and two years later parents and careproviders were asked to rate the children's current adjustment to daycare, using similar rating scales.

Ability to Play Alone. When children averaged 28 months of age they were observed at home. To assess their ability to play alone, the observer presented them with a variety of interesting toys in the mother's presence. After the child had a chance to play with the toys for a couple of minutes, the mother instructed the child to continue to play with the toys and then left the room. The observer stayed with the child for 1 minute, and then went to join the mother. The mother was instructed to encourage the child to return to the toys if the child followed her. The child's behavior was rated on an 8-point scale ranging from "child was never away from mother more than 15 seconds and was distressed when the mother encouraged the child to return to play" (1) to "child plays alone during the whole observation period and makes no attempt to contact the mother" (8).

Reliability

All observations and ratings of parental impressions were made by one of three individuals who trained together using videotapes and with pilot subjects until achieving criterial degrees of reliability. For the peer interaction measures criterion was set at 80% exact agreement; for sociability, play alone, and the ratings of parental impressions, the criterion was set at 90%. Once data collection began, 15% of the sessions were conducted by two of the observers, working simultaneously but independently. Reliability coefficients were within 5% of the criterial levels in each of these reliability assessments. It was impossible to keep observers blind with respect to the group status of the children, but they were not aware of the specific questions being explored.

RESULTS

Preliminary analyses of all the dependent variables showed that children in the family daycare group had means close to, and not significantly different from, those of children in the daycare center group. This fact and the small size of the family daycare group (27 at the 1-year follow-up and 16 at the 2-year follow-up) led us to combine children in family and center-based daycare into one group, hereafter called the out-of-home care (or DC) group, for purposes of the analyses reported here.

Correlations between Composite Measures of Inhibition and their Components

As is shown in Table 8.1, composite measures of inhibition were not only significantly correlated with component measures, but they were also related cross-situationally and over time. Inhibition at home correlated significantly with careproviders ratings of inhibition in the out-of-home

TABLE 8.1
Correlations between Composite and Discrete Measures of Inhibition

	Composite Measures of Inhibition				
Components of Inhibition	Home I (n = 146)	Home II (n = 138)	Home III (n = 136)	Daycare II (n = 81)	Daycare III (n = 71)
	At Home				
Sociability I	(.71)	−.23**	−.22**	n.s.	n.s.
Sociability II	−.28***	(−.68)	−.44***	n.s.	n.s.
Sociability III	−.35***	−.35***	(−.71)	−.21 +	−.32**
Peer noninv. I	(.68)	.19*	.27***	n.s.	n.s.
Peer noninv. II	.18*	(.67)	.26**	.20 +	n.s.
Peer noninv. III	.23**	.17*	(.60)	n.s.	n.s.
IBQ-Fear I	(.68)	.24**	.35***	n.s.	.29*
CCQ-Inhibition II	.20*	(.71)	.42***	.23*	n.s.
CCQ-Inhibition III	.21*	.54***	(.64)	n.s.	.25*
	In Daycare				
Peer noninv. II	n.s.	n.s.	n.s.	(.73)	.28*
Peer noninv. III	n.s.	n.s.	.32**	n.s.	(.72)
CCQ-Inhibition II	n.s.	.29**	.25*	(.72)	.28*
PBQ-Inhibition III	.29**	.25*	.26*	.41***	(.73)

I, II, and III refer to waves of data collection, i.e., when children averaged 16, 28, and 40 months of age, respectively.

Coefficients in parenthesis refer to correlations between a composite measure and its components.

$+p < .10$; $*p < .05$; $**p < .01$; $***p < .001$; two-tailed.

care settings, and inhibition measured in the daycare setting in Phase III was related to sociability as measured at home in Phase III, maternal ratings of fear in Phase I, and inhibition as measured at home in Phase III. Overall, then, the composite measures of inhibition showed consistent although moderate correlations with most of the component measures.

Temporal and Situational Stability of Inhibition

As is shown in Table 8.2, the composite measures of inhibition were moderately but significantly correlated over time, confirming earlier findings of temporal stability of the inhibition construct from 16 months of age. Correlations across settings were lower but significant.

In order further to explore the temporal stability of inhibition, a median split was performed on the composite measures of inhibition in the home setting in Phases I, II, and III. Each subject was placed in one of five different categories: (1) consistently uninhibited (i.e., below median in all three phases); (2) moving from inhibited to uninhibited (either above-above-below, or above-below-below the median); (3) fluctuating (below-

TABLE 8.2
Correlations between Composite Measures of Inhibition

| | n | Composite Measures of Inhibition | | | |
		Home I	Home II	Home III	Daycare II
Home I	146	1.00			
Home II	138	.32***	1.00		
Home III	136	.41***	.55***	1.00	
Daycare II	81	n.s.	.24*	.19 +	1.00
Daycare III	71	.22 +	.25*	.39***	.31***

I, II, and III refer to waves of data collection, i.e., when children averaged 16, 28, and 40 months of age, respectively.
$+p < .10$; $*p < .05$; $**p < .01$; $***p < .001$; two-tailed.

above-below or above-below-above); (4) moving from uninhibited to inhibited (below-above-above or below-below-above); and finally (5) consistently inhibited children (above median on all three measures). Because there are 2 possibilities for a child to be placed in each of categories 2, 3, and 4, but only one possibility each to be placed in categories 1 and 5, the number of children in each category expected by chance would be 17 in categories 1 and 5 and 34 in categories 2, 3, and 4 (based on $N = 136$). As is shown in Table 8.3, children were much more likely to stay on the same side of the median split than they were to cross that border over the time period studied (i.e., when children averaged 16 to 40 months of age) (χ^2 [4, $N = 136$] $= 62.89$, $p < .001$).

Computing Mega-Composite Measures of Inhibition

Based on the temporal stability of inhibition and on the intercorrelations between the measures of inhibition, we proceeded by constructing a "mega-composite" measure of inhibition at home by summing the standardized scores of inhibition at home at 16, 28, and 40 months of age into a single measure, called *Inhibition at home*. The reliability of this measure was .67 (Cronbach's α). For those children that were in out-of-home care in

TABLE 8.3
Stability of Inhibition

Group	Exp. Freq.	Obs. Freq.	Obs. %	Standard Residuals
Consist. inhibited	17	38	28	5.09
Uninhib > inhibited	34	21	15	2.23
Fluctuating	34	20	15	2.40
Inhib > uninhibited	34	21	15	2.23
Consist. uninhibited	17	36	27	3.17

both Phase II and Phase III (N = 57), we also constructed a "mega-composite" measure of inhibition by summing the 4 standardized indicators of inhibition in the daycare settings (at 28 and 40 months of age) and the 9 standardized indicators of inhibition at home into a single measure, called *Inhibition at home and in day care* (Cronbach's α = .67). Correlation coefficients between our different indices of inhibition seem to imply that the inhibition construct becomes more stable over time. Not only is the relation between inhibition measured at home stronger between Phases II and III then between Phases I and II or I and III, but the relation between measures at home and in daycare settings also becomes stronger over time.

Inhibition as a Continuous versus a Dichotomous Construct

In order to address this question, the mega-composite score of inhibition at home was used. Instead of using the standardized components, raw scores of the 9 measures constituting the mega-composite were summed into a single measure. The range of the different components varied between 27 and 59, except for sociability in Phase III, which had a range of only 8. The value of that variable was therefore multiplied by 5 to give it a range roughly equal to the other variables. The sum of all the components of inhibition at home resulted in a variable with a mean of 200, a range of 206, and a standard deviation of 45. Of the 136 subjects only 19 fell above and 21 fell below one standard deviation. As is shown in Fig. 8.1, the distribution, although slightly negatively skewed, clearly indicates a continuous rather than dichotomous distribution.

Inhibition and Peer Play in the Context of Out-of-Home Care

Relation Between Inhibition and Peer Play Behavior at Home.   Our next step was to relate inhibition to the children's behavior in the peer play situation at home. There was no relation between inhibition and children's peer play behaviors in Phase I, when children averaged 16 months of age. One and two years later, however, clear differences emerged, as is shown in Table 8.4. By that time, children who scored high on inhibition were consistently less likely than children scoring low on inhibition to display positive peer play behaviors and, in particular, to play at a qualitatively high level. The relation between inhibition and quality of peer play was evident regardless of whether inhibition had been measured at home, or in the out-of-home care setting, and there were no significant differences between children reared only at home and children with experience of

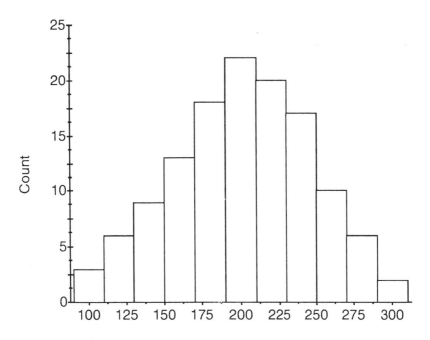

FIG. 8.1 Distribution of raw scores on the inhibition mega-composite.

out-of-home care regarding the relation between inhibition and peer play behaviors.

Table 8.5 shows the relation between inhibition and some other behaviors displayed in the peer play situation at home. Again there was no relation between inhibition and peer play behaviors when children averaged 16 months of age, whereas one and two years later clear differences were evident.

At 28 months of age, children with high scores on inhibition interacted more with adults, were more aimless, vocalized less, and cried more than did children scoring low on inhibition. At 40 months of age, mothers of children with high scores on inhibition were found to initiate more interaction with their children than did mothers of children scoring low on inhibition, whereas there were no differences between children with high scores or low on inhibition with regard to the amount of interaction with adults that was child initiated. Children with high scores on inhibition displayed more undirected vocalizations, and they were less likely to engage in direct communicative vocalizations with their peers.

In order to determine whether the differences in vocalization patterns were a question of performance or of ability, the relations between vocalizations, Griffiths' score, and inhibition were determined. At 28 months of age, the correlation between vocalizations and inhibition, when the effect of the Griffiths' score had been partialled out, was $-.33$ ($t = 4.05$, $p < .001$). A year later, the partial correlation between "undirected vocalizations" and inhibition was .25 ($t = 2.99$, $p < .01$), and the partial correlation between "positive vocalizations" and inhibition was $-.36$ ($t = 4.45$, $p < .001$). The relation between inhibition and vocalization, therefore, does not seem to reflect a delayed language ability on the part of the more inhibited children.

Relation Between Inhibition and Peer Play Behavior in the Daycare Setting. Our next step was to determine whether the relation between inhibition and children's behavior in the peer play situation was evident also in the daycare setting. As at home, there was no relation between inhibition and peer play behaviors in Phase I, when children averaged 16 months of age, but clear differences emerged one and two years later. As is shown in Table 8.6, children with high scores on inhibition were less likely to display positive peer play behaviors, and they were less likely to play at a qualitatively high level, than were their more uninhibited counterparts. Observed in the daycare settings at 28 and 40 months of age, children with high scores on inhibition were more often observed "aimless" ($r = .26$, $p < .05$ in both Phase II and III), and they vocalized less ($r = -.43$, $p < .001$ in Phase II; $r = -.30$, $p < .05$ in Phase III) than did their uninhibited counterparts. Unlike mothers, careproviders did not initiate more adult-child interaction with children with high scores on inhibition than with children scoring in the lower end.

Inhibition measured at home and inhibition measured in the daycare

TABLE 8.4
Correlations between Mega-Items of Inhibition and Peer Play Variables at Home in Phases II and III

	Mega-Inhibition as Measured			
	At Home			At Home plus in Daycare
Peer Play Variables	W grp[a]	HC[b]	DC[c]	ODC[d]
	In Phase II			
Positive peer play	$-.42$***	$-.46$***	$-.40$***	$-.33$**
High qual. peer pl.	$-.37$***	$-.24$+	$-.46$***	$-.54$***
	In Phase III			
Positive peer play	$-.15$	$-.15$	$-.35$*	$-.19$
High qual. peer pl.	$-.41$***	$-.58$***	$-.60$***	$-.51$***

[a]The whole group, regardless of care status ($n = 136$); [b]children consistently in home care ($n = 49$ in Phase II and $n = 39$ in Phase III); [c]children in daycare ($n = 80$ in Phase II and $n = 70$ in Phase III); and [d]children who were in daycare during all three phases ($n = 57$).
$+p < .10$; *$p < .05$; **$p < .01$; ***$p < .001$; two-tailed.

TABLE 8.5
Correlations between Mega-Items of Inhibition and Play Situational Variables
at Home in Phases II and III

| | Mega-Inhibition as Measured | | | |
| | At Home | | | At Home plus in Daycare |
Peer Situational Variables	W grp[a]	HC[b]	DC[c]	ODC[d]
	In Phase II			
Interaction w adult	.22**	.10	.38***	.36**
Aimless	.19*	− .07 ‡	.37**	.44***
Vocalize	− .38***	− .51***	− .33**	− .24 +
Cry	.15 +	.28*	.14	.12
	In Phase III			
Int. w ad; ad. init.	.23**	.20	.45***	.42***
Int. w ad; ch. init.	.19*	.25	.18	.15
Aimless	.20*	.37*	.10	.04
Undir voc.	.26**	.36*	.38**	.31*
Positive vocal.	− .37***	− .40***	− .63***	− .41***
Negative vocal.	− .05	− .03	− .02	− .05
Cry	.17*	.12	.35**	.24 +

[a]The whole group regardless of care status ($n = 136$); [b]children consistently in home care ($n = 49$ [Phase II] & $n = 39$ [Phase III]); [c]children in daycare ($n = 80$ [Phase II] & $n = 70$ [Phase III]); and [d]children who were in daycare during all three phases ($n = 57$).
   $+ p < .10$; $*p < .05$; $**p < .01$; $***p < .001$; two-tailed.
   ‡ indicates that the difference between HC and DC children is significant.

setting were both related to peer play behaviors, and the combined inhibition composite showed the strongest relation with peer play behaviors.

Inhibition and Children's Adjustment to Out-of-Home Care

For the children who had experienced out-of-home care, our next step was to relate inhibition to children's adjustment to the out-of-home care settings, as rated by their parents and careproviders. Inhibition as measured only at home correlated significantly with parents' ratings of adjustment at 16 months ($r = −.26$, $p < .05$). The effect seemed, however, to be transient because all subsequent ratings of adjustment were unrelated to inhibition as measured at home.

Careproviders' ratings of children's adjustment, however, showed a somewhat different picture. They were unrelated to inhibition as measured only at home in all three phases, but they approached significance with the

TABLE 8.6

Correlations between Mega-Items of Inhibition and Peer Play Variables in Day Care in Phases II and III

Peer Play Variables	Mega-Inhibition as Measured	
	At Home[a]	At Home plus in Daycare[b]
In Phase II		
Positive peer play	− .14	− .46***
High qual. peer play	− .34**	− .36**
In Phase III		
Positive peer play	.04	− .10
High qual. peer play	− .26*	− .41**

[a]Children in daycare (n = 80 in Phase II and n = 70 in Phase III); [b]children who were in daycare during all three phases (n = 57).
*p < .05; **p < .01; ***p < .001; two-tailed.

combined inhibition measure in Phase I (r = − .22, p < .10) and Phase III (r = − .23, p < .10). Adjustment to daycare, as rated by teachers, was also significantly related to inhibition as measured only in the out-of-home care setting in all three phases ($r_{16months}$ = − .29, p < .05; $r_{28months}$ = − .27, p < .05; $r_{40months}$ = − .39, p < .01). According to careproviders, then, inhibition is related to adjustment, and the effect is not transient. If anything, the opposite seemed to be the case.

Inhibition in Relation to Gender and Out-of-Home Care

There were no overall differences relating inhibition to gender or to children's experiences of home versus out-of-home care. A gender by type-of-care ANOVA, however, showed a tendency toward interaction between gender and type of care (F = 2.92, p = .06), implying that DC-boys had the lowest means on inhibition, followed by HC-girls, and DC-girls, with HC-boys scoring highest on the inhibition composite. A gender by type-of-care analysis on stability of inhibition also showed an interaction between DC-boys and the other groups. Compared to HC-boys, HC-girls, or DC-girls, fewer DC-boys scored in the two stable categories (inhibited or uninhibited in all three phases) and more DC-boys either fluctuated or scored above median on inhibition after having scored below (χ^2DC-boys vs. HC-boys [4, N = 42] = 4.50, p < .05).

Play Alone.   A 2-way ANOVA (Inhibition by quartiles and type of care, HC vs. DC), showed that children reared exclusively at home were much better able, than were children with one year's experience of out-of-home care, to play alone during a short separation from their mothers ($F = 9.45$, $p < .01$). The findings further showed a significant interaction between inhibition and group status ($F = 15.26$, $p < .001$), indicating that HC-children with high scores on inhibition and DC-children scoring low on inhibition were least able to play alone in their mothers' absence.

Inhibition and Ratings of Children's Emerging Personality Styles

A number of items on the CCQ and PBQ were significantly correlated with inhibition. We report only those relations where, for at least one of the correlations, the probability of its occurrence by chance is less than .01. As is shown in Table 8.7, the following items (N.B. items with negative correlations have been reworded accordingly) showed the most consistent correlations with inhibition: "does not behave in dominating manners with others," "is not self-reliant and confident, does not trust own judgment," "is not vital, energetic, lively," "is not an interesting, arresting child," "is reflective, thinks and deliberates before speaking or acting," "does not like to compete, does not test or compare self against others," "is not admired or sought out by other children," "is physically cautious," "does not seek to be independent and autonomous," "when in conflict or disagreement with others tends to give in," "tends to brood and ruminate or worry," and "is not a talkative child."

For mothers, but not for careproviders, the following CCQ–items also correlated with inhibition: "is not cheerful" ($r = .18$ $p <. 05$ [Phase II]; $r = .27$ $p < .01$ [Phase III]), "overreacts to minor frustrations" ($r = .32$ $p < .001$ [Phase II]), and "is not warm and responsive" ($r = -.24$ $p < .01$ [Phase II]). For careproviders, but not for mothers, the following CCQ-items were correlated with inhibition in Phase II: "tends not to arouse liking and acceptance in adults" ($r = .41$ $p < .01$), "does not try to be the center of attention" ($r = .37$ $p < .01$), "daydreams, tends to get lost in reverie" ($r = .34$ $p < .01$), "can be trusted, is dependable" ($r = .49$ $p < .001$), "tends to keep thoughts feelings or products to self" ($r = .35$ $p < .01$), and "can delay gratification, can wait for satisfaction" ($r = .34$ $p < .01$).

In Phase III, careproviders used the Baumrind's (1971) PBQ instead of Block and Block's (1979) CCQ to describe children. As is shown in Table 8.8, the result was strikingly similar to that arrived at by using the CCQ. The five items that showed the highest correlations with inhibition were: "Does not bully other children," "is not paid attention to by other children," "not a content, cheerful attitude," "characteristically unoccupied," and "hits only in self-defense, or does not hit at all."

TABLE 8.7
Correlation between Inhibition and Maternal or Careproviders CCQ-ratings of Children's Personality

| | Mega-Inhibition as Measured | | | |
| | Only at Home | | | At Home plus in Daycare |
CCQ – Items	W grp[a]	HC[b]	DC[c]	ODC[d]
93[e] m[f] II[g] Behaves in dominating manners with others	−.19*	−.29*	−.15	−.24+
mIII	−.19*	−.21	−.37**	−.23+
aII			−.36**	−.52***
88mII Is self-reliant, confident; trusts own jdgmnt		−.30*	.01‡	
mIII	−.25**	−.29+	−.03	−.26+
aII			−.32**	−.41***
28mIII Is vital energetic lively	−.22**	−.30*	−.34*	−.35**
aII			−.43***	−.54
42mII Is an interesting, arresting child	−.23**	−.21	−.30**	−.26*
mIII	−.24**			
aII			−.22+	−.45***
99mII Is rflctv; thnks & dliberates bfr speakng or actng		.17*	.18	.22+
mIII	.21**	.31*	.10	.31*
aII		.41***		.46***
37mII Lks to cmpte; tsts & cmprs slf agnst othrs	−.17*			−.29*
mIII			−.30*	
aII			−.26*	−.53***
5mIII Is admired and sought out by other children	−.25**	−.16	−.25+	−.40**
aII			−.31*	
52mIII Is physically cautious	.27**			.27*
aII			.23+	.45***
83mIII Seeks to be independent and autonomous	−.26**	−.36*	−.18	
aII			−.23+	−.30*
44mII When in cnflct or dsgrmnt w othrs tnds t gve in	.29***		.44**	.16
aII				.31*
24mIII Tends to brood and ruminate or worry	.19*	.44**	−.14‡	
aII		.39***		.41**
84mIII Is a talkative child	−.24**	−.33*	−.26+	−.22+
aII				
22mII Tries to manipulate others by ingratiation			.03	−.37**‡
aII			−.42***	
86mIII Likes to be by h/hself enjoys solitary actvts				.26*
aII			.31**	.49***

[a]The whole group, regardless of care status ($n = 136$); [b]children consistently in home care ($n = 49$ in Phase II and $n = 39$ in Phase III); [c]children in daycare ($n = 80$ in Phase II and $n = 70$ in Phase III); and [d]children who were in daycare during all three phases ($n = 57$); [e]CCQ item number; [f]respondent (m = mother, a = alternative care provider); [g]wave of data collection.

$+p < .10$; $*p < .05$; $**p < .01$; $***p < .001$; two-tailed; ‡ indicates that the difference between HC and DC children is significant.

TABLE 8.8
Correlations between Inhibition and Careproviders PBQ-Ratings of Children's
Personality

	Mega-Inhibition as Measured	
PBQ-Items	Only At Home DC[a]	At Home plus in Daycare ODC[b]
54[c] Bullies other children	− .38**	− .43***
24 Paid attention to by other children		− .40**
56 Content, cheerful attitude		− .37**
14 Characteristically unoccupied		.36**
67 Hits only in self-def. or doesn't hit at all	.34*	.34**
1 Expr. neg. feelings openly and directly	− .27*	− .33**
69 Resp ab following stand oper proc at school	.45***	.30*

[a]Children in daycare in Phase III ($n = 70$); [b]children who were in daycare during all three phases ($n = 57$); [c]PBQ item number.
*$p < .05$; **$p < .01$; ***$p < .001$; two-tailed.

DISCUSSION

The results reported here confirm the importance of inhibition as a dimension of toddlers' and pre-schoolers' temperament and emerging personality styles. Taken together, individual differences in observed noninvolvement in peer play at home, observed lack of sociability in relation to the approach of an unfamiliar adult at home, and maternal ratings of inhibition formed reliable composite measures of inhibition that were stable over time (from 16 to 40 months of age). Aggregation of the nine different indicators of inhibition resulted in a single mega-measure of inhibition with acceptable internal reliability. Another mega-measure of inhibition was formed summing up the indicators of inhibition both at home and in the daycare settings. The correlations between component scores, and the robust predictive validity of the composite scores, confirm that inhibition should be viewed as a complex, multifaceted dimension, which should be assessed using a variety of measures (Kagan, 1989).

In their definition of inhibition, Kagan, Reznick, Clarke, Snidman, and Garcia-Coll (1984) emphasized initial reactions to unfamiliar events, and especially unfamiliar people, noting that the typical inhibited child was slow to explore unfamiliar environments, was more likely to withdraw from novel stimuli, generally was more fearful, and reacted much more strongly to stressful events than did children in general. The profile of ratings that together formed coherent rating-scales of inhibition in the present study confirmed these descriptions. Mothers and careproviders rating children high on the two "basic variables" (i.e., "is shy and reserved, makes social contacts slowly," and "is socially withdrawn"), also rated children high on items describing, fearfulness, anxiety, and low stress tolerance.

Another aspect of the temperament of inhibited children, suggested by the CCQ–ratings, is that of emerging introversion. According to Rubin and Mills (1988), a distinction between "passive-anxious withdrawal" and "active-immature withdrawal" is warranted. They describe passively withdrawn children as children "whose isolation from the peer group reflects social anxiety and negative self-perceptions of social competence" (Rubin & Mills, 1988, p. 921). Although Rubin and Mill's description refer to much older children (7 to 10-year-olds), our inhibited children could fit into their passive-anxious category, especially given some of the PBQ-items included in the careprovider's rating-scale in Phase III ("spectator," "timid with other children," "typically in the role of the listener").

The distributional characteristics of our composite measure of inhibition are that of a continuous rather than dichotomous variable. Our findings support that of Reznick et al. (1989), who found that, given a normal sample of at least 100 subjects, measures of inhibition tend to be approximately normally distributed. According to Kagan (1989) measures of inhibition, although possibly continuously distributed, should be stable over time and have predictive validity only for a specific subgroup of children that are "truly inhibited." This was clearly not the case in our sample. Correlational analyses using all subjects (see also regression analyses in Broberg et al., 1990) produced the most consistent results, relating inhibition to a number of outcome variables. It is worth noting that our subjects were firstborns and that on average they had very low scores on a scale of stressful life events, which according to Kagan (1989) should make the sample even less well suited for these types of predictive relations. At least among Swedish toddlers and pre-schoolers, inhibition seemed to be best construed on a continuum.

The increased contact with adults and other children that followed from enrollment in out-of-home care did not affect children's inhibition at 28 and 40 months of age, which suggests that inhibition in the first years of life is best viewed as a fairly stable dimension that is not systematically affected by ordinary life changes like those implicit in the initiation of out-of-home care.

Further, we did not replicate American reports of sex differences in inhibition and sociability. There were no overall differences between boys and girls either in mean levels or stability of inhibition. This is consistent with other findings (Lamb, Hwang, & Broberg, 1989) suggesting a greater tendency among Swedish parents and preschool teachers than among their North American counterparts to treat boys and girls similarly. There was, however, an interaction between gender and type-of-care showing that DC-boys had the lowest mean levels of inhibition. DC-boys were also likely to be stable in inhibition over the three years of the study (i.e., either inhibited or uninhibited). Although this finding is generally consistent with those showing that boys are generally more vulnerable than girls (Jacklin, 1989), the number of DC-boys (23 altogether) scoring in each category (7 moved towards inhibition, 3 moved towards "uninhibition," and 6 fluctuated) was too low to allow any definite interpretation as to the direction of change relative to the other groups.

Overall, our composite measures of inhibition were related to the quality of peer play in the expected manner, but only for two- and three-year-old children. As Eckerman, Davis, & Didow (1989) and Howes (1987) have pointed out, a relatively sudden, almost qualitative, difference in children's ability to engage in social play takes place during the second half of children's second year of life. In Phase I, therefore, our subjects were probably too young (16 months of age on average) for meaningful individual differences to manifest themselves. One and two years later, however, inhibited children were less engaged in high-quality peer play, were more often observed standing aimlessly, and vocalized less towards the peer during the peer play observations at home and in the daycare settings. These findings are in accordance with the description of passive-anxious withdrawal given by Rubin and Mills (1988).

At home, but not in the daycare settings, inhibited children also interacted more with adults and cried more often during the peer play observation. Data from Phase III (when our subjects averaged 40 months of age) showed that mothers of inhibited DC-children were especially prone to intervene during the peer play session by initiating interaction with their children. One could speculate that mothers of DC-children, who generally were less used to seeing their children play with other children at home, were more eager to "help" their child interact with his or her peer, whereas HC-mothers (and careproviders in the day care settings) who were more used to the inhibited children's behavioral peer play style, were less inclined to intervene. Inhibited children were also much less engaged in verbal interactions with their peers both at 28 and 40 months of age, and at home they were also more often observed talking "on their own" (i.e., undirected vocalizations).

Controlling for language ability, these differences remained, showing that the inhibited children's vocalization patterns were not due to delayed language development. Furthermore, as Broberg, Hwang, Lamb, and Bookstein (1990) have pointed out, scores on the Griffiths' language scale are themselves affected by children's sociability towards an unfamiliar adult, also indicating that inhibited children's less frequent communicative vocalizations are not the result of delayed language development. Defects in some aspects of language development can, however, be a long-term consequence of not using language as interactive communication (see Evans, this volume).

Although out-of-home care did not affect later inhibition, it was related to children's dependency on their mothers, and it interacted strongly with type of care in this respect. According to our hypothesis, inhibited children should have been more dependent on their mothers, and consequently less able to play alone, than their uninhibited counterparts. This was indeed true for children who remained at home. For children that had been in out-of-home care for one year, on the other hand, contrasting results were obtained — uninhibited children were less able or willing to play alone in their mothers' absence. The meaning of these differences is not clear: somehow, being left alone for a couple of minutes with a set of interesting toys has divergent psychological meaning for toddlers with and without out-of-home care experience. One could speculate that inhibited toddlers in home care seek the comforting proximity of their mothers when separated from them and left with another adult; that is, their attachment systems are activated. Inhibited DC-children, on the other hand, may find separation from the mother less threatening and are therefore content with a couple of minutes of solitary play with a new set of interesting toys. Uninhibited toddlers with out-of-home care experience may seek to engage their mothers as playmates (rather than as a secure base), thus preventing their mothers from interacting with the other adult (a pattern they may have learned in the out-of-home care setting).

Our finding that, according to both parents and day careproviders, inhibited children had more difficulty adjusting to out-of-home care than did uninhibited children suggests that inhibition should be regarded as a risk factor, as conceptualized by Rutter and Garmezy (1983). The fact that differences in adjustment in Phases II and III were consolidated only in relation to inhibition as measured in the out-of-home care settings, and that they were most clearly related to contemporaneous measures of inhibition in those settings, suggests that careproviders' ratings of adjustment were more closely related to the aspects of inhibition that were least stable over time and situations.

A number of items on the CCQ and PBQ were significantly correlated with inhibition. Overall these correlations are in accordance with other researchers' descriptions of inhibited or passively withdrawn children, showing that at least in the views of mothers and careproviders these behavioral patterns are already evident in inhibited three-year-olds. These findings supports the usefulness of mothers as raters of children's inhibition; a finding consistent with that of Lancaster, Prior, & Adler (1989), who found that mothers' descriptions of children's anxious behaviors are much less influenced by maternal characteristics compared to children's hostile-aggressive behaviors.

Consistent with suggestions that early inhibition/shyness/social withdrawal may be risk factors for future internalizing problems (Rubin &

Mills, 1988) or panic or anxiety disorders (Rosenbaum et al., 1989), the mothers and careproviders described inhibited children as being less interesting and rewarding to interact with, and as having negative moods and poor self-evaluations. One should, however, keep in mind that we refer to between-group differences on items that in some cases have low (or high) means — most mothers, for example, rated their children as interesting, although mothers of children scoring low on inhibition rated their children as more interesting than mothers of children with high scores on inhibition. The fact that there exists a correlation between inhibition and maternal ratings of how interesting they find their children does not mean that mothers of inhibited children on average find them "uninteresting." Some do, however, and it is these children who are probably the least well off in the long run.

In summary, mothers and careproviders described children with high scores on inhibition as being more thoughtful, reserved, and uncommunicative than children with low scores. Children with high scores on inhibition were also seen as less cheerful and outgoing than children scoring low on inhibition, and despite the fact that they were not seen as aggressive, they were not, according to their mothers and careproviders, highly appreciated by other children or by adults. In peer contacts they were viewed as ignored rather than rejected, and in relation to adults they were pictured as more dull and not so interesting to interact with as uninhibited children.

Overall, our results confirm that individual differences in inhibited behavior, whatever their origin, are stable across the toddler and preschool years. The results also demonstrate that inhibition affects children's behavior in a variety of contexts and circumstances, and that it is not affected by contrasting childcare histories. Our data further suggest that being a two to three-year-old child with an inhibited temperament may have profound effects on the image that significant others hold of that child. As Lancaster et al., have pointed out "how the mother perceives her child is likely to be both a cause and effect of her interaction with her child" (Lancaster, et al., 1989, p. 146). In some cases a vicious cycle may begin, causing the child to internalize a negative self image, and later develop a range of internalizing problems in middle childhood, adolescence, or adulthood.

ACKNOWLEDGMENTS

This research was supported by Riksbankens Jubileumsfond of Stockholm, Sweden, whose assistance is gratefully acknowledged. We appreciate the cooperation of the parents, children, and care providers without whose help this study would not have been possible. Gunilla Hult and Majt Frodi greatly assisted in the collection of the data. Many thanks also to Drs. Michael Lamb and Philip Hwang for their constructive comments on earlier versions of this chapter.

This study was completed while the author was a visiting fellow at the National Institute of Child Health and Human Development.

REFERENCES

Alin-Åkerman, B., & Norberg, L. (1980). *Griffiths Utvecklingsskalor I och II*. Stockholm: Psykologiförlaget.

Asendorpf, J. (1989). Shyness as a final common pathway for two different kinds of inhibition. *Journal of Personality and Social Psychology, 57*, 481–492.

Baumrind, D. (1971). Current patterns of parental authority. *Developmental Psychology Monographs, 4*, 1–102.

Beckwith, L. (1972). Relationships between infants' social behavior and their mothers' behavior. *Child Development, 43*, 397–411.

Block, J. H. (1965). *The child-rearing practises report: A technique for evaluating parental socialization orientations*. Unpublished manuscript, Institute of Human Development. Berkeley: University of California.

Block, J. H. (1976). Issues, problems, and pitfalls in assessing sex differences: a critical review of the psychology of sex differences. *Merrill-Palmer Quarterly, 22*, 283–308.

Block, J., & Block, J. (1979). *Instructions for the California child Q-set*. Unpublished manuscript, University of California, Institute of Human Development, Berkeley.

Block, J., & Block, J. (1980). The Role of ego-control and ego-resiliency in the organization of behavior. In W. A. Collins (Ed.), *Minnesota symposium on child psychology* (Vol. 13, pp. 39–101). Hillsdale, NJ: Lawrence Erlbaum Associates.

Bretherton, I. (1978). Making friends with one-year-olds: An experimental study of infant-stranger interaction. *Merrill-Palmer Quarterly, 24*, 29–51.

Broberg, A., & Hwang, P. (1986). *Barnomsorg i Göteborg*. Unpublished manuscript. Department of Psychology: University of Göteborg.

Broberg, A., & Hwang, P. (1991). Child care in Sweden. In E. Melhuish & P. Moss (Eds.), *Day care and young children—International perspectives*. London: Routledge.

Broberg, A., Lamb, M. E., & Hwang, P. (1990). Inhibition: Its stability and correlates in sixteen to forty-month-old children. *Child Development, 61*, 1153–1163.

Broberg, A., Lamb, M. E., Hwang, C. P., Bookstein, F. L. (1990). Factors related to verbal abilities in Swedish preschoolers. *British Journal of Developmental Psychology, 8*, 335–349.

Bronson, W. C. (1966). Central orientations: A study of behavior organization from childhood to adolescence. *Child Development, 37*, 125–155.

Buss, A. H. (1986). A theory of shyness. In W. H. Jones, J. M. Cheek, & S. R. Briggs (Eds.), *Shyness: Perspectives on research and treatment* (pp. 39–46). New York: Plenum.

Caspi, A., Elder, G. H. Jr., & Bem, D. J. (1988). Moving away from the world: Life course patterns of shy children. *Developmental Psychology, 24*, 824–831.

Clarke-Stewart, K. A., Umeh, B. J., Snow, M. E., & Pederson, J. A. (1980). Development and prediction of childrens' sociability from 1 to $2\frac{1}{2}$ years. *Developmental Psychology, 16*, 290–302.

Daniels, D., & Plomin, R. (1985). Origins of individual differences in shyness. *Developmental Psychology, 21*, 118–121.

Eckerman, C. O., Davis, C. C., & Didow, S. M. (1989). Toddlers' emerging ways of achieving social coordinations with a peer. *Child Development, 60*, 440–453.

Garcia-Coll, C. T., Kagan, J., & Reznick, J. S. (1984). Behavioral inhibition in young children. *Child Development, 55*, 1005–1019.

Gersten, J. C., Langner, T. S., Eisenberg, J. G., Simcha-Fagan, O., & McCarthy, E. D. (1976). Stability and change in types of behavioral disturbance of children and adolescents. *Journal of Abnormal Child Psychology, 4,* 111–127.

Griffiths, R. (1954). *The abilities of babies.* London: University of London Press.

Griffiths, R. (1970). *The abilities of young children.* London: University of London Press.

Hinde, R. A., Stevenson-Hinde, J., & Tamplin, A. (1985). Characteristics of three- to four-year olds assessed at home and their interactions in preschool. *Developmental Psychology, 21,* 130–140.

Hollingshead, A. B. (1975). *The four factor index of social position.* Manuscript available from the Department of Sociology, Yale University, New Haven, CT 06520.

Howes, C. (1980). Peer play scale as an index of complexity of peer interaction. *Developmental Psychology, 16,* 371–372.

Howes, C. (1987). Social competence with peers in young children: Developmental sequences. *Developmental Review, 7,* 252–272.

Jacklin, C. N. (1989). Female and Male: Issues of Gender. *American Psychologist, 44,* 127–133.

Kagan, J. (1989). *Unstable ideas; Temperament, cognition, and self.* Harvard University Press: Cambridge, Massachusetts.

Kagan, J., & Moss, H. A. (1962). *Birth to maturity: A study in psychological development.* New York: Wiley.

Kagan, J., Reznick, J. S., & Snidman, N. (1987). The physiology and psychology of behavioral inhibition in children. *Child Development, 58,* 1459–1473.

Kagan, J., Reznick, J. S., & Snidman, N. (1988). Biological bases of childhood shyness. *Science, 240,* 167–171.

Kagan, J., Reznick, J. S., & Snidman, N. (1990). The temperamental qualities of inhibition and lack of inhibition. In M. Lewis & S. M. Miller (Eds.), *Handbook of developmental psychopathology* (pp. 219–226). New York: Plenum.

Kagan, J., Reznick, J. S., Clarke, C., Snidman, N., & Garcia-Coll, C. (1984). Behavioral inhibition to the unfamiliar. *Child Development, 55,* 2212–2225.

Lamb, M. E. (1982). Individual differences in infant sociability: Their origins and implications for cognitive development. In H. W. Reese & L. P. Lipsitt (Eds.), *Advances in child development and behavior.* (Vol. 16, pp. 213–239), NY: Academic Press.

Lamb, M. E., Hwang, C-P., & Broberg, A. (1989). Associations between parental agreement regarding child-rearing and the characteristics of families and children in Sweden. *International Journal of Behavioral Development, 12,* 115–129.

Lancaster, S., Prior, M., & Adler, R. (1989). Child behavior ratings: The influence of maternal characteristics and child temperament. *Journal of Child Psychology and Psychiatry, 30,* 137–149.

Maccoby, E. E., & Feldman, S. (1972). Mother-attachment and stranger-reactions in the third year of life. *Monographs of Society for Research in Child Development, 37,* No. 1.

Marks, I. M. (1987). *Fears, phobias and rituals.* New York: Oxford University Press.

Moskowitz, D. S., Schwartzman, A. E., & Ledingham, J. E. (1985). Stability and change in aggression and withdrawal in middle childhood and early adolescence. *Journal of Abnormal Psychology, 94,* 30–41.

Plomin, R., & Daniels, D. (1986). Genetics and shyness. In W. H. Jones, J. M. Cheek, & S. R. Briggs (Eds.), *Shyness: Perspectives on research and treatment* (pp. 63–80). New York: Plenum.

Plomin, R., & Stocker, C. (1989). Behavioral genetics and emotionality. In S. Reznick (Ed.), *Perspectives on behavioral inhibition* (pp. 219–240). Chicago: University of Chicago Press.

Reznick, S., Gibbons, J., Johnson, M., & McDonough, P. (1989). Behavioral inhibition in a normative sample. In S. Reznick (Ed.), *Perspectives on behavioral inhibition* (pp. 25–49). Chicago: University of Chicago Press.

Rosenbaum, J. F., Biederman, J., & Gersten, M. (1989). Anxiety Disorders and behavioral inhibition. In S. Reznick (Ed.), *Perspectives on behavioral inhibition* (pp. 255–270). Chicago: University of Chicago Press.

Rosenberg, A. A., & Kagan, J. (1989). Physical and physiological correlates of behavioral inhibition. *Developmental Psychobiology, 22,* 753–770.

Rothbart, M. K. (1981). Measurement of temperament in infancy. *Child Development, 52,* 569–578.

Rubin, K. H. (1985). Socially withdrawn children: An "at risk" population? In B. H. Schneider, K. H. Rubin, & J. E. Ledingham (Eds.), *Peer relationships and social skills in childhood: Issues in assessment and training* (pp. 125–139). New York: Springer-Verlag.

Rubin, K. H., & Lollis, S. (1988). Origins and consequences of social withdrawal. In J. Belsky & T. Nezworski (Eds.), *Clinical implications of attachment.* (pp. 219–252). Hillsdale, NJ: Lawrence Erlbaum Associates.

Rubin, K. H., & Mills, R. S. L. (1988). The Many Faces of Social Isolation in Childhood. *Journal of Consulting and Clinical Psychology, 56,* 916–924.

Rubin, K. H., Hymel, S., & Mills, R. S. (1988). Sociability and social withdrawal in childhood: Stability and Outcomes. *Journal of Personality.*

Rutter, M., & Garmezy, N. (1983). Developmental psychopathology. In E. M. Hetherington (Ed.), P. H. Mussen (Series Ed.), *Handbook of child psychology: Vol. 4 Socialization, personality and social development.* (pp. 775–911). New York: Wiley.

Stevenson, M. B., & Lamb, M. E. (1979). Effects of infant sociability and the caretaking environment on infant cognitive performance. *Child Development, 50,* 340–349.

Stevenson-Hinde, J., Stillwell-Barnes, R., & Zunz, M. (1980). Subjective assessment of rhesus monkeys over four successive years. *Primates, 21,* 66–82.

Suomi, S. J. (1987). Genetic and maternal contributions to individual differences in rhesus monkey biobehavioral development. In N. A. Krasnegor, E. M. Blass, M. A. Hofer, & W. P. Smotherman (Eds.), *Perinatal development: A psychobiological perspective* (pp. 397–420). New York: Academic Press.

Thomas, A., Chess, S., Birch, H., Herzig, M. E., & Korn, S. (1963). *Behavioral individuality in early childhood.* New York: New York University Press.

Thompson, R. A., & Lamb, M. E. (1982). Stranger sociability and its relationships to temperament and social experience during the second year. *Infant Behavior and Development, 5,* 277–287.

Thompson, R. A., & Lamb, M. E. (1983). Security of attachment and stranger sociability in infancy. *Developmental Psychology, 19,* 184–191.

Tizard, J., & Tizard, B. (1971). The social development of two-year old children in residential nurseries. In H. R. Schaffer (Ed.), *The origins of human social relations* (pp. 127–151). New York: Academic Press.

Younger, A. J., Schwartzman, A. E., & Ledingham, J. (1986). Age-related differences in children's perceptions of social deviance: Changes in behavior or in perspective? *Developmental Psychology, 22,* 531–542.

9 Features of Speech in Inhibited and Uninhibited Children

Maureen Rezendes, Nancy Snidman, Jerome Kagan, and Jane Gibbons
Harvard University

The rise of interest in temperamental qualities has raised the consciousness of investigators regarding the best way to conceptualize and to measure this class of psychological characteristics. The tension surrounding conceptualization turns on the difference between a continuous trait compared with a discrete category. For example, one can regard a temperamental characteristic, like approach-withdrawal, as continuous, and to treat extremely shy and extremely sociable children as belonging on a single dimension. The implication of this assumption is that the processes that mediate a very sociable child are the complements of those that produce a very shy child.

Historical analysis reveals that nineteenth century investigators preferred to regard temperamental types as categorical rather than continuous. The hysterical personality in psychoanalytic theory was not on a continuum with an obsessive-compulsive personality; rather, the two were regarded as distinct categorical types. The work of Clarke, Mason, and Moberg (1988) on closely related strains of macaque monkeys demonstrates that one cannot place members of the two strains on either a continuum of arousal or physiological reactivity; each shows a distinct profile of reactivity. Magnusson and Allen (1983) and Hinde and Dennis (1986) make similar arguments for the utility of assigning subjects to psychological categories.

A more pragmatic issue, and the one this chapter addresses, deals with the task of discovering the most sensitive indexes of each of the temperamental constructs at various ages. The dramatic maturational changes in behavior that occur over the first six years of life require investigators to find different referents for temperamental qualities that are presumed to be moderately stable from infancy forward. Earlier work in our laboratory revealed that after three years of age, spontaneous speech with an unfamiliar adult (or child) was an unusually sensitive index of inhibition, where inhibition refers to restraint, avoidance, or distress to an unfamiliar person, object, or event. Inhibited children tend to be wary of and show distress in unfamiliar situations while uninhibited children tend to approach them (Kagan, 1989; Kagan, Reznick, & Snidman, 1988; Reznick, Kagan, Snidman, Gersten, Baak, & Rosenberg, 1986). The children in our first two longitudinal cohorts selected as inhibited at 2 years of age, were, at $7\frac{1}{2}$ years of age, quiet with unfamiliar examiners and spoke very little when interacting with a large group of unfamiliar children (Kagan, 1989).

Asendorpf (in press) has affirmed this result in samples of 4 to 6 year old children, as well as adults. Briefly, observations of children and adults in a setting where each was with an unfamiliar adult revealed that latency to the first spontaneous comment and percent of time silent were extremely sensitive indexes of the quality of shyness as judged by observers.

This chapter reports the results of a recent investigation from our laboratory that supports the assumption that the presence or absence of speech with unfamiliar people may be one of the best indexes of an inhibited temperament in children over three years of age.

A previous report (Kagan, Reznick, & Gibbons, 1989) summarized data on a longitudinal sample of 100 Caucasian children who had not been selected on any a priori qualities and were observed at 14, 20, 32, and 48 months of age.

BASES FOR THE INITIAL CLASSIFICATIONS

Each child participated in a 90-minute laboratory session at 14 and 20 months, which evaluated cognitive and language functioning and included six procedures to assess inhibited and uninhibited behavior to unfamiliar people, contexts, and objects (See Reznick, Gibbons, Johnson, & McDonough, 1989, for details). The index of behavioral inhibition was based on the child's behavior to the following events at 14 and 20 months: (1) a 5- and a 10-minute unstructured free play session conducted in two different rooms; (2) reaction to a large mask of a dog's face an experimenter placed in the corner of a room; (3) reaction to an unfamiliar female adult; (4) reaction to the sudden sound of an alarm clock ringing; and (5) reaction to a large robot constructed from tin cans and light bulbs. The mother was with the child continually throughout all the episodes.

The index of behavioral inhibition was based on scores reflecting approach or withdrawal to the unfamiliar events, as well as fretting or crying. The specific variables coded from videotapes of the sessions at 14 and 20 months were: latency to leave the parent initially, latency to touch the first toy in the initial 5-minute free play session, proportion of time the child was proximal to the parent, and the presence or absence of fretting or crying in each situation.

At 32 months of age the index of inhibition was based on the child's behavior in a 30-minute free play situation with three unfamiliar children of the same age and sex with all mothers present. The index of inhibition was based on the frequency of approaches to another child, entering another child's territory, seizing an object from another child, entering a plastic tunnel, and total time in social interaction with another child. These variables, which were positively correlated, were converted to standard scores and averaged to form an aggregate index of inhibition.

The index of inhibition at four years of age represented the most extensive evaluation of these two temperamental types and was based on behavior in three separate situations. The three situations were: (1) individual testing session with an unfamiliar examiner; (2) a 30-minute peer play session with an unfamiliar child of the same sex and age; and, finally, (3) a five minute play situation in two small unfamiliar rooms containing novel objects.

The individual testing session yielded two variables indexing inhibition: latency to the child's first spontaneous comment and the total number of spontaneous comments across the entire battery. The peer play situation yielded five variables indexing inhibition: total time proximal to the mother while not playing with any toys; total time the child was not in social interaction with the other child but was staring at the unfamiliar child; latency to touch the first toy; latency to utter the first vocalization; and total amount of time the child spoke over the 30-minute session. The mean standard score across these five standardized variables (reversing the score for total time talking) became the index of inhibition.

Finally, the index of inhibition for the final five minute free play situation in an unfamiliar room containing novel objects was based on: (1) latency to touch the first object; (2) latency to the first vocalization; and (3) total amount of time playing with the objects across the five minutes. The correlations among the three indexes of inhibition were all positive and an aggregate index was created by averaging the three standard scores based on the three assessment situations.

These data revealed preservation of the two temperamental profiles from 14 and 20 to 48 months of age, but only for those children who were in the top and bottom 20% of the distribution of the aggregate index of behavioral inhibition. (It should be noted that in all of our previous work, the 20th and 80th percentiles tend to be the criterial scores that best differentiate consistently inhibited and consistently uninhibited children from other children whose behavior is less extreme and less consistent.) There was no comparable stability of behavior over time for the children who were in percentiles 21 to 79 and who were therefore less extreme in their early behavior.

We now summarize the results of a follow-up study of a selected subset of these 100 children when they were $5\frac{1}{2}$ years of age in order to determine if speech behavior provided a sensitive index of inhibition at this later age.

METHOD

Subjects.   The subjects were 44 $5\frac{1}{2}$ year old children (23 girls and 21 boys) who had been part of the larger sample of 100 children observed at 14, 20, 32, and 48 months. All the children who had been extremely inhibited or uninhibited at either 14 or 20 months (early), or 32 or 48 months (late), were asked to participate in the sessions at $5\frac{1}{2}$ years. Because of the long interval of almost $4\frac{1}{2}$ years, many subjects were not available and some refused to cooperate. As a result, 44 children participated in a laboratory testing situation and 28 children in a peer play situation.

Twenty-nine of these children had been classified as either extremely inhibited ($n = 14$) or uninhibited ($n = 15$) on the early observations at 14 or 20 months. As noted, the criteria for classification as inhibited required the child's score to fall in the top 20% of the distribution of scores for all children on the aggregate index of inhibition at each age, while the classification as uninhibited required the child's score to fall in the bottom 20% of the distribution for that age. In the original study, 26 children were classified as inhibited or uninhibited because we required the child to be inhibited or uninhibited at both 14 and 20 months. When we changed the criterion so that classification was possible if the child was inhibited or uninhibited at either one of those early ages, three additional children were included, yielding 14 inhibited and 15 uninhibited children.

A second group of 15 children was classified as extremely inhibited ($n = 8$) or extremely uninhibited ($n = 7$) based on their behavior at 32 or 48 months of age; these children had not been either inhibited or uninhibited at 14 or 20 months. Of the 14 children classified as inhibited at 14 or 20 months, 6 were also inhibited at 32 or 48 months; of the 15 children classified as uninhibited at 14 or 20 months, 9 continued to be uninhibited at 32 or 48 months, yielding a total of 22 inhibited and 22 uninhibited children.

PROCEDURES AT FIVE AND ONE-HALF YEARS

Laboratory Test Session.   Each child, accompanied by a parent, came to a small laboratory room that had been used on the earlier assessments. All 44 children participated in this session. The child and parent were greeted by a female examiner who was unaware of the child's prior classification.

After a brief warm-up period the examiner then applied three heart rate electrodes to the child's chest and back. A battery that consisted of 14 episodes and took about 90 minutes included sitting and standing heart rate baselines with the child quiet, sitting and standing blood pressure baselines, and a set of recognition and recall memory tasks designed to evaluate the child's response to stressful, cognitive tasks. In the recognition memory task, children viewed 24 familiarization slides of objects or people with various facial expressions. Twenty minutes later the children were shown a second set of slides containing half of the previously viewed slides and 12 new slides. They were asked whether they had previously seen each slide. There were also two immediate recall tasks. In one, the child was asked to repeat after the experimenter a series of three to six words. In another situation, children were asked to recall a sequence of tones played on a xylophone.

Two coders who had no knowledge of the child's prior classification coded the videotapes of the test session for: (a) latency to each of the first 10 spontaneous comments (a spontaneous comment was an unprovoked utterance and not a reply to the examiner's question); and (b) frequency of spontaneous comments to the examiner during each of the episodes.

Four randomly selected videotapes were recoded by a second coder. Reliability for the two variables (latency to the child's first 10 spontaneous comments and frequency of spontaneous comments), was high ($r = .98$, and .99, respectively).

Free Play With Peers.   Two to four months prior to the test session each child was also observed in a play session with other children. Four separate same age, same sex play groups, composed of seven to ten children who were unfamiliar with each other, were videotaped. Each child entered a large laboratory playroom approximately 20′ by 40′. A piece of paper on which a number and the child's first name were written was attached to the child's clothing on both the chest and back. Each of the four playgroups contained approximately equal proportions of inhibited and uninhibited children based on their earlier classifications. After the first six children had arrived, the group was led to the playroom by two unfamiliar female examiners. The room was equipped with age and sex appropriate toys as well as food and beverages. The children were told to play until the remaining children arrived; the examiners then left the room. The parents viewed their children's activities through a television monitor in another room.

When all the children had arrived, within about 10 minutes, the two female examiners reentered the room and told the children that various team games would be played and they would be given stamps to be exchanged for toys at the end of the session based on the group performance in the games. Each child was assigned to one of two teams for each of the five games. New teams were formed for each game and each team contained equivalent proportions of each temperamental category of the child. Each game was followed by four minutes of free play during which the experimenters left the room under the guise of preparing for the next game.

The first game was a hopping race in which pairs of children competed by hopping across the length of the room and returning to the starting position. The second game was "Pin the Tail on the Donkey." The third game was ball toss in which each child had three opportunities to throw a ball into a box that was set at a fixed distance. The fourth game was an egg race in which a pair of competing children had to balance a small wooden egg on a spoon while racing the length of the room and returning to the starting position. The fifth game was musical chairs. Approximately 50 minutes were devoted to these five games and 30 minutes to the unstructured free play intervals before the games began and between each of the games.

The entire session was recorded on videotape from behind a one way screen. In addition, each child was assigned an observer who had no knowledge of the child's behavioral classification. The observer narrated the behaviors of that single child during the entire session. Two additional observers were assigned to two different children who were already being described by another coder in order to evaluate reliability of the first coder's narrated descriptions. Each observer narrated into an audiotape recorder a continuous description of five selected behaviors previously shown to differentiate inhibited and uninhibited children in the same social situation (Kagan et al., 1988). These five variables were: time when the child was greater than arm's distance from any other child, talking to an adult, talking to a child, smiling-laughter, and yelling-cheering. Internarrator reliabilities for these variables ranged from .81 for smiling and laughter to .94 for talking.

The narrations and videotapes were coded for the above five variables by two different coders who did not view the original session and had no knowledge of the child's prior classification. The coders relied on both the videotapes and audiotaped narration for each child to code the frequency of duration of the five variables noted above for each game and each free play session.

A randomly selected set of nine audio and videotapes (for nine children) were scored by another coder. Intercoder reliabilities were high: percent time not proximal to a peer ($r = .98$), total number of spontaneous comments ($r = .97$), frequency of smiling-laughing ($r = .91$), frequency of yelling or cheering ($r = .66$).

RESULTS

Laboratory Testing Session.   Table 9.1 contains the mean raw scores of the speech variables for inhibited and uninhibited children (early and late

TABLE 9.1
Means and Standard Scores for Variables in Test and Free Play Sessions for Children Classified as Inhibited or Uninhibited Early or Late

Session	Early Classification		Late Classification		t^a	p^a
	I	U	I	U		
Laboratory Test						
N	14	15	8	7		
Latency to 1st	1584.70	546.13	750.75	43.43	3.06	<.01
Comments (sec.)	(1401.54)	(429.53)	(788.50)	(51.05)		
No. Comments	32.07	66.33	33.88	112.00	2.90	<.01
	(33.42)	(55.71)	(41.99)	(88.85)		
Free Play						
N	5	10	7	6		
No. Comments	16.60	54.60	19.57	82.00	3.77	<.001
	(9.37)	(42.00)	(13.38)	(37.64)		
Percentage Time Not	53.45	47.32	63.14	41.30	2.45	<.05
Proximal to Peer	(16.30)	(15.32)	(17.65)	(9.05)		

[a] t-tests were conducted between pooled early and late classifications for inhibited (I) and uninhibited (U) subjects.

classification) in the laboratory and the free play sessions. The two variables that were selected to index inhibited and uninhibited behavior in the testing session had differentiated the temperamental groups in earlier research on other samples. The variables were number of spontaneous comments during the session (the score was reversed to reflect inhibited behavior) and the latency to the first spontaneous comment. Across all children, there was a great deal of variability in the amount of speech; latencies to the first spontaneous comments ranged from one second to the end of the test session; frequency of spontaneous comments ranged from zero to 250. Two children failed to make any spontaneous comments during the session; their latencies to the first comment were adjusted by giving them a value equal to three standard deviations from the mean for the group. These two variables were standardized within sex; and the index of inhibition for the laboratory test session was the mean of the two standard scores.

The correlation between the latency to the first spontaneous comment and the frequency of spontaneous comments was significant ($r = -.33$, $p < .05$). The scores for number of spontaneous comments were not adjusted for the length of the testing session because the time differences across the sessions were very small. In addition, the inhibited children made fewer spontaneous comments despite the fact that their test sessions were slightly longer.

There was a significant difference in both the latency to the first comment and the number of comments between the inhibited and uninhibited children (for both $p < .01$).

Free Play Situation. The two behaviors that differentiated the two groups in prior research were frequency of spontaneous comments to any child or adult during the entire session and the duration of time the child was not proximal to any other child during the free play intervals (Reznick et al., 1986). The timing of the sessions was constant across all the free-play groups. There was a great deal of variability in the number of comments made to peers (0 to 47) and adults (0 to 19) as well as in the percentage of time a child was not proximal to a peer during the free play intervals (28% to 80%). The number of spontaneous comments was reversed so that a high value indicated behavioral inhibition. Both percentage of time not proximal to a peer and the number of spontaneous comments made to both peers and adults differentiated the inhibited from uninhibited children. An inhibited child was characterized by a high proportion of time not proximal to any other peer and very few comments to peers or adults, while the uninhibited child had the opposite profile.

There was a significant correlation for all children in the number of spontaneous comments produced in the test and free play sessions ($r = .56$, $p < .01$). In addition, there was a significant correlation for all children between the index of behavior in the laboratory test session and behavior in the free play session with peers ($r = .48$, $p < .01$).

Inhibited children differed from uninhibited children in an expected fashion on all variables. Inhibition of speech was, as expected, an extremely sensitive index of inhibition in both situations. For example, subjects classified as inhibited at 14 or 20 months spoke half as often as children classified as uninhibited. At 32 or 48 months, uninhibited children spoke $3\frac{1}{2}$ times more often as inhibited children. In a peer play situation, total time not proximal to an unfamiliar child was less sensitive than inhibition of speech in differentiating the two groups of children.

Figure 9.1 presents the standard scores for each child in each of the four groups (inhibited early, inhibited late, uninhibited early, uninhibited late) for the laboratory test and free play sessions.

The behavioral differences between inhibited and uninhibited children were preserved to $5\frac{1}{2}$ years of age. When the subjects in both the early and late classification groups were pooled into inhibited versus uninhibited groups, the behavioral differences between the two groups at $5\frac{1}{2}$ years of age were significant for both situations ($t(42) = 3.04$, $p < .01$ for the laboratory test situation; $t(26) = 3.75$, $p < .001$ for free play situation).

Among the inhibited children, 29% of those who were classified as inhibited early and 50% of those who were classified as inhibited late had positive standard scores on the index of inhibition in the laboratory test session. By contrast, not one of the uninhibited children classified early and only 14% of those classified late had positive standard scores (not significant, $\chi^2 < .10$, for early and late groups pooled).

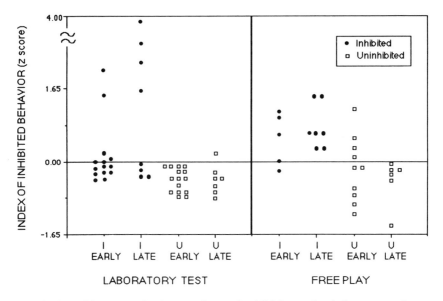

FIG. 9.1. Mean standard score for each child in each of the groups for the two evaluative sessions.

In the free play situation, four of the five early inhibited group and every one of the late inhibited children had positive standard scores on the inhibition index. The comparable proportions for the uninhibited subjects were 40% for those classified early and 0% for those classified late (χ^2 = 12.3, p < .001).

DISCUSSION

The preservation of the behavioral differences between inhibited and uninhibited children from the second to the sixth year of life in this selected sample represents the third demonstration in our laboratory of the stability of a diverse set of behaviors that characterize these contrasting temperamental types. More important, these data affirm both our earlier research, as well as the findings of Asendorpf, that among older children, inhibition of speech with an unfamiliar child or adult is an unusually sensitive index of inhibition.

As we suggested in an earlier paper (Kagan, 1989), differential excitability of the amygdala, especially the central nucleus and its projections to the central gray, may be a salient characteristic of inhibited children. Projections from the central gray to the vocal cords and larynx create high levels of muscle tension in these structures. One of the consequences of the higher muscle tension is the decrease in the variability of the pitch periods of phonation of spoken words. We have reported elsewhere that inhibited, compared with uninhibited, children show significantly larger decreases in the variability of pitch periods when speaking single, familiar words under mild stress (Kagan, Reznick, & Snidman, 1988). If inhibited children had markedly lower thresholds in this circuit, we would expect the restriction of speech, especially in uncertain contexts.

It is relevant in this discussion to note that unpublished data from two longitudinal cohorts that have been followed from 4 to 21 months of age reveal that children who are inhibited at 14 and 21 months showed significantly less spontaneous vocalization to unfamiliar visual and auditory stimuli when they were 4 and 9 months of age as well as less vocalization in speech at 14 and 21 months (See Kagan & Snidman, 1991 for details of the procedure).

We have interpreted this robust result as reflecting greater excitability in the amygdala and the circuit to the central gray and the vocal cords. Thus, restraint on speech, which is such a consistent feature of older, inhibited children, may reflect a fundamental characteristic of shy, fearful children that can be detected in early infancy.

Many animal species are characterized by a distinctive reaction to unexpected threat, novelty, or intrusion. Cats crouch and hiss; rabbits freeze, monkeys grimace and squeal. It may be that restraint of vocalization and speech is a biologically prepared reaction in humans.

It is hoped that future research will provide a more detailed understanding of why restriction on speech is such a pervasive accompaniment to states of uncertainty in children and a sensitive index of the temperamental quality of inhibition.

ACKNOWLEDGMENTS

This research was supported by a grant from the John D. and Catherine T. MacArthur Foundation. We thank Hilary Sokolowski for her contributions to this research.

REFERENCES

Asendorpf, J. B. (in press). A Brunswikean approach to trait continuity: Application to shyness. *Journal of Personality.*

Clarke, A. S., Mason, W. A., & Moberg G. P. (1988). Differential behavioral and adrenocortical responses to stress among three macaques species. *American Journal of Primatology, 14,* 37–52.

Hinde, R. A., & Dennis, A. (1986). Categorizing individuals. *International Journal of Behavioral Development, 9,* 105–119.

Kagan, J. (1989). Temperamental contributions to social behavior. *American Psychologist, 44,* 668–674.

Kagan, J., Reznick, J. S., & Gibbons J. (1989). Inhibited and uninhibited types of children. *Child Development, 60,* 838–845.

Kagan, J., Reznick, J. S., & Snidman N. (1988). Biological bases of childhood shyness. *Science, 240,* 167–171.

Kagan, J., & Snidman, N. (1991). Infant predictors of inhibited and uninhibited profiles. *Psychological Science, 2,* 40–44.

Magnusson, D., & Allen, V. I. (1983). *Human Development: An Interactional Perspective.* New York: Academic Press.

Reznick, J. S., Gibbons, J., Johnson, M. O., & McDonough, P. (1989). Behavioral inhibition in a normative sample. In J. S. Reznick (Ed.), *Perspectives on behavioral inhibition* (pp. 25–50). Chicago: University of Chicago Press.

Reznick, J. S., Kagan, J., Snidman, N., Gersten, M., Baak, K., & Rosenberg, A. (1986). Inhibited and uninhibited behavior: A follow-up study. *Child Development, 57,* 660–680.

10 Communicative Competence as a Dimension of Shyness

Mary Ann Evans
University of Guelph

INTRODUCTION

Talk, or rather the lack thereof, is a prominent component across a variety of concepts used to describe those who appear awkward, uncomfortable, and inhibited in social interaction. These include shyness, social withdrawal, social inhibition, social anxiety, reticence, and communication apprehension. Although there are the conceptual distinctions between these terms (see Asendorpf, 1990a; Clevenger, 1984; Leary, 1983), both the quality and quantity of talk emerge as marker variables that cut across them. It is the intent of this chapter to review and integrate a variety of studies in the literature that comments on the communicative behavior of these groups of children. When referring to the various studies, I use the terms used by the authors of the studies to denote their subject groups. However, when generalizing across the studies, the word "shy" is used. While "shy" and "shyness" are probably what Meehl (1978) would call "fuzzy verbalisms" lacking scientific precision, in English they nonetheless carry meaning as used in everyday language similar to the various terms of the research literature reviewed (Zimbardo, 1977).

   The second intent of the chapter is to provide a more detailed description of the language and discourse skills of children identified by their teachers as untalkative, by describing recent research carried out by this author and students at the University of Guelph. Because much of this research has not been published elsewhere, some descriptive statistics are included in this chapter. In this research we have followed Leary (1983) and adopted the term *reticent* to refer to our subjects, who according to teachers, rarely volunteer to answer questions, rarely participate in classroom discussions, and speak minimally when they do so.

Finally the chapter closes by moving beyond the studies reviewed to consider the dynamic interplay between communicative competence and shyness, and the potential ramifications for social relations, self perceptions, and cognitive development.

TALKATIVENESS

Individual differences in the frequency and amount that people talk have been documented in both children and adults since the 1930s and 1940s. In the early so-called "count studies" of language development, which documented growth in the amount and rate of talking without reference to the quality of what was said or how it was expressed, marked individual differences were noted. These studies are reviewed by Dorothea McCarthy in her chapter, "Language Development in Children," in Carmichael's 1954 *Manual of Child Psychology*. From these studies it appeared that, although sheer increase in the quantity of talk within a given time period proved to be an reasonable indicator of language development until age four (Jerslid & Ritzman, 1938; Smith, 1926; Young, 1941), the "variability [was] too great from child to child for it to be an adequate criterion" (Smith, 1926, p. 17). Other early researchers attempted to examine correlates of amount of talk—extroversion (McCarthy, 1929), mental age (Jerslid & Ritzman, 1938), and sex (Jerslid & Ritzman, 1938; Olson & Koetzle, 1936)—and observed only low associations in favor of girls, extroverts, and those with higher mental ages, leaving the question of what accounted for individual differences in fluency largely unanswered.

Throughout these early reports examining developmental trends in the amount of talk, the terms "shy," "quiet," and "unexpressive" were used to refer to the "less voluble" children. Throughout more recent reports of shy children, there are numerous indications that they are "less voluble." For example, children identified as behaviorally inhibited at 21 months have been observed at age 5 to spend less time talking during free play, and to make fewer spontaneous comments in a formal assessment situation (Kagan, Reznick, Snidman, Gibbons, & Johnson, 1988; Reznick, Kagan, Snidman, Gersten, Baak, & Rosenberg, 1986). Asendorpf (1992) observed similar results among both adults and children in that latency of their first spontaneous utterance, the percentage of speech, and the length of pauses when conversing with an unfamiliar adult partner were highly correlated with parent, self, and observer ratings of shyness. (See also Pilkonis, 1977, for observations of adults). Finally four year olds define shyness by talk, identifying the shy puppet as the one who doesn't like to talk to others, and who doesn't take a turn at Show & Tell (Zimbardo & Radl, 1981).

This construct of shyness as defined by young children shares substantial similarity with definitions of shyness in the research literature, many of which mention reduced quantity of talk as an observable index or marker of shyness. To quote some examples, for Jones, Briggs, and Smith (1986) shyness includes "self-consciousness and reticence in social situations," for Buss (1984) a tendency to "not speak up, mumble minimal replies if addressed, and fail to hold up one's end of the interaction," and for McCroskey and Richmond (1982) "to be timid, reserved, and most specifically, talk less." It could hardly be the case otherwise. Both talking to others and shyness are social phenomenon, and talking to others is a major vehicle — except for young children perhaps the major vehicle — by which interaction occurs and by which social relations are formed and maintained. (See for example, the importance of exchanging information verbally for friendship formation and peer group entry as documented by Altman & Taylor, 1973; Dodge, 1983; Duck & Craig, 1977; Gottman, 1983; Putallaz & Gottman, 1981; Putallaz, 1983.)

The difficulty some children have in exchanging information in social groups is illustrated by the behavior of children in the classroom activity "Show & Tell." In this activity, children volunteer to tell their teacher and classmates about events, people, and objects in their lives. Some children, in my experience, about 3 in a class of 30, rarely participate. When they do, their speech is almost painfully limited. The following samples of "Show and Tell" conversations collected by Evans (1987) give some sense of this stylistic difference. Both conversations involve kindergarten girls who have brought their dolls to "Show and Tell." *T* denotes teacher, *PG* denotes peer girl, and *RG* denotes reticent girl.

Sample 1	Sample 2
T: Tell us what you brought today.	*T:* Erica [fictional name]
RG: (pulls rag doll out of bag; does up button on doll's dress) A doll.	*PG:* (takes out and shows doll)
T: Can you tell us about it?	*T:* Can you tell us who you brought today?
RG: It can stand up.	*PG:* Crying Baby. You give her a bottle and pull the string out. (pulls string to demonstrate) And then she cries.
T: Can you tell us anything else?	
RG: (no response)	
T: Does she have a name?	*T:* Did you get her for Christmas?
RG: (no response)	*PG:* (nods)
T: Where did you get her?	*T:* I see you've got some more clothes for her.
RG: For Christmas.	*PG:* I got a whole bunch in my room.
T: Did you? She's very nice.	*T:* Do you have a bed for her at your house?
	C: She sleeps with me.
	T: Oh does she.

In response to the same query, "Tell us what you brought today," the peer girl responds at length with its name and a description of how she plays with it complete with demonstration, and continues to volunteer information beyond the required answers to the teacher's questions. The reticent girl answers with a single redundant label and subsequent terse responses to the teacher's questions. Data gathered across fifteen Show & Tell sessions (Evans, 1987) showed that when children who infrequently participated did take a turn in this activity, they spoke two-thirds fewer words, spoke utterances half as long, and commented on two-thirds fewer topics. They also were asked more questions by their teacher than were their classmates, and responded twice as frequently to these questions with no response or a minimal response as in the preceding excerpt.

A FRAMEWORK FOR EXAMINING TALKATIVENESS

What causes the apparent unwillingness or reluctance of individuals to talk as fluently as their more verbal peers and what consequences this might have are broad and complex questions addressed by researchers in both the fields of psychology and speech communication, the latter of which tend to use the terms "reticence" (Phillips, 1984; Van Kleeck & Street, 1982) unwillingness to communicate (Burgoon, 1976), communication apprehension (McCroskey, 1977, 1984), and pragmatic disorders (McTear, 1985). Within both fields, hypothesized contributors to shyness include both the affective aspects of anxiety, inhibition, or apprehension, which may include a genetic component, and the cognitive components of knowing and understanding appropriate communicative behaviors as well as being able to produce them, or in other words, communicative competence. The resulting product is verbal fluency, and in the case of shy individuals, nonfluency.

In a paper entitled "On fluency," Charles Fillmore (1971) outlined several criteria by which speakers are judged to be fluent. These include the ability to talk at length with few pauses and to fill time with talk, to speak easily in a compact and careful way, to be verbally at ease in many different settings, and to be creative and imaginative in language use. These criteria outline the linguistic domain of pragmatics, or the use of language, but phrased in the negative effectively describe those who are shy. They are not verbally at ease in a variety of settings and do not talk at length. They violate Grice's (1967) conversational maxim called the co-operative principal by which participants are assumed to mutually contribute to conversations. They frequently fail to take a speaking turn when offered one, to answer questions directed to them, and to initiate topics associated with those of their partners.

Filmore elaborates on six sets of proposed sources for individual differences in fluency, or how each person uses language. They include: (a) knowledge of fixed linguistic forms (morphemes, words, idioms) and phrases (cliche's, politeness formulas); (b) the ability to create new expressions through, for example, knowledge of syntactic devices; (c) rich semantic encodings; (d) knowledge of various interactional schemata for conversations; (e) knowledge of discourse schemata such as narratives and expositions; and (f) knowledge of the appropriateness of particular words and forms or registers for particular situations. Thus fluency may be viewed as rooted in both what may be termed language skill, corresponding roughly to the first three items, and discourse skill, corresponding roughly to the last three. While Fillmore acknowledges the role of personality factors in language performance, application of his framework suggests that researchers in the area of shyness should focus not only on early development and responses to unfamiliarity and stress, but also on language and discourse abilities in later development and the environmental circumstances that might nurture them.

OBSERVED LINGUISTIC AND COMMUNICATIVE SKILL DIFFERENCES

The data from studies examining the language and discourse skills of "shy" children (See Table 10.1 for an overview) appear to fall into three general areas grouped accordingly for presentation here: (a) their scores from formal language measures including standardized tests of linguistic ability and indices of linguistic maturity from naturalistic speech samples; (b) their discourse performance in social situations coded according to various pragmatic schemes; and (c) their responses to various hypothetical social situations. Studies comparing socially withdrawn, reticent, and communicatively apprehensive subjects with normal peers have usually been conducted with children at a given grade. Some are cross-sectional in design or have tracked children across grades to give some sense of the developmental course. Others are correlational in design, examining what communication behaviors are associated with child characteristics reflecting shyness.

Formal Language Test Performance. Several studies indicate that shy children fare less well, although not necessarily below average, on formal tests of language than do their more talkative peers. In a paper entitled "Talkativeness and children's linguistic abilities," Landon and Sommers (1979) reported that preschool and kindergarten children who were identified by their teachers as "quiet" versus those identified as "chatterboxes" obtained lower scores on tests of articulation, expressive morphology, and

TABLE 10.1
Studies Examining Communicative Competence Grouped by Type of Measure

Study	Sample	Variable and Results
A. FORMAL LANGUAGE PERFORMANCE		
Landon & Sommers (1979)	20 reticent vs 20 verbal age 3–6	< ITPA expressive morphology < NSST receptive syntax < Deep Test of Articulation > Menyuk Sentence Repetition errors
Van Kleeck & Street (1982)	2 reticent vs 2 verbal preschoolers	PPVT 69/64 vs 87/88 Carrow ACL 75/84 vs 54/83 DSS 85/26 vs 47/39 < MLU in dyad < TTR in dyad < complex sentences in dyad ns modifiers & word length in dyad
Rubin (1982)	17 isolate vs. 17 sociable, 17 average per kindergarten, grade one	< PPVT
Rubin & Krasnor (1986)	85 isolate vs 10 sociable, 30 average kindergarten through grade one	ns PPVT
Vriniotis & Evans (1988)	14 reticent vs 14 verbal per grade 2, 4, 6	< WISC-R Vocabulary < CELF Word Associations
Evans (1989)	37 reticent vs 27 improved 64 verbal kindergarten through grade one	< Verbal Comm. Scale-Parent < Verbal Comm. Scale-Teacher < EOWPVT < Binet-4 Absurdities ns PPVT-R < CELF Production ns CELF Reception > prop at risk
B. DISCOURSE PERFORMANCE		
Van Kleeck & Street (1982)	as above	< requests for action in dyad > direct requests in dyad
Rubin, Daniels-Beirness & Bream (1984)	52 Kindergarten	− r utterances with isolate play − r requests with isolate play
Rubin & Borwick (1984)	5 dyads of isolate with sociable per preschool, kindergarten	> attention requests < action & object requests ns number of requests
Evans & Ellis (1992)	8 dyads of reticent with verbal friends grade one	> low cost requests > simple requests > nonverbal requests > information requests re here-and-now
Evans (1987)	7 reticent vs 7 verbal kindergarten Show & Tell	> present object topics < absent object topics < narratives ns simple reports < MLU

194

TABLE 10.1 (*Continued*)

Study	Sample	Variable and Results
C. HYPOTHETICAL-REFLECTIVE PERFORMANCE		
Rubin, et al. (1984)	as above correlations with isolate play	− r SPST relevant categories − r SPST flexibility + r SPST adult interventions
Rubin & Krasnor (1986)	as above	< SPST alternatives in Kin. < SPST flexibility in Kin. ns............................ in grade 1
	8 isolate vs 11 early isolate, 13 average, 10 sociable Kindergarten through 2	ns SPST variables
Vriniotis & Evans (1988)	as above	< variety intents < variety strategies ns variety pooled intents < variety pooled strategies

receptive syntax, and made more errors repeating model sentences. However, their battery did not include any tests of semantic ability and their subjects ranged from age 36 to 77 months, making one wonder whether the differences observed might be isolated to the younger untalkative children.

Another study by Van Kleeck and Street (1982) described formal language test results and naturalistic speech observations of two talkative and two reticent three-year-old girls. The talkative girls were nominated as such by their teacher, and the reticent girls had been observed in a previous study to make few spontaneous comments to an adult. To describe the sample, they list the scores of the four children on three language measures. No consistent difference between the two sets of girls was apparent on the Auditory Comprehension of Language Test (Carrow, 1973), (a measure of receptive syntax), or in the complexity of spontaneous expressive language as indexed by Lee and Canter's (1971) Developmental Syntax Scoring procedure. However on the Peabody Picture Vocabulary Test (Dunn & Dunn, 1959) on which children point to which of four pictures is named, reticent girls obtained percentile ranks of 69 and 64 versus 87 and 88 for the talkative girls. This observation is similar to that of Rubin (1982) who reported lower PPVT scores for 34 isolate preschool and kindergarten children (average test age equivalent of 68 months) than for their sociable and normal peers (average test age equivalents of 82 and 75 months, respectively). Rubin did not report chronological ages for these groups. However, assuming his groups were both roughly 60 months of age, the sociable children, like Van Kleeck and Street's two talkative girls, would appear to be somewhat above average in semantic development.

As part of a study assessing conversational skills in the context of social problem solving, Vriniotis and Evans (1988) administered two language tests to grade 2, 4, and 6 children selected by their teachers in January of the school year as "quiet and rarely participating in classroom discussions" versus "verbal and participating readily." At each grade level, reticent children obtained significantly lower scores on the Vocabulary subtest of the WISC-R (Wechsler, 1974), which requires children to state the meanings of various words. The standard score means for reticent versus verbal children were 11.3 versus 13.9; 12.8 versus 14.9, and 10.4 versus 12.3 for grade 2, 4, and 6 children respectively. They also obtained significantly lower scores on the Producing Word Associations subtest of the Clinical Evaluation of Language Functioning (Semel & Wiig, 1980), which assesses fluency and speed of word retrieval by requiring children to name as many different animals and then foods as they can in one minute. The average number of items named by the reticent versus peer groups was 22 versus 27; 29 versus 35, and 31 versus 39. No differences were noted on the Block Design subtests of the WISC-R as an estimate of nonverbal intelligence.

In Van Kleeck and Street's (1982) study, the children subsequently played with seven unfamiliar adults, each in a separate play session, these interactions being videotaped, transcribed, and scored. Data analyses showed that the speech of the talkative girls contained longer utterances, a more varied vocabulary, and a larger proportion of complex sentences. No differences were observed in the frequency of adverb and adjective modifiers or in mean word length. Van Kleeck and Street concluded that the reticent children did not use the full range of their linguistic competence, and that in practicing language less, "they may eventually fall behind in their knowledge of language form" (p. 622). No longitudinal studies are available to evaluate this speculation. However, it might be noted that among college students a negative correlation has been observed between communication apprehension and scores on the verbal portion of the College Entrance Examination Board (Bashore, 1971), English portions of the American College Test (McCroskey & Anderson, 1976), and group IQ tests (Davis & Scott, 1978).

While the studies above suggest significant language skill differences between shy and non-shy children, the data are derived from very small sample sizes, from samples of mixed ages, or from isolated assessments of language skill that were ancillary to other research questions. To arrive at a more comprehensive picture of the performance of shy children on language tests, Evans (1989) conducted a study of 128 children. To select the subjects, twenty kindergarten teachers were asked to consider the extent to which each child in their class volunteered to speak in class discussions and the expansiveness of their speaking turns. The teachers then rank-ordered the children, dividing the list into "very quiet," "somewhat quiet," "somewhat verbal," and "very verbal" groups. As many or as few children could be placed in each group as the teacher wished. This rating was done in November to allow time for the children to become familiar with their new school setting, and was repeated again in March. Initially, two groups of subjects were formed that excluded children who spoke little English at home, or had mental or physical handicaps, or were listed as the two most verbal children. Half of the 128 subjects were very quiet children and half, matched on sex, were somewhat or very verbal children. However, according to the March ranking, the very quiet children were separated into two groups — 37 children called the *reticent* group who were "very quiet" at both time periods, and 27 children called the *improved* group who in March were described as "somewhat verbal" and were listed at least six ranks higher in the rank-ordered list. The *verbal* group remained intact.

With the parental consent forms, parents returned a rating of their child's verbal performance (Verbal Communication Scales — Parent Version, Bryant & Bryant, 1983) and teachers completed a teacher version of the same scale. Three testing sessions were then held with the children, summary data from which are reported in Table 10.2. The first session, held partially to establish contact with the children, included a drawing task (Geometric Design subtest of the Wechsler Preschool and Primary Scale of Intelligence, Wechsler, 1967), and a construction task (Block Design subtest of the WPPSI). On both of these tasks, boys in the reticent group obtained lower scores than boys in the improved and verbal groups. In two later sessions a battery of formal language tests was individually administered, interspersed with two game-like tasks from the Stanford Binet Intelligence Scale-IV

TABLE 10.2
Descriptive statistics for language and communications variables
(Evans, 1989).

	Group means (standard deviations)		
Variable	*Stable Reticent* N = 37	*Improved* N = 27	*Verbal* N = 64
End of Kindergarten			
Communication Scale: Parent	84.84[a] (8.61)	87.96[ab] (7.64)	89.21[b] (7.74)
Communication Scale: Teacher	73.76[a](14.81)	84.22[b] (11.17)	92.83[c] (8.59)
Communication Scale: Examiner	18.12[a] (5.41)	19.82[a] (5.64)	24.49[b] (6.64)
Fall of Grade One			
Communication Scale: Teacher	73.35[a](11.33)	76.46[a] (15.09)	86.41[b](11.97)
Production CELF	99.19[a](11.76)	106.26[bc] (9.64)	104.92[c](10.05)
Expressive OWPVT	106.80[a](19.26)	112.11[ab](13.83)	117.30[b](12.58)
Peabody PVT-R	105.70 (15.86)	108.26 (14.44)	109.66 (14.23)
Processing CELF	94.38 (12.96)	99.81 (10.05)	99.91 (12.55)
Absurdities (Binet-N)	48.46[a] (3.72)	50.07[ab] (3.23)	51.95[bc](5.73)

Note: Superscripts indicate significant differences on Scheffé test at alpha .05

(Thorndike, Hagen, & Sattler, 1986): Pattern Analysis for which the child constructs designs from blocks, and Absurdities for which the child states what's funny about given pictures. The language battery consisted of The Clinical Evaluation of Language Functioning or CELF (Semel & Wiig, 1980), which yields two composite scores. The Processing Composite reflects the ability to process, interpret, and recall semantic and syntactic information through pointing, yes/no, or wh-answer responses. The Production Composite reflects accuracy, fluency, and control in retrieving words and formulating sentences and in repeating modelled sentences. The battery also included the Expressive One Word Picture Vocabulary Test (Gardner, 1979) for which the children name line drawings and the Peabody Picture Vocabulary Test–Revised (Dunn & Dunn, 1981).

Data analyses revealed that the improved and verbal groups differed only on the teacher version of the Verbal Communication Scale, with verbal children receiving higher ratings in both kindergarten and grade one. Compared to both the improved and verbal groups, reticent children obtained lower scores on the teacher version of the Verbal Communication Scale completed in kindergarten, and on the Production Composite of the Clinical Evaluation of Language Functioning. Compared to the verbal group, reticent children also obtained significantly lower scores on the parent version of the Verbal Communication Scale completed in kindergarten, on the Expressive One Word Picture Vocabulary Test, and on the Absurdities subtest. Only on the receptive tests—the Revised Peabody Picture Vocabulary Test and Processing Composite of the CELF—were the scores of reticent children comparable to the other groups. In addition, examination of the individual subtests scores of the CELF revealed that a greater proportion of reticent children than verbal and improved children combined fell below the 20th percentile on the following subtests: Processing Word and Sentence Structure, in which the child matches a picture to a spoken sentence, Processing Paragraphs, in which the child recalls information from short spoken paragraphs of increasing length and complexity, Producing Model Sentences, in which the child repeats spoken sentences increasing in length and complexity of vocabulary and syntax, and Producing Formulated Sentences, in which the child makes up 12 sentences each of which are to include a specified word (e.g., what, herself, nothing). In the test manual, Semel and Wiig (1980) suggest that scoring below the 20th percentile on 3 or more subtests is indicative of possible language deficits. With a more stringent rule of five or more subtests as the criterion, 27% of the reticent children versus 14% of the improved and verbal children would be suspected of language deficits, a marginally significant difference. Finally, on the Pattern Analysis subtest, reticent boys had lower scores than the other male subgroups, mirroring the earlier findings.

This study, along with those presented earlier, clearly shows that children who across time are less socially outgoing in kindergartens and nursery schools perform less well on a wide variety of formal language measures assessing articulation, automaticity, and the comprehension and production of syntax and semantics. Although the difference is most apparent in the expressive language domain, some of the tasks required only a minimal verbal response such as naming an object, or repeating a sentence. Moreover, the data show that care should be taken in distinguishing between children who appear verbally inhibited across time versus those whose participation improves. It is only the former group that obtained significantly lower language scores than children who readily verbally participated throughout kindergarten. This suggests that there are different types of "shy" children. Some children (corresponding to the improved group of the above study) may be apprehensive and inhibited with unfamiliar people and social settings, such as a new class and new teacher. These children would be expected to speak less in the early months of school despite good communication skills, but become non-shy across time as the context becomes familiar. Other children (corresponding to the reticent group) may be less communicatively competent, and less able to verbally contribute and compete in both new and established social groups. Their shyness would be expected to remain stable and in some circumstances become even more entrenched over time (see Asendorpf, 1990b). More longitudinal studies are needed to address this possibility.

Discourse Performance. Relatively little research has examined the discourse performance of shy children, or how they socially interact with others through language. Most of the research has used play dyads as the context for social interaction. Although many of the studies code children's requests, the ways in which utterances are coded is quite variable from study to study, a problem that pervades research attempting to apply speech act theory to coding and counting real speech (see McTear, 1985).

Van Kleeck and Street (1982), in the aforementioned study, observed that their two reticent girls made proportionately fewer requests for action to their adult play partners than did the two verbal girls, and that they phrased a higher proportion of their requests in a direct as opposed to indirect form. Similarly, Rubin, Daniels-Beirness, and Bream (1984) using a correlational design, observed a negative relation between social withdrawal and the number of requests children made in play groups with a same-sex schoolmate. In contrast, Rubin and Borwick (1984), who reported frequencies, did not find any difference in the number of direct or indirect requests made by isolate preschoolers and kindergarteners, and neutral or "non-friend" classmates with whom they were paired in play dyads. However, the purpose of the requests distinguished the two groups. Isolate children made proportionately more requests to gain attention, fewer requests to elicit action, and fewer requests to acquire objects than did their playmates.

These studies have paired shy children with nonfriends, allowing the possibility that inhibition with a non-preferred play partner might have contributed to their verbal behavior. However, findings from a study by Evans and Ellis (1992), pairing reticent children with classmates with whom they preferred to play and for whom teachers gave somewhat or very verbal ratings, has shown similar results. Data analyses revealed that compared to their preferred playmates, reticent children made significantly more low cost requests for attention (8.9% vs. 1.5% of all utterances), more simple requests (19.8% vs. 6.8%), more non-verbal requests (4.4% vs. 1.4%), and more requests for information concerning the here-and-now (71.0% vs. 41.3% of all information requests). Particularly prominent was the routine of calling their partner's name. Some sense of the different interactional styles of reticent children and their more verbal friends is provided by the following excerpt of two boys playing with playdough. John (fictitious name) was the reticent child and Kyle (fictitious name) his more verbal friend:

John: Kyle, Kyle.
Kyle: hmm?
John: (shows him playdough construction)
Kyle: I know what this will be.
A hot dog with lines on it (laughs).
Eeeeoooow (while making line indentations).
John: (laughs)
Kyle: Eeow eeow (pause) eeow.
John: I'll make a hot dog.
Kyle: A hot dog.
There.
John: I'm making a big one, Kyle.
Kyle: (glances) There (puts own dough in pretend oven).
John: (laughs at Kyle's big glob of playdough)
Kyle: I think that it's too much.
John: (laughs)

Differences are also apparent in shy children's speech when talking to a group. Through observing and audiotaping kindergarten Show & Tell sessions, Evans (1987) found that reticent children not only talked less as outlined earlier, but spoke about less varied topics than their more talkative peers. Two-thirds of their participatory turns consisted of simply naming and briefly commenting on an object they had brought to show, while their peers frequently related personal narratives, described objects they had at home, and reported on events. Often the reticent children simply held the objects in front of them and named them, prompting the teacher to ask questions to solicit further information.

These observations of discourse skills by no means form a coherent or complete body of empirical data, but they suggest that many socially withdrawn and reticent children do not just talk less when interacting with others, but interact differently, employing a higher percentage of strategies that emerge earlier in development — direct requests (Ervin-Tripp, 1977; Garvey, 1975), nonverbal speech acts (Bates, 1976; Bates, Camaioni, & Volterra, 1975; Snyder, 1978), talk about the here and now (Bloom, Rocissano, & Hood, 1976; Evans, 1985; Keenan & Schieffelin, 1976), and bids for attention (Ervin-Tripp, O'Connor, & Rosenberg, 1984).

Hypothetical-Reflective Performance. Lastly this review considers studies using hypothetical-reflective procedures in which children are asked to imagine being in a certain situation and to report what they would say, or do. While what children say they would say in these analogues is not necessarily what they in fact would say in real life situations (Enright & Sutterfield, 1980; Kazdin, Matson, & Esveldt-Dawson, 1984; McLure, Chinsky, & Larcen, 1978), the hypothetical-reflective paradigm nonetheless provides some sense of the child's social situational repertoire. Two studies (Rubin, Daniels-Beirness, & Bream, 1984; Rubin & Krasnor, 1986) have asked children to indicate what they could say or do in five scenarios in which they are to try to gain an object from someone else. Rubin, Daniels-Beirness, and Bream (1984) in a correlational study observed low to moderate correlations between the extent to which preschool and kindergarten children engaged in isolate behavior during free play and both the number of relevant solutions and flexibility of solutions generated for these object conflict scenarios. Similarly, Rubin and Krasnor (1986), using a design comparing sociable versus isolate and average children's responses to these scenarios, found that sociable kindergartners offered more alternatives and more flexible alternatives than isolate and average children. However, they observed no differences between these groups among first graders or children tracked through grades one and two, although these negative results may be due to ceiling effects.

In all of these studies both verbal and nonverbal strategies were scored and a restricted range of social scenarios were presented. In order to explore children's verbal response strategies to a variety of social scenarios, Vriniotis and Evans (1988) asked children in grades 2, 4, and 6 to role play what they would *say* in nine different scenarios. Half of the children at each grade had been identified by their teachers as verbal and half as very quiet in classroom discussions at mid-school year. The nine social scenarios, each verbally described and supported by photographs, included situations requiring peer entry, making a new acquaintance, renewing an old acquaintance, receiving a gift, and comforting a friend. For example, "A friend you've invited to your birthday party telephones you to say he can't come to your birthday party. What would you say to him?"; "An aunt you've never met before comes to visit you and you meet her at the door. What would you say?" Responding to these scenarios requires the child to imagine him- or herself and the social partner(s) in the scenario, to formulate general communicative intents such as expressing gratitude, greeting, comforting, offering help, introducing self, and so on appropriate to the scenario, and to encode those communicative intents into verbal strategies for accomplishing them. For example, one may express gratitude for a gift through the verbal strategies of directly saying thank you, though ingratiating oneself by saying "Oh, you shouldn't have," or by offering a token exchange such as "You can come over and play with this, too."

Analyses of variance revealed that younger children and reticent children did not differ from older children and verbal children respectively in terms of the number of utterances with which they responded to the scenarios. However, the utterances of younger children and of reticent children reflected fewer different communicative intents within each scenario, and fewer different verbal strategies to accomplish each of these intents. We also pooled across the scenarios and found that reticent children generated an equal variety of different communicative intents at least once across the nine scenarios but fewer different strategies for verbally encoding those intents at least once across the nine scenarios. Thus they appear to have similar knowledge of what can be accomplished socially through language, but less sophistication in the various ways of using language to do so. Finally, the differences noted in the studies above do not appear to be limited to studies of shy versus non-shy children. Bruch, Giordano, and Pearl (1986) scored written responses of what college students indicated they would say in various social and educational situations. The responses of fearful shy students to making requests and expressing feelings were rated as less competent than those of non-shy students.

The above studies suggest that isolate and reticent children hold similar basic knowledge of how to respond to social-problem scenarios, but differ when presented with a variety of scenarios that are scored according to criteria on the specific verbal formulations employed. Another interpretation is that the these children have less well elaborated social scripts (see Nelson, 1981; Schank & Abelson, 1977) for these situations to guide their responses as to what they might say.

DISCUSSION

What accounts for these differences? Are they real or artifactual? If real, what implications do they have? Regardless of whether one views scores on various tests as estimates of verbal IQ or as more specifically of language development, the data suggest that many shy individuals are less verbally competent than their non-shy peers. The difficulty in drawing this conclusion is that measures of verbal intelligence, language development, and communication skill that require a verbal response may be confounded by the affective components of anxiety and inhibition that are hypothesized to underlie shyness, reticence, and communication apprehension and interfere with discourse performance. Compared to those who are low anxious, high anxious adults are less comprehensible (Freimuth, 1976; 1982), offer fewer ideas (Jablin, Seibold, & Sorenson, 1977), and use less varied language (Lerea, 1956) in conversations and small-group exchanges. Thus it may be the case that shy children who have been observed in the above studies to show weaker linguistic and communicative skills across a variety of contexts such as the classroom, home, test situation, and play group, or who remain reticent across time within a given context, constitute a more anxious group for whom the difference between knowledge and observed competence is most marked, and who under nonanxious familiar conditions would perform as well as their peers. This interpretation is consistent with the hypothesized inverted U-shaped relationship between anxiety and performance outlined by Hebb (1955) and reviewed by Murray (1971). Observations of shy versus non-shy children interacting with close friends or family members and in familiar contexts as opposed to the standard paradigm of observing them with neutral or unfamiliar partners, and studies in which the same children are observed with familiar and unfamiliar social partners would be ways to address this question (see e.g., Asendorpf, 1990b, Evans & Ellis, 1992).

However, while anxiety and inhibition are undoubtedly factors, they may not be the whole story. The observed differences in verbal fluency and social competence may not be artifactual but at least partly real, and a true reflection of less well developed verbal knowledge and communication skill. Different threads of evidence can be drawn together to support this position. First, it could be argued that, although being interviewed by an unfamiliar experimenter and asked how to respond to hypothetical social scenarios can arouse fear of the unfamiliar, it may be less anxiety-inducing than actually being in the real situation (Cooney & Selman, 1978), and thus reduce the effect of confounding affective variables. Secondly, some of the test performances on which shy children have been observed to perform less well require no verbal response or only single word answers, or in the case of parent ratings, reflect behavior in familiar contexts. Thirdly, no differences (except for lower scores for shy boys) are displayed on nonverbal tasks, so that if anxiety is the only factor, one would have to explain how anxiety is induced in test and observational circumstances where verbal problems are to be solved but not in circumstances where nonverbal problems are to be solved. Fourthly, background experiences, which would be expected to influence language and social discourse skills, differ between shy and non-shy children.

This last point stems from a PRINCALS analyses (Gifi, 1985) that I have completed of interviews with parents of 119 of the 128 children in the study of Evans (1989). As explained earlier, some of the children were reticent throughout kindergarten, some were reticent in only the first few months, and some of the children were verbal throughout. Two solutions accounted for 20% of the variance in the data set and indicated that participation in classroom discourse throughout kindergarten was associated with the following background factors: a higher level of maternal and paternal education, child attendance at nursery school, more frequent outings with the mother, more frequent book reading experiences with parents, more educationally oriented family hobbies according to television and recreational activities, and more encouragement by mothers to participate in the interaction when the parent's friends visited. Similar findings suggesting an environmental basis for shyness are scattered throughout other reports. For example, more sophisticated discourse skills in children are associated with the variety of social networks in the home (Stohl, 1989). Daniels and Plomin (1985) report an association between shyness in children and the extent to which their adoptive families like to explore new things, express their feelings, and have friends over to visit. Others have observed communication apprehension to be associated with the extent of social stimulation in the environment (Phillips, 1984; Sibinga & Friedman, 1971) and encouragement of communication in the home (Daly & Friedrich, 1981). Lastly, numerous studies have demonstrated the contribution of joint book reading activities to linguistic and discourse skills (Evans & Schmidt, 1991; Wells, 1985; Whitehurst, Falco, Lonigan, Fischel, DeBaryshe, Valdez-Menchaca, & Caufield, 1988; Wolf & Dickinson, 1985). Together this research suggests that environments having reduced emphasis on social and verbal activities and reduced availability of role models and experiences for the development of communication skills may make a direct contribution to poorer communicative competence and shy behavior.

One might hypothesize that both reticent children who remain quiet across kindergarten and those who are quiet only initially may lack backgrounds that foster the social and communication skills that would make for easy and comfortable discourse participation in novel settings such as the classroom, but that those children who remain quiet across the school year within the increasingly familiar context of kindergarten constitute a different group of children from those who are shy in only the initial term. They may be a more inhibited and anxious group whose inhibition is not substantially reduced under normal circumstances. Alternatively or additionally, their language and communication skills may be too discrepant from those of their peers to make the adjustment within the school year. Hence they remain quiet in school, obtain lower scores on a wide variety of language and communication tasks, and engage in less mature verbal strategies at play. Discourse moves very quickly. Conversational turn-taking latencies are typically less than one second (Jaffe & Feldstein 1970; Matarazzo & Wiens, 1972; Rowe, 1974). One must be motivated to participate in conversations, know how to proceed, and be able to easily make rapid syntactical and lexical choices to encode one's thoughts and intentions. The potential consequence of not being able to express oneself easily is illustrated by the observation that language-delayed children (Kolvin, Fundidis, George, Wrate, & Scarth, 1979; Petrie, 1975; Rutter, 1972; Caceres as cited by Baker & Cantwell, 1985) and stutterers (Robinson, 1966) are frequently shy and withdrawn.

The exact ways in which communication competence, affective factors such as anxiety, motivation, and self-efficacy, and experience contribute to shyness is complex, and any model needs to be a dynamic one which takes into consideration the developmental nature of the phenomena. Communicative competence can simultaneously be conceived of as a contributor to or source of shyness, as a means or process by which shyness is maintained and even exacerbated, and as an outcome of shy behavior. As a source, poorer communicative competence handicaps the child in readily and effectively conversing with others as demonstrated in the research reviewed in this chapter. As a means, poorer communicative competence may increase the likelihood of negative feedback, negative self-perceptions, and anxiety, and restrict opportunities to develop social skills, thereby maintaining shyness. There is substantial research documenting higher incidence of lower self-esteem and self-perceptions of competence in shy adolescents and adults (e.g. Buss, 1984; Clark & Arkowitz, 1975; Crozier, 1979; Duran, 1983; McCroskey, Daly Richmond, & Falcione, 1977; Zimbardo, 1977), and Asendorpf (1990b) has recently demonstrated the development of inhibition in familiar contexts through repeated social failure. Finally, poorer communicative competence may be an outcome of a vicious cycle in which shy individuals have less experience through personal choice or the lack of opportunities afforded them to observe, try out, and practice interactional strategies. As Cazden (1972) has noted, "communication skills as with other complex skills must be learned through practice to the point where performance is automatic" (p. 236).

The dynamic interplay between communication experiences, communicative competence, and affect with respect to shyness also suggests that efforts to develop communication skills should help alleviate shyness. Glass and Shea (1986) report that 10- to 20% of shy adults who volunteer for their therapeutic program seem not to know what to do in conversations and benefit from social skills training. Similarly, training studies in which specific communication skills have been coached have demonstrated beneficial effects on the recipients of this training. Specifically, Bierman and Furman (1984) trained children who were both deficient in communication skills and low in peer acceptance on a specific set of conversational skills linked to social competence—self-expression or sharing information about oneself, questioning or asking other about themselves, and leadership bids such as offering help, invitations, and advice. Follow-up six weeks after training indicated improvements in children's conversational performance in dyadic and peer group interactions and higher rates of interaction with peers at lunchtime among the trained than untrained subjects. Videotapes of selected training sessions indicated that the use of these conversational skills was associated with positive peer responses during the treatment (Bierman, 1986).

These studies highlight the point that how one converses influences how one is regarded in day-to-day interactions. The label "shy" is colloquially applied to those who less frequently participate in verbal interaction, but research suggests that negative perceptions in others are also formed. Although independent of sociometric status in early childhood, by age 10 or 11 shyness becomes associated with negative peer status (Rubin, Hymel, & Mills, 1989; Rubin & Mills, 1988) and the less talkative child is viewed as less approachable by peers (Richmond, Beatty, & Dyba, 1985), less socially competent (Kelly, 1982), and a less desirable social partner (Hurt & Priess, 1978). In addition, adults regard those who are less verbally fluent as less attractive and credible (Duran & Kelly, 1988; Hayes & Metzger, 1972), and teachers regard them as less competent, less likely to be successful in school, and less effective in social relationships (McCroskey & Daly, 1976; Smythe & Powers, 1978). There may be some truth to these expectations in that verbal fluency in kindergarten correlates positively with reading achievement in grade three (Stevenson, Parker, Wilkinson, Hegion, & Fish, 1976) and communication apprehension correlates negatively with achievement in older students (Comadena & Prusank, 1988; Hurt & Preiss, 1978).

One needs to consider the role that expectations and behaviors of others may play in contributing to these outcomes. For example, Van Kleeck and Street (1982) report that adults used simpler speech, made fewer comments, and asked more questions when talking to the reticent preschoolers than when talking to the more outgoing children. Similarly, Evans (1987) found that some 60% of teacher remarks to reticent children were questions, often occurring in chains of up to four successive questions in an attempt to get a response. Evans, Hauer, and Bienert (1991) demonstrated that when teachers asked a question, they waited the same amount of time for reticent children to make a reply as their classmates, but responded more quickly to the reticent child's speaking turn, effectively taking back the turn more quickly and providing less discourse space. In support of these studies is the following quote from Simons (1981),

> How to interview inarticulate pupils is one of the problems for which I have no adequate solution. . . . Often the interview becomes a question and answer session, with the questions getting longer and the answer getting shorter. Faced with a lack of response, the temptation is to try to articulate the problem for them. (p. 42)

While I have no adequate solution either, this chapter closes with what should begin another. Evans and Bienert (in press), who studied reticent children, Mirenda and Donnellan (1986), who studied mentally retarded children, and Wood and Wood (1984), who studied hearing impaired children have all shown that fewer questions from adults result in longer speaking turns and more spontaneous speech from these children. Instead of focusing only on shy children, research should turn towards studying how their interactional partners affect these children's shyness.

REFERENCES

Altman, I., & Taylor, D. A. (1973). *Social penetration: The development of interpersonal relationships*. New York: Holt, Rinehart & Winston.

Asendorpf, J. B. (1990a). Beyond social withdrawal: Shyness, unsociability, and peer avoidance. *Human Development, 33,* 250–259.

Asendorpf, J. B. (1990b). The development of inhibition during childhood: Evidence for situational specificity and a two-factor model. *Developmental Psychology, 26,* 721–730.

Asendorpf, J. B. (1992). A Brunswikean approach to trait continuity: Application to shyness. *Journal of Personality, 60,* 53–77.

Baker, L., & Cantwell, D. P. (1985). Psychiatric and learning disorders in children with communication disorders: A critical review. In K. D. Gadow (Ed.), *Advances in learning and behavioral disabilities*. Vol 4. Greenwich, CT: JAI Press.

Bashore, D. N. (1971). *Relationships among speech anxiety, IQ, and high school achievement*. Unpublished masters thesis, Illinois State University.

Bates, E. (1976). *Language in context: the acquisition of pragmatics*. New York: Academic Press.

Bates, E., Camaioni, L., & Volterra, V. (1975). The acquisition of performatives prior to speech. *Merrill Palmer Quarterly, 21,* 205–226.

Bierman, K. L. (1986). Process of change during social skills training with preadolescents and its relation to treatment outcome. *Child Development, 57,* 230–240.

Bierman, K. L., & Furman, W. (1984). The effects of social skills training and peer involvement on the social adjustment of preadolescents. *Child Development, 55,* 151–162.

Bloom, L., Rocissano, L., & Hood, L. (1976). Adult-child discourse: Developmental interaction between information processing and linguistic interactions. *Cognitive Psychology, 8,* 521–552.

Bruch, M., Giordano, S., & Pearl, L. (1986). Differences between fearful and self-conscious shy subtypes in background and current adjustment. *Journal of Research in Personality, 20,* 172–186.

Bryant, B. R., & Bryant, D. L. (1983). *The Verbal Communication Scales*. Austin, TX: Pro-ed.

Burgoon, J. K. (1976). The willingness to communicate scale: Development and validation. *Communication Monographs, 43,* 60–69.

Buss, A. H. (1984). A conception of shyness. In J. A. Daly & J. C. McCroskey (Eds.), *Avoiding communication: shyness, reticence and communication apprehension* (pp. 39–49). Beverly Hills: Sage.

Carrow, E. (1973). *Test for Auditory Comprehension of Language*. Austin, TX: Urban Research Group.

Cazden, C. B. (1972). *Child language and education*. New York: Holt, Rinehart & Winston.

Clark, J. V., & Arkowitz, H. (1975). Social anxiety and self evaluation of interpersonal performance. *Psychological Reports, 36,* 211–221.

Clevenger, T., Jr. (1984). An analysis of research on the social anxieties. In J. A. Daly & J. C. McCroskey (Eds.), *Avoiding communication* (pp. 219–236). Beverly Hills: Sage.

Comadena, M. E., & Prusank, D. T. (1988). Communication apprehension and academic achievement among elementary and middle school students. *Communication Education, 37,* 270–277.

Cooney, E., & Selman, R. (1978). Children's use of social conceptions: Towards a dynamic model of social cognition. In W. Damon (Ed.), *Social cognition* (pp. 23–44). San Francisco: Jossey-Bass.

Crozier, W. A. (1979). Shyness as a dimension of personality. *British Journal of Social and Clinical Psychology, 18,* 121–128.

Daly, J. A., & Friedrich, G. (1981). The development of communication apprehension: A retrospective analysis of contributory correlates. *Communication Quarterly, 29,* 243–155.

Daniels, D., & Plomin, R. (1985). Origins of individual differences in infant shyness. *Developmental Psychology, 21,* 118–21.

Davis, G. F., & Scott, M. D. (1978). Communication apprehension, intelligence and achievement among secondary school students. In B. D. Ruben (Ed.), *Communication Yearbook II* (pp. 457–472). New Brunswick, NJ: Transaction Books.

Dodge, K. A. (1983). Behavioral antecedents of peer status. *Child Development, 54,* 1386–1399.

Duck, S. W., & Craig, G. (1977). The relative attractiveness of different types of information about another person. *British Journal of Social and Clinical Psychology, 16,* 229–233.

Dunn, L. M., & Dunn, L. M. (1959). *Peabody Picture Vocabulary Test*. Circle Pines, MN: American Guidance Services.

Dunn, L. M., & Dunn, L. M. (1981). *Peabody Picture Vocabulary Test-Revised*. Circle Pines, MN: American Guidance Services.

Duran, R. L. (1983). Communication adaptability: A means of social communicative competence. *Communication Quarterly, 31,* 320–326.

Duran, R. L., & Kelly, L. (1988). The influence of communication competence on perceived task, social, and physical attraction. *Communication Quarterly, 36,* 41–49.

Enright, R., & Sutterfield, S. (1980). An ecological validation of social cognitive development. *Child Development, 51,* 93–100.

Ervin-Tripp, S. (1977). "Wait for me roller skate." In S. Ervin-Tripp & C. Mitchell-Kernan (Eds.), *Child Discourse* (pp. 165–188). New York: Academic Press.

Ervin-Tripp, S., O'Connor, M., & Rosenberg, J. (1984). Language and power in the family. In C. Kramerae, M. Schulz, & W. M. O'Brien (Eds.), *Language and power* (pp. 116–135). Urbana: University of Illinois Press.

Evans, M. A. (1985). Play beyond play: It's role in formal informative speech. In A. Pellegrini & L. Galda (Eds.), *Play, language and stories* (pp. 124–143). Norwood, NJ: Ablex.

Evans, M. A. (1987). Discourse characteristics of reticent children. *Applied Psycholinguistics, 8,* 171–184.

Evans, M. A. (1989). Classroom reticence: What it looks like and what might account for it. In G. Bonitatibus (chair), *Background and conversational influences on literacy and communication skills in the classroom*. Symposium conducted at the American Educational Research Association, San Francisco.

Evans, M. A., & Bienert, H. (in press). Control and paradox in teacher conversations with shy children. *Canadian Journal of Behavioural Science*.

Evans, M. A., & Ellis, P. A. (1992). *Requestive strategies of reticent and verbal children at play. Paper presented at the Biennial University of Waterloo Conference on Child Development, Waterloo*.

Evans, M. A., Hauer, R., & Bienert, H. (1991). *Conversational response latencies of teachers and reticent children*. Paper presented at the Biennial Meeting of the Society for Research in Child Development, Seattle.

Evans, M. A., & Schmidt, F. (1991). Repeated maternal book reading with two children: Language normal and language impaired. *First Language, 11,* 269–287.

Fillmore, C. J. (1971). On fluency. In C. J. Fillmore, D. Kemple, & W. S. Wang (Eds.), *Individual differences in language and language behavior* (pp. 85–101). New York: Academic Press.

Freimuth, V. S. (1976). The effects of communication apprehension on communication effectiveness. *Human Communication Research, 2,* 289–295.

Freimuth, V. S. (1982). Communication apprehension in the classroom. In L. Barker (Ed.), *Communication in the classroom*. Englewood Cliffs, NJ: Prentice-Hall.

Gardner, M. F. (1979). *Expressive One-Word Picture Vocabulary Test*. Novato, CA: Academic Therapy.

Garvey, C. (1975). Requests and responses in children's speech. *Journal of Child Language, 2,* 41–63.

Gifi, A. (1985). *PRINCALS*. Leiden, The Netherlands: Department of Data Theory.

Glass, C. R., & Shea, C. A. (1986). Cognitive therapy for shyness and social anxiety. In W. H. Jones, J. M. Cheek, & S. R. Briggs (Eds.), *Shyness: Perspectives on research and treatment* (pp. 315–327). New York: Plenum.

Gottman, J. M. (1983). How children become friends. *Monographs of the Society for Research in Child Development, 48,* (3, Serial No. 201).

Grice, H. P. (1967). Logic and conversation. In P. Cole & J. L. Morgan (Eds.), *Syntax and semantics: Speech acts* (pp. 41–59). New York: Academic Press.

Hayes, D. P., & Metzger, L. (1972). Interpersonal judgements based on talkativeness: Fact or artifact. *Sociometry, 33,* 538–561.

Hebb, D. O. (1955). Drives and the C.N.S. (conceptual nervous system). *Psychological Review, 62,* 243–254.

Hurt, H. T., & Preiss, R. (1978). Silence isn't necessarily golden: Communication apprehension, desired social choice and academic success among middle-school students. *Human Communication Research, 4,* 315–328.

Jablin, F., Seibold, D. R., & Sorenson, R. L., (1977). Potential inhibitory effects of group participation on brainstorming performance. *Central States Speech Journal, 28,* 113–121.

Jaffe, J., & Feldstein, S. (1970). *Rhythms of dialogue*. New York: Academic Press.

Jerslid, A. T., & Ritzman, R. (1938). Aspects of language development: The growth of loquacity and vocabulary. *Child Development, 9,* 243–259.

Jones, W. H., Briggs, S., & Smith, T. (1986). Shyness: conceptualization and measurement. *Journal of Personality and Social Psychology, 51,* 629–639.

Kagan, J., Reznick, J. S., Snidman, N., Gibbons, J., & Johnson, M. O. (1988). Childhood derivatives of inhibition and lack of inhibition to the unfamiliar. *Child Development, 59,* 1580–1589.

Kazdin, A. E., Matson, J. L., & Esveldt-Dawson, K. (1984). The relationship of role-play assessment of children's social skills to multiple measures of social competence. *Behavioral Research and Therapy, 22,* 129–139.

Keenan, E. O., & Schieffelin, B. (1976). Topic as a discourse notion: A study of topic in the conversations of children and adults. In C. Li (Ed.), *Subject and topic* (pp. 336–384). New York: Academic Press.

Kelly, J. A. (1982). *Social skills training.* New York: Springer.

Kolvin, I., Fundidis, T., George, G. S., Wrate, R. M., & Scarth, L. (1979). Predictive importance: behaviour. In T. Fundidis, I. Kolvin, & R. Garside, (Eds.), *Speech retarded and deaf children: Their psychological development* (pp. 69–76). London: Academic Press.

Landon, S. J., & Sommers, R. K. (1979). Talkativeness and children's linguistic abilities. *Language and Speech, 22,* 269–275.

Lerea, L. A. (1956). A preliminary study of verbal behavior and speech fright. *Speech Monographs, 23,* 220–223.

Leary, M. (1983). The conceptual distinctions are important: Another look at communication apprehension and related constructs. *Human Communication Research, 10,* 305–312.

Lee, L. L., & Canter, S. H. (1971). Developmental syntax scoring: A clinical procedure for estimating syntactic development in children's spontaneous speech. *Journal of Speech and Hearing Disorders, 40,* 315–340.

Matarazzo, J., & Wiens, A. (1972). *The interview: Research on it's anatomy and structure.* Chicago: Aldine.

McCarthy, D. (1929). A comparison of children's language in different situations and its' relation to personality traits. *Journal of Genetic Psychology, 36,* 583–591.

McCarthy, D. (1954). Language development in children. In L. Carmichael (Ed.), *Manual of Child Psychology* (pp. 492–630). New York: Wiley.

McLure, L. F., Chinsky, J. M., & Larcen, S. W. (1978). Enhancing problem solving performance in an elementary school setting. *Journal of Educational Psychology, 70,* 504–513.

McCroskey, J. C. (1977). *Quiet children and the classroom teacher.* Falls Church, VA: Speech Communication Association.

McCroskey, J. C. (1984). The communication apprehensive perspective. In J. A. Daly, & J. C. McCroskey (Eds.), *Avoiding communication* (pp. 13–38). Beverly Hills: Sage.

McCroskey, J. C., & Anderson, J. F. (1976). The relationship between communication apprehension and academic achievement among college students. *Human Communication Research, 3,* 73–81.

McCroskey, J. C., & Daly, J. A. (1976). Teachers expectations of the communication apprehensive child in the elementary school. *Human Communication Research, 3,* 67–72.

McCroskey, J. C., Daly, J. A., Richmond, V., & Falcione, R. (1977). Studies of the relationship between communication apprehension and self-esteem. *Human Communication Research, 3,* 264–277.

McCroskey, J. C., & Richmond, V. P. (1982). Communication apprehension and shyness: conceptual and operational distinctions. *Central States Speech Journal, 33,* 458–468.

McTear, M. (1985). Pragmatic disorders: A case study of conversational disability. *British Journal of Disorders of Communication, 20,* 119–127.

Meehl, P. E. (1978). Theoretical risks and tabular asterisks: Sir Karl, Sir Ronald, and the slow progress of soft psychology. *Journal of Consulting and Clinical Psychology, 46,* 806–834.

Mirenda, P. L., & Donnellan, A. M. (1986). Effects of adult interaction style on conversational behavior in students with severe communication problems. *Language, Speech and Hearing Services in the Schools, 17,* 126–141.

Murray, D. C. (1971). Talk, silence, and anxiety. *Psychological Bulletin, 75,* 244–260.

Nelson, K. (1981). Social cognition in a script framework. In J. H. Flavell & L. Ross (Eds.), *Social cognitive development: Frontiers and possible futures* (pp. 97–118). New York: Cambridge University Press.

Olson, W., & Koetzle V. (1936). Amount and rate of talking of young children. *Journal of Experimental Education, 5,* 175-179.

Petrie, I. (1975). Characteristics and progress of a group of language disordered children with severe receptive difficulties. *British Journal of Disorders of Communication, 10,* 123-133.

Phillips, G. M. (1984). Reticence — A perspective on social withdrawal. In J. A. Daly & J. C. McCroskey (Eds.), *Avoiding communication* (pp. 51-56) Beverly Hills: Sage.

Pilkonis, P. A. (1977). The behavioral consequences of shyness. *Journal of Personality, 45,* 596-611.

Puttalaz, M. (1983). Predicting children's sociometric status from their behavior. *Child Development, 54,* 1417-1426.

Putallaz, M., & Gottman, J. (1981). An interactional model of children's entry into peer groups. *Child Development, 52,* 986-994.

Reznick, J., Kagan, J., Snidman, N., Gersten, M., Baak, K., & Rosenberg, A. (1986). Inhibited and uninhibited children: A follow-up study. *Child Development, 57,* 660-680.

Richmond, V. P., Beatty, M. J., & Dyba, P. (1985). Shyness and popularity: Children's views. *Western Journal of Speech Communication, 49,* 116-125.

Robinson, F. B. (1966). What parents and teachers should know about children who stutter. I. *Hearing and Speech News, 34,* 8-10.

Rowe, M. B. (1974). Wait-time and rewards as instructional variables, their influence on language, logic, and fate control. Part one — Wait time. *Journal of Research in Science Teaching, 11,* 81-94.

Rubin, K. H. (1982). Social and social-cognitive characteristics of young isolate, normal, and sociable children. In K. H. Rubin & H. S. Ross (Eds.), *Peer relationships and social skills in childhood* (pp. 353-374). New York: Springer-Verlag.

Rubin, K. H., & Borwick, D. (1984). The communicative skills of children who vary with regard to sociability. In H. Sypher & J. Applegate (Eds.), *Communication by children and adults: Social cognitive and strategic processes* (pp 152-170). Beverly Hills: Sage.

Rubin, K. H., Daniels-Beirness, T., & Bream, L. (1984). Social isolation and social problem solving: A longitudinal study. *Journal of Consulting and Clinical Psychology, 52,* 17-25.

Rubin, K. H., Hymel, S., & Mills, R. (1989). Sociability and social withdrawal in childhood stability and outcomes. *Journal of Personality, 57,* 237-255.

Rubin, K. H., & Krasnor, L. R. (1986). Social-cognitive and social perspectives on problem solving. In M. Perlmutter (Ed.), *Cognitive perspectives on children's social and behavioural development (The Minnesota Symposium on Child Development)* (Vol. 18, pp 1-68). Hillsdale, NJ: Lawrence Erlbaum Associates.

Rubin, K. H., & Mills, R. S. (1988). The many faces of social isolation in childhood. *Journal of Consulting and Clinical Psychology, 56,* 916-924.

Rutter, M. (1972). The effect of language delay on development. In M. Rutter & J. A. Martin, (Eds.), *The child with delayed speech* (pp 176-188). Clinics in Developmental Medicine, No 43. London: Heinemann Medical Books.

Schank, R., & Abelson, R. P. (1977). *Scripts, plans, goals and understanding.* Hillsdale, NJ: Lawrence Erlbaum Associates.

Semel, E. M., & Wiig, L. (1980). *Clinical evaluation of language functions.* Columbus, OH: Merrill.

Sibinga, M. S., & Friedman, C. J. (1971). Restraint of speech. *Pediatrics, 48,* 116-122.

Simons, H. (1981). Conversation piece: The practice of interviewing in case study research. In C. Adelman (Ed.), *Uttering, muttering* (pp 27-50). London: Grant McIntyre.

Smith, M. E. (1926). An investigation of the development of the sentence and the extent of vocabulary in young children. *University of Iowa Studies in Child Welfare, 3.* No. 8.

Smythe, M. J., & Powers, W. G. (1978). When Galatea is apprehensive: the effect on communication apprehension of teacher expectations. In B. D. Ruben (Ed.), *Communication yearbook 2* (pp 487-491). New Brunswick, NJ: Transaction Books.

Snyder, L. (1978). Communication and cognitive abilities and disabilities in the sensori-motor period. *Merrill-Palmer Quarterly, 24,* 161–180.

Stevenson, H. W., Parker, T., Wilkinson, A. M., Hegion, A., & Fish, F. (1976). Predictive value of teacher's ratings of young children. *Journal of Educational Psychology, 68,* 507–515.

Stohl, C. (1989). Children's social networks and the development of communicative competence. In J. F. Nussbaum (Ed.), *Lifespan communication: Normative processes* (pp 53–77). Hillsdale, NJ: Lawrence Erlbaum Associates.

Thorndike, R. L., Hagen, E. P., & Sattler, J. M. (1986). *Stanford-Binet Intelligence Scale Fourth Edition.* Chicago: Riverside.

Van Kleeck, A., & Street, R. (1982). Does reticence just mean talking less? Qualitative differences in the language of talkative and reticent preschoolers. *Journal of Psycholinguistic Research, 11,* 609–629.

Vriniotis, C., Evans, M. A. (1988). *Children's social communicative competence and its relationship to classroom participation.* Paper presented at the Biennial meeting of the University of Waterloo Conference on Child Development, Waterloo, Ontario.

Wechsler, D. (1967). *Wechsler Preschool and Primary Scale of Intelligence.* New York: Psychological Corporation.

Wechsler, D. (1974). *Wechsler Intelligence Scale for Children – Revised.* New York: Psychological Corporation.

Wells, G. (1985). Preschool literacy related activities and success in school. In D. R. Olson, N. Torrance, & A. Hildygard (Eds.), *Literacy, language, and learning: The nature and consequences of reading and writing* (pp. 229–255). New York: Cambridge University Press.

Whitehurst, G. J., Falco, F. L., Lonigan, C. J., Fischel, J. E., DeBaryshe, B. D., Valdez-Menchaca, M. C., & Caufield, M. (1988). Accelerating language development through book reading. *Developmental Psychology, 24,* 552–559.

Wolf, M., & Dickinson, D. (1985). From oral to written language: Transitions in the school years. In J. B. Gleason (Ed.), *The development of language* (pp. 227–276). Columbus, OH: Merrill.

Wood, H. A., & Wood, D. J. (1984). An experimental evaluation of the effects of five styles of teacher conversation in the language of hearing impaired children. *Journal of Child Psychology and Psychiatry, 25,* 45–62.

Young, F. M. (1941). An analysis of certain variables in a developmental study of language. *Genetic Psychology Monographs, 23,* 3–141.

Zimbardo, P. G. (1977). *Shyness: What it is, what to do about it.* Reading MA: Addison-Wesley.

Zimbardo, P. G., & Radl, S. L. (1981). *The shy child: A parent's guide to preventing and overcoming shyness from infancy to adulthood.* New York: McGraw Hill.

IV PEER AND SELF PERCEPTION

11 Children's Perceptions of Social Withdrawal: Changes Across Age

Alastair Younger, Carole Gentile, and Kim Burgess
University of Ottawa

Over the past 20 years, peer relationships in childhood have assumed an increasingly important role in the study of children's social development. Social maladjustment in children is of particular concern to many investigators because of a number of studies linking it with later adjustment problems and psychopathology in adolescence and adulthood (see Parker & Asher, 1987, for a comprehensive review of this area). Two patterns of social maladjustment are frequently described: aggression and social withdrawal. Aggression (also labeled Conduct Problems, Undercontrolled, or Externalizing behavior) is a broad factor that includes physical and verbal aggression, disruptiveness, and attention-seeking. Social Withdrawal (also labeled Personality Problems, Overcontrolled, or Internalizing behavior) is an equally broad factor that includes shyness, anxiety, oversensitivity, and social isolation. These two patterns of behavior have been consistently identified as broad, independent factors underlying ratings of maladjusted childhood behavior provided by teachers, parents, and clinicians (see Achenbach, 1980; Achenbach & Edelbrock, 1978; Kohn, 1977; Quay, 1986; and Ross, 1980, for comprehensive reviews of this literature).

Although central to adult perceptions of childhood maladjustment, however, the aggression — social withdrawal distinction may not be as central to how children view and categorize maladjusted behavior in their peers (Younger, Schwartzman, & Ledingham, 1985). Differences in children's and adults' views of maladjustment are important because of the increasing tendency among researchers in the area of children's peer relationships to employ children as assessors of the social adjustment of their peers. The research discussed in this chapter focuses on the issues of how children view aggression and social withdrawal in their peers, how this view changes across age, and what social-cognitive factors may underlie age-related changes in children's views of aggression and social withdrawal. This research has been guided by the underlying practical need to determine the ability of children at different ages to serve as assessors of the social maladjustment of their peers; that is, to report accurately on aggressive and socially withdrawn behaviors their peers have displayed.

PEER ASSESSMENT

Investigators of children's peer relationships frequently employ children as assessors of the social functioning of their peers. The popularity of such peer assessment derives from the fact that children represent not only observers of, but also participants in, the social behavior of their peers; therefore, their opinions offer the investigator unique assessment information (Wiggins & Winder, 1961). Indeed, the value of peer assessment is underscored by findings that childhood peer evaluations can predict later psychopathology in adulthood, and may identify "at risk" children better than ratings by adults such as teachers or parents (Cowen, Pederson, Babigian, Izzo, & Trost, 1973; Rolf, 1972; 1976).

Peer assessment procedures have taken various forms. Some investigators have focused primarily upon the dimension of peer acceptance versus rejection, collecting measures of liking or disliking by the peer group. Such sociometric procedures provide an overall indication of a child's positive or negative reputation among his or her peers, but provide little indication why such a reputation exists (Asher & Hymel, 1981). Consequently, other investigators have moved away from such undifferentiated evaluations, toward peer assessments of specific patterns of maladjusted behavior. Such behaviorally specific procedures involve presenting child assessors with a list of maladjusted social behaviors and asking them to nominate those of their peers who are best described by each behavior. This latter type of peer assessment measure, the best known of which are the Revised Class Play (RCP; Masten, Morison, & Pelligrini, 1985) and the Pupil Evaluation Inventory (PEI; Pekarik, Prinz, Liebert, Weintraub, & Neale, 1976), has been considered valuable by both researchers and clinicians because it provides a parallel to behavior-rating scales frequently employed with adult assessors, focusing on the broad factors of aggression and social withdrawal.

CHILDREN'S VIEWS OF AGGRESSION AND SOCIAL WITHDRAWAL

Our interest in children's views of aggression and social withdrawal developed from findings suggesting that these two patterns of behavior are not as reliably assessed by child raters as by adult raters and perhaps are not central to children's view of maladjustment in their peers at all ages. This notion that children view maladjustment differently than do adults emerged from the initial findings of a longitudinal study conducted by Ledingham (1981). This investigator identified children who were highly aggressive, highly withdrawn, or high on both aggression and social withdrawal concurrently. Using peer nominations on the Pupil Evaluation Inventory (Pekarik et al., 1976), Ledingham identified these three groups of malad-justed children at three grade levels — grades one, four, and seven. An interesting grade-related shift appeared in the joint distribution of the children's peer nominations of aggression and social withdrawal. First graders nominated the same peers concurrently for both aggression and social withdrawal items far more often than had been expected, and for either aggression or social withdrawal alone far less frequently than predicted. The same pattern was evident, though to a lesser degree, in the assessments of fourth graders. However, in the assessments of the seventh graders, the pattern was reversed. Children in this grade nominated few peers concurrently for both aggression and social withdrawal items, se-lecting many more instead as either high on aggression alone or high on social withdrawal alone. Considering the large body of literature indicating the orthogonality of these two factors in adult assessments of child maladjustment (cf. Quay, 1986), these findings raised questions as to whether children's views of maladjustment differed from those of adults. Thus, this intriguing age-related shift in children's peer nominations provided the impetus for a series of studies we conducted to examine children's perceptions of social withdrawal and aggression in their peers, and how these perceptions changed across age.

AGE CHANGES IN CHILDREN'S PEER NOMINATIONS

Our initial studies of children's perceptions of aggression and social withdrawal (Younger, Schwartzman, & Ledingham, 1985, 1986) employed multidimensional scaling to examine children's views of these patterns of maladjustment in their peers at different ages. Multidimensional scaling is a geometric model that is used to uncover the structure or organization underlying measures of similarity or association among various stimuli (see Kruskal & Wish, 1978). It is a procedure that has gained popularity in studies of social perception (e.g., Rosenberg & Sedlack, 1972) because of its ability to represent measures of similarity among sets of stimuli as measures of distance between points in Euclidian space. It enables investigators to "map out" the conceptual structure underlying subjects' social perceptions in such a way that stimuli that are perceived as very similar are located near one another, whereas those that are perceived as different are located far from one another in the spatial representation. We believed that multidimensional scaling would prove useful in examining the organization underlying children's peer nominations for aggression and social withdrawal, allowing us to determine the cohesiveness of these patterns of behavior, their distinctness from other behaviors, as well as dimensions of social perception underlying children's peer assessments.

Peer Nominations on the PEI.   Our initial investigation focused on children's peer nominations. In this study (Younger et al., 1985), we examined the peer nominations of 325 first-grade, 356 fourth-grade, and 298 seventh-grade children. Following Ledingham's (1981) procedure, the children were required to select up to four peers who they felt were best described by each item on the PEI. This measure contains 19 aggression items (e.g., "Someone who says he can beat everybody up," "Someone who gets into trouble a lot), 9 social withdrawal items (e.g., "Someone who is too shy to make friends easily," "Someone whose feelings get hurt easily"), and 5 likability items (e.g., "Someone who helps others," "Someone who is especially nice"). With first graders, because of their limited reading and attentional abilities, we used the abbreviated 16-item version of the measure that Ledingham (1981) and Pekarik et al. (1976) employed with younger children; this version includes 9 aggression, 5 social withdrawal, and 2 likability items, all drawn from the longer version of the instrument (see Fig. 11.1 for the full set of PEI items).

To examine children's *perceptions* of aggression and social withdrawal in their peers on the basis of their PEI nominations, the usual scoring procedure for the instrument had to be modified. Typically, scoring a measure such as the PEI involves summing across all the nominations received by a particular child on each item, to get an index of the child's total score on that item. Such a procedure, however, would have obscured the perceptions of the child evaluators. That is, although the usual scoring procedure would indicate how the class as a whole viewed these behaviors in each peer, it would not reveal how each child evaluator viewed aggression and social withdrawal in his or her peers. Because we were interested in children's *perceptions* of these patterns of maladjustment in their peers, we focused on the way each peer nominator used the items in assessing his or her classmates. Thus, we derived a measure of inter-item association that was based on co-occurring nominations. That is, for all pairs of items, we calculated the number of times each child evaluator picked the same peer as best described by *both* items. The rationale behind this procedure was that the more frequently a child evaluator nominated the same peers for both members of a pair of items, the more similar or associated those items must be in the perceptions of that peer rater. In fact, similar measures of co-occurrence have been used in other multidimensional scaling studies to

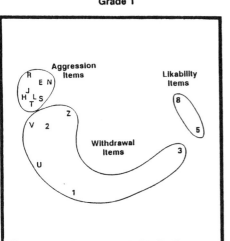

Grade 1

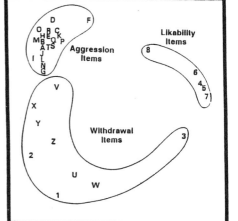

Grade 4

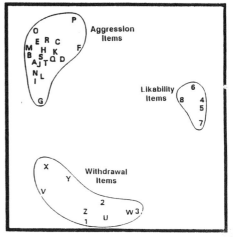

Grade 7

AGGRESSION ITEMS
A. Can't sit still
B. Get others into trouble
C. Act stuck-up
D. Play the clown
E. Start fights
F. Tell others what to do
G. Get into trouble
H. Make fun of others
I. Do strange things
J. Bother others
K. Get mad easily
L. Don't pay attention to the teacher
M. Rude to teacher
N. Act like babies
O. Mean and cruel
P. Give dirty looks
Q. Show-off
R. Say can beat up peers
S. Exaggerate
T. Complain

WITHDRAWAL ITEMS
U. Too shy to make friends
V. Feelings easily hurt
W. Never have a good time
X. Upset when called on in class
Y. Chosen last for activities
Z. Have few friends
1. Unhappy or sad
2. Don't want to play
3. Not noticed much

LIKABILITY ITEMS
4. Help others
5. Liked by everyone
6. Best friend
7. Especially nice
8. Always seem to understand things

FIG. 11.1. Multidimensional scaling representations of the similarity among the PEI items derived from children's peer nominations. Reproduced from Younger, Schwartzman, & Ledingham, 1985, © American Psychological Association.

produce "derived" measures of inter-item similarity (cf. Kruskal & Wish, 1978). These derived measures of inter-item similarity were then analyzed separately at each grade level using Kruskal, Young, and Seery's (1978) KYST multidimensional scaling procedure.

The results of the multidimensional scaling analyses are shown in Fig.

11.1. As can be seen, there was a clear grade effect in the organization of the PEI items. At lower grades (particularly the first grade), the items were largely organized with reference to a single dimension that differentiated prosocial behaviors from maladjusted behaviors. We labeled this an evaluative (or good-bad) dimension. As grade level increased, however, a second dimension that distinguished withdrawn forms of maladjustment from aggressive maladjustment became increasingly prominent. This second dimension we labeled an active-passive dimension. In addition, the three categories of items were not viewed equivalently at all grades. Aggression and likability items clustered into cohesive categories at all grades. Social withdrawal items, however, did not cluster into a distinct category at the first grade. Rather, some social withdrawal items were more closely associated with aggression items than with other social withdrawal items in first graders' peer ratings, and some were more closely associated with likability. Moreover, whereas aggression items and likability items were located at opposite poles of the evaluative dimension, social withdrawal items were scattered between the two poles. With increasing grade, social withdrawal items became increasingly distinct from the other two categories and formed an increasingly cohesive category.

Thus, the multidimensional scaling analyses of children's peer nominations revealed two major findings. First, unlike aggression, social withdrawal did not appear to be a well-defined component of young children's views of maladjusted behavior in their peers, although it became better defined with age. In fact, at older ages social withdrawal was as well defined as aggression. Second, at least to some extent, social withdrawal may have been poorly defined in the perceptions of younger children because it did not fit well into a good-bad, or social evaluative distinction that appeared to dominate the perspective of younger children.

Existing literature offered partial support for this notion that young children do not have a well-defined view of social withdrawal. For example, several factor analytic studies of children's peer nominations had failed to identify a distinct social withdrawal factor (Mitchel, 1956; Rubenstein, Fisher, & Iker, 1975), despite identifying a clear aggression factor. In addition, other researchers had reported age differences in the reliability of children's peer nominations for social withdrawal, paralleling the age shift we observed. Moscowitz, Schwartzman, and Ledingham (1985) reported poorer test-retest reliability of peer nominations for social withdrawal than for aggression at the first grade. However, the reliability increased across grade, such that in the fourth and seventh grades peer nominations for social withdrawal were as reliable as those for aggression. Finally, Coie and Pennington (1976) reported findings concerning children's perceptions of social withdrawal that were highly germane to our observations. These researchers examined children's descriptions of the behavior of maladjusted peers and reported that, until the seventh grade, when children described maladjustment they described aggression — social withdrawal was conspicuously absent in the peer descriptions of younger children. However, at older ages, the reverse was true: older children focused on social withdrawal when describing maladjusted peers, while aggression was featured with considerably less frequency in their descriptions. Our findings fit well with these latter reports, clearly underscoring the notion that social withdrawal played an increasingly important role in children's perceptions of maladjustment as age increased.

The literature also supported our finding that social perception in young children may be dominated by a social evaluative, or good versus bad, distinction (Livesley & Bromley, 1973; Saltz, Dunin-Markiewicz, & Rourke, 1975; Yarrow & Campbell, 1963) into which aggression may fit better than social withdrawal. The age trends we observed in the organization of children's peer nominations of aggression and social withdrawal, therefore, fit well with existing findings concerning children's social perception.

Age Trends in Perception or in Behavior? Although the results of our analysis of children's peer nominations revealed an indisputable age difference, it was less certain that the effect represented changes solely in the perceptions of the peer nominators. That is, despite the fact that our measure of inter-item similarity was derived to reflect the raters' perceptions of their peers' behaviors, the measure was nonetheless derived from actual peer assessments of behavior. Thus, it was impossible to say for certain whether the age shift was the result of assessor-specific age differences in social perception or peer-specific age differences in behavior. This is because when using peer assessments, age of assessor and age of "assessee" are confounded — peers are almost always age-mates. Consequently, we conducted three studies designed to tease apart the perceptions of assessors from the behaviors of peers (Younger et al. 1986).

In the first study, we analyzed teacher nominations of aggression, social withdrawal, and likability, using the PEI with teachers from the same three grade levels as the children. Examining teacher nominations allowed us to hold age of assessor constant across grade level, permitting age differences attributable to the behavior of the "assessees" to be examined. Had the age effects in children's peer nominations represented differences in the aggressive and withdrawn behaviors actually displayed by their peers, similar trends should have been observed across grade in the organization of the teacher nominations. Such was not the case. No grade-related differences were found in the organization of the teacher nominations — aggression, social withdrawal, and likability items clustered into cohesive categories that were distinct from one another at all three grade levels.

In the second study, we collected children's nominations for peers who were not their age-mates. In this study, we examined first-grade children's assessments of the behavior of seventh-grade peers, and seventh-grade children's assessments of the behavior of first-grade peers. Results of this study also pointed to differences in the perceptions of the peer assessors playing a greater role than age differences in the behavior of those who were assessed. First graders' assessments of even the behavior of older peers were organized largely with respect to an undifferentiated evaluative dimension, much like their assessments of the behavior of same-age peers. In contrast, seventh graders' assessments of even younger peers reflected their use of both social-evaluative and active-passive dimensions.

In the third study, we examined how children conceptually organize their perceptions of aggressive and socially withdrawn behaviors, asking them whether a peer who displayed one aggressive, socially withdrawn, or likable behavior might also display a second behavior, comparing all possible pairs of behaviors. We thus assessed their existing beliefs concerning how behaviors co-occur in others. Multidimensional scaling revealed an age effect in the organization of such beliefs about how behaviors co-occur, paralleling the shift observed in children's peer nominations. Thus, results of all three studies emphasized the importance of changes across age in how children view maladjustment in their peers, specifically their views of socially withdrawn peer behavior.

SOCIAL-COGNITIVE FACTORS IN CHILDREN'S PERCEPTIONS OF WITHDRAWAL

Our more recent research has delineated factors responsible for this age shift in children's perceptions of social withdrawal. In two recent studies (Younger & Boyko, 1987; Younger & Piccinin, 1989), we have examined social-cognitive factors that may underlie the shift. We have proposed that the age changes in children's peer perceptions of social withdrawal reported by Younger et al. (1985) may be attributable to age differences in the relative ease with which children process information concerning these patterns of maladjustment in their peers. It is our contention that schema theory in social psychology is highly relevant to the understanding of children's views of social withdrawal and other maladjusted behaviors in their peers.

Schema Theory.   Theory and research in cognitive-social psychology suggest that social perception may be guided by cognitive structures, or social schemas, that help organize and give meaning to social information. Such schemas represent our experience-based abstractions about the typical behavior, traits, or other characteristics of certain types of people (such as the typical extravert, the typical introvert, the typical socially withdrawn child, etc.). These schemas guide perception, memory, and social inference. According to schema theory, we categorize people according to our person schemas. The schema then functions to: (a) direct our attention to schema-relevant information about that person; (b) influence how we categorize and encode such information into memory; (c) facilitate our recalling of schema-consistent information about the person; and (d) assist in our making predictions about the person's future behavior, and so on (see Cantor & Kihlstrom, 1987; Cantor & Mischel, 1977, 1979a, 1979b; Fiske & Taylor, 1984; Taylor & Crocker, 1981). In other words, social schemas facilitate the processing of social information.

The information-processing function of social schemas has frequently been assessed by researchers through the use of memory tasks. Typically, individuals are presented with a description of an individual and later their memory for the behaviors that were included in the description is assessed (e.g., Cantor & Mischel, 1977, 1979a). Both free recall (i.e., "Tell me all you can remember about what the person did?") and recognition memory (i.e., "which of the following list of behaviors did the person display?") have been assessed. Using these procedures, it has been found that if individuals possess a well-defined social schema pertaining to the traits, behaviors, or other characteristics presented to them, they are able to encode them readily into memory and recall them easily later. But, social information that doesn't fit such a schema is less attended to, less readily encoded into memory, and not easily recalled (see Fiske & Taylor, 1984, for a review of this literature).

One of the best examples of the functioning of such social schemas in children can be found in research on gender-role stereotypes. Researchers in this field describe a "gender schema" (Bem, 1981) that affects children's perceptions and memory of the behavior of others. Consistent with schema theory, it has been observed that, after hearing a description of an individual engaging in a certain activity, children more readily recall gender-consistent over gender-inconsistent information, and may even inaccurately recall the information such that the activity and the gender of the actor are consistent (Bradbard & Endsley, 1983; Koblinsky & Cruse, 1981; Liben & Signorella, 1980; Martin & Halverson, 1983; Nesdale & McLaughlin, 1987). Such research with gender stereotypes illustrates quite well the selective information-processing and recall functions of social schemas.

Aggression and Withdrawal as Social Schemas. We maintain that schema theory is also highly relevant to the study of children's perceptions of aggression and social withdrawal. The results of the multidimensional scaling analyses strongly suggested that it may be easier for young children to categorize a peer as aggressive than as socially withdrawn. Certainly, aggression comprised a better-defined category of behavior at young ages, suggesting that perhaps aggression is a better-defined or better-used social schema for young children. The relevance of schema theory to peer assessment becomes more obvious when we consider the similarities between the recall and recognition-memory tasks that cognitive-social psychologists have used to assess the functioning of social schemas and the peer nomination procedures used to collect peer assessments of social maladjustment. Both procedures are memory tasks. That is, in the peer assessment situation children are not asked to systematically and objectively record their peers' on-going behavior (although there is evidence that even systematic observation can be influenced by the observer's social schemas — see Lyons & Serbin, 1986). Rather, they are asked to report on behaviors they have seen their classmates perform in the past. Typically, children are presented with a list of classroom behaviors, including aggressive and socially withdrawn behaviors, and asked: "Check off (or list) who in your class best fit each item" (see Masten et al., 1986, or Pekarik et al., 1976, for descriptions of the peer nomination procedure). Such a procedure, in our view, clearly involves memory. In fact, the peer nomination procedure is not very different from the previously discussed procedures used by cognitive-social psychologists to assess individuals' memories for behaviors and traits of others. Thus, it may well be that what we are assessing using peer nominations is not just the behavior of a child's peers, but also how well the rater has processed and can recall the behavior of his or her peers — in other words, the functions of the rater's social schemas (see Younger & Piccinin, 1989, for further discussion of the relevance of schema theory to children's peer assessments).

In two studies, we examined the roles of aggression and withdrawal as social schemas underlying children's peer perceptions. Borrowing from cognitive-social psychology, we employed memory tasks to assess the ease with which children of different ages encode and recall descriptions of the behavior of aggressive and socially withdrawn peers. Children from grades 1, 3, 5, and 7 were presented descriptions of hypothetical aggressive and socially withdrawn age-mates, following which their memory for the behaviors of these hypothetical characters was assessed. These hypothetical characters were developed using items from existing peer and teacher assessment instruments. The aggressive character was described as physically and verbally aggressive, disruptive, and attention-seeking (e.g., "is mean and cruel to other children," "tells other children what to do," "complains a lot," "gets into trouble a lot," "starts a fight over nothing," "makes fun of people"). The socially withdrawn character was described as shy, oversensitive, and socially withdrawn or isolated (e.g., "has very few friends," "cries for nothing," "feelings get hurt easily," "is usually chosen last to join in a group," "isn't noticed much by the other kids," "gets scared easily"). Consistent with schema theory, we had expected that in listening to these character descriptions, children, like adults, would employ relevant social schemas to make sense out of, organize, store, and recall the descriptors. Consequently, if the age differences found earlier in children's peer nominations of aggression and social withdrawal reflected differences in the social schemas underlying their peer perceptions, then parallel age-related trends should also have emerged in their recall for the items. In other words, at all grades children should have readily recalled the behaviors of the aggressive child, implying the existence of a well-defined schema for that type of person at all ages. In contrast, only older children should have readily recalled the behaviors of the socially withdrawn child, reflecting their increasing use, across age, of the schema for social withdrawal.

We assessed memory for these descriptions using free recall (Younger & Boyko, 1987) and recognition memory (Younger & Piccinin, 1989). In both studies, our hypotheses were confirmed. Regardless of type of memory task used, younger children recalled aggression much better than social withdrawal. Moreover, as predicted, recall for social withdrawal improved markedly with increasing age. Interestingly, the free recall study indicated that recall for social withdrawal not only improved with increasing age, but was superior to recall for aggression at older ages (Younger & Boyko, 1987). This finding bore remarkable similarity to Coie and Pennington's (1976) observation that whereas younger children described maladjusted peers almost exclusively as aggressive, older children described such peers more frequently as socially withdrawn than as aggressive. Thus, these results highlighted even further differences in the salience of aggressive and socially withdrawn behaviors to children at different ages. Children's free recall for the aggressive and socially withdrawn descriptions is illustrated in Fig. 11.2

These findings support the notion of age-related differences in the ease with which children process information about aggressive and socially withdrawn behaviors displayed by other children. Even children as young as six- or seven-years-old readily attend to and easily recall information about aggressive peer behaviors. This does not appear to be the case, however, for social withdrawal. Our younger subjects were inclined to pay less attention to social withdrawal and were less able to recall or identify instances of socially withdrawn behavior in other children. This observation has been confirmed in a recent replication of these recall studies, conducted by Bukowski (1990), in which similarly striking differences between younger and older children's recall for instances of socially withdrawn behavior were observed. We interpret these differences as evidence of the early emergence

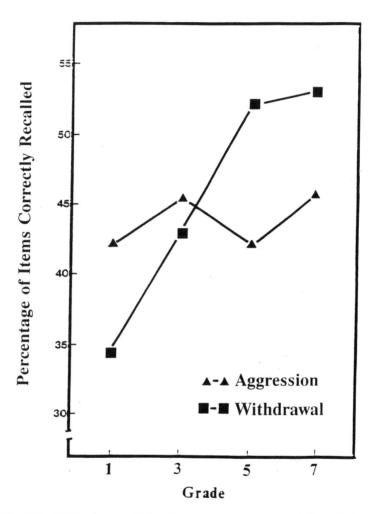

FIG. 11.2 Children's recall for the aggressive and socially withdrawn character descriptions. Derived from Younger & Boyko, 1987, © Society for Research in Child Development.

of a social schema into which children can encode aggressive behaviors, but the later emergence of a schema into which socially withdrawn behaviors fit.

Reasons for the Later emergence of the Social Withdrawal Schema. There may be several reasons why children develop the aggression schema earlier than the schema for social withdrawal. One possible explanation that we have examined explains the age effect with reference to the social-evaluative dimension found to underlie children's peer nominations. As discussed earlier in this chapter, young children's perceptions of aggression and social withdrawal in their peers, as revealed through the organization of their peer nominations, seemed strongly influenced by a good versus bad distinction—the social-evaluative dimension (Younger et al., 1985). Schemas for aggressive and socially withdrawn behaviors may emerge at different points in development because they are not equally well described in terms of such a social-evaluative distinction. Thus, one explanation why the schema for aggression emerges early is that it fits quite well into this fundamental good versus bad distinction. There is plenty of evidence that children view aggression negatively—aggressive behavior is probably the most reliable correlate of peer rejection that has been identified (Coie, Dodge, & Kupersmidt, 1990; Hartup, 1983). Moreover, this negative view of aggression may be strengthened by the fact that children frequently serve as targets of their peers' aggressive behaviors. Socially withdrawn behaviors, on the other hand, are not so easy to categorize. Especially at younger ages, when solitary activity is relatively common (Rubin, 1985; Rubin, Fein, & Vandenberg, 1983), socially withdrawn behaviors may not be viewed negatively by children. Certainly, such behavior is seldom targeted towards other peers and seldom hurts anyone. Thus, at young ages, social withdrawal likely does not fit easily into the fundamental good-bad distinction. With age, however, as children become increasingly interactive (Greenwood, Todd, Hops, & Walker, 1982), socially withdrawn behavior may be viewed more negatively because it appears more atypical and dysfunctional. In other words, social withdrawal may be viewed in an increasingly negative fashion across age. Although there are less data concerning the association of social withdrawal and rejection, the evidence does indicate that, at least by about grade 4 or 5, socially withdrawn children are also rejected by their peers (Hymel & Rubin, 1985; Rubin, 1990; Rubin, Hymel, LeMare, & Rowden, 1989). Consequently, the early emergence of the schema for aggression and the later emergence of the schema for social withdrawal may reflect how well these patterns of behavior fit the more basic evaluative dimension underlying children's peer perceptions.

We examined this hypothesis by assessing children's opinions of aggressive and socially withdrawn behavior (Younger & Piccinin, 1989). In addition to examining their recognition memory for behaviors of the aggressive and socially withdrawn characters, we questioned children about whether they and their classmates would like the hypothetical aggressive and socially withdrawn peers as friends. Children's assessments of the likability of the characters are illustrated in Fig. 11.3. As can be seen, these results provided clear support for the hypothesized link between children's increasingly negative view of social withdrawal across age and the emergence of their social schema for this pattern of behavior. Again, we

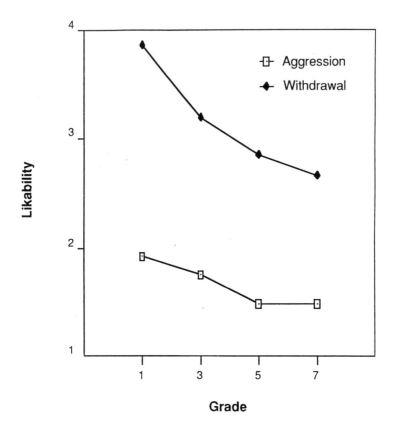

FIG. 11.3 Likability of the aggressive and socially withdrawn characters. Derived from Younger & Piccinin, 1989, which is © Society for Research in Child Development.

observed a grade-related shift in children's perceptions of the socially withdrawn character, but no such shift for the aggressive character. Likability of the aggressive character was consistently low across all four grade levels (i.e., grades 1, 3, 5, and 7), whereas the socially withdrawn character, though favorably viewed by young children, declined significantly in likability across grade. This age-related shift in likability parallels similar shifts in children's recall (Younger & Boyko, 1987) and recognition memory of the socially withdrawn character's behavior (Younger & Piccinin, 1989), as well as in the cohesiveness of their peer nominations of social withdrawal (Younger et al., 1985).

There are likely other factors, in addition to likability, that contribute to age differences in the emergence of schemas for aggression and social withdrawal. The literature indicates, for example, that in their conceptions of others, young children focus on concrete, observable behavior, whereas older children view others in terms of underlying dispositions, traits, motives, and so on (Barenboim, 1981; Livesley & Bromley, 1973; Peevers & Secord, 1973; Rholes & Ruble, 1984). Aggression and social withdrawal differ with respect to this dimension as well. Aggression is largely a behavioral construct, referring to things a person *does*. In contrast, although social withdrawal can also be described behaviorally, more frequently it refers to inner states and dispositions — what a peer *is like* or how a peer *feels*. Thus, the early development of the aggression schema contrasted with the later emergence of the social withdrawal schema may reflect such differences in how these two patterns of maladjustment fit with children's characteristic ways of viewing others at different ages.

SUBTYPES OF SOCIAL WITHDRAWAL

It appears from the studies just described that social withdrawal, as a category of maladjustment, becomes increasingly important to children's view of maladjustment across age. Moreover, it also appears that social withdrawal becomes increasingly negative in children's view with increasing age. However, do these age-related differences apply to all forms of social withdrawal, or only to certain types of withdrawal? This question is important, because, as Rubin and Mills (1988) point out, the construct of social withdrawal, as used in the peer relationships literature, and as assessed by peer nomination instruments, is heterogeneous; it confuses shyness and oversensitivity (i.e., passive withdrawal *from* the peer group) with peer rejection (i.e., active isolation *by* the peer group). Although these different "subtypes" of social withdrawal have not tended to emerge as distinct in factor analyses of children's peer nominations (cf. Masten et al., 1986; Pekarik et al., 1976), there is some evidence that children do distinguish between these constructs when nominating their peers for social withdrawal items. The multidimensional scaling analyses of children's peer nominations on the PEI (Younger et al., 1985) revealed that certain social withdrawal items were more associated with the negative pole of the evaluative dimension, where aggressive behaviors were located, than were others, although this effect declined with age as social withdrawal became a more cohesive category. PEI social withdrawal items such as "Those who are chosen last for group activities" and "Those who have few friends" seemed more negatively viewed than others, such as "Those who are not noticed much." Similarly, Rubin and associates (Rubin & Mills, 1988; Rubin, Hymel, Mills, & Rose-Krasnor, 1991) point out that two social withdrawal items on the Revised Class Play (Masten et al., 1986) — "Those who have trouble making friends" and "Someone who is often left out" — have substantial loadings on the aggressive factor of this instrument in addition to loading on the social withdrawal factor. Thus, an examination of children's peer nominations indicates that children may differentiate to some degree between these two types of social withdrawal.

The memory studies we conducted provide further evidence of such a distinction, although we believe this evidence must be interpreted cautiously as these studies were not designed a priori to examine children's schemas for passive withdrawal versus active isolation (to do so would involve presenting descriptions of two such socially withdrawn characters, comparing relative recall for each). Nevertheless, item analysis of our free-recall results (Younger & Boyko, 1987) revealed that some social withdrawal items were better recalled than others. The best recalled included crying for nothing, chosen last to join in a group, and having very few friends, whereas those least-well recalled included feelings being easily hurt, not being noticed much, giving in to other kids, and getting scared easily. These two clusters of best recalled versus least-well recalled items seem to fit the active-isolation versus passive-withdrawal distinction, with active isolation items better recalled than passive withdrawal items. Such differences in recall suggest that it is likely passive withdrawal, in contrast with active isolation, to which young children are least sensitive.

In a recent study (Younger & Daniels, in press), we directly examined children's ability to distinguish between these two forms of withdrawal by questioning them about the reasons for their peer nominations for the social withdrawal items on the Revised Class Play (RCP) peer nomination measure. Eighty-six children from grades one, three, and five completed the RCP, and then, in individual interviews, were asked about the reasons for their nominations (e.g., "You picked Billy for this item—What made him best suited for that item?"). Subsequently, their answers were categorized as reflecting either passive withdrawal (e.g., shyness, oversensitivity) or active isolation (e.g., peer rejection). For three items— "Someone who would rather play alone than with others," "Someone whose feelings get hurt easily," and "Someone who is very shy"—children's reasons for their nominations involved predominantly passive withdrawal. For three other items—"Someone who has trouble making friends," "Someone who can't get others to listen," and "Someone who is often left out"—children's reasons included largely active isolation. Children's reasons for their nominations for the remaining social withdrawal item— "Someone who is usually sad"—included both types of social withdrawal. These findings, therefore, provide evidence that children do differentiate between different forms of social withdrawal, and, in conjunction with the findings reported above, suggest that children may be more sensitive to and react less favorably to some forms of social withdrawal than to others.

SUMMARY AND DISCUSSION

The studies described indicate age differences in children's perceptions of social withdrawal in their peers. Young children do not seem to view social withdrawal as a cohesive category of co-occurring behaviors in their peers, in contrast to their view of aggression. With increasing age, however, their view of social withdrawal becomes better defined, such that by about 10–11 years old, children view social withdrawal as a category of maladjustment that is as cohesive as aggression. This shift across age in children's view of social withdrawal seems mediated by changes in the ease with which children process information concerning socially withdrawn behaviors in their peers. Based on children's recall for descriptions of socially withdrawn peers, we concluded that younger children do not easily fit socially withdrawn behaviors into their existing social schemas; however, a schema for social withdrawal emerges with age, and by about age 10 is used to process information concerning socially withdrawn behaviors as effectively as the schema for aggressive behavior. The age-related emergence of the withdrawal schema, moreover, does not appear affected by gender. The withdrawal schema emerges at about the same age in both girls and boys (Younger & Boyko, 1987; Younger & Piccinin, 1989) and is equally relevant to the behavior of girl and boy peers (Bukowski, 1990; Younger & Piccinin, 1989). In contrast, there is some evidence that the aggression schema may be used at an earlier age to process information about boys' than about girls' behavior (Bukowski, 1990).

The lack of a clear schema for social withdrawal in younger children appears related to their relatively neutral view of such behavior. That is, behavior that is either very positive or very negative seems to fit best into children's view of their peers (Younger & Piccinin, 1989). Young children do not appear to view social withdrawal negatively, though, with increasing age, children's view of social withdrawal becomes increasingly negative. In addition to differences in children's evaluative reactions to social withdrawal and aggression, social withdrawal differs from aggression in its reference to inner states as opposed to concrete behaviors. Thus, social withdrawal may not easily fit into young children's characteristic way of viewing others in terms of observable behavior. Even young children, however, differentiate between passive withdrawal from the peer group and active isolation by the peer group, and better remember the latter than the former in their peers.

Our initial reasons for looking at peer perceptions of social withdrawal came from an interest in the use of children as assessors of the social adjustment of their peers. As such, we believe our findings have important implications for the use of peer assessment with children. Whether children should be employed as assessors of social withdrawal in their peers depends on their age or level of cognitive maturity. Social withdrawal is not as salient or well-recalled by younger as by older children. It may be wiser, therefore, to employ some other means of assessing social withdrawal in young children. Of the two subtypes of social withdrawal, young children are likely better able to assess active isolation by the peer group than passive withdrawal from the peer group. By about grade four, however, children appear quite sensitive to socially withdrawn behavior and thus are likely more adept at assessing this form of maladjustment.

These findings, moreover, have implications extending beyond assessment issues. Age differences in the salience of social withdrawal to children may also indicate possible differences in the extent to which behaviors are problematic at different ages. That is, the peer group perspective is important because children not only observe behavior but also react to it. Such reaction to behavior, moreover, can exacerbate existing problems in a peer (Cowen et al., 1972). Our findings indicate that even young children notice, remember, and do not like aggression. Consequently, it seems likely that a child's reputation as aggressive develops quite early. However, children do not recall as well and do not dislike socially withdrawn behavior at young ages. Thus, children may not be labeled by their peers as socially withdrawn nor are socially withdrawn children likely to be rejected at young ages. By middle childhood, however, this has changed. In other words, as Rubin's (1990) findings also suggest, as social withdrawal increases in importance in children's social perceptions, it may also increase as an indicator and possibly as a predictor of maladjustment. Our findings suggest that such an increase across age in the importance of social withdrawal as a predictor of maladjustment may be at least partially attributable to changes in how the peer group views and reacts to socially withdrawn children.

REFERENCES

Achenbach, T. M. (1980). Behavior disorders of children and adolescents. In R. H. Woody (Ed.), *Encyclopedia of clinical assessment* (Vol. 1, pp. 113–127). Washington: Jossey-Bass.

Achenbach, T. M., & Edelbrock, C. G. (1978). The classification of child psychopathology: A review and analysis of empirical efforts. *Psychological Bulletin, 85,* 1275–1301.

Asher, S. R., & Hymel, S. (1981). Children's social competence in peer relations: Sociometric and behavioral assessment. In J. D. Wine & M. D. Smye (Eds.), *Social competence.* New York: Guilford.

Barenboim, C. (1981). The development of person perception in childhood and adolescence: from behavioral comparisons to psychological constructs to psychological comparisons. *Child Development, 52,* 129–144.

Bradbard, M. R., & Endsley, R. C. (1983). The effects of sex-typed labeling on children's information seeking and retention. *Sex Roles, 9,* 247–260.

Bem, S. (1981). Gender schema theory: A cognitive account of sex typing. *Psychological Review, 88,* 354–364.

Bukowski, W. (1990). Age differences in children's memory of information about aggressive, socially withdrawn, and prosociable boys and girls. *Child Development, 61,* 1326–1334.

Cantor, N., & Kihlstrom, J. F. (1987). *Personality and social intelligence,* Englewood Cliffs, NJ: Prentice-Hall.

Cantor, N., & Mischel, W. (1977). Traits as prototypes: Effects on recognition memory. *Journal of Personality and Social Psychology, 35,* 38–48.

Cantor, N., & Mischel, W. (1979a). Prototypicality and personality: Effects on free recall and personality impressions. *Journal of Research in Personality, 13,* 187–205.

Cantor, N., & Mischel, W. (1979b). Prototypes in person perception. In L. Berkowitz (Ed.), *Advances in experimental social psychology,* Volume 12 (pp. 3–52). New York: Academic Press.

Coie, J. D., Dodge, K. A., & Kupersmidt, J. B. (1990). Peer group behavior and social status. In S. R. Asher & J. D. Coie (Eds.), *Peer rejection in childhood* (pp 17–59). New York: Cambridge University Press.

Coie, J. D., & Pennington, B. F. (1976). Children's perceptions of deviance and disorder. *Child Development, 47,* 400–413.

Cowen, E. L., Pederson, A., Babigian, H., Izzo, L. D., & Trost, M. A. (1972). Long term follow up of early detected vulnerable children. *Journal of Consulting and Clinical Psychology, 41,* 438–446.

Fiske, S. T., & Taylor, S. E. (1984). *Social cognition.* New York: Random House.

Greenwood, C. R., Todd, N. M., Hops, H., & Walker, H. M. (1982). Behavior change targets in the assessment and treatment of socially withdrawn preschool children. *Behavioral Assessment, 4,* 273–297.

Hartup, W. W. (1983). Peer relations. In E. M. Hetherington (Ed.), *Handbook of child psychology, Vol. 4. Socialization, personality, and social development* (pp. 103–196, 4th ed.). New York: Wiley.

Hymel, S., & Rubin, K. H. (1985). Children with peer relationship and social skills problems: Conceptual, methodological, and developmental issues. In G. W. Whitehurst (Ed.), *Annals of child development* (Vol. 2, pp. 251–297). Greenwich, CT: JAI Press.

Koblinsky, S. A., & Cruse, D. F. (1981). The role of frameworks in children's retention of sex-related story content. *Journal of Experimental Psychology, 31,* 321–331.

Kohn, M. (1977). *Social competence, symptoms and underachievement in childhood: A longitudinal perspective.* Washington: Winston-Wiley.

Kruskal, J. B., & Wish, M. (1978). *Multidimensional scaling.* Beverly Hills, CA: Sage.

Kruskal, J. B., Young, F. W., & Seery, J. B. (1978). *How to use KYST-2A: A very flexible program to do multidimensional scaling and unfolding.* Murray Hill, NJ: Bell Telephone Laboratories.

Ledingham, J. E. (1981). Developmental patterns of aggressive and withdrawn behavior in childhood: A possible method for identifying preschizophrenics. *Journal of Abnormal Child Psychology, 9,* 1–22.

Liben, L. S., & Signorella, M. L. (1980). Gender related schemata and constructive memory in children. *Child Development, 51,* 11–18.

Livesley, W. J., & Bromley, D. B. (1973). *Person perception in childhood and adolescence.* London: Wiley.

Lyons, J. A., & Serbin, L. A. (1986). Observer bias in scoring boys' and girls' aggression. *Sex Roles, 14,* 301–313.

Martin, C. L., & Halverson, C. F. (1983). The effects of sex-typing schemas on young children's memory. *Child Development, 54,* 563-574.

Masten, A. S., Morison, P., & Pelligrini, D. S. (1985). A revised class play method of peer assessment. *Developmental Psychology, 21,* 523-533.

Mitchell, J. (1956). The factor analysis of a guess who questionnaire designed to identify significant patterns of behavior in children. *Journal of Personality, 24,* 376-386.

Moscowitz, D. E., Schwartzman, A. E., & Ledingham, J. E. (1985). Stability and change in aggression and withdrawal in middle childhood and adolescence. *Journal of Abnormal Psychology, 94,* 30-41.

Nesdale, A. R., & McLaughlin, K. (1987). Effects of sex stereotyping on young children's memories, prediction, and liking. *British Journal of Developmental Psychology, 5,* 231-241.

Parker, J. G., & Asher, S. R. (1987). Peer relations and later personal adjustment: Are low-accepted children at risk? *Psychological Bulletin, 102,* 357-389.

Peevers, B. H., & Secord, P. F. (1973). Developmental changes in attribution of descriptive concepts to persons. *Journal of Personality and Social Psychology, 27,* 120-128.

Pekarik, E. G., Prinz, R. J., Liebert, D. E., Weintraub, S., & Neale, J. M. (1976). The Pupil Evaluation Inventory: A sociometric technique for assessing children's social behavior. *Journal of Abnormal Child Psychology, 4,* 83-97.

Quay, H. C. (1986). Classification. In H. C. Quay & J. S. Werry (Eds.), *Psychopathological disorders of childhood* (third edition, pp. 1-34). New York: Wiley.

Rholes, W. S., & Ruble, D. N. (1984). Children's understanding of dispositional characteristics of others. *Child Development, 55,* 550-560.

Rolf, J. (1972). The social and academic competence of children vulnerable to schizophrenia and other behavior pathologies. *Journal of Abnormal Psychology, 80,* 225-243.

Rolf, J. (1976). Peer status and the directionality of symptomatic behavior. *American Journal of Orthopsychiatry, 46,* 74-81.

Rosenberg, S., & Sedlack, A. (1972). Structural representations of implicit personality theory. In L. Berkowitz (Ed.), *Advances in experimental social psychology* Vol. 6, (pp. 235-297) New York: Academic Press.

Ross, A. O. (1980). *Psychopathological disorders of children* (second edition). New York: McGraw-Hill.

Rubenstein, G., Fisher, L., & Iker, H. (1975). Peer observation of student behavior in elementary school classrooms. *Developmental Psychology, 11,* 867-868.

Rubin, K. H. (1985). Socially-withdrawn children: An "at risk" population? In B. H. Schneider, K. H. Rubin, & J. E. Ledingham (Eds.), *Children's peer relations: Issues in assessment and intervention* (pp. 125-139). New York: Springer-Verlag.

Rubin, K. H. (1990). The Waterloo Longitudinal Project: The long-term predictive "outcomes" of passive withdrawal in childhood. In K. H. Rubin (Ed.), *Shyness, withdrawal, and social inhibition.* Chicago: University of Chicago Press.

Rubin, K. H., Fein, G. G., & Vandenberg B. (1983). Play. In E. M. Hetherington (Ed.) *Handbook of child psychology, Vol. 4. Socialization, personality, and social development* (pp. 693-774, 4th ed.). New York: Wiley.

Rubin, K. H., Hymel, S., Mills, R., & Rose-Krasnor, L. (1991). Conceptualizing different developmental pathways to and from social isolation in childhood. In D. Cicchetti (Ed.) *Rochester symposium on developmental psychology,* Vol. 2, (pp. xxx-xxx). Hillsdale, NJ: Lawrence Erlbaum Associates.

Rubin, K. H., Hymel, S., LeMare, L., & Rowden, L. (1989). Children experiencing social difficulties: Sociometric neglect reconsidered. *Canadian Journal of Behavioural Science, 21,* 94-111.

Rubin, K. H., & Mills, R. S. (1988). The many faces of social isolation in childhood. *Journal of Consulting and Clinical Psychology, 56,* 916-924.

Saltz, E., Dunin-Markiewicz, A., & Rourke, D. (1975). The development of natural language concepts. II Developmental changes in attribute structure. *Child Development, 46,* 913–921.

Taylor, S. E., & Crocker, J. (1981). Schematic bases of social information processing. In E. T. Higgins, C. P. Herman, & M. P. Zanna (Eds.), *Social cognition: The Ontario symposium,* Volume 1, (pp. 89–134). Hillsdale, NJ: Lawrence Erlbaum Associates.

Wiggins, J. S., & Winder, C. L. (1961). The Peer Nomination Inventory: An empirically derived sociometric measure of adjustment in preadolescent boys. *Psychological Reports, 9,* 643–677.

Yarrow, M. R., & Campbell, J. D. (1963). Person perception in children. *Merrill-Palmer Quarterly, 9,* 57–92.

Younger, A. J., & Boyko, K. A. (1987). Aggression and withdrawal as social schemas underlying children's peer perceptions. *Child Development, 58,* 1094–1100.

Younger, A. J., & Daniels, T. M. (in press). Children's peer nominations for withdrawal: Passive withdrawal vs. active isolation. *Developmental Psychology.*

Younger, A. J., & Piccinin, A. M. (1989). Children's recall of aggressive and withdrawn behaviors: Recognition memory and likability judgements. *Child Development, 60,* 580–590.

Younger, A. J., Schwartzman, A. E., & Ledingham, J. E. (1985). Age-related changes in children's perceptions of aggression and withdrawal in their peers. *Developmental Psychology, 21,* 70–75.

Younger, A. J., Schwartzman, A. E., & Ledingham, J. E. (1986). Age-related differences in children's perceptions of social deviance: Changes in behavior or in perspective? *Developmental Psychology, 22,* 531–542.

12

Social Withdrawal in Childhood: Considering the Child's Perspective

Shelley Hymel, Erik Woody, and Anne Bowker
University of Waterloo

Despite an ever increasing literature on children's peer relations (e.g., Asher & Coie, 1990, Berndt & Ladd, 1989; Rubin & Ross, 1982; Schneider, Rubin, & Ledingham, 1985; Wine & Smye, 1981), the child's perspective on his or her social difficulties has been a relatively neglected topic (Hymel & Franke, 1985). This general failure is at least in part attributable to the fact that researchers generally question the validity of children's self reports, owing primarily to evidence indicating rather positive bias in children's self evaluations (see Kagan, Hans, Markowitz, Lopez, & Sigal, 1982). When one considers the child's perspective, self appraisals and self assessments, by necessity, are of primary interest. However, self-report measures have and do receive mixed reviews as an assessment tool within psychology. As Beharry (1990) has pointed out, self-report measures are often regarded as biased, unreliable, and inaccurate, making them a less than adequate scientific tool. Such concern is not entirely unwarranted, according to Beharry; after all, self-report data is not necessarily a true reflection of behavior and, more often than not, bears little relationship to objective observations of behavior (Hetherington & Parke, 1986; Kochanska, Kuczynski, & Radke-Yarrow, 1989) or to evaluations by others (e.g., Hymel, Woody, Ditner, & LeMare, 1988; Shrauger & Schoeneman, 1979). Moreover, Kagan (1984) notes that "because so much information is viewed by the person as evaluative of self, a verbal report is often an extremely distorted sign of the essential quality the scientist wishes to know in its less disguised form" (p. 24).

Despite these acknowledged limitations, self reports may be a unique and potentially critical part of child assessment. Kagan (1984) distinguishes subjective and objective frames of reference within psychology—that is, the perspective of the subject him/herself versus the perspective of another who is trying to understand the subject. Kagan argues that it is not necessary to decide between these two frames nor to determine whether the subjective or objective frame is correct. Rather, it is important to understand the distinction between the two frames of reference as well as the implications of each. So how might an understanding of children's subjective evaluations of their social difficulties benefit us?

First, self appraisals are the only way to tap directly children's own beliefs and feelings about their social situations. Considering the advantages of self-report assessments, Beharry (1990) argues that self-reports provide "perspectival information on human relations—that is, how people understand and discuss their relationships" (p. 4). Beharry also reminds us that, in some cases, self perceptions may provide critical information, since "people responding to self report measures use information based on many experiences to which the researcher has not had access" (p. 4). Similarly, Zill (1985, as cited in Hetherington & Parke, 1986) suggests that considering children's self appraisals "permits a glimpse at a child's life from his or her unique perspective. The child is the best authority on his own feelings, even if he has some trouble verbalizing those feelings. And even in matters of fact—where adults have the advantage of a more fully developed sense of where, of when and of how many—there are aspects of a child's daily life that his parents or teacher know little or nothing about" (Zill, 1985, pp. 23–24). In some cases, the individual's perceptions and interpretations of events may be as important as, if not more important, than the events themselves (Hetherington & Parke, 1986; McGillicuddy-Delisi, 1982).

Second, an understanding of the child's perspective may have important implications for the treatment of problems such as withdrawal. Within the clinical literature on social problems in children, several authors have recognized that consideration of the child's own thoughts, feelings, and perceptions is an important, if not critical component of assessment and treatment (e.g., Meichenbaum, Bream, & Cohen, 1984; Yule, 1981). For example, arguing for the application of a cognitive-behavioral perspective to the treatment of social isolation in childhood, Meichenbaum et al. emphasized the need to consider the interaction of the child's own thoughts and feelings with observable social behavior. Also, research by Evers-Pasquale (1978; Evers-Pasquale & Sherman, 1975) has demonstrated that the effectiveness of at least some forms of social skill intervention in modifying isolation behavior varies as a function of the value the children themselves place on peer interaction.

Third, research by Kagan and his colleagues (Kagan et al., 1982; Kagan, 1989), evaluating the accuracy of children's self reports in various domains of their lives (including peer relations), has indicated that children's self reports did provide a relatively valid data source, as compared with peer and teacher evaluations, *when self-reports acknowledged negative or undesirable attributes.* Positive self evaluations were suspect in about one-third of the cases in which children overestimated their own abilities relative to the perceptions of teachers and peers. At least for children who express *negative* self-perceptions, then, self appraisals may provide an important indicator of difficulty for the child. Further, failure to acknowledge and utilize such information is to ignore a valid (at least in some cases) and theoretically important data source that could contribute substantially to our understanding of childhood risk. It is in this light that we attempt to understand the child's perspective on his or her social withdrawal.

Evaluating the self perceptions of *socially withdrawn* children may be particularly helpful in clarifying research on childhood social rejection. Within the clinical literature on developmental psychopathology, an important distinction is made between internalizing and externalizing difficulties (Achenbach, 1982; Achenbach & Edelbrock, 1981). To date, externalizing problems, including outcomes such as aggression, hostility, and acting-out behavior or delinquency, have been emphasized in the literature on rejected children. For example, in a recent review of the long-term predictive correlates of early social problems (such as peer rejection), Parker and Asher (1987) concluded that there is reasonable evidence to support the contention that early rejection and aggressive behavior within the peer group is predictive of subsequent externalizing problems in adolescent and adult life. More recently, Rubin and Hymel and colleagues (Hymel, Rubin, Rowden, & LeMare, 1990; Rubin, Hymel, & Mills, 1989) have pointed out that the possible links between early social difficulties and subsequent *internalizing* problems have not been adequately addressed, despite theoretical arguments that peer rejection might be associated with later internalizing (as well as externalizing) outcomes with age, as the child becomes increasingly aware of his or her poor status within the peer group (See Rubin & Lollis, 1988). According to Achenbach, internalizing problems are usually defined in terms of a constellation of difficulties including fearfulness, anxiety, low self concept, and social withdrawal. With social withdrawal usually considered to be a symptom or behavioral reflection of internalizing problems (e.g., Achenbach & Edelbrock, 1981), one would expect that children who are extremely withdrawn from their peers would be more likely to exhibit affective and cognitive difficulties within the self-system.

Understanding the self perceptions of withdrawn children is also important in determining whether social withdrawal is in fact a potential indicator of risk. Although socially withdrawn behavior is considered an index of peer difficulty by parents, practitioners, and clinicians (Mills & Rubin, 1990), some have argued that social withdrawal in childhood is not a predictor of negative developmental outcomes (e.g., Michael, Morris, & Soroker, 1957; Robins, 1966). Given that, until recently, there has not been clear evidence that early social withdrawal is predictive of later maladjustment (Kohlberg, La Crosse, & Ricks, 1972; Parker & Asher, 1987), and given the hypothesized links just mentioned between withdrawal and internalizing problems, it then becomes important to determine whether socially withdrawn children are in fact at risk for internalizing difficulties, both concurrently and predictively. This determination would seem to require the study of children's self reports of affect (e.g., loneliness) and satisfaction with their peer relations, as well as subjective states such as fearfulness, anxiety, sadness, and so forth.

Alternatively, particular patterns of self evaluations may serve a positive function, buffering the child from the long-term risks associated with early peer rejection. As argued in Hymel and Franke (1985), at present there is clearly no one-to-one correspondence between early peer difficulties and later maladjustment. The longitudinal research on which this link is based (see Parker & Asher, 1987) has resulted in significant but modest predictive correlations between early social difficulties and later problems, suggesting that not all poorly accepted children are destined to face adjustment difficulties in later life. Given the heterogenous nature of rejected subgroups (Bierman, Miller, & Stabb, 1987; Coie, 1985; Coie, Dodge, & Kupersmidt, 1990; French, 1988, 1990; Hymel & Rubin, 1985) and the fact that there appear to be multiple pathways for the development of social difficulties (Rubin, LeMare, & Lollis, 1990), it is intriguing to speculate that how children themselves perceive and interpret their social difficulties may influence subsequent behavior and, in turn, the likelihood of negative interpersonal outcomes.

In the paragraphs that follow, we review evidence concerning the relations between social withdrawal during middle childhood and a variety of children's self perceptions. We begin with an examination of the correlations between social withdrawal and self perceptions as observed in two different samples of middle elementary school aged children (grades 4–6). In these samples, social withdrawal was assessed by means of peer evaluations, and self perceptions were assessed by a variety of different self-report measures, including social self concept, global self esteem, loneliness, and perceived social support within the peer group. A brief discussion of the assessment procedures employed follows.

ASSESSING SOCIAL WITHDRAWAL

Within research on children's social difficulties, peer assessments of social status and social behavior have become commonplace (see Hymel & Rubin,

1985). Peers provide a face-valid source of information on children's social standing within a primary peer group—usually the school classroom. Also, such information can be obtained in a relatively short period of time from multiple peer observers who have varied experiences with the children being assessed. However, although peer evaluations can provide a face-valid and efficient means of assessing children's typical social behavior, research by Younger and colleagues (Younger & Daniels, in press; Younger, & Boyko, 1987; Younger, Schwartzman, & Ledingham, 1985; 1986) has raised questions regarding the ability of children to provide an accurate assessment of socially withdrawn behavior, especially at younger ages. According to Younger, Gentile, and Burgess (this volume), however, children's conceptions of withdrawal appear to have achieved a reasonable degree of coherence and validity by the fourth-grade level. Thus, in the work described here, we consider peer assessments of social withdrawal among children of at least the fourth-grade level.

Of additional concern in peer assessments of social withdrawal is the nature of the criteria employed to tap social withdrawal. Two of the most often-used peer assessment devices, the Revised Class Play (Masten, Morison, & Pelligrini, 1985) and the Pupil Evaluation Inventory (Pekarik, Printz, Liebert, Weintraub, & Neale, 1976), include a subscale or factor that assesses sensitive, isolated, and/or withdrawn social behavior. However, several authors have recently noted that the items included in these assessments of withdrawal are varied and reflect social isolation that may result from peer rejection or exclusion, as well as passive-withdrawn behavior on the part of the child (Coie, Dodge, & Kupersmidt, 1990; Rubin & Mills, 1988; Younger & Daniels, in press). Accordingly, in the present samples, peer assessments were limited to those items which clearly reflect passive withdrawal on the part of the child, as recommended by Rubin and Mills (1988). In addition, we omitted from consideration items typically included in the withdrawal factor that reflect sensitivity or internal affect (e.g., "It is easy to hurt this person's feelings," "This person is usually sad"). Of concern here was the possibility that such items may be more closely related to negative self perceptions than withdrawn behavior per se, making relations between indices of withdrawal and self-report assessments more likely in a possibly rather artifactual manner.

Finally, in the present samples, peers were required to rate, on 5-point scales, each same-sex classmate in terms of each of two withdrawal items. Previous peer assessment measures (e.g., Masten et al., 1985; Pekarik et al., 1976) have typically employed a nomination procedure in which children select a limited number of classmates from a provided list according to who best fits the criteria under consideration. Thus, peer assessments are based on the sum of nominations provided by classmates, although the interpretation of non-nominations is unclear. Peer ratings, on the other hand, provide a collective evaluation of each child on each item, based on the average ratings received from all same-sex classmates. Thus, in contrast to nomination data, peer ratings provide a more psychometrically sound assessment, with the evaluations of each participating classmate contributing to the overall score.

Accordingly, in each of two samples of fourth through sixth grade children, peer assessments of withdrawal were derived from ratings received from same-sex peers on two items: "This person would rather play alone rather than with others," and "This person is shy," providing the purest peer assessment of social withdrawal possible within the limits of existing data sets. Although these two items tap somewhat different aspects of withdrawal (e.g., unsociability versus ambivalence due to shyness), recent empirical research (Asendorpf, 1991) suggests that by Grade 2, shyness/ inhibition and unsociability have become associated and occur together as coping responses to social difficulties. Thus, social withdrawal as assessed by a combination of these two items was considered appropriate for this sample of later elementary-school-aged children. In each sample, the ratings received from same-sex peers on these two items were standardized within class and sex groups in order to permit comparisons across classrooms differing in size and sex-role composition. Higher scores were indicative of greater social withdrawal, according to peers.

ASSESSING SELF PERCEPTIONS

Research on children's self perceptions has waxed and waned over the past few decades (see Harter, 1986 for a historical review), and has been fraught with difficulties, particularly with regard to the development of reliable and valid assessment instruments (Wylie, 1974, 1979). In the 1980s, however, we have witnessed a resurgence of interest in the self system and its development and the emergence of a new conceptualization of the self, with new assessment approaches (see Wylie, 1989). In particular, research by Harter, Marsh, and Shavelson and their colleagues (e.g., Harter, 1982, 1985; Marsh, Smith, & Barnes, 1983, 1985; Marsh, Byrne, & Shavelson, 1988; Shavelson & Bolus, 1982) has emphasized a multidimensional model of self that requires the separate assessment of self concept in various domains of one's life (e.g., academic and athletic competence, peer relations, appearance, etc.). General self esteem, or self worth as it is referred to in recent work, is assessed as a separate component of the self system. In light of this recent focus on multidimensional or domain-specific assessments of self, we examined the self perceptions of withdrawn children across multiple domains using the Self Description Questionnaire (SDQ, Marsh et al., 1983, 1985) in the first sample considered herein. On this self-report scale, following procedures outlined by Marsh et al., self concept was assessed in five distinct domains—academics, athletics, relations with peers, relations with parents, and appearance—with a separate subscale assessing feelings of general self esteem. Across domains, higher scores were indicative of more positive self concept.

Given the obvious implications of social withdrawal for children's relations within the peer group, we also wanted to include a more in-depth assessment of children's self perceptions within the social domain. Until recently, however, few assessment instruments have been developed for tapping children's feelings about their social relations with peers (see Hymel & Franke, 1985). However, within the last decade, researchers have attempted to develop reliable and valid measures of children's feelings of loneliness (Asher, Hymel, & Renshaw, 1984) and satisfaction with available social support (Hayden, 1989), instruments that more directly tap children's feelings about their own social relations (see Asher, Parkhurst, Hymel, & Williams, 1990 for a review). Accordingly, in the second sample, we considered more directly children's feelings about their peer relations by assessing children's affect and self appraisals in the social domain. Social self concept and general self esteem were evaluated using the SDQ (Marsh et al., 1983, 1985), as in the first sample. Children's feelings of loneliness and social dissatisfaction were assessed using a self-report measure developed by Asher et al. (1984), on which children were asked about their feelings of competence in their relations with peers (e.g., "It's hard for me to make new friends at school," "I don't get along with other children in school," "I am well liked by the kids in my class," etc.), their feelings of loneliness (e.g., "I'm lonely," "I feel alone at school," etc.), their appraisals of their current peer relations (e.g., "I don't have any friends," "I feel left out of things at school," etc.), and their perceptions of the degree to which relationship provisions are being met (e.g., "There's no other kids I can go to when I need help in school," "I have nobody to talk to in class," etc.). In addition, children's perceptions of the social support available from peers was assessed using a self-report measure of relational provisions developed by Hayden (1989), which distinguishes two different types of relational provisions, based on Weiss's (1973) model of social versus emotional loneliness: group integration needs and intimacy needs. Social loneliness was assessed in terms of the degree to which children felt that they belonged to a group of peers with whom they could share activities (e.g., "I feel part of a group of friends that does things together," "I feel like other children want to be with me," etc.); while emotional loneliness was assessed in terms of the degree to which the children felt that they had access to peers with whom they could share their intimate thoughts and feelings (e.g., "There is someone my age I could go to if I were feeling down," "I have a friend I can tell everything to," etc.). Each of these measures was developed for use with middle elementary school age children, and has demonstrated reliability, validity and utility within this age group. For all three of these measures (loneliness, peer intimacy, and peer group integration), higher scores were indicative of greater negative affect or dissatisfaction with peer relations (i.e., greater loneliness, and a lack of peer group intimacy and peer group integration).

RELATIONS BETWEEN WITHDRAWAL AND SELF PERCEPTIONS

Correlational analyses were conducted in order to examine the relations between peer perceptions of social withdrawal and various self perceptions in each of two samples of fourth through sixth grade children (approximately half male and half female in each sample). In the first sample, we examined the relations of withdrawal to self concept in multiple domains as well as to overall self esteem; in the second sample, we examined the relations of withdrawal to particular social self perceptions (social self concept, loneliness, and satisfaction with peer intimacy and peer group integration) as well as to overall self esteem. Results of these analyses are presented in Table 12.1.

As can be seen in the table, withdrawn children reported significantly

TABLE 12.1
Relations Between Peer-Perceived Withdrawal and Self-Perceptions

	Withdrawal	
	Sample A (N = 322–335)	Sample B (N = 293–301)
Self Concept Domains:		
Academic Competence	− .02	
Athletic Competence	− .21***	
Appearance	− .10*	
Relations with Parents	− .01	
Relations with Peers	− .31***	− .24***
General Self Esteem	− .13**	− .09ᵗ
Social Self Perceptions:		
Loneliness		.28***
Lack of Peer Group Intimacy		.21***
Lack of Peer Group Integration		.32***

All correlations reported are one-tailed.
***$p < .001$
**$p < .01$
*$p < .05$
ᵗ$p < .10$

more negative self appraisals of their competence in the athletic, but not the academic domain. Also, withdrawn children were slightly but significantly more likely to view themselves as unattractive. Although withdrawn children did not report more negative relations with their parents, they did report more negative relations with peers in both samples. In addition, withdrawn children tended to report more negative overall self esteem. Finally, greater withdrawal was associated with significantly greater reported dissatisfaction with peer relations, as reflected in self reports of loneliness and a perceived lack of social support with regard to both intimacy and group integration (belongingness). These data certainly reflect a rather negative pattern of self perceptions associated with withdrawal, although the magnitude of these correlations is never large.[1] Moreover, the same pattern of relations were observed for males and females, when evaluated separately, lending greater confidence to the generality of these findings.[2]

The findings reported here regarding the relatively negative pattern of self perceptions associated with social withdrawal are consistent with the results of other studies on the self perceptions of socially withdrawn children. Particularly relevant to the present discussion are results of recent longitudinal research by Hymel, Rubin, Rowden, and LeMare (1990). They examined the concurrent as well as predictive relations between early social withdrawal, as well as aggression, and later internalizing difficulties, including children's self evaluations, as measured by self-report measures of loneliness (Asher et al., 1984) and both social self concept and general self esteem (Harter, 1982, 1985). Children were evaluated for both withdrawn and aggressive behavior (as assessed by peers, teachers, and observational assessments) in both the second and fifth grades. Concurrently, in the second grade, social withdrawal, as assessed by peer nominations on the Revised Class Play (Masten et al., 1985), was significantly and negatively related to social self concept. In contrast, teacher ratings of internalizing difficulties (which included fearful, anxious, and solitary behaviors) and observed isolated play behavior were not significantly related to social self concept in the second grade. In grade five, again, peer assessments of social withdrawal (Masten et al., 1985) were significantly associated with poor

---

[1]It is worth noting that a virtually identical pattern of relations was obtained when peer assessments of withdrawal were based on both withdrawal items (e.g., "This person plays alone rather than with others"; "This person is shy") and internal affect items (e.g., "It is easy to hurt this person's feelings"; "Someone who is usually sad"), although the magnitude of the correlations was sometimes larger, as would be expected.

[2]For the interested reader, it is also worth noting that these relations were maintained in partial correlational analyses when peer perceptions of popularity (peer acceptance based on rating scale sociometric measures) and/or peer perceptions of aggressive behavior were partialled out.

social self concept and feelings of loneliness. Also, teacher ratings of shy-anxious behavior in grade five were associated with poor social self concept. In terms of concurrent relations, then, withdrawn children were more likely to report low self concept in the social domain (grades 2 and 5) and reported greater loneliness and social dissatisfaction (grade 5).

Predictively, a similar pattern of findings emerged, with peer perceptions of socially withdrawn behavior in grade two significantly related to negative self appraisals three years later. Children who were nominated by peers as sensitive and isolated in their social behavior in grade two were significantly more likely to report low social self concept and greater feelings of loneliness in grade five. General self esteem was not significantly related to peer perceptions of withdrawal, although low self esteem was associated with negative self appraisals in the social domain (social self concept, loneliness) both concurrently and predictively. The finding that peer perceptions of sensitive-withdrawn social behavior in the second grade were predictive of later negative self perceptions is particularly noteworthy in light of evidence (Younger et al., this volume) that young children's conceptions of social withdrawal are not well articulated at this age (grade 2).

Of additional interest here is the fact that Hymel et al. (1990) found relations between social self perceptions and withdrawal, but not aggression. Peer assessments of aggressive-disruptive social behavior (Masten et al., 1985) were significantly related to teacher ratings of externalizing difficulties (acting-out behavior), both concurrently and predictively, replicating previous findings on the stability of aggressive behavior and its links to externalizing outcomes (see Parker & Asher, 1987). However, aggression and negative self perceptions were *not* significantly related in either grades two or five, and grade two assessments of aggression (peer nominations) and externalizing problems (teacher ratings) were *not* predictive of subsequent negative self perceptions. As Hymel et al. noted, previous research on children's social difficulties has emphasized peer rejection and/or aggression and subsequent externalizing outcomes. Far less attention has been directed toward the long-term outcomes associated with early social withdrawal. These data, however, suggest that early social withdrawal, at least as perceived by peers, is indeed associated with concurrent and subsequent difficulties, but difficulties of an internalizing sort, including negative self perceptions.

The findings reported above take on added significance when one considers the research on peer rejection in childhood. Given that socially withdrawn or isolated behavior as well as aggressive behavior is characteristic of children who are rejected or unpopular among their peers at this age (Rubin, Hymel, LeMare, & Rowden, 1989), these data fit within a larger literature on childhood rejection. Although children's social self perceptions have not been a major focus within this literature (Hymel & Franke, 1985), results of several recent studies have indicated that global indices of children's peer acceptance/rejection are significantly, but only modestly related to children's self perceptions, including self-report indices of social self concept (e.g., Hymel, 1983; Hymel, Woody, Ditner, & LeMare, 1988), social anxiety (Hymel & Franke, 1985; LaGreca, Dandes, Wick, Shaw, & Stone, 1988), and loneliness (Asher, Hymel, & Renshaw, 1984; Asher, Parkhurst, Hymel, & Williams, 1990). While some unpopular or rejected children acknowledge their poor peer acceptance and report greater negative affect (loneliness, social anxiety), others do not, leading some researchers to consider self perceptions as an important individual difference variable (Hymel & Franke, 1985). Of interest to this chapter is whether social self perceptions vary systematically as a function of the particular pattern of social behavior exhibited by unpopular or socially rejected children — specifically, withdrawn versus aggressive behavior. We turn now to an examination of research relevant to this issue.

SELF PERCEPTIONS OF REJECTED SUBGROUPS

Within the literature on childhood peer rejection, researchers have increasingly recognized the heterogeneous nature of rejected children (e.g., Bierman, Miller, & Stabb, 1987; Coie, 1985; Coie, Dodge, & Kupersmidt, 1990; French, 1988, 1990). Several recent studies have attempted to distinguish between particular subgroups of rejected children in terms of various characteristics. Behaviorally, the primary distinction among subgroups of rejected children appears to be that between aggressive and withdrawn, unpopular children (e.g., French, 1988, 1990), which is not surprising, given previous evidence that unpopular and/or rejected children can exhibit both aggressive as well as withdrawn social behavior (Hymel & Rubin, 1985; Ledingham, 1981; Ledingham & Schwartzman, 1984; Rubin et al., 1989). Within this literature, a few studies have considered variations in children's self perceptions as a function of rejected subgroups. An examination of their findings follows.

In an initial study, Boivin and Bégin (1989) distinguished two subgroups of socially rejected children: those who expressed positive self concepts and those who expressed negative self-concepts in the social as well as other domains. Although Boivin and Begin speculated that behavioral differences between these two subgroups, such as aggression versus withdrawal, might be systematically related to observed differences in self perceptions, such behavioral data were not available in their study. Subsequent studies comparing aggressive versus non-aggressive subgroups of rejected children (e.g., Patterson, Kupersmidt, & Greisler, 1990) failed to identify clear differences between the subgroups in terms of self concept measures in multiple domains. However, other studies, comparing subgroups of aggressive versus withdrawn or submissive rejected children have identified systematic variations in self perceptions. In particular, Williams and Asher (1987) found that submissive-rejected children reported significantly greater loneliness than did aggressive-rejected children. Similarly, Boivin, Thomassin, and Alain (1989) found that withdrawn-rejected children, but not aggressive-rejected children, expressed greater loneliness and social dissatisfaction, as compared with average status peers. In addition, Boivin et al. reported that withdrawn-rejected children, relative to average status peers, perceived themselves to be less well accepted by peers and less competent academically and behaviorally. In contrast, aggressive-rejected children perceived themselves to be less competent, relative to average peers, only in terms of behavioral conduct.

In extending this research on variations in self perceptions across rejected subgroups, we (Hymel, Bowker, & Woody, forthcoming) examined variations in self perceptions of competence in both social and nonsocial domains for subgroups of aggressive unpopular, withdrawn unpopular, aggressive-withdrawn unpopular, and average status children. These subgroups were distinguished on the basis of peer ratings of popularity (rating-scale sociometric measures), aggression (based on two rating criteria: "This person starts fights and arguments with others," and "This person picks on and teases others too much"), and withdrawal (based on two rating criteria: "This person plays alone rather than with others," and "This person is shy"), using a mean, half-standard deviation split in each case. Thus, for example, aggressive unpopular children ($n = 13$) were those whose score on the standardized average aggression composite was at least one-half standard deviation above the mean for their class and sex group, while their standardized average composite for withdrawal and their standardized score for popularity were both at least one-half standard deviation below the mean. Similarly, withdrawn unpopular children ($n = 14$) were those who scored at least one-half standard deviation below the mean on both popularity and aggression, but who scored at least one-half standard deviation above the mean on withdrawal. Unpopular children who were both aggressive and withdrawn ($n = 29$) received scores at least one-half standard deviation above the mean on both aggression and withdrawal criterion measures and at least one-half standard deviation below the mean for popularity. Research by Ledingham and colleagues (Ledingham, 1981; Ledingham & Schwartzman, 1984) has suggested that children who exhibit *both* withdrawn and aggressive behavioral tendencies may be at particular risk for later difficulties, making them an important consideration in evaluating variations as a function of unpopular subgroups. Finally, for comparison purposes, a fourth group of average status children ($n = 30$)

was also considered — children whose scores on all three indices (popularity, aggression and withdrawal) fell within one-half standard deviation of the mean. Self-perceptions of competence were assessed using the SDQ (Marsh et al., 1983, 1985) in four domains — academics, athletics, appearance, and relations with peers.

Results of the Hymel et al. (forthcoming) study indicated that withdrawn unpopular children reported the lowest (i.e., least positive) self concept of all the subgroups across domains, although significant differences were only evident in two of the four areas: athletic competence and peer relations. Withdrawn unpopular children viewed themselves as significantly less athletically competent than did average status children, and as significantly less competent in their relations with peers than did average status or aggressive unpopular children. Consistent with research described earlier, these findings might simply be taken as corroborating evidence that withdrawn unpopular children are more negative in their self appraisals. Subsequent analyses considered the accuracy of children's self-concept scores by examining subgroup differences in the discrepancies between self evaluations in each of the four domains and peer evaluations of competence in each area (self minus other standardized scores). Although peer assessments do not constitute a purely "objective" evaluation of actual competence, they do reflect the collective views of one of the child's primary reference groups and hence may be particularly important in terms of social relations with these classmates. When discrepancies between self and peer evaluations were examined, significant differences across subgroups were observed in all four domains. Average status and withdrawn unpopular children tended to evaluate their self concept accurately (i.e., near zero discrepancies), while aggressive and aggressive-withdrawn unpopular children were likely to overestimate their competencies in each area.

In understanding these variations in self perceptions, it is important to consider self perceptions as a function of indices of actual competence in each domain. Relevant here are peer ratings of the children's competence in both nonsocial (academic and athletic competence, appearance, style) and social domains (social competence or popularity with peers, relations with adults, behavioral conduct in school, cooperativeness, leadership qualities, sense of humor, and being left out). A comparison of subgroup differences in actual competence (peer assessments) was particularly interesting in clarifying the nature of the subgroup differences observed in self appraisals across domains. Consider, first, the finding that withdrawn unpopular children reported more negative self perceptions in the athletic domain, relative to average status children. According to peer perceptions of actual competence in this domain, withdrawn unpopular children were rated as relatively less athletically competent (as were aggressive-withdrawn unpopular children), while aggressive unpopular children were not (relative to average peers). Thus, it would appear that withdrawn unpopular children were merely acknowledging their deficiencies in this area. In contrast, aggressive unpopular children did not differ from average status children in athletic competence, according to peers, and thus had no clear deficiencies to acknowledge. In this light, one might argue that withdrawn unpopular children were simply reporting an accurate, albeit negative, appraisal of themselves. One interesting question, then, is why aggressive-withdrawn unpopular children, who were also viewed as deficient in athletic competence (as well as other areas), failed to acknowledge their difficulties in their self reports.

Differences in self perceptions of social competence (peer relations) between withdrawn unpopular and aggressive unpopular children become particularly interesting when one considers the actual social behaviors and characteristics of these subgroups, as perceived by peers. Withdrawn but nonaggressive unpopular children reported more accurate, but negative self appraisals in the social domain, while aggressive and aggressive withdrawn unpopular children tended to overestimate their social competence. Similar results have been reported by Boivin et al. (1989), comparing aggressive rejected and withdrawn rejected third-grade children in terms of social self-concept. Again, one might argue that the lower social self-concept reported by withdrawn unpopular children is simply a recognition or acknowledgment of their poor peer acceptance. When one considers various indices of actual social competence, however, it appears that aggressive unpopular and withdrawn unpopular subgroups exhibited a mix of positive and negative social qualities. Thus, why did aggressive unpopular children fail to acknowledge their social difficulties? By examining the nature of the relative social strengths and weaknesses of each subgroup, a possible answer to this question is suggested.

Peers viewed withdrawn unpopular children as low in social competence (i.e., less popular), lacking in leadership qualities and a sense of humor, and likely to be left out of peer activities, relative to average status peers. Also, relative to average peers, withdrawn unpopular children did *not* possess other, nonsocial qualities that are likely valued by the peer group and that may have contributed to their marginal status among peers—athletic competence and attractiveness. However, there was also some evidence of positive social qualities on the part of withdrawn unpopular children. Specifically, withdrawn unpopular children were viewed by peers as comparable to average status children in terms of cooperativeness, behavioral conduct, and relations with adults. Thus, despite some evidence of acknowledged positive social skills, withdrawn unpopular children nevertheless perceived themselves to be socially incompetent in their relations with peers.

A somewhat different pattern of results emerged for aggressive (nonwithdrawn) unpopular children, who did *not* report low self concept in the social domain. Like withdrawn unpopular children, aggressive unpopular children by definition were not well accepted within the peer group, at least according to their same-sex classmates. Peers also indicated that aggressive unpopular children, relative to average peers, were poor leaders, uncooperative with peers, and lacked a sense of humor. Moreover, aggressive unpopular children were seen as exhibiting poor behavioral conduct at school, and not getting along well with adults. Despite these rather negative qualities, aggressive unpopular children were not necessarily left out of peer activities. For these aggressive unpopular children, then, despite clear social deficits (e.g., poor relations with adults, poor behavioral conduct, lack of cooperativeness, etc.), some positive aspects of their social relations were evident. In addition, aggressive unpopular children possessed certain qualities that might well be valued within the peer group, such as athletic competence.

Thus, while both subgroups were perceived as exhibiting some positive qualities in the social domain, they also exhibited problematic social characteristics. However, it would also appear that aggressive unpopular and withdrawn unpopular children might well be faced with different behavioral indicators suggestive of peer acceptance/rejection — specifically, whether they are or are not left out of peer activities. Previous research has indicated that children tend to base their self perceptions of social competence on rather subjective interpretations of the sometimes ambiguous behavior directed towards them by others (Hymel et al., 1988). Being left out (withdrawn unpopular children) or not left out (aggressive unpopular children) of peer activities, for example, would seem one such behavioral indicator to which the children would have access. Perhaps the positive aspects of peer relations are more salient to the optimistic eyes of the aggressive unpopular self-perceiver, suggesting some positivity in terms of their self evaluations of social competence. In contrast, the withdrawn unpopular children may be faced with more negative behavioral "feedback" from their social environment, hence they more readily acknowledge their social difficulties.

The general failure of unpopular children who were both aggressive *and* withdrawn to acknowledge their social difficulties is less readily explained. Interestingly, peers rated these children as even more unpopular than the other rejected subgroups, and peers viewed them as deficient in terms of relations with adults, as lacking in terms of a sense of humor, as poor leaders, as uncooperative, and as left out of peer activities. Given these rather negative social qualities and the absence of positive, redeeming social qualities, at least among the areas tapped, one might well expect that aggressive withdrawn children should express the most negative self perceptions of their social competence. Yet, aggressive withdrawn unpopular children did not differ significantly from average status children in terms of social self-concept. Like aggressive unpopular children, they were likely to overestimate their social competence. The reasons for their general failure to admit to their social difficulties remains an important question for future research.

Replication of these subgroup variations in the accuracy of children's self appraisals is certainly warranted. One concern in the research reported here is the use of peer judgments as "objective" standards that may provide an underestimate of unpopular children's actual competence. In the case of children who are perceived by their peers to be aggressive, such perceptions may lead to biased (overly negative) estimates of other social deficiencies. As well, both withdrawn children themselves and their evaluators may underestimate some of their skills, such as athletic competence. While this area has traditionally used teacher and peer ratings as measures of "objective reality," future research may well consider including more "objective" criteria such as academic grades, tests of motoric ability, and social skills assessments as additional measures of children's actual competencies. Nevertheless, the findings described here do suggest that one's own perceptions and those of others may be rather consistent for unpopular children who are withdrawn but nonaggressive, but quite discrepant for unpopular children who are withdrawn and aggressive.

In summary, a growing body of research consistently demonstrates that withdrawn children who are unpopular or rejected within their peer group are likely to be aware of and/or acknowledge their social difficulties. Other rejected or unpopular children, particularly those who are aggressive or aggressive as well as withdrawn, are less likely to acknowledge their social difficulties, at least on self-report questionnaires. The tendency for withdrawn rejected children to be aware of and acknowledge their difficulties, however, is not limited to the social domain alone, but appears to be evident in other domains as well. While previous research on the self perceptions of unpopular or rejected children has indicated only modest relations between self perceptions and actual social competence, more recent research has demonstrated that the links between actual and perceived competence vary systematically as a function of the type of social difficulty experienced. In particular, it is withdrawn unpopular children who are likely to express negative, albeit accurate perceptions of their own competencies in the social domain, as well as other domains. Finally, the findings described here suggest that an important avenue for future research would be consideration of the nature of the "feedback" that children receive from their social world, with suggestions that such feedback may play an important role in how at least some unpopular children interpret their social standing in the classroom.

It is important to note, however, that the pattern of strengths and weaknesses exhibited by particular unpopular children may well vary across children and samples, both in terms of social qualities, per se, and other competencies across domains. Relevant here is the fact that in the Boivin et al. (1989) research, withdrawn-rejected children perceived themselves to be less socially and academically competent (consistent with teacher evaluations), but not necessarily less competent in the domains of athletics and appearance (despite negative teacher evaluations in these domains). In our research (Hymel et al., forthcoming), withdrawn unpopular children viewed themselves as less socially and athletically competent, consistent with peer evaluations, but were not viewed as academically incompetent by themselves or peers. Thus, while the exact nature of the deficits may vary, at least two studies now have found withdrawn unpopular/rejected children to be the ones most likely to acknowledge their inadequacies.

IMPLICATIONS AND FUTURE DIRECTIONS

The research presented and reviewed in this chapter indicates that social withdrawal is associated with relatively negative self perceptions, both concurrently and predictively. However, like previous research on the self perceptions of unpopular children (see Hymel & Franke, 1985), the magnitude of these correlations is low. Such low correlations may be due to asymmetry in the predictor variables (e.g., high withdrawal predicts low social self-concept but low withdrawal does not predict high social self-concept) or may suggest considerable individual variation. Whether or not withdrawn children will express negative self perceptions appears to depend on the degree to which they also exhibit aggressive behavior, at least among unpopular children. Withdrawn, but nonaggressive unpopular children express a particularly negative, although accurate pattern of self perceptions within both social and nonsocial domains. In contrast, unpopular children who exhibit withdrawn as well as aggressive behavior do not necessarily express negative self appraisals, despite the fact that peers view these children as deficient in terms of social and nonsocial characteristics. In evaluating the implications of these findings, we wish to return to three issues raised at the outset of this chapter: (1) whether children's self-reported beliefs and feelings are valid and useful in understanding their social adjustment; (2) whether these self-reports contribute to a fuller account of the possible risks associated with social withdrawal, and (3) whether such self-reports may have implications for the treatment of social difficulties. Let us consider each of these points in turn.

First, our results, as well as those of other researchers, suggest that the self evaluations of withdrawn (nonaggressive) unpopular children, are reasonably valid—these children seem to report negative characteristics accurately across domains. Accuracy in self perceptions is much less likely in the case of aggressive and aggressive-withdrawn unpopular children, who seem to provide strikingly inflated self evaluations, and thereby exhibit the credibility problem discussed by Kagan and his colleagues (e.g., Kagan et al., 1982; Kagan, 1989). Why aggressive-withdrawn unpopular children fail to acknowledge their difficulties remains an important question for future research. One might speculate that aggressive social tendencies seem related to a repressive or self-deceptive ego-enhancing style (cf. Paulhus, 1984; Sackeim, 1983), and withdrawal to a sensitizing or non-self-deceptive style. In any case, our data, distinguishing aggressive and nonaggressive withdrawn unpopular children, underscores the need to consider both aggression and withdrawal in assessing a child's social problems, particularly if one is concerned with the child's perspective on his or her social difficulties. Children's social self perceptions do appear to vary systematically as a function the nature of their social difficulties, making continued exploration of rejected subgroups an important consideration in future research.

Second, it seems important to consider the implications of these findings for understanding the long-term risks associated with social withdrawal. Previous research has generally failed to establish consistent links between social withdrawal and later maladaptive outcomes (e.g., see Kohlberg et al., 1972; Parker & Asher, 1987 for reviews). For example, results of earlier, retrospective studies indicated that withdrawal in childhood was more frequently cited in case histories of schizophrenics (e.g., Bower, Shelhammer, & Daily, 1968; Flemming & Ricks, 1970). Also, predictive links between early withdrawal and later (adolescent) psychopathology were reported by Janes and Hesselbrock (1978) and by John, Mednick, and Schulsinger (1982), but only for girls, not boys. However, other studies failed to demonstrate a predictive link between withdrawal and psychological disorders (e.g., Janes, Hesselbrock, Myers, & Penniman, 1979; Michael, Morris, & Soroker, 1957; Morris, Soroker, & Burruss, 1954; Robins, 1966). On the basis of these rather equivocal findings, some conclude that withdrawn children are not at risk for later psychopathology (e.g., Coie, 1985). However, Rubin and colleagues (e.g., Hymel, Rubin, Rowden, & LeMare, 1990; Rubin, Hymel, Mills, & Rose-Krasnor, 1991) have argued that the general failure of previous research to demonstrate the "risk" status of withdrawn children is in part attributable to methodological flaws: use of high-risk samples with an attenuated range of observed behavior, use of teacher assessments of questionable or unknown validity, emphasis on externalizing rather than internalizing outcome measures, and the failure to distinguish between active versus passive withdrawn behavior. Our research points to an additional problem that may have limited the success of previous studies in this area: the failure to distinguish withdrawn children who were aggressive from those who were nonaggressive.

In evaluating the likelihood of long-term "risk" for withdrawn children, we must ask whether it is more adaptive to be accurate but negative in one's self perceptions (withdrawn unpopular children), or to be inaccurate but positive in one's self perceptions (aggressive and aggressive-withdrawn unpopular children). The implications of these findings are difficult to determine given the current debate that exists regarding the role of accurate versus distorted self-perceptions for one's mental health. Taylor and Brown (1988) point out that, on one hand, traditional views of mental health (see Jourard & Landsman, 1980) suggest that accurate perceptions of self and reality are critical to healthy development and effective functioning. In contrast, Taylor and Brown review research from social, personality, clinical, and developmental psychology that indicates that the healthy or "normal" individual typically possesses unrealistic and positively biased views of themselves. Indeed, in their review, Taylor and Brown point out that it is "individuals who are low in self esteem, moderately depressed, or both who are more balanced in self perceptions (see Coyne & Gotlieb, 1983; Ruehlman, West, & Pasahow, 1985; Watson & Clark, 1984 for reviews) . . . and offer self appraisals that coincide more closely with appraisals by objective observers (e.g., Lewinson, Mischel, Chaplin, & Barton, 1980)." (Taylor & Brown, 1988, p. 196).

In light of these findings, Rubin's (e.g., Hymel et al., 1990; Rubin et al., 1991) arguments concerning the appropriate long-term outcomes to consider in evaluating the risk status of withdrawn children are particularly relevant. Increasing evidence has demonstrated that early social withdrawal, particularly passive withdrawal, is concurrently associated with negative affect (e.g., loneliness) and negative self perceptions (e.g., Boivin, et al., 1989; Hymel et al., 1990; Rubin & Mills, 1988) and also linked, concurrently and predictively to internalizing difficulties such as depression (Altmann & Gotlib, 1988; Erickson, Bacon, & Egeland, 1987; Quay & LaGreca, 1986; Rubin & Mills, 1988; Rubin et al., 1991). Thus, withdrawn children, particularly those who are aware of and acknowledge their social difficulties (e.g., nonaggressive, unpopular withdrawn children) would appear to be at greater risk for subsequent internalizing problems such as low self esteem and/or depression. Although further research on the internalizing outcomes associated with early social withdrawal is needed, a growing body of studies has begun to demonstrate just where these links are likely to be found.

Third, the accuracy of children's self perceptions (or lack thereof) may play an important role in the success of intervention efforts aimed at ameliorating children's social difficulties. The accurate, but negative self perceptions expressed by withdrawn unpopular children may well reflect internalizing difficulties, but they might also aid the possibilities of therapeutic intervention, since such children seem more likely to acknowledge their problems and be motivated to try and change them due to their displeasing implications. Arriving at a mutual understanding of the problem that merits intervention might be more difficult with the aggressive and aggressive-withdrawn children, who appear rather unaware of their shortcomings. Consistent with this argument are recent data presented by Asher and his colleagues (personal communication, December, 1990; Asher, 1991; Asher, Zelis, Parker, & Bruene, 1991). Results from several studies by these authors indicate that unpopular or poorly accepted children in the third through sixth grades were more likely to refer themselves for help with their peer relationship problems if they exhibited withdrawn rather than aggressive social behavior.

Given that it is withdrawn (nonaggressive) unpopular children who are more likely to acknowledge their own difficulties (Hymel et al., forthcoming) and consider seeking help (self-referral, Asher et al., 1991), it is possible that such children would indeed attempt to modify their social difficulties. One might speculate that the acknowledgment of social difficulties among withdrawn individuals (Hymel et al., forthcoming) and their greater likelihood of seeking help (Asher et al., 1991) in part accounts for the failure of some studies to demonstrate a predictive link between withdrawal and later psychological disorder (e.g., Janes et al., 1979; Morris et al., 1954; Michael et al., 1957; Robins, 1966). In contrast, unpopular children who exhibit both aggressive and withdrawn behavior do not appear to admit to their difficulties (Hymel et al., forthcoming) and are less likely to self-refer (Asher et al., 1991), making the likelihood of later problems greater.

In terms of future research, one potentially fruitful approach would be to consider the mechanisms involved in the development and maintenance of social self perceptions. For example, one might ask whether particular types of withdrawn children utilize different strategies in their efforts to protect their self conceptions, be they positive or negative. Within the literature on stress and coping, researchers have begun to examine variations in the strategies which children and adolescents use to cope with stress and conflict in their lives. Compas, Malcarne, and Fondacaro (1988) examined the relations between behavioral problems, including aggression, unpopularity and depression/withdrawal, as reported by mothers and the children themselves on the Child Behavior Checklist (CBCL, Achenbach & Edelbrock, 1983, 1987) and the strategies that the children suggested for coping with one interpersonal and one academic stressful event. Results indicated significant relations between reported behavior problems and the likelihood of emotion-focused versus problem-focused coping strategies. Relevant to the present discussion is the finding that females rated by mothers as depressive/withdrawn or rated by themselves as unpopular were more likely to suggest emotion-focused coping strategies and less likely to suggest problem-focused coping strategies in response to stressful life events. As well, recent research by Bowker and Hymel (1991) has indicated that lonelier children (self-reported) were more likely to report negative coping strategies in dealing with daily hassles in several domains (family, peer relations, academics) than were nonlonely children. Specifically, lonely children were more likely to suggest the use of potentially aggressive strategies (e.g., revenge/retaliation, displacement, blaming others) and/or avoidant strategies (e.g., denial, engaging in alternate activities) and were less likely to seek social support in coping with these hassles. Given previous evidence that withdrawn rejected children are more likely to express feelings of loneliness (e.g., Boivin et al., 1989; Williams & Asher, 1987), these data are suggestive of the possibility that social withdrawal may indeed by associated with particular forms of coping. In an extension of these findings in our own research on aggressive versus withdrawn unpopular subgroups, we are currently examining variations in children's strategies and mechanisms for sustaining positive self-regard in the face of social failure experiences. Such research may help us to understand the processes by which children's self perceptions, and their efforts to maintain them, influence their social behavior.

Finally, we might speculate briefly on how children's self perceptions could maintain and exacerbate current social problems. Personality psychologists of the interpersonal school (e.g., Carson, 1969), as well as some social psychologists (e.g., Jones, 1977; Snyder & Swann, 1978) have long emphasized the role of vicious circles in which self perceptions lead one to behave socially in ways that elicit experiences that verify these self perceptions. Unlike the possibly buffering effect of aggressive children's unrealistically positive self perceptions, the accurate but negative self perceptions of withdrawn children may lead them to behave anxiously and tentatively with peers and avoid corrective experiences in which they might learn other, possibly more rewarding patterns of social behavior. By contrast, the difficulty with aggressive and aggressive-withdrawn children may be their relative imperviousness to negative feedback, which sustains a rosy picture of self and thereby subverts the motivation to learn other patterns of social behavior (see Dodge, 1991; Rubin, Bream, & Rose-Krasnor, 1991). In both cases, the basic theme would be that what one believes about oneself may come to have self-perpetuating qualities that hamper aspects of one's social development.

ACKNOWLEDGMENTS

The research reported herein was supported in part by research grants from the Social Sciences and Humanities Research Council of Canada.

REFERENCES

Achenbach, T. M. (1982). *Developmental psychopathology,* Second Edition. New York: Wiley.

Achenbach, T. M., & Edelbrock, C. S. (1981). Behavioral problems and competencies reported by parents of normal and disturbed children aged four through sixteen. *Monographs of the Society for Research in Child Development, 46,* (Serial no. 188).

Achenbach, T. M., & Edelbrock, C. S. (1983). Behavioral problems and competencies reported by parents of normal and disturbed children. *Monographs of the Society for Research in Child Development, 46* (1, Serial No. 188).

Achenbach, T. M., & Edelbrock, C. S. (1987). *Manual for the Youth self-report and profile.* Burlington: University of Vermont, Department of Psychiatry.

Altmann, E. O., & Gotlib, I. H. (1988). The social behavior of depressed children: An observational study. *Journal of Abnormal Child Psychology, 16,* 29–44.

Asendorpf, J. B. (1991). Development of inhibited children's coping with unfamiliarity. *Child Development, 62,* 1460–1474.

Asher, S. R. (1991). *Loneliness and self-referral among aggressive-rejected and withdrawn-rejected children.* Paper presented at the biennial meeting of the International Society for the Study of Behavioral Development, Minneapolis, MN.

Asher, S. R., & Coie, J. D. (1990). *Peer rejection in childhood.* New York: Cambridge University Press.

Asher, S. R., Hymel, S., & Renshaw, P. D. (1984). Loneliness in children. *Child Development, 55,* 1456–1464.

Asher, S. R., Parkhurst, J. T., Hymel, S., & Williams, G. A. (1990). Peer rejection and loneliness in childhood. In S. R. Asher & J. D. Coie (Eds.), *Peer rejection in childhood.* (253–273). New York: Cambridge University Press.

Asher, S. R., Zelis, K., Parker, J., & Bruene, C. (1991). *Self-referral for peer relationship problems among aggressive and withdrawn low-accepted children.* Paper presented at the biennial meeting of the Society for Research in Child Development, Seattle, WA.

Beharry, P. J. (1990). *Interviews with parents and children: A qualitative analysis.* Paper presented at the biennial University of Waterloo Conference on Child Development, Waterloo, Ontario.

Berndt, T. J., & Ladd, G. W. (1989). *Peer Relationships in Child Development.* NY: Wiley.

Bierman, K. L., Miller, C. L., & Stabb, S. D. (1987). Improving the social behavior and peer acceptance of rejected boys: Effects of social skill training with instructions and prohibitions. *Journal of Consulting and Clinical Psychology, 55,* 194–200.

Boivin, M., & Bégin, G. (1989). Peer status and self-perception among early elementary school children: The case of the rejected children. *Child Development, 60,* 591–596.

Boivin, M., Thomassin, L., & Alain, M. (1989). Peer rejection and self-perceptions among early elementary school children: Aggressive rejectees versus withdrawn rejectees. In B. H. Schneider, G. Attili, J. Nadel, & R. P. Weissberg (Eds.) *Social competence in developmental perspective* (pp. 392–393). Boston, MA: Kluwer Academic Publishing.

Bower, E. M., Shelhammer, T. A., & Daily, J. M. (1968). Social characteristics of male adolescents who later became schizophrenics. *American Journal of Orthopsychiatry, 30,* 712–729.

Bowker, A., & Hymel, S. (1991). *Coping with daily hassles in early adolescence.* Paper presented at the biennial meeting of the Society for Research in Child Development, Seattle, WA.

Carson, R. C. (1969). *Interaction concepts of personality.* Chicago: Aldine.

Coie, J. D. (1985). Fitting social skills intervention to the target group. In B. H. Schneider, K. H., Rubin, & J. E. Ledingham (Eds.), *Children's peer relations: Issues in assessment and intervention.* (pp. 141–156). New York: Springer-Verlag.

Coie, J. D., Dodge, K. A., & Kupersmidt, J. (1990). Peer group behavior and social status. In S. R. Asher and J. D. Coie (Eds.), *Peer rejection in childhood* (pp. 17–59). New York: Cambridge University Press.

Compas, B. E., Malcarne, V. L., & Fondacaro, K. M. (1988). Coping with stressful events in older children and young adolescents. *Journal of Consulting and Clinical Psychology, 56,* 405–411.

Coyne, J. C., & Gotlieb, I. H. (1983). The role of cognition in depression: A critical appraisal. *Psychological Bulletin, 94,* 472–505.

Dodge, K. A. (1991). The structure and function of reactive and proactive aggression. In D. J. Pepler & K. H. Rubin (Eds.), *The development and treatment of childhood aggression* (pp. 201–218). Hillsdale, NJ: Lawrence Erlbaum Associates.

Erickson, M. F., Bacon, M., & Egeland, B. (1987). *Developmental antecedents and concomitants of depressive symptoms in preschool children.* Paper presented at the biennial meeting of the Society for Research in Child Development.

Evers-Pasquale, W. (1978). The Peer Preference Test as a measure of reward value: Item analysis, cross validation, concurrent validation, and replication. *Journal of Abnormal Child Psychology, 6,* 175–188.

Evers-Pasquale, W., & Sherman, M. (1975). The reward value of peers: A variable influencing the efficacy of filmed modeling in modifying social isolation in preschoolers. *Journal of Abnormal Child Psychology, 3,* 179–189.

Flemming, D., & Ricks, D. F. (1970). Emotions of children before schizophrenia and before character disorder. In M. Roff & D. F. Ricks (Eds.), *Life history research in psychopathology,* Vol. 1. Minneapolis: University of Minnesota Press.

French, D. C. (1988). Heterogeneity of peer-rejected boys: Aggressive and non-aggressive types. *Child Development, 59,* 976–985.

French, D. C. (1990). Heterogeneity of peer-rejected girls. *Child Development, 61,* 2028–2031.

Harter, S. (1982). The perceived competence scale for children. *Child Development, 53,* 87–97.

Harter, S. (1985). *Manual for the Self-Perception Profile for Children.* Unpublished manuscript, University of Denver.

Harter, S. (1986). Processes underlying the construction, maintenance, and enhancement of the self-concept in children. In J. Suls & A. G. Greenwald (Eds.), *Psychological perspectives on the Self,* Vol. 3. Hillsdale, NJ: Lawrence Erlbaum Associates.

Hayden, L. (1989). *The development of the Relational Provisions Loneliness Questionnaire for children.* Unpublished doctoral dissertation, University of Waterloo, Waterloo, Ontario.

Hetherington, E. M., & Parke, R. D. (1986). *Child Psychology: A contemporary viewpoint,* Third Edition. New York: McGraw-Hill.

Hymel, S. (1983). *Social isolation and rejection in children: Considering the child's perspective.* Paper presented at the biennial meeting of the Society for Research in Child Development, Detroit, MI.

Hymel, S., Bowker, A., & Woody, E. (forthcoming). *Aggressive versus withdrawn unpopular children: Variations in peer, teacher and self-perceptions in multiple domains.* Manuscript submitted for publication.

Hymel, S., & Franke, S. (1985). Children's peer relations: Assessing self-perceptions. In B. H. Schneider, K. H. Rubin, & J. E. Ledingham (Eds.). *Children's peer relations: Issues in assessment and intervention.* (pp. 75–91). New York: Springer-Verlag.

Hymel, S., & Rubin, K. H. (1985). Children with peer relationship and social skills problems: Conceptual, methodological, and developmental issues. In G. J. Whitehurst (Ed.), *Annals of child development,* Vol. 2 (pp. 251–297). Greenwich, CT: JAI Press.

Hymel, S., & Rubin, K. H., Rowden, L., & LeMare, L. (1990). Children's peer relationships: Longitudinal prediction of internalizing and externalizing problems from middle to late childhood. *Child Development, 61,* 2004–2021.

Hymel, S., Woody, E., Ditner, E., & LeMare, L. (1988). *Children's self perceptions in different domains: Are children consistent across measures and do they see what others see?* Paper presented at the biennial University of Waterloo Conference on Child Development, Waterloo, Ontario.

Janes, C. L., & Hesselbrock, V. M. (1978). Problem children's adult adjustment predicted from teacher's ratings. *American Journal of Orthopsychiatry, 48,* 200–309.

Janes, C. L., & Hesselbrock, V. M., Myers, D. G., & Penniman, J. H. (1979). Problem boys in young adulthood: Teachers' ratings and twelve-year follow-up. *Journal of Youth and Adolescence, 8,* 453–472.

John, R. S., Mednick, S. A., & Schulsinger, F. (1982). Teacher reports as a predictor of schizophrenia and borderline schizophrenia: A Bayesian decision analysis. *Journal of Abnormal Psychology, 6,* 399–413.

Jones, R. A. (1977). *Self-fulfilling prophecies: Social, psychological, and physiological effects of expectancies.* Hillsdale, NJ: Lawrence Erlbaum Associates.

Jourard, S. M., & Landsman, T. (1980). *Healthy personality: An approach from the viewpoint of humanistic psychology* (Fourth Edition). New York: MacMillan.

Kagan, J. (1984). *The nature of the child.* New York: Basic Books.

Kagan, J. (1989). *Unstable ideas: Temperament, cognition and self.* Cambridge, MA: Harvard University Press.

Kagan, J., Hans, S., Markowitz, A., Lopez, D., & Sigal, H. (1982). Validity of children's self reports of psychological qualities. In B. Maher (Ed.) *Progress in experimental personality research,* Vol. II (pp. 171–211). New York: Academic Press.

Kochanska, G., Kuczynski, L., & Radke-Yarrow, M. (1989). Correspondence between mothers' self-reported and observed child-rearing practices. *Child Development, 60,* 56–63.

Kohlberg, L., LaCrosse, I., & Ricks, D. (1972). The predictability of adult mental health from childhood behavior. In B. B. Wolman (Ed.), *Manual of child psychopathology* (pp. 1217–1284). New York: McGraw-Hill.

LaGreca, A. M., Dandes, S. K., Wick, P., Shaw, K., & Stone, W. L. (1988). Development of the Social Anxiety Scale for Children: Reliability and concurrent validity. *Journal of Clinical Child Psychology, 17,* 84–91.

Ledingham, J. E. (1981). Developmental patterns of aggressive and withdrawn behavior in childhood: A possible method of identifying preschizophrenics. *Journal of Abnormal Child Psychology, 9,* 1–22.

Ledingham, J. E., & Schwartzman, A. E. (1984). A 3-year follow-up of aggressive and withdrawn behavior in childhood: Preliminary findings. *Journal of Abnormal Child Psychology, 12,* 157–168.

Lewinsohn, P. M., Mischel, W., Chaplin, W., & Barton, R. (1980). Social competence and depression: The role of illusory self perceptions. *Journal of Abnormal Psychology, 89,* 203–212.

Marsh, H. W., Byrne, B. M., & Shavelson, R. J. (1988). A multifaceted academic self-concept: Its hierarchical structure and its relation to academic achievement. *Journal of Psychology, 80,* (3), 336–380.

Marsh, H. W., Smith, I. D., & Barnes, J. (1983). Multitrait-multimethod analyses of the Self Description Questionnaire: Student-teacher agreement on multidimensional ratings of student self-concept. *American Educational Research Journal, 20,* 333–357.

Marsh, H. W., Smith, I. D., & Barnes, J. (1985). Multidimensional self-concepts: Relations with sex and academic achievement. *Journal of Educational Psychology, 77,* 581–596.

Masten, A., Morison, P., & Pelligrini, D. (1985). A revised class play method of peer assessment. *Developmental Psychology, 21,* 523–533.

McGillicuddy-DeLisi, A. V. (1982). Parental beliefs about developmental processes. *Human Development, 25,* 192–200.

Meichenbaum, D., Bream, L. A., & Cohen, J. S. (1984). A cognitive-behavioral perspective of child psychology: Implications for assessment and training. In R. J. McMahon & R. D. Peters (Eds.), *Childhood disorders: Behavioral-developmental approaches.* New York: Brunner-Mazel.

Michael, C. M., Morris, D. P., & Soroker, E. (1957). Follow-up studies of shy, withdrawn children II: Relative incidence of schizophrenia. *American Journal of Orthopsychiatry, 27,* 331-337.

Mills, R. S. L., & Rubin, K. H. (1990). Parental beliefs about problematic social behaviors in early childhood. *Child Development, 61,* 138-151.

Morris, D. P., Soroker, E., & Burruss, G. (1954). Follow-up studies of shy, withdrawn children − 1: Evaluation of later adjustment. *American Journal of Orthopsychiatry, 24,* 743-754.

Parker, J. G., & Asher, S. R. (1987). Peer relations and later personal adjustment: Are low-accepted children at risk? *Psychological Bulletin, 102,* 289-357.

Patterson, G. J., Kupersmidt, J. B., & Greisler, P. C. (1990). Children's perceptions of self and of relations with others as a function of sociometric status. *Child Development, 61,* 1335-1349.

Paulhus, D. L. (1984). Two-component models of socially desireable responding. *Journal of Personality and Social Psychology, 46,* 598-609.

Pekarik, E. G., Printz, R. J., Liebert, D. E., Weintraub, S., & Neale, J. M. (1976). The Pupil Evaluation Inventory: A sociometric technique for assessing children's social behavior. *Journal of Abnormal Child Psychology, 4,* 83-97.

Quay, H. C., & LaGreca, L. M. (1986). Disorders of anxiety, withdrawal, and dysphoria. In H. C. Quay & J. S. Werry (Eds.), *Psychopathological disorders of childhood* (pp. 73-110). New York: Wiley.

Robins, L. N. (1966). *Deviant children grow up.* Baltimore: Williams & Wilkins.

Rubin, K. H., Bream, L. A., & Rose-Krasnor, L. (1991). Social problem solving and aggression in childhood. In D. J. Pepler & K. H. Rubin (Eds.), *The development and treatment of childhood aggression* (pp. 219-248). Hillsdale, NJ: Lawrence Erlbaum Associates.

Rubin, K. H., Hymel, S., LeMare, L., & Rowden, L. (1989). Children experiencing social difficulties: Sociometric neglect reconsidered. *Canadian Journal of Behavioral Science, 21,* 94-111.

Rubin, K. H., Hymel, S., & Mills, R. S. L. (1989). Sociability and social withdrawal in childhood: Stability and outcomes. *Journal of Personality, 57,* 237-256.

Rubin, K. H., Hymel, S., Mills, R. S. L., & Rose-Krasnor, L. (1991). Conceptualizing different developmental pathways to and from social isolation in childhood. In D. Cicchetti (Ed.), *Rochester Symposium on Developmental Psychopathology,* Vol. 2 (pp. 91-122). Hillsdale, NJ: Lawrence Erlbaum Associates.

Rubin, K. H., LeMare, L., & Lollis, S. (1990). Social withdrawal in childhood: Developmental pathways to peer rejection. In S. R. Asher & J. D. Coie (Eds.), *Peer rejection in childhood.* New York: Cambridge University Press.

Rubin, K. H., & Lollis, S. (1988). Origins and consequences of social withdrawal. In J. Belsky & T. Nezworski (Eds.), *Clinical implications of attachment* (pp. 219-252). Hillsdale, NJ: Lawrence Erlbaum Associates.

Rubin, K. H., & Mills, R. (1988). The many faces of social isolation in childhood. *Journal of Consulting and Clinical Psychology, 6,* 916-924.

Rubin, K. H., & Ross, H. S. (1982). *Peer relationships and social skills in childhood.* New York: Springer-Verlag.

Ruehlman, L. S., West, S. G., & Pasahow, R. J. (1985). Depression and evaluative schemata. *Journal of Personality, 53,* 46-92.

Sackeim, H. A. (1983). Self-deception, self-esteem, and depression: The adaptive value of lying to oneself. In J. Masling (Ed.), *Empirical studies of psychoanalytic theories* (pp. 101-157). Hillsdale, NJ: Lawrence Erlbaum Associates.

Schneider, B. H., Rubin, K. H., & Ledingham, J. E. (Eds.) (1985). *Children's peer relations: Issues in assessment and intervention.* New York: Springer-Verlag.

Shavelson, R. J., & Bolus, R. (1982). Self-concept: The interplay of therapy and methods. *Journal of Educational Psychology, 74,* 3–17.

Shrauger, J. S., & Schoeneman, S. (1979). Symbolic interactionist view of self-concept: Through the looking glass darkly. *Psychological Bulletin, 86,* 549–573.

Snyder, M., & Swann, W. B. (1978). Behavioral confirmation in social interaction: From social perception to social reality. *Journal of Experimental Social Psychology, 14,* 148–160.

Taylor, S. E., & Brown, J. D. (1988). Illusion and well-being: A social psychological perspective on mental health. *Psychological Bulletin, 103,* 193–210.

Watson, D., & Clark, L. A. (1984). Negative affectivity: The disposition to experience aversive emotional states. *Psychological Bulletin, 96,* 465–490.

Weiss, R. S. (1973). *Loneliness: The experience of emotional and social isolation.* Cambridge, MA: MIT Press.

Williams, G. A., & Asher, S. R. (1987). *Peer and self-perceptions of peer rejected children: Issues in classification and subgrouping.* Paper presented at the biennial meeting of the Society for Research in Child Development, Baltimore, Maryland.

Wine, J. D., & Smye, M. D. (1981). *Social Competence.* New York: Guilford Press.

Wylie, R. C. (1974). *The self-concept: A review of methodological considerations and measuring instruments,* Volume 1. Lincoln, Nebraska: University of Nebraska Press.

Wylie, R. C. (1979). *The self-concept (Volume 2): Theory and research on selected topics.* Lincoln: University of Nebraska Press.

Wylie, R. C. (1989). *Measures of self concept.* Lincoln, Nebraska: University of Nebraska Press.

Younger, A. J., & Boyko, K. A. (1987). Aggression and withdrawal as social schemas underlying children's peer perceptions. *Child Development, 58,* 1094–1100.

Younger, A. J., & Daniels, T. (in press). Children's peer nominations for withdrawal: What are the reasons for their choices? *Developmental Psychology.*

Younger, A. J., Schwartzman, A. E., & Ledingham, J. E. (1985). Grade-related changes in children's perceptions of aggression and withdrawal in their peers. *Developmental Psychology, 21,* 70–75.

Younger, A. J., Schwartzman, A. E., & Ledingham, J. E. (1986). Age-related differences in children's perceptions of social deviance: Changes in behavior or perspective? *Developmental Psychology, 22,* 531–542.

Yule, W. (1981). Epidemiology of child psychopathology. In B. Lahey & A. Kazdin (Eds.), *Advances in child-clinical psychology,* Vol. 4. NY: Plenum Press.

V LONGITUDINAL PERSPECTIVES ON SOCIAL WITHDRAWAL AND INHIBITION

13 Beyond Temperament: A Two-Factorial Coping Model of the Development of Inhibition during Childhood

Jens B. Asendorpf
Max-Planck-Institut für Psychologische Forschung

Why do some children react with inhibition when they encounter strangers but other children do not? Why do some of these initially inhibited children overcome their shyness quickly and become immersed in social interaction whereas others need a long time to warm up, and still others escape to splendid isolation, ignoring the stranger? Why do some children act so shy in groups of familiar peers whereas others fly around like butterflies? In this chapter I try to provide some tentative answers to these questions.

The answers are based on my preoccupation with empirical studies of shyness, inhibition, and social withdrawal in adults and children in the last seven years. During this period, my research team has scrutinized some 250 university students in various social situations, and has closely followed a cohort of 99 children from the start of preschool at age 4 for 5 years through grade 2, both in strictly controlled laboratory settings and in their school environment. The latter longitudinal data were obtained from the Munich Longitudinal Study on the Genesis of Individual Competencies (LOGIC), a collaborative study on various aspects of children's emerging cognitive and social competence (Weinert & Schneider, 1986).

The university student studies (Asendorpf, 1987, 1989a,b) suggested a two-factorial view of inhibition. Inhibited behavior is a final common pathway of two different kinds of inhibitory processes. It is triggered both by the unfamiliarity of interaction partners and by the anticipation of social evaluation. This view of inhibition proved to be quite helpful for analyzing the longitudinal data on children's inhibition. Inhibition toward strangers was surprisingly stable over time whereas inhibition in the preschool/kindergarten class was less stable. The longer children stayed in class, the less their inhibition toward classmates was predictable by their inhibition toward strangers, and the more it was predictable by negative relations with classmates (Asendorpf, 1990a). This chapter presents new data supporting this domain-specificity of inhibition: In grade one, teacher ratings of children's inhibition in class were predictable from their inhibition toward strangers, but teacher ratings of inhibition in grade two were not.

Together, these data suggest a two-factorial view of inhibited behavior. Inhibition is triggered both by unfamiliarity and by social-evaluative concerns. Whereas inhibition toward strangers can be accounted for by a static temperamental trait, social-evaluative concerns are due to the nature of the social relationships that emerge in stable social settings. Because a relationship between two children cannot be reduced to the temperamental trait of one of them, children's inhibited behavior with *familiar* people cannot be fully accounted for by a temperamental trait. This was the first observation that forced me to transcend the notion that individual differences in inhibition could be sufficiently explained by a biological disposition to react with inhibition to conspecifics. There was more in the data than just temperament.

A second observation challenged the assumption of a simple relation between temperament and behavior even further. When I correlated children's inhibition toward adult strangers with their behavior toward unfamiliar peers, I found an interesting age-related change in the correlations that suggested a developmental shift in children's coping strategies with unfamiliarity. Between the ages of 5 and 8 years, normal children became increasingly social with an unfamiliar peer but most highly inhibited children continued to be rather unsocial. When they faced an unfamiliar peer, they retreated to passive solitude (comprising solitary-exploratory and solitary-constructive play; Rubin & Mills, 1988) quite often.

I interpreted this divergence of the inhibited children from the normal path of development as a failure to cope with unfamiliarity (Asendorpf, 1991). Normal children learned how to overcome their shyness in the face of an unfamiliar peer, but inhibited children failed to do so. This developmental divergence could not be explained by temperamental differences alone. But the data were quite plausible if it was assumed that temperamental differences were moderated by coping strategies. Most uninhibited (and some inhibited) children learned how to overcome their inhibition rather quickly whereas most inhibited children remained unable to do so.

The bottom line is that children's inhibited behavior cannot be fully explained by a temperamental disposition. Beyond temperament, children's emerging social relationships with peers in stable social settings and their coping strategies in dealing with unfamiliarity (and perhaps also with negative peer relationships) have to be taken into account if we want to explain children's inhibition in social situations. In this chapter, I discuss this view of children's inhibition and its relation to unsociability in more detail.

INHIBITION TOWARD STRANGERS

Assessment

Inhibition toward adult strangers and toward peer strangers were assessed both by a parental scale in each year of observation and by one behavioral observation with a stranger in each year; adult and peer strangers changed systematically between years.

Parental Scale.   Table 13.1 presents the 8 items of the parental inhibition scale. The items had to be rated on a 7-point scale ("never" - "always"); items were randomly distributed among 40 other items of the same response format. Parallel items referred to adult versus peer strangers. The two 4-item subscales "inhibition toward adult strangers" and "inhibition toward peer strangers" showed little discriminant validity (intercorrelations between .64 and .76 in all 5 years of assessment and only small differences in correlations with external variables); therefore they are not distinguished in the analyses reported here. The internal consistency of the 8-item scale was above $\alpha = .84$ in each year.

Observation of Inhibition toward Adult Strangers.   In research on wariness toward strangers (Sroufe, 1977) and attachment (Ainsworth, Blehar, Waters, & Wall, 1978), a stranger approaches an infant or child; it is assumed that the child is interested in the stranger and that aversive reactions indicate wariness or inhibition but not a lacking social interest. If this classic procedure is applied to older children, it can be difficult to distinguish between children who are inhibited and those who are simply disinterested in the stranger. In order to overcome this problem, in the first two assessments at an age of 3.9 and 5.9 years the children were explicitly motivated to get in contact with the stranger as follows (see Fig. 13.1).

The child and mother sat in an observation room. At the beginning of the

TABLE 13.1
Items of the Parental Inhibition Scale

When my child meets unknown xxx s/he needs a long time to warm up
My child is shy toward unknown xxx
My child is somewhat inhibited toward unknown xxx
My child easily approaches unknown xxx (item reversed)

In four items, "xxx" is replaced by "adults," and in the other four items by "children."

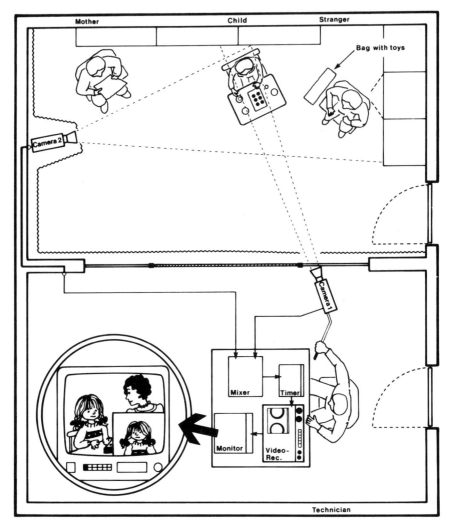

FIG. 13.1   Observational setting for adult strangers.

session, the child had rather uninteresting toys to play with. If the child lost interest in the toys (usually after 1–3 minutes), a female stranger appeared with a transparent bag full of interesting toys; all children in a given year of observation met the same woman. The stranger greeted the mother and child briefly, sat down and started unpacking the bag. The stranger only responded to verbal initiations of the child but did not actively approach the child. If the child did not initiate a conversation within three minutes, the stranger started speaking about the toys. In any case, there was a preinteraction period of 0–3 minutes, and an interaction period of 2 minutes following contact initiation by the child or the stranger. Both periods were videotaped.

When the children of the LOGIC study were 7.9 years old, this no longer seemed an age-appropriate procedure. At this age, the child and the female stranger sat at a table facing each other; no parent was in the room. The stranger started a conversation about visiting a circus (every child had experience with that). She asked only short questions (e.g., have you already been in a circus?) and waited up to 10 seconds for the child to respond. After each child response, she waited 10 seconds before asking the next question. This slow interviewing style put the burden of the conversation on the children. The interviewer had a repertoire of 6 questions available. Each interview lasted for at least 2 minutes and was videotaped.

Although the videotapes of these situations were extensively coded for various aspects of children's verbal and nonverbal behavior, a rather simple measure turned out to be the best according to its stability over time and its correlations with the parental inhibition scale: the latency toward children's first *unsolicited* utterance toward the stranger. This latency showed a high variance between children and in the first two assessments a ceiling effect: The maximum latency of 300 sec was obtained by 41% of the children at age 3.9 years and by 12% at age 5.9 years. Therefore, correlations with these latencies had to be corrected (method proposed by Alliger, Hanges, & Alexander, 1988).

Observation of Inhibition toward Peer Strangers.   Obviously it was not possible to confront the children with an unfamiliar peer in a way that was exactly comparable with the adult stranger procedure. Instead, we observed dyads of unfamiliar children in a free play situation for 10–15 minutes. The disadvantage of such an approach is that different children had different partners; hence each child's behavior was affected not only by the child's inhibition but also by the inhibition of the partner. The advantage of this approach is that children's adaptation to a peer stranger could be studied for a longer period of time.

There were three play sessions that took place in an observation room of the Max Planck Institute when the children were 4.9, 6.9, and 8.1 years old. Thus, there was an age difference of exactly one year between the first five stranger confrontations; only the last one at age 8.1 followed the last adult confrontation at age 7.9 at a time span of 3 months.

The children were randomly paired with a same-gender child whom they had never met. The room was equipped with age-appropriate toys that were changed at each year of observation. At age 4.9, the parent of each child sat quietly in the room and was instructed to answer a long questionnaire. In the other two play sessions, a female experimenter well known to the children sat in the room pretending to read a book. Adults were instructed to ignore the children as much as possible. All play sessions were videotaped (see Fig. 13.2).

The videotapes of the play sessions were extensively coded for children's social and cognitive play behavior (Rubin, 1985), the requests directed toward their partner (Rubin & Emptage, 1985), and the partner's response to these social initiatives. But similarly to the adult stranger situation, one rather simple latency score was superior to all other observational measures in terms of its stability over time and its correlations with the parental inhibition scale: the latency toward children's first *request* directed toward their partner (requests rather than unsolicited utterances were used here

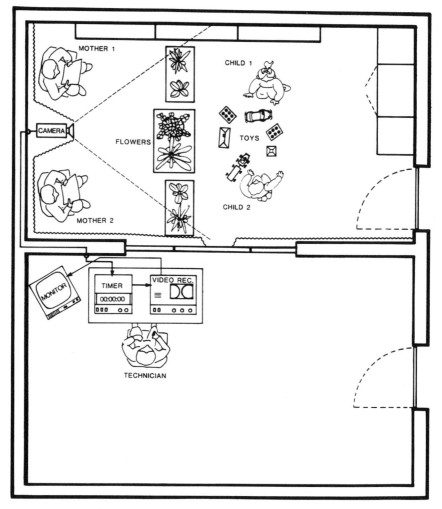

FIG. 13.2 Observational setting for peer strangers.

because some children directed nonverbal requests to the partner). Again, these latency scores showed ceiling effects; about 30% of the children at each year of observation did not produce any requests and thus reached ceiling (the duration of the play session). Therefore, correlations with these latencies were corrected for this ceiling effect.

Continuity between Childhood and Adulthood. Is the *construct* of inhibition toward strangers *continuous* over time in terms of its behavioral expression, or do people express their inhibition differently at different ages? One of the most important but least understood problems of personality development is the fact that the "same" construct of individual differences relates to different characteristic behaviors at different ages. For example, the typical aggressive behavior of a three-year-old boy is quite different from a typical aggressive behavior of a 30-year-old man. Is inhibition toward strangers expressed similarly at different ages?

Recently, I proposed a new method to answer this question *empirically* (Asendorpf, 1992). First, a construct is defined separately from the observed behavior by some criterion measure. This criterion measure is correlated with the frequency or intensity of many behaviors. A crucial point is that these behaviors are not selected exclusively for high correlations with the criterion. Instead, behaviors are sampled "representatively," that is, in a way that represents the whole continuum from very valid to completely invalid behaviors. For example, if speech is analyzed, various indices of speech are assessed independently of the question whether these indices are valid indicators of inhibition or not. The temporal stability of the rank-order of the validity coefficients of these behaviors reflects the continuity of the construct. This approach to the continuity of personality traits follows the perspective of functional probabilism (Brunswik, 1956; Petrinovich, 1979).

In the present case, the parental inhibition scale can serve as the criterion measure for the construct "inhibition toward strangers," and it can be related to a wide variety of behaviors toward strangers such as measures of verbal activity, gazing, and body movement. Because I had data available from previous studies with university students that were quite comparable with the data on children's behavior toward adult strangers (Asendorpf, 1987, 1988), I studied the continuity of the expression of inhibition toward adult strangers. Are highly inhibited children during conversations with adult strangers characterized by the same behaviors that describe highly inhibited university students when they confront adult strangers (i.e., in this case peers)? In order to answer this question empirically, I compared the rank-order of the validity coefficients of 17 different behaviors for inhibition between children and adults (see Table 13.2).

For the children, the four items of the parental inhibition scale that

TABLE 13.2
Behavioral Correlates of Inhibition in Children and Adults

Behavioral measures	88 Children age 4yrs		70 Students age 19–32yrs	
	r^a	rank[b]	r^a	rank[b]
Latency to first spontaneous utterance	.64***	1	.46***	1
Percent speaking alone	− .55***	17	− .40***	17
Mean length speaking alone	− .14	10	− .11	10
Percent listening	− .21	14	− .09	9
Mean length listening	.17	5	.07	5
Percent silence	.55***	3	.41***	2
Mean length silence	.59***	2	.38**	3
Percent double talk[c]	− .40***	16	− .33**	15
Mean length double talk	− .15	13	− .14	14
Percent gazing during speaking	− .09	8	− .13	13
Mean length gazing during speaking	− .01	7	− .07	8
Percent gazing during silence	− .35**	15	− .35**	16
Mean length gazing during silence	− .11	9	.04	7
Mean length gaze aversion during speaking	− .15	12	.05	6
Mean length gaze aversion during silence	.39***	4	.31*	4
Percent self-adaptors	− .14	11	− .11	12
Mean length self-adaptors	.16	6	− .11	11

[a]Spearman correlations with parental scale (children) or with shyness scale (students) except for children's latencies for which Pearson correlations are reported that were corrected for the ceiling effect in the latencies (see text).
[b]Rank of correlation among all behaviors.
[c]Percent of observation time when both partners were speaking at the same time.
*$p < .05$ **$p < .01$ ***$p < .001$

referred to adult strangers were used as the criterion measure of inhibition; for the university students, a 4–item self-rating scale with similar items and the same response format was used (see Asendorpf, 1987, 1989a,b). The students were confronted with a same-gender confederate of the experimenter who pretended to be another subject (see also Asendorpf, 1987). The conversational behavior of children and adults was coded with identical methods.

Table 13.2 indicates that the rank order of the 17 behaviors for the children was very similar to the rank order found for the university students; a Spearman correlation of .84 was found between the two rank orders. This high correlation could be inflated, however, if the differences among the short-term stabilities of the behaviors were also stable between childhood and adulthood. However, the rank orders of the stabilities of the 16 behaviors between the first and the second half of the conversations were not significantly stable between childhood and adulthood (obviously, the latency measure could not be evaluated for short-term stability), and when the validity coefficients in Table 13.2 were each corrected for their short-term stability (correction for attenuation), the rank orders of children and adults still correlated .84 with each other. Thus, 4-year-olds and university students expressed their inhibition toward strangers by a very similar pattern of conversational behaviors. Less surprisingly, this was also true for a comparison between the three assessments of children's conversations with adult strangers (see Asendorpf, 1992, for the comparison of the first two assessments).

Stability

Because the parental inhibition scale showed significant positive correlations with the latency measure in each year of observation, the parental inhibition score and the latency measure were made comparable by a z-transformation and were then aggregated, yielding one inhibition index per assessment. The stability of the individual differences in children's inhibition toward strangers was evaluated by correlating this index between different ages. These correlations showed that inhibition was quite stable even if it was compared between the differently designed assessments involving adults versus peers (see Table 13.3).

Inhibition toward adult strangers was quite stable between 4 and 8 years of age. The four-year stability of .62 was higher than the stability of IQ tests in this age range (in the LOGIC study, the four-year stability for the Columbia Mental Maturity Scale, a nonverbal intelligence test, was .43, and the 4-year stability for the verbal IQ of the Wechsler test was .45). Kagan and Moss (1962) and Kagan, Reznick, Snidman, Gibbons, and Johnson (1988) also reported high stabilities of inhibition, although the Kagan and Moss data refer to older ages, and the stabilities that were reported by Kagan et al. (1988) are inflated because they used extreme groups of highly inhibited and uninhibited children.

TABLE 13.3
Stabilities of Inhibition toward Strangers

Stranger	Age	Age				
		4.9	5.9	6.9	7.9	8.1
Adult	3.9	.68	.75	.64	.62	.49
Peer	4.9		.58	.59	.58	.51
Adult	5.9			.68	.63	.58
Peer	6.9				.69	.65
Adult	7.9					—[a]
Peer	8.1					

N varies between 55 and 80 due to missing values.

[a]Correlation is not meaningful because the compared indices contain the same parental scale.

The stabilities of inhibition toward peer strangers were somewhat lower than the stabilities of inhibition toward adult strangers (e.g., a 3.2-year stability of .51). This can be attributed to the fact that inhibition toward unfamiliar peers was affected by the inhibition of the partners who varied from child to child whereas the adult stranger was the same for all children of one age group. Consistent with this interpretation, the stabilities between assessments involving an adult at one measurement point and a peer at the other assessment ranged between the comparable stabilities for the adult assessments and the peer assessments.

The relatively high temporal stability (when compared with other personality differences in this age range) and the high consistency of inhibition toward adult versus peer strangers suggests that inhibition toward strangers is an individual characteristic of a child that is independent of the age of the unfamiliar partner. It is a temperamental trait par excellence (for the concept of temperament, see Buss & Plomin, 1984; Kagan, 1989; Thomas & Chess, 1980).

Specificity

So far we have seen that inhibition toward strangers is a relatively stable temperamental trait in childhood. How general is this trait? Does it affect only children's behavior toward strangers, or does it also influence their behavior toward familiar people? In order to explore this specificity question, the children were observed not only in the three play sessions with unfamiliar peers but also in two play sessions with familiar peers.

These sessions took place in the familiar environment of the kindergarten and were quite comparable with the laboratory play observation in terms of the size of the room, the toys, and the length of the play session. The only major difference was that children played together with a *classmate* of their regular kindergarten group whom they knew for at least 8 months. The two assessments were scheduled 6 months after the first play session with a peer stranger and 6 months before the second play session with a peer stranger.

The two types of play sessions were compared by contrasting the correlations between the concurrently assessed parental inhibition scales and children's behavior in the sessions. Besides the most important latency measure, three other measures relating to inhibition were assessed: the percentage of the observation time when children did not show any particular activity (e.g., staring into space) or when they watched their partner from a distance without playing, called *isolation;* the percentage of time when they did not interact with the partner, called *lack of interaction* (this category includes isolation as well as solitary and parallel play); and the frequency of requests or role initiations directed to their partner, which was inversed in order to show positive correlations with inhibition, called *lack of initiatives.* Figure 13.3 shows the correlations between the parental inhibition scale and these four behavioral measures for each of the four play sessions.

Figure 13.3 indicates that the parental inhibition scale correlated positively with all four measures of inhibition in both play sessions involving peer strangers; all 8 correlations were significant at least at the $p = .02$ level. The correlations with the two play sessions involving classmates were much lower; none of the 8 correlations was even marginally significant. Furthermore, when the correlations with a particular behavior were compared between the sessions involving unfamiliar versus familiar peers, 12 of the 16 comparisons revealed significantly higher correlations for the unfamiliar condition (see Asendorpf, 1990a, for details). Thus, inhibition toward strangers as judged by the parents predicted children's behavior toward peer strangers but was *unrelated* to their behavior toward classmates.

The specific relation between inhibition and unfamiliarity is perhaps most dramatically demonstrated by comparing an extreme group of *continuously* inhibited children (inhibition scores in the upper quartile of the distribution of the parental inhibition scale at age 4, age 5, and age 6) with a control group of children who had inhibition scores below the median at all three

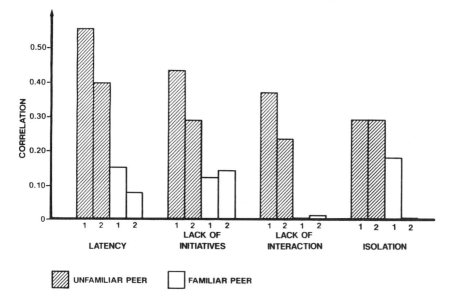

FIG. 13.3 Concurrent correlations between parental inhibition scale and children's behavior toward unfamiliar and familiar peers (adapted from Asendorpf, 1990a; reprinted with permission of the American Psychological Association).

ages. Figure 13.4 shows the "survival functions" of the latency of children's first request directed to their partner for the two play sessions with unfamiliar peers as well as for the first two play sessions with familiar classmates (the data of the two sessions with unfamiliar peers were pooled in one analysis and the data of the two sessions with familiar peers were pooled in another analysis). These survival functions describe the probability that a child does not direct a request toward the partner (these survival functions are estimated by survival analysis, a statistical method of analyzing ceilinged latency variables; cf. Kalbfleisch & Prentice, 1980).

Figure 13.4 indicates that inhibited children were much less likely than controls to request something from an unfamiliar peer whereas they were as likely as controls when the partner was familiar; in the latter case, the survival functions were virtually identical. These data also demonstrate that the critical difference is the one between highly inhibited children and average children, not the one between children very low in inhibition and average ones (correlational analyses cannot distinguish between these two alternatives but an extreme group approach does).

The findings reported so far show that it makes good sense to assume a temperamental trait "inhibition toward strangers" that is expressed in the behavior of children and young adults in the same way, shows a considerable stability over time between age 4 and 8, and is specific to encounters with strangers; children's behavior toward familiar classmates in dyadic play situations was not affected by this trait. Thus, inhibition toward

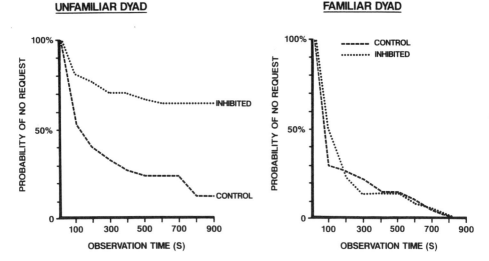

FIG. 13.4 Survival functions for inhibited and control children's latency to their first request directed to unfamiliar and familiar peers.

strangers reflects a lack of social *performance* in certain social situations but *not* a general lack of social *competence.*

Coping with Unfamiliarity

Continuously inhibited children were found to have much longer latencies toward a peer stranger also in the third play session at age 8.1. Furthermore, they showed a significantly higher rate of isolated behaviors (unoccupied or watching the partner without playing; see Fig. 13.3) in all three play sessions. In this respect, they did not change with increasing age; analyses of variance did not find significant age × group interactions for the latencies or for isolated behavior (see Asendorpf, 1991, for details).

But for children's rate of interaction and for their solitary play, interesting differential-developmental changes were found. Continuously inhibited children's rate of social interaction remained low throughout the play sessions but the interactional behavior of the control children doubled between the second and the third year of observation (see Fig. 13.5). This was reflected in a significant group × quadratic age effect in an analysis of variance that took the unequal spacing of the play sessions into account (see Asendorpf, 1991, for details).

This relative increase of the control children's interactional behavior was mirrored by a relative increase of the inhibited children's *solitary-passive play.* Among solitary play, two different forms can be distinguished: solitary-

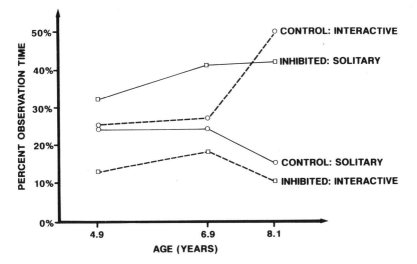

FIG. 13.5 Percentages of solitary-passive and interactive play of inhibited and control children in three years of observation.

passive play comprising exploration or constructive play, and solitary-active play consisting of functional or dramatic play. According to Rubin and colleagues (Rubin, Hymel, & Mills, 1989; Rubin, LeMare, & Lollis, 1990; Rubin & Mills, 1988), a preference for solitary-passive play in kindergarten and grade 2 predicts internalizing problems in later years (negative social self esteem and self-reported loneliness and depression) whereas a high rate of solitary-active play is related to teacher ratings of externalizing problems (particularly aggressiveness) and cognitive immaturity. Thus, it is important to distinguish between these two types of solitary play. In fact, continuously inhibited children tended to show *less* solitary-active play and *more* solitary-passive play than controls in all three years of observation.

The shift of inhibited children to relatively more solitary-passive play was also found in correlational analyses that used the full sample of children. The rate of solitary-passive play correlated increasingly positively with increasing age with concurrent assessments of the parental inhibition scale, the latency measure, and the rate of isolated behavior (see Asendorpf, 1991, for details).

I have interpreted this developmental shift of inhibited children toward more solitary-passive play relative to controls in terms of an emerging difference in *coping strategies.* Uninhibited children learned, over the years, how to deal with an unfamiliar peer; hence, by Grade 2, they achieved an average rate of 50% of social interaction within a play session and spent only 15% of their time playing passively alone. Inhibited children failed to develop this successful style of coping with unfamiliarity. In Grade 2, they spent 42% of their time in solitary-passive play but only 10% in social interaction. Even in nonsolitary forms of play (parallel or group play) inhibited children of this age spent 91% of the play time in passive activities as compared to a rate of 67% among uninhibited children (see Asendorpf, 1991, for details). Thus, inhibited children tended to cope with their inhibition in the face of an unfamiliar peer by *social withdrawal:* They retreated to passive solitude.

In light of the findings of Rubin et al. (1989, 1990) that for older children the rate of passive solitude in groups of familiar peers is predictive of later internalizing problems, the relatively high rate of passive-solitary play among older inhibited children when they face unfamiliar peers may indicate a major problem for their future development *if* these children tend to retreat to solitude in groups of *familiar* peers as well. Presently, there do not seem to exist data that address this issue directly.[1]

---

[1]Our most recent results of the LOGIC study indicate that high and chronic inhibition to strangers between 4 and 6 or 6 and 7 years of age is *not* predictive of internalizing problems at 8, 9, or 10 years of age, even if among the 6 and 7-year-olds only those inhibited children were considered who retreated to passive solitude in the presence of unfamiliar peers. This result suggests that this coping style may not generalize to familiar peers for most highly inhibited children.

At a conceptual level, the developmental shift in the association between inhibition and solitary-passive play suggests a distinction between *initial inhibition* toward strangers and *later adaptation* to strangers. The temperamental trait of inhibition toward strangers may exert a similar effect on all children only in the first few minutes of an encounter with strangers. Later on, it may become much more important how children *cope* with their initial inhibition than how inhibited they were in the beginning.

For example, some children may be trapped for a long time in the state of inhibition; at age 4 and 5 years, a few children of the LOGIC study literally froze for five minutes when they faced the adult or the peer stranger; with increasing age, however, this dramatic expression of inhibition became shorter and shorter. Other children may learn how to overcome their inhibition quickly and may appear completely sociable after a short time. And many inhibited children may respond to their inhibition with social withdrawal; they "give up" their social interests and instead become object-focused (see Jennings, 1975, for the distinction between "people-orientation" and "object-orientation" among children). The preference for solitude may have its emotional price, though, if it generalizes to familiar peers. As the studies of Rubin and colleagues suggest, these children may be prone to later internalizing problems.

This coping view of inhibition also speaks to the issue of how inhibition and unsociability might be related. Earlier I suggested that it is important to distinguish clearly between these two constructs because inhibition involves an approach-avoidance conflict whereas unsociability can be characterized by both a low social approach motivation and a low social avoidance motivation (Asendorpf, 1990b). Many have attributed a lack of social approach motivation to a temperamental trait (e.g., Buss & Plomin, 1984), and this seems to be one reason indeed why some children appear to lack social interest. The coping view of inhibition, however, assumes that there may exist a different developmental pathway leading to unsociable behavior: coping with inhibition by becoming unsociable. At a behavioral level, these two forms of unsociability may be distinguishable only by the immediate response to strangers but not by gross indices of social participation.

BEHAVIOR IN GROUPS OF PEERS

In the preceding section, the study of inhibition was restricted to highly controlled dyadic situations, mainly including unfamiliar interaction partners with whom children had no social relationships. In light of the two-factorial view of inhibition, these data on inhibition to strangers provide a one-sided view of inhibition because they neglect inhibition due to social-evaluative concerns. Such concerns can be studied in long-lasting peer groups such as preschool or elementary school classes where stable relationships can develop between classmates. Negative relationships can arouse social-evaluative concerns and social-evaluate inhibition. Therefore we observed the same longitudinal sample of children also during free play in their preschool class.

Assessment

The German School System.   The German school system is different in some respects from Angloamerican countries. Children often enter Kindergarten at an age of 3–4 years and remain in the *same* class with the same teachers for three years; every year, the oldest third of the class is replaced by a new, youngest third. This provides a more stable class environment and hence the development of more stable relationships with classmates than the typical North American system where children change classes every year before they enter Grade 1. All children of the LOGIC study started Kindergarten at an age of 3–4 years.

Furthermore, German children usually enter grade school later than in North America. Therefore, very few children of the LOGIC study left their Kindergarten after 2 years. Over 80% spent three years and about 15% even four years in Kindergarten. Thus, when German children enter grade school, their average age is about 6.7 years — nearly one year higher than in North America.

Observation of Contact Initiations in Kindergarten.   Children's contact initiation behavior during the regular free play period in their class in the morning was coded by an observer sitting in the classroom with the Contact Initiation Coding System (Asendorpf, 1985). Each child was observed for at least eight 10–minute periods on at least five different days in each of the three years of observation; the average observation time per child and year was 98–111 minutes.

In this chapter, only two variables are of interest: the rate of "wait-and-hover" as the behavioral measure of inhibition, and the success rate in contact initiation attempts as an index of peer acceptance. According to definitions of Gottman (1977) and Dodge, Schlundt, Schocken, and Delugach (1983), "wait-and-hover" was coded whenever the child approached a single person or a group, stopped before reaching them, and looked at them for at least 3 seconds without speaking. The rate of these "inhibited approaches" appeared to be a good measure of children's inhibition in the group because they were independent of the number of initiation attempts or the rate of interaction that may reflect sociability rather than inhibition.

Each contact initiation attempt of the observed child was also coded either for success or for failure. Success was coded whenever the partner responded positively to the initiation attempt; failure was coded whenever the partner did not react to the initiation within 10 seconds, or reacted negatively (cf. Asendorpf, 1985, for details). The rate of successful initiations appeared to be a good measure of the child's acceptance in the peer group.

Teacher Q-sort Measure of Inhibition in Kindergarten. In each of the first three years of observation, the children's main Kindergarten teacher provided a Q-sort description of the child, using a German 54–item short form of the California Child–Q-set of Block and Block (1980) (Göttert & Asendorpf, 1989). Thus, the teacher had to assign 54 items describing personality characteristics of children to nine categories of increasing saliency for the particular child; six items had to be assigned to each category (forced equal distribution that maximizes interindividual differences).

Four teachers of different Kindergartens also independently provided a prototypic Q-sort description for a "Shy-inhibited child"; their agreement was high ($\alpha = .92$). The correlation between each child's Q-sort and the averaged Q-sorts of the four teachers is a measure of the similarity between the child's personality and the personality pattern of a typical shy-inhibited child; this correlation served as the teacher judgment of the child's inhibition in Kindergarten. This index had a split-half reliability of above .82 in each year of observation (see Asendorpf, 1990a, for details).

Teacher Rating of Inhibition in Grade School. About 80% of the children of the LOGIC sample entered Grade 1 in the fourth year of observation. Because the children were dispersed among more than 50 different classrooms and because it was difficult to get permission to observe children in the schools, inhibition could no longer be observed in the school setting. Also, teacher judgments could be obtained for only about 60% of the LOGIC sample. Therefore, a single teacher judgment of inhibition, based on a 9–point scale, could be obtained for only 58 children of the original sample of 99 children.

Consistency and Stability. In each of the three years of observation in Kindergarten, the teacher Q-sort measure and the observed rate of wait-and-hover (inhibited contact initiation attempts) were significantly correlated. Therefore they were z-transformed and aggregated, yielding one index of inhibition in class per year. This index showed a stability of .44 over two years, which was significantly lower than the two-year stability of .75 for inhibition toward strangers.

The teacher inhibition rating in Grade 1 correlated .40 ($p < .01$) with the aggregated inhibition index in the last year of Kindergarten. Thus, there was some stability between inhibition in Kindergarten and inhibition in Grade 1. The teacher rating of inhibition in Grade 2, however, was neither significantly related to the teacher rating in Grade 1 nor to the previously assessed measures of inhibition in Kindergarten. This drop in the correlations suggests a major differential shift in children's inhibition in grade school between Grades 1 and 2.

CHANGING RELATIONS BETWEEN INHIBITION TOWARD STRANGERS AND INHIBITION IN CLASS

Figure 13.6 presents the stability data for inhibition toward strangers and inhibition in class as well as the concurrent correlations between these two kinds of inhibition.

Figure 13.6 suggests a decreasing consistency between inhibition toward strangers and inhibition in class with increasing familiarity of the class setting. In Kindergarten, the correlations dropped from .47 in the first year to a nonsignificant .23 in the third year; this decrease was significant (cf. Asendorpf, 1990a, for details). In the first year of grade school, the correlation between inhibition toward strangers and inhibition in class was again high (in fact surprisingly high given the fact that inhibition in class was measured by only one rating); in Grade 2, it dropped again significantly to a zero correlation. This drop is particularly noteworthy because the teachers remained the same in Grade 1 and 2 in nearly all cases.

This decreasing consistency between inhibition toward strangers and inhibition in class and the lower stability of inhibition in the class setting could be attributed to a familiarity effect. Because nearly all children remained in the same class in Kindergarten and grade school, the class setting became more familiar to them; thus, their temperament-based inhibition toward strangers should have decreased strongly.

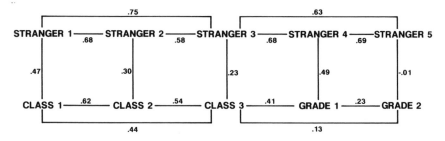

FIG. 13.6 Consistency of inhibition toward strangers and inhibition in class in five years of observation.

However, the means and standard deviations of children's inhibition in Kindergarten decreased only slightly, and this decrease was comparable in size with a decrease of their inhibition toward strangers (cf. Asendorpf, 1990a, for details). The teacher rating of children's inhibition in class actually *increased* from Grade 1 to Grade 2. This increase might reflect the fact that children in Grade 1 often have difficulty in focusing on their learning tasks. In the eyes of an elementary school teacher they may appear quite impulsive and distractable. In Grade 2, children are usually quieter in class, and the increased inhibition rating may well be due to this change. Thus, the increasing familiarity of the class setting alone cannot fully explain the decreasing consistency between the two kinds of inhibition.

CHANGING RELATIONS BETWEEN INHIBITION IN CLASS AND PEER ACCEPTANCE

The two-factorial view of inhibition suggests that individual differences in children's inhibition in class may at least partly be due to social-evaluative concerns because of a low acceptance by the classmates. Indeed, the rate of children's success in contact initiation attempts in class was nonsignificantly related to their inhibition in class in the first year in Kindergarten, but in the second and third years, it became significantly and negatively related to their inhibition in the classroom, and this increase in correlations was significant (see Asendorpf, 1990a, for details; in particular, inhibition in the classroom was controlled for the influence of inhibition toward strangers in this analysis, that is, the effect was independent of possible changes in inhibition toward strangers).

Thus, the more children were ignored or rejected by their classmates, the more inhibited they became in the classroom. Because this effect showed up only in the second and third year in Kindergarten, it may be attributed to the emerging peer relationships in the class setting. Children with negative peer relations as indicated by a low rate of peer acceptance in contact initiations may have anticipated neglect or rejection when they tried to approach classmates, and this anticipation may have led to inhibition.[2]

This effect could not be demonstrated in grade school because no behavioral observations or sociometric measures were available. But a

---

[2]Our most recent results of the LOGIC study indicate that those children who were observed to be highly inhibited in the familiar peer group at the end of Kindergarten developed internalizing problems during grade school. At 8, 9, and 10 years of age, they were characterized by a low social self esteem, and at age 9 and 10 by high loneliness. This result, when contrasted with the negative findings for inhibition to strangers, demonstrates the developmental significance of inhibition in the peer group.

similar increasing influence of emerging social relationships also might have been partly responsible for the decreasing consistency between inhibition toward strangers and inhibition in class in grade school.

A TWO-FACTORIAL COPING MODEL OF INHIBITION DURING CHILDHOOD

The findings of all of these studies on the inhibition of adults and children can be summarized in a simple model of inhibition. This model rests upon the notion of a common "behavioral inhibition system" that interacts with various behavioral activation systems (Gray, 1982, 1987). According to this view, the behavioral inhibition system mediates the inhibition of behavior in response to three different classes of behavior: novel stimuli, conditioned cues for punishment, and conditioned cues for frustrative nonreward. If the behavioral inhibition system is triggered by one or many of these cues, its activation leads to the inhibition of overt behavior, to an increment in arousal, and to an increased attention to the external situation (cf. Fig. 13.7).

Gray (1982) has provided empirical support for this model mainly in terms of animal conditioning studies and pharmacology. If his model is applied to human social behavior, the conditioning paradigm must, in my view, be transcended by including more complex situational evaluations, such as checking one's coping potential or comparing one's behavior with social norms or self-presentational goals (see Scherer, 1984, for a model of emotion that takes such evaluations into account).

Furthermore, if we are interested not only in the immediate effects of inhibition on behavior but also in the subsequent adaptation to the

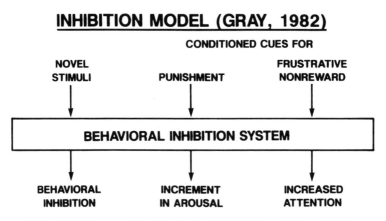

FIG. 13.7   The model of behavioral inhibition of Gray (1982).

situation, coping strategies for dealing with inhibition must be included in the model (e.g., Lazarus & Launier, 1978).

Despite this double expansion of the mediating processes between situation and response, the tripartite classification of inhibiting situations proposed by Gray (1982) can be maintained in order to describe inhibition in social situations. Social inhibition is triggered by the unfamiliarity of the interaction partner as well as by the anticipation of negative or insufficiently positive evaluation by others (i.e., being rejected or ignored). The full model is summarized in Fig. 13.8.

So far, the model describes *intra*individual changes in inhibition from a general-psychological perspective: Under what conditions do people react with inhibition, and what effects does inhibition have on social behavior? But the model is also useful for describing *inter*individual differences in inhibition. The model is suggestive of three sources of interindividual differences.

First, interindividual differences in the "strength" of the behavioral inhibition system (its threshold and intensity of responding) mediate the inhibiting effects of strangers or social-evaluative situations. The temperamental view of inhibition focuses on this source of individual differences. It is a source that rests within persons and may reflect stable physiological differences between persons. The best way of assessing the influence of this source of inhibition on behavior would be to study people's responses to strangers, because in these situations the stimulus side (the unfamiliarity of

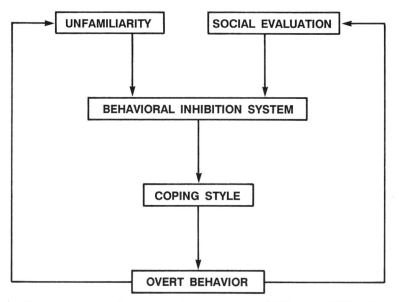

FIG. 13.8 A two-factorial coping model of inhibition in childhood.

the stranger) can be experimentally controlled more easily than the social-evaluative meaning of interaction partners. I suspect that the robustness of the construct of inhibition toward strangers, with its high temporal stability and cross-partner consistency, is due to this good experimental control of the situation.

Furthermore, people's characteristic style of coping with inhibiting situations represent a second source of interindividual differences. Some cope with inhibition more successfully than others, and among nonsuccessful copers different styles may be distinguished (e.g., retreating quickly to passive solitude versus being trapped in the state of inhibition for a long time).

And third, depending on their history of social interactions in a particular social setting, different members of the setting develop different social relationships with other members of the setting. They are familiar with them to different degrees, and they anticipate social acceptance by them to different degrees. Thus, the same person can have a different inhibiting potential on others.

All three sources can contribute to observed interindividual differences in a particular social setting, and they are different in terms of their temporal stability and cross-situational generality. The first source, the strength of the behavioral inhibition system, is expected to be cross-situationally general and to be quite stable over time when it has been crystallized due to genetic and early environmental influences. The second source, coping styles, may be also relatively consistent across different situations and stable over time, but only after a longer period of learning how to cope; coping styles might not stabilize before children enter grade school.

And the third source, the inhibiting potential of others, is expected to be consistent across potential interaction partners only as far as these are comparable in terms of familiarity and social-evaluative meaning. Because the inhibiting potential of a person is based upon the quality of the social relationship with that person and because most people have highly differentiated relationships, no high cross-partner consistency can be expected. Also, the temporal stability of the inhibiting potential of others should be high only in stable social settings with a long history of social interaction between the members of the setting.

HYPOTHESES FOR FUTURE INVESTIGATION

Although the discussion of the three sources of interindividual differences is highly speculative, it allows the derivation of hypotheses that can be put to empirical test. Thus, the model not only explains past findings on inhibition, but it also helps in generating new, testable hypotheses. I conclude this chapter with six such hypotheses.

1. *Unfamiliarity and the anticipation of being rejected or ignored by others contribute to intraindividual differences in inhibition independently of each other.* This has been confirmed for adults by Asendorpf (1989a) by a systematic, independent variation of the unfamiliarity and the social-evaluative potential of interaction partners; similar studies could be done with children.

2. *Children who are temperamentally disposed to high inhibition do not lack general social skill. They behave normal in social interactions with familiar peers if they feel accepted by them.* This hypothesis is supported by the findings on children's play with strangers versus classmates (Asendorpf, 1990a, and this chapter), but it must find additional support before it can be concluded that interventions aimed at enhancing inhibited children's general social skill are of limited value, particularly by the demonstration that temperamental inhibition is not a risk factor for developing internalizing difficulties.

3. *The influence of the temperamental factor on inhibited behavior is strongest when people enter new social settings.* Thus, during the life course, this temperamental factor can be best studied during major social life transitions. This effect has been already replicated in the LOGIC study (see Fig. 13.6), but it should be also studied in other kinds of new settings, such as entering a new job environment or moving to a new town.

4. *The longer people share a particular social setting, the more their mean level of inhibition can be predicted from their mean level of acceptance by members of the setting. Furthermore, to the extent that stable social relationships emerge in the setting, people's inhibition to a particular person in the setting will be predictable from their level of experienced acceptance in this relationship.* Only the first part of this hypothesis has been supported by Asendorpf (1990a, and this chapter), and only for Kindergarten classes. It needs more support in other social settings such as grade school classes, sport clubs, or job teams by a method of observing inhibition and social acceptance that also tests the second part of the hypothesis.

5. *The behavioral effects of an inhibiting situation are more consistent across individuals in infancy and early childhood than at older ages because coping styles need some time to develop and to stabilize. At later ages, social withdrawal is a frequent style of coping with inhibition.* This hypothesis relates the coping factor in inhibition to developmental issues. It has found preliminary support by Asendorpf (1991, and this chapter) and is in need of further confirmation.

6. *Those who are temperamentally disposed to high inhibition are highly resistant to interventions aimed at reducing inhibition, but if interventions focus on teaching coping strategies, these persons can learn how to overcome inhibition quickly in the presence of strangers or when they fear being rejected or neglected by others.* This hypothesis relates the coping factor in inhibition to issues of intervention.

ACKNOWLEDGMENTS

The studies reported here were conducted as part of the Munich Longitudinal Study on the Genesis of Individual Competencies (LOGIC) funded by the Max Planck Society. Part of the studies were supported by NATO grant 0467/86 to the author and Kenneth H. Rubin. I wish to thank Ken Rubin for many stimulating discussions and detailed comments on an earlier version of this chapter.

REFERENCES

Ainsworth, M. D. S., Blehar, M. C., Waters, E., & Wall, S. (1978). *Patterns of attachment.* Hillsdale, NJ: Lawrence Erlbaum Associates.

Alliger, G. M., Hanges, P. J., & Alexander, R. A. (1988). A method for correcting parameter estimates in samples subject to a ceiling. *Psychological Bulletin, 103,* 424–430.

Asendorpf, J. (1985). *Manual for coding the behavior of young children during contact initiation episodes* (Res. Rep.). Munich, F. R. G.: Max-Planck-Institut für psychologische Forschung.

Asendorpf, J. B. (1987). Videotape reconstruction of emotions and cognitions related to shyness. *Journal of Personality and Social Psychology, 53,* 542–549.

Asendorpf, J. B. (1988). Individual response profiles in the behavioral assessment of personality. *European Journal of Personality, 2,* 155–167.

Asendorpf, J. B. (1989a). Shyness as a final common pathway for two different kinds of inhibition. *Journal of Personality and Social Psychology, 57,* 481–492.

Asendorpf, J. (1989b). *Soziale Gehemmtheit und ihre Entwicklung* (Social inhibition and its development). Berlin: Springer-Verlag.

Asendorpf, J. B. (1990a). Development of inhibition during childhood: Evidence for situational specificity and a two-factor model. *Developmental Psychology, 26,* 721–730.

Asendorpf, J. B. (1990b). Beyond social withdrawal: Shyness, unsociability, and peer avoidance. *Human Development, 33,* 250–259.

Asendorpf, J. B. (1991). Development of inhibited children's coping with unfamiliarity. *Child Development, 62.* 1460–1472

Asendorpf, J. B. (1992). A Brunswikean approach to trait continuity: Application to shyness. *Journal of Personality, 60,* 53–77.

Block, J. H., & Block, J. (1980). The role of ego-control and ego-resiliency in the organization of behavior. In W. A. Collins (Ed.), *Minnesota Symposium on Child Psychology* (Vol. 13, pp. 39–101). Hillsdale, NJ: Lawrence Erlbaum Associates.

Brunswik, E. (1956). *Perception and the representative design of psychological experiments* (2nd ed.). Berkeley: University of California Press.

Buss, A. H., & Plomin, R. (1984). *Temperament: Early developing personality traits.* Hillsdale, NJ: Lawrence Erlbaum Associates.

Dodge, K. A., Schlundt, D. C., Schocken, I., & Delugach, I. D. (1983). Social competence and children's sociometric status: The role of peer group entry strategies. *Merrill-Palmer Quarterly, 29,* 309–336.

Göttert, R., & Asendorpf, J. (1989). Eine deutsche Version des California-Child-Q-Set, Kurzform (A German short version of the California-Child-Q-Set). *Zeitschrift für Entwicklungspsychologie und Pädagogische Psychologie, 21,* 70–82.

Gottman, J. M. (1977). Toward a definition of social isolation in children. *Child Development, 48,* 513–517.

Gray, J. A. (1982). *The neuropsychology of anxiety: An enquiry into the functions of the septo-hippocampal system.* Oxford: Oxford University Press.

Gray, J. A. (1987). Perspectives on anxiety and impulsivity. *Journal of Research in Personality, 21,* 493–509.

Jennings, K. D. (1975). People versus object orientation, social behavior, and intellectual abilities in children. *Developmental Psychology, 11,* 511–519.

Kagan, J. (1989). Temperamental contributions to social behavior. *American Psychologist, 44,* 668–674.

Kagan, J., & Moss, H. A. (1962). *Birth to maturity.* New York: Wiley.

Kagan, J., Reznick, J. S., Snidman, N., Gibbons, J., & Johnson, M. O. (1988). Childhood derivatives of inhibition and lack of inhibition toward the unfamiliar. *Child Development, 59,* 1580–1589.

Kalbfleisch, J. D., & Prentice, R. L. (1980). *The statistical analysis of failure time data.* New York: Wiley.

Lazarus, R. S., & Launier, R. (1978). Stress-related transactions between person and environment. In L. A. Pervin & M. Lewis (Eds.), *Perspectives in interactional psychology* (pp. 287–327). New York: Plenum Press.

Petrinovich, L. (1979). Probabilistic functionalism: A conception of research method. *American Psychologist, 34,* 373–390.

Rubin, K. H. (1985). *The play observation scale (POS)* (Tech. Rep.). Waterloo, Canada: University of Waterloo.

Rubin, K. H., & Emptage, A. (1985). *A manual for coding communicative and social competence in children* (Tech. Rep.). Waterloo, Canada: University of Waterloo.

Rubin, K. H., Hymel, S., & Mills, R. S. L. (1989). Sociability and social withdrawal in childhood: Stability and outcomes. *Journal of Personality, 57,* 237–255.

Rubin, K. H., LeMare, L. J., & Lollis, S. (1990). Social withdrawal in childhood: Developmental pathways to peer rejection. In S. R. Asher & J. D. Coie (Eds.), *Peer rejection in childhood* (pp. 217–249). Cambridge: Cambridge University Press.

Rubin, K. H., & Mills, R. S. L. (1988). The many faces of social isolation in childhood. *Journal of Consulting and Clinical Psychology, 56,* 919–924.

Scherer, K. R. (1984). On the nature and function of emotion: A component process approach. In K. R. Scherer & P. Ekman (Eds.), *Approaches to emotion* (pp. 293–317). Hillsdale, NJ: Lawrence Erlbaum Associates.

Sroufe, L. A. (1977). Wariness of strangers and the study of infant development. *Child Development, 48,* 731–746.

Thomas, A., & Chess, S. (1980). *The dynamics of psychological development.* New York: Brunner/Mazel.

Weinert, F. E., & Schneider, W. (Eds.) (1986). *First report on the Munich Longitudinal Study on the Genesis of Individual Competencies (LOGIC)* (Res. Rep.). München: Max-Planck-Institut für psychologische Forschung.

The Waterloo Longitudinal Project: Correlates and Consequences of Social Withdrawal from Childhood to Adolescence

14

Kenneth H. Rubin
University of Waterloo

The purpose of this chapter is to describe findings from the Waterloo Longitudinal Project *(WLP),* an ongoing 10–year study of normal, school attending children. The central focus of the *WLP* has been to chart the developmental course of social competence (e.g., Rubin & Rose-Krasnor, in press), social withdrawal (e.g., Rubin & Mills, 1988), and aggression (e.g., Hymel, Rubin, Rowden, & LeMare, 1990; Rubin, Bream & Rose-Krasnor, 1991) from early childhood to adolescence. In this chapter, a conceptual and empirical analysis of the developmental causes, correlates, and consequences of *social withdrawal* is documented.

THE DEVELOPMENTAL SIGNIFICANCE OF SOCIAL WITHDRAWAL

Social withdrawal has long been associated with the literature on internalizing disorders in childhood (e.g., Achenbach & Edelbrock, 1981). To a large extent, it is viewed as a behavioral reflection of psychological overcontrol (e.g., Lewis & Miller, 1990). Yet, despite the conceptual "clustering" of social withdrawal with indices of anxiety, depression, and negative self-regard, the literature concerning this phenomenon has had a relatively checkered history. For example, it has been reported that behavioral manifestations of overcontrol in childhood have limited developmental significance; social withdrawal has been described as relatively unstable and nonsignificantly predictive of psychological maladjustment during adolescence and adulthood (Kohlberg, LaCrosse, & Ricks, 1972;

Parker & Asher, 1987; Robins, 1966). The data supportive of this "non-risk" perspective on social withdrawal, when combined with the long-standing psychoanalytic position that childhood internalizing disorders (more specifically, depression) cannot be experienced until the superego has been fully developed in adolescence (Kashani, Husain, Shekim, Hodges, Cytryn, & McKnew, 1981), has failed to provide a "raison d'etre" for the clinical-developmental study of social withdrawal.

In spite of these traditional clinical perspectives, however, a primary focus of our research program has been to understand, conceptually and empirically, the etiology of internalizing problems in childhood, and most specifically, the development of social withdrawal — the prime *behavioral* manifestation of psychological overcontrol. Our persistence in tracking what had been, heretofore, a problem of relatively insignificant proportions, has been spurred on by several theoretical, conceptual, and methodological factors.

Theoretical Underpinnings.   In the opening chapter, several theoretical perspectives on the significance of peer interaction and the lack thereof were described. Rather than reiterate these perspectives, in length, herein, the reader is presented with a brief reminder of these early conceptual under-pinnings. First, in the 1920s and 1930s, Piaget (1926, 1932) contended that it was through peer interaction, particularly episodes of conflict and the opportunities for negotiation that they create, that children come to develop the capacity for sensitive perspective-taking in interpersonal relationships and for the understanding of cause-effect relations in social interaction. At approximately the same time, Mead (1934) proposed that the ability to self-reflect, to consider the self in relation to others, and to understand the perspectives of others was largely a function of participation in organized, rule-governed activities with peers.

The classic personality theory of Sullivan (1953) has also served as a guide for much of the current research concerning children's peer relationships and social skills. Sullivan suggested that the foundations of mutual respect, cooperation, and interpersonal sensitivity derived initially from children's peer and friendship relationships. And finally, theorists in the social learning camp have long suggested (and found) that children learn social behaviors and social norms directly through peer tutelage, reinforcement and punishment, and indirectly by observing peers "in action" (Bandura & Walters, 1963).

Taken together, these early theories and the data supportive of them (see Hartup, in press; Rubin & Coplan, in press for recent reviews) have led psychologists to conclude that peer interaction is an important force in the development of normal social relationships and social skills. The questions raised in our program of research have been, "What happens to children who, for whatever reason, fail to take advantage of their opportunities to interact with peers?; Will such socially withdrawn children fail to develop acceptable social skills; will they fail to develop normal thoughts and feelings of self-regard?" Our hunch has been that the child who does not have adequate peer interactive experiences may indeed be at risk for later maladjustment.

Clinical Confusions and Conundrums. Given the aforementioned theoretical statements about the significance of peer interaction for *normal* growth and development, it is curious to note that many of those who study *abnormal* development have been reticent to acknowledge the possibility that socially withdrawn children may have difficulties in socioemotional development. In actuality, there is a rather confusing and confused contradiction in clinical views regarding the significance of social withdrawal in childhood. On the one hand, there has been the above noted reporting that social withdrawal is a transient phenomenon that is unrelated to adolescent or adult maladjustment (e.g., Ensminger, Kellam, & Rubin, 1983). Yet, on the other hand, psychologists have persisted in regarding social withdrawal as a behavioral manifestation, in childhood, of emotional and behavioral overcontrol (e.g., Achenbach & Edelbrock, 1981; Cicchetti & Toth, 1991), and as warranting intervention (e.g., Conger & Keane, 1981; Wanlass & Prinz, 1982).

These confusions and conundrums aside, it is also the case that the clinical research on social withdrawal in childhood has been, in many respects, conceptually and methodologically impoverished. For example, of the handful of prospective longitudinal studies in which the risk status of childhood social withdrawal has been examined (Janes & Hesselbrock, 1978; Janes, Hesselbrock, Myers, & Penniman, 1979; John, Mednick, & Schulsinger, 1982; Michael, Morris, & Soroker, 1957; Morris, Soroker, & Burruss, 1954; Robins, 1966), *all* have used clinic or high-risk samples. This procedure tends to result in an attenuated range of observed behavior and an underestimate of the correlation between withdrawal and later outcomes. Moreover, in each of these studies, social withdrawal has been assessed by some form of teacher assessment, the validity of which has been largely unknown (Hymel & Rubin, 1985). In addition, the long-term "outcome" measure typically assessed has been some form of *externalizing* disorder. This latter procedure has seemed odd to us given that withdrawal has long been regarded as a reflection of internalizing difficulties.

Finally, in the original clinical research on social withdrawal, different forms of social isolation have been studied in aggregation. It has been argued recently, on the other hand, that social isolation can occur for a variety of different reasons, ranging from ostracism *by* the peer group, to anxious withdrawal *from* the peer group, to strong disinterest *in* the peer group (Asendorpf, this volume; Rubin & Mills, 1988). One reason for the lack of evidence that social withdrawal presages later maladjustment may be the failure to differentiate between different subtypes of the phenomenon.

It has been clear to us, from these methodological and conceptual flaws, that the study of internalizing difficulties in general, and social withdrawal in particular, has been severely hampered by the lack of a guiding conceptual framework. One purpose of this chapter, therefore, is to describe the working models that have guided our research. A second purpose of this chapter is to describe initial findings that begin to provide an empirical base for our developmental models. These data are drawn from several sources including our longitudinal study of the concurrent and predictive correlates of social withdrawal, loneliness, and depression in children.

A "FANTASYLAND" MODEL OF BEHAVIORAL ADJUSTMENT

A basic tenet of developmental psychopathology is that one can better understand deviations from the norm by examining normal developmental processes and content (Sroufe & Rutter, 1984). Thus, in our own work, we began with a paradigm case for studying the optimal development of psychological adjustment. The description of the "Fantasyland" pathway offered in the following is probably beyond the reach of any "real" human child and her or his family. Albeit very simplistic, the model nevertheless represents a highly useful, heuristic scenario of normal socioemotional development.

It seems reasonable to suggest that socioemotional adjustment derives from the interaction of intra-individual, inter-individual, and macro-systemic forces. Basically, we have proposed that the combination of (a) an even-tempered, easy disposition, (b) the experience of sensitive and responsive parenting, and (c) the general lack of major stresses or crises during infancy and early childhood predict the development of secure parent-child attachment relationships (Rubin & Mills, 1991). In turn, these secure primary relationships are hypothesized to predict the development of social and emotional adjustment (e.g., Grossman & Grossman, in press; Sroufe, 1983).

This viewpoint derives from our understanding of some of the general functions of parent-child relationships (Hartup, 1985). First, parent-child relationships constitute emotional and cognitive resources that allow children to explore their social and non-social worlds. Second, the early parent-child relationship may serve as the precursor or model of all subsequent relationships (e.g., Bowlby, 1973). Given these perspectives, it is not difficult to understand how secure parent-child relationships, once established, can contribute to behavioral adjustment.

Most infants and toddlers do have relatively easy-going dispositions (Thomas & Chess, 1977) and most come to develop *secure* relationships with their parents (Ainsworth, Blehar, Waters, & Wall, 1978). These relationships appear to be caused and maintained, in part, by sensitive and responsive parents who are in tune with the child's needs and behaviors, and who respond effectively and appropriately to the child (Isabella, Belsky, & van Eye, 1989). Moreover, although the sensitive and responsive parent may, from time-to-time become irritated by the child's behavior, the parent is accepting of the child and does not remain angry, hostile, or resentful. It should be noted, as a modest after-thought, that it is probably easiest to behave in a responsive and sensitive manner (a) when one's infant is relatively easy-going; (b) when the birth of the infant was planned and desired; and (c) when the family unit is relatively stress-free to begin with.

Within the context of a *secure* relationship, then, a conceptual link to the development of behavioral adjustment can be suggested. This link draws its underpinnings from the notion that a primary attachment relationship results in the child's development of a belief system that incorporates the parent as available and responsive to his or her needs. This "internal working model" allows the child to feel secure, confident, and self-assured when introduced to novel settings, and this sense of "felt security" fosters the child's active exploration of the social environment (Sroufe, 1983). In turn, exploration of the social milieu allows the child to address a number of significant "other-directed" questions such as "What are the properties of this other person?"; "What is she/he like?"; "What can and does she/he do?" Once these exploratory questions are answered, the child can begin to address "self-directed" questions such as "What can *I* do with this person?" Thus, from our perspective, the construct of felt security plays a critical role in socioemotional development. It enhances social exploration, and exploration results in peer play (Rubin, Fein, & Vandenberg, 1983).

During play with peers, children experience the interpersonal exchange of ideas, perspectives, roles, and actions; and from social negotiation, discussion, and conflict with peers, children learn to understand *others'* thoughts, emotions, motives, and intentions (e.g., Doise & Mugny, 1981). Armed with these new social understandings, children are able to think about the consequences of their social behaviors, not only for themselves but also for others. As noted earlier, the development of these social-cognitive abilities has long been thought to result in the production of socially competent behaviors (e.g., Selman & Schultz, 1990).

Once socially competent behavior is demonstrated by the child and recognized by the parent, the secure parent-child relationship will be nurtured and maintained by the dialectic between (a) the child who is willing and able to explore and play competently in a social milieu, and who is able to benefit social-cognitively and socially from peer interactive experiences, and (b) a competent parent who is emotionally available, sharply attuned to social situations and to the thoughts and emotions of the child, able to anticipate the child's behaviors and the consequences of the child's actions, and able to predict the outcomes of her or his own actions for the child. This competent, secure relationship system serves both parent and child well, *and barring any undue circumstances,* a socioemotional outcome of positive intra- and interpersonal adjustment is predicted.

A DEVELOPMENTAL PATHWAY TO MALADJUSTMENT

Not all children and their parents are fortunate enough to experience the "Fantasyland" scenario described above. For example, few families are immune to the experience of stress, crises, and daily hassles. These stressors, if they occur with regularity and intensity, can influence both the quality of the parent-child relationship and the social and emotional well-being of children (Cohen & Wills, 1985). For example, stressors may presage positive and negative developmental "outcomes" by influencing (a) parental values, attitudes, and expectations concerning children and (b) the quality of parent-child interaction. Thus, economic poverty and the stress that often accompanies it are associated with parental conflict (Elder, Caspi, & Burton, 1987); in turn, both poverty and marital conflict are associated with parental anger, insensitivity, inconsistency, and punitiveness in childrearing (e.g., Gottman & Katz, 1989; Radke-Yarrow, Richters, & Wilson, 1988). In short, stress may produce a generalized maladaptive response set in parents that leads to the neglect or overdirection of the child (Crnic & Greenberg, 1990; Patterson, 1983; Wahler & Dumas, 1987).

Another stressor, of course, is the child him- or herself. Interestingly, there have been few attempts to examine the contributions of infant dispositional factors to the development of social and emotional adjustment in childhood. Yet, it is not difficult to imagine how such factors may be influential. We have described, in our recent writings, a developmental scenario that begins with the infant dispositional characteristic generally referred to as *behavioral inhibition* (Rubin, LeMare, & Lollis, 1990; Rubin & Lollis, 1988; Rubin & Mills, 1991). As noted throughout this volume (e.g., chapters by Davidson; Fox & Calkins; Kagan & Snidman), some newborns may be biologically predisposed to have a low threshold for arousal when confronted with social (or non-social) stimulation and novelty. Researchers have demonstrated that under conditions of novelty or uncertainty, some babies demonstrate physical and physiological changes that suggest that they are "hyperarousable" (e.g., Kagan 1989; Fox & Calkins, this volume)—a characteristic that may make them extremely difficult for their parents to soothe and comfort. Indeed, some parents do find such infantile responses of hyperarousal aversive (Kagan, Reznick, Clarke, Snidman, & Garcia-Coll, 1984). It is probably the case that most parents will respond to the consistent production by their infants and toddlers of wary behavior with sensitivity, concern, and the delivery of appropriate support. Parents who are experiencing a good deal of stress and who also lack social support, however, may react to easily aroused and wary babies with hostility, insensitivity, and/or non-responsivity (e.g., Engfer & Gavranidou, 1987). Thus, we posit that an interplay of endogenous, socialization, and early relationships factors, as they co-exist under the "umbrella" of negative setting conditions, will lead to a sense of felt insecurity. It is hypothesized, therefore, that the internal working models of insecurely attached, temperamentally inhibited children may lead them to "shrink from" (Bowlby, 1973, p. 208) their social milieus.

Children who "shrink" anxiously away from their peers, preclude themselves from the aforementioned positive outcomes associated with social exploration and peer play. Thus, one can predict a developmental sequence in which an inhibited, fearful, insecure child withdraws from the social world of peers, fails to develop those skills derived from peer interaction and, because of this, becomes increasingly anxious and isolated from the peer group.

Furthermore, by the mid-years of childhood, social reticence or withdrawal is salient to, and recognized as deviant by, the peer group (Younger & Boyko, 1987; Younger, Gentile, & Burgess, this volume). Given that deviation from age-appropriate social behavior is often associated with the establishment of negative peer reputations, we predict that by the mid-to-late years of childhood, social withdrawal and social anxiety will be strongly associated with peer rejection and unpopularity.

It is likely also, that at some point *before* peers identify social withdrawal as deviant from the norm, teachers and parents will recognize the social insecurities and anxieties of withdrawn children and will respond in some fashion. Given their reticence to explore their environments, these children may demonstrate difficulties in getting social "jobs" done or social problems ameliorated. Sensing the young child's difficulties and perceived helplessness, the concerned parent may attempt to help in a very direct fashion by either manipulating their child's social behaviors through power assertion (e.g., telling the child how to act or what to do) or by actually intervening and taking over for the child (e.g., intervening during object disputes; inviting a potential playmate to the home). An association between overcontrolling, overinvolved socialization strategies and social withdrawal in early childhood has long been posited, although seldom directly investigated (e.g., Hetherington & Martin, 1986; see also Mills & Rubin, this volume).

Parental overdirectiveness is likely to maintain rather than to ameliorate the postulated problems associated with social inhibition. It likely will not help the young child deal first-hand with his or her social interchanges and dilemmas; it probably does little to aid in the development of a belief system of social self-efficacy, and it likely perpetuates feelings of insecurity within and outside of the family.

In summary, an inhibited temperament, when responded to with insensitivity or overcontrol is hypothesized to predict an insecure attachment relationship (see also, Mangelsdorf, Gunnar, Kestenbaum, Lang, & Andreas, 1990). Felt insecurity may lead to an impoverished exploratory style that precludes the opportunity to experience those forms of peer exchanges hypothesized to promote the development of social competence. The relatively slow development of social competence, when combined with "wariness" and felt insecurity may lead to the development of negative self appraisals of competence, which in turn exacerbate withdrawal from peers. These factors, *taken together,* are hypothesized to predict difficulties of an internalizing nature, such as loneliness and depression (Rubin et al., 1990; Rubin & Lollis, 1988).

It is essential to note our belief that an infant with a fearful, wary inhibited temperament may be "deflected" to a pathway leading to the development of social and emotional well-being by responsive and sensitive caregiving and by a relatively stress-free environment. Thus, as noted earlier, it is probable that many, if not most, dispositionally inhibited babies will develop secure relationships with their parents and will not experience the sort of parental overcontrol that we posit to be debilitating. Likewise, an inhibited temperament is *not* necessary for the development of internalizing problems. We hypothesize that parental overcontrol and overinvolvement, especially when accompanied by familial stress and a lack of social support, may deflect the temperamentally easy-going infant to pathways of maladaptation (see also Rubin et al., 1990).

Evidence for the Pathway to Maladjustment

In recent years, research has begun to emerge in partial support of the pathway to maladjustment just described. For example, significant associations have been found between temperamental hyperreactivity, insecure attachment, and socially inhibited behavior; between patterns of parenting and social withdrawal; and between social withdrawal, social skill deficits, and internalizing difficulties.

Temperament, Attachment, and Behavioral Inhibition.   The model described here suggests that individual factors (temperament) and interindividual factors (the quality of the parent-child attachment relationship) may conspire, especially under stressful circumstances, to predict the development of an inhibited behavioral style. First, is there evidence for the posited relations between temperament and attachment? Recently, Thompson, Connell, and Bridges (1988) reported that the temperamental characteristic of proneness to fear was predictive of infant distress to maternal separation. Such distress usually marks a child for "C" classification in the traditional attachment paradigm. Furthermore, Belsky and Rovine (1987) argued, from both conceptual and empirical bases, that the temperamental characteristic, proneness to distress, is predictive of "B3" through "C2" attachment classifications. The most promising data, however, appear to stem from the research program of Fox and colleagues (Fox & Calkins, this volume), who have demonstrated that infants who are behaviorally and physiologically reactive to mildly stressful, *novel* social events are more likely to be classified as insecurely attached "C" (anxious-resistant) babies than are their less reactive counterparts.

Following from these findings, the literature suggests also that insecure "C" status *predicts* the production of inhibited and passive-withdrawn behavior in early childhood (Calkins & Fox, in press; Renken, Egeland, Marvinney, Sroufe, & Mangelsdorf, 1989). Furthermore, Kagan and colleagues have revealed that high levels of motor arousal and high, stable heart rates in response to mildly stressful stimulation in very early childhood predict subsequent displays of socially inhibited behavior (e.g., Kagan, Reznick, & Gibbons, 1989). Taken together, there is growing reason to believe that a relation exists between dispositionally based reactivity to novel stimulation, the quality of the parent-infant attachment relationship, and subsequent socially inhibited behavior.

Social Withdrawal, Social Skill Deficits, and Internalizing Difficulties.
The developmental model offered above suggests that children who preclude themselves from interacting with others may place themselves at risk of not developing, at a normal rate, those social and social-cognitive skills that are derived from peer interaction, and the opportunities it affords to develop skill in negotiation, persuasion, and conflict-resolution (Doise & Mugny, 1981). Further, it is argued that when socially withdrawn children come to recognize their own difficulties, and when others behave toward them in a rejecting manner, they may begin to develop negative self-perceptions and emotions.

Data that address the above noted speculations are few and far between. Much of the relevant research extant derives from a single data base, namely the Waterloo Longitudinal Project *(WLP)*. This project is an ongoing 10–year study of normal, school-attending children, which focuses on the concurrent and predictive correlates of social withdrawal in childhood and adolescence. In the following sections, we describe the *WLP*. It is important to note that, in this study, the hypothesized infant-toddler precursors of social withdrawal have not been examined. The corpus of data, however, do allow for a close inspection of the characteristics of extremely withdrawn children in the age period 5–11 years. Moreover, the data have allowed for an analysis of the stability and the long-term "outcomes" of social withdrawal from childhood through early adolescence.

THE WATERLOO LONGITUDINAL PROJECT *(WLP)*

The *WLP* has been guided by the belief that peers influence growth and development and that socially withdrawn children who, by definition, do not interact with their peers to a normal degree, may be deprived of opportunities that significantly influence later development. The particular foci of this chapter are the assessment, the stability, and the concurrent and long-term correlates of social withdrawal during childhood and early adolescence.

THE IDENTIFICATION OF SOCIALLY WITHDRAWN CHILDREN

The participants in the *WLP* included two cohorts of children who entered the study at 5 years of age. Cohort 1 was composed of 110 kindergarteners; Cohort 2 entered the study two years later with 70 kindergarten participants. Data were collected on as many of the participants as possible in each of Grades 2, 4 (Cohort 1 only), and 5. All of the children attended regular public schools in Waterloo County, a community of about 250,000 people in southwestern Ontario. Thus, in Grade 2, we had access to 105 of the original group of 180 children. By Grade 5, we had access to only 76 members of the original sample.

In each year of the project, however, we added children to the sample whenever parental permission could be obtained. Thus, in grade 2, the actual number of participants was 153; in Grade 5, the actual number of participants was 231 (87 for whom we had data in Grade 2). Finally, in 1990, when the *first cohort* of children entered high school, we were able to track down one-third of the original kindergarten participants.

In the course of the WLP, we have used two procedures to study social withdrawal and sociability in childhood. In kindergarten and Grades 2 and 4 (Cohort 1 only), children were observed, during free play, with their peers. Each kindergartener was observed in the classroom following procedures outlined, in detail, elsewhere (e.g., Rubin, 1982, 1986; Rubin, Hymel, Mills, & Rose-Krasnor, 1991). Basically, each child was observed for six 10–sec time samples each day over a 30–day period. Because there were no opportunities to observe free-play in elementary school classrooms, each Grade 2 and Grade 4 child was invited to play with three same-sex age-mates for four 15–minute free play sessions in a laboratory playroom. The child's playmates differed in each of the four sessions, thus allowing observations to be made with 12 different playmates. All elementary school observations were made from behind one-way mirrors. The Grades 2 and 4 children were observed for 42 10–sec time intervals during each of the four sessions.

All behaviors were coded on a checklist that included the cognitive play categories of functional-sensorimotor, exploratory, constructive, dramatic, and games-with-rules behaviors nested within the social participation categories of solitary, parallel, and group activities. Other categories included unoccupied and onlooker behaviors, aggression, and conversations with peers. After recording play behavior, the observers noted the names of the focal child's play partners and who it was that initiated the activity. Finally, the affective quality of each interaction was coded as positive, neutral, or negative.

From these time-sampled data, each child received a score for the frequency with which she or he was observed engaging in social behavior (all forms of group play and conversations = *SOCPLAY*), and non-social behavior (unoccupied + onlooker + all forms of solitary play = *ISO-PLAY*).

In Grades 2, 4 (Cohort 1 only), and 5 the children were administered The Revised Class Play (Masten, Morison, & Pelligrini, 1985). Children were requested to nominate up to three classmates who would best fit each of 30 behavioral descriptors. Subsequently, nominations received from same-sex peers were used to compute each of three factor scores for each child following procedures outlined by Masten et al. (1985): Sociability-leadership, Aggression-disruption, and Sensitivity-isolation *(CPISO)*. For each summary score, the number of nominations received by each child was standardized within class and gender groups to permit appropriate comparisons. Higher scores were indicative of stronger peer perceptions of the identified behavior in each case.

A close inspection of the items that comprise the *CPISO* factor revealed, however, that this factor actually consists of two sub-clusters of items (Rubin, Hymel, LeMare & Rowden, 1989; Rubin & Mills, 1988). Four of the items appear to describe passive-anxious withdrawal ("someone who would rather play alone than with others," "someone whose feelings get hurt easily," "someone who is very shy," and "someone who is usually sad"), which reflects our conceptualization of a child who is socially isolated from the peer group *(CPISOW)*. The remaining three items appear indicative of peer rejection or isolation by the peer group (*CPISOR,* "a person who can't get others to listen," "someone who has trouble making friends," and "someone who is often left out"). In support of this conceptual analysis, we recently factor analyzed the Revised Class Play in two large Grade 2 and 4 Canadian samples (Chen, Rubin, & Sun, in press). These conceptually distinct clusters of items *did* load on two orthogonal factors. As in Masten et al. (1985), the first two items on *CPISOR* actually loaded significantly on both the aggression-disruption and sensitivity-isolation factors. Given the above, and given that peer rejection is associated with high frequencies of aggressive and disruptive behaviors (Coie & Kupersmidt, 1983; Dodge, 1983) as well as with social withdrawal (French, 1988; Rubin, Hymel, & Mills, 1989), it appeared to us important to examine separately the Revised Class Play items that reflected rejection *by* peers *(CPISOR)* and those that reflected passive, fearful withdrawal *from* peers *(CPISOW)*. In this report, therefore, we describe results based only on those items characterizing *CPISOW.*

THE STABILITY OF SOCIAL WITHDRAWAL

Extreme Group Identification. In kindergarten, socially withdrawn children were identified as those whose ISOPLAY scores were 1 *SD* above the *M* for their age group plus 10% above their class *M*s (this latter criterion was used for kindergarteners only to control for variations in classroom ecologies and hence opportunities of peer interaction; for the older children the materials available for use in the playroom were identical) and whose SOCPLAY scores were below their age-group *M*s (see Rubin, 1982, 1985, for additional details). This procedure resulted in the identification of 18 Isolates in Cohort 1 and 8 Isolates in Cohort 2 in kindergarten (or 14.44% of the total sample).

In Grade 2, 153 children were observed, of whom 105 had been observed previously in kindergarten. Sixteen Isolates were identified from the group of 153 children (or 10.46% of the total sample); data were available from kindergarten for 12 of these children. Eight of these 12 children (or 66.7%) had been earlier identified as extremely withdrawn.

These behavioral data suggest that extreme social withdrawal in the early-to-mid years of childhood is highly stable. Unfortunately, because data were available only for Cohort 1 in the fourth grade, it was impossible to examine further the stability of withdrawal using the extreme targeting procedure.

A similar extreme-groups targeting procedure was employed with the Revised Class Play. In this case, stability data from Grades 2, 4, and 5 were available only for the children in Cohort 1. Isolates were identified as those children whose CPISOW scores were one *SD* above the age group *M* and whose CPSOC scores were below the *M*. These criteria allowed the identification of 16 socially withdrawn children in Grade 2 (*n* for sample = 88; 18.18% = "isolates"), 18 in Grade 4 (*n* = 81; 22.22%), and 18 in Grade 5 (*n* = 77; 23.37%).

Of the 13 social isolates in Grade 4 for whom data were available in Grade 2, nine had been likewise identified (or 69.23% stability). Of the 11 social isolates in Grade 5 for whom data were available in Grade 2, six had been so identified (i.e., 54.54% stability), and of the 15 Grade 5 isolates for whom data were available in at least one of the previous years, 10 had been identified earlier as withdrawn (or 66.67% stability).

Correlational Stability. Given the relatively small numbers of extreme cases, we examined the stability of social withdrawal in a second way, by running a series of grade-by-grade correlational analyses. Observational indices of withdrawal were available in kindergarten and Grade 2 for both cohorts, and in Grade 4 for Cohort 1. It is important to note, however, that observational settings differed considerably for the kindergarten versus elementary school age samples (i.e., regular free play periods versus laboratory free play in quartets respectively). The most direct test of stability, then, was examination of the two year stability correlations (one-tailed) obtained across the second to fourth grade period, available for a longitudinal sample of 58 children. Some modest degree of stability was observed across the two-year period for ISOPLAY, r (56) = .37, p < .002.

Although observational data obtained in kindergarten were not directly comparable to those obtained in Grades 2 and 4 due to methodological variations, the relations between the index of withdrawal was, nonetheless, of interest. Some degree of stability was observed across the kindergarten to Grade 2 period for overall social withdrawal, r (105) = .25, p < .01; however, the kindergarten to Grade 4 correlation was nonsignificant. Thus, these data suggest some degree of stability for observed overall social withdrawal, at least across two-year periods and despite methodological variations.

Somewhat higher stability correlations were obtained when peer assessments of withdrawal were considered. Grade-by-grade correlations for peer assessed isolation (CPISOW) were: Grade 2 to 4, r (55) = .53, p < .001; Grade 2 to 5, r (49) = .38, p < .001; Grade 4 to 5, r (67) = .40, p < .001.

In summary, it appears that social withdrawal in childhood is a relatively stable phenomenon. When *extreme-group targeting procedures* are used, most children identified as extremely withdrawn in any given year appear to have been similarly identified in earlier years. This finding is in keeping with that of Kagan and colleagues (e.g. Kagan, 1989), who argue that the developmental continuity of inhibition is strongest when the longitudinal sample is composed of children who represent behavioral extremes. Year-to-year correlations of observed and peer nominated withdrawal were consistently, albeit modestly, stable. Nevertheless, taken together, the relative stability reported herein bolsters the existing evidence documenting the longitudinal continuity of social withdrawal (Bronson, 1966; Kagan & Moss, 1962; Moskowitz, Schwartzman, & Ledingham, 1985; Olweus, 1984). Although these studies vary considerably in time spans covered, developmental periods involved, and measures employed, they show quite consistently that social withdrawal tends to persist over time.

It is one thing to suggest that a phenomenon is stable; it is altogether different to argue that a given phenomenon is reflective of psychological risk. To examine the risk status of social withdrawal, the psychological concomitants of the construct were examined throughout childhood.

CHARACTERISTICS OF SOCIALLY WITHDRAWN YOUNG CHILDREN

In our first study of social withdrawal, our sample included 126 4-year-old preschoolers and 111 5-year-old kindergarteners (Rubin, 1982). For the most part, children identified observationally as extremely withdrawn were not rated by their teachers as problematic and their peers did not dislike or reject them (Rubin, 1982). This first "cut" of data analysis was clearly in keeping with the traditional clinical view that social withdrawal is not a risk factor for future maladaptive development.

Close inspection of the *dyadic play* of withdrawn children with average partners revealed a number of potential difficulties. First, withdrawn children directed fewer requests to their play partners (e.g., "Can you give me that crayon?"; "Come over here!"). These data confirmed the classroom observations that led to their being identified as socially withdrawn. Moreover, this finding indicated that socially withdrawn children take less social initiative than their non-withdrawn counterparts (Rubin & Borwick, 1984; Rubin & Krasnor, 1986).

Second, when young, withdrawn children did issue requests, they were likely to be of a "low cost" nature; that is, they were more likely to try to get the attention of their playmates (e.g., "Look at this car.") than to try to gain access to objects in their partner's possession, to stop their partner's activity, or to get their partner to join them in play (Rubin & Borwick, 1984; Rubin & Krasnor, 1986). The latter goals would require much more expenditure of energy by the play partner than the goal of "gain partner's attention." We interpret these data as indicating that the withdrawn children are less socially assertive than their more sociable age-mates.

Despite issuing more "low cost" requests, it was nevertheless the case that when withdrawn children attempted to obtain partner compliance, they were more likely than their average counterparts to fail (Rubin & Borwick, 1984; Rubin & Krasnor, 1986). Thus, within these dyadic groupings, withdrawn children *did* experience rejection in the form of non-compliance and non-responsiveness.

Finally, when we interviewed young children and asked them how they would go about acquiring objects or initiating social activities with peers, we found that withdrawn youngsters were more likely than average children to suggest "adult intervention" solutions; that is they often suggested that they would get an adult to help them solve their interpersonal problems (Rubin, 1982; Rubin, Daniels-Beirness, & Bream, 1984; Rubin & Krasnor, 1986).

In summary, preschool and kindergarten withdrawn children were quiet, highly compliant, and submissive. They also experienced a higher than average degree of social failure. Perhaps the best way to characterize them is as "easy marks."

CHARACTERISTICS OF SOCIALLY WITHDRAWN CHILDREN: MIDDLE CHILDHOOD

By the age of seven, children who are identified as extremely withdrawn have more severe difficulties than their younger preschool and kindergarten aged counterparts. Withdrawn second graders are *not* unpopular among their peers. They are recognized, however, by their peers as sensitive, shy, fearful, and withdrawn (Rubin, 1985). We also found that teachers rated as withdrawn, anxious, and fearful those children observed and rated by peers as most socially withdrawn (Moller & Rubin, 1988). Furthermore, in keeping with the Piagetian position that peer interaction aids in the development of social cognition (Piaget, 1926), we found that socially withdrawn children were less able than their more sociable agemates to comprehend the perspectives of others (LeMare & Rubin, 1987).

We also observed 7-year-old socially withdrawn children while they played in dyads with a same-age, same-sex partner. The frequency with which each of the dyad participants displayed managerial and teaching behaviors directed at the play partner was coded (Rubin, 1985). We took these particular behaviors to reflect the degree to which children attempted to assert themselves and dominate their playmates. We found that the withdrawn children were less likely to play the managerial or teacher roles than their dyadic partners, and when they did try to take the dominant role they were more often rebuffed. In this case, just as we found in early childhood, observations of rebuff occurring in dyads indicated that withdrawn children did experience a form of rejection by their play partners.

Given that the withdrawn children did experience a higher than average rate of social rebuff, it is not surprising that we discovered that withdrawn children think more poorly of themselves and of their competencies than non-withdrawn children (Rubin, 1985).

In summary, seven-year-olds who are identified observationally as extremely withdrawn are recognized as such by their teachers and peers. Indeed, in more recent work we have found that, in addition to peers and teachers, the *parents* of withdrawn second graders perceive their children as withdrawn (Rubin, Bigras, & Mills, 1992). Yet, these children are not rejected sociometrically by their peers. They are rejected, however, when they attempt to manage the behaviors of their agemates during play. Furthermore, they view themselves and their skills in a negative light. As such, given the data from early and middle childhood, it would appear that social withdrawal is associated with an anxious, submissive interpersonal behavioral style that reflects internalized feelings of anxiety and negative thoughts about the self and one's own skills.

CHARACTERISTICS OF SOCIALLY WITHDRAWN CHILDREN: EARLY ADOLESCENCE

In early adolescence (11 years), we have used the Revised Class Play (Masten et al., 1985) to identify extremely withdrawn and passive fifth graders (Rubin, Chen, & Hymel, in press). Our data indicate clearly that socially withdrawn early adolescents are (a) disliked by their peers, (b) view themselves as lacking in social competence, and (c) express greater feelings of loneliness and depression than their average-normal agemates. In addition, their teachers rate extremely withdrawn young adolescents as being less competently assertive and as having more learning difficulties than average pre-adolescents. These data provide support for our contention that with age, social withdrawal becomes increasingly negatively evaluated by the peer group. In addition, social withdrawal continues to reflect internalizing difficulties during early adolescence.

In conclusion, the findings reported in this chapter indicate that for those children who have been identified as extremely withdrawn, their social and emotional lives deviate from the norm in pessimistic ways. As such, we must disagree strongly with previous assertions that social withdrawal is not a risk factor in child development. It is important, however, to strengthen this argument by examining those indices of maladaptation that may be predicted from the frequent experience of social solitude in childhood. We do so in the following section.

Predicting from Social Withdrawal and its Concomitants

The primary goal of the WLP has been to examine the hypothesis that social withdrawal does predict negative psychological outcomes for children and young adolescents. More specifically, we have argued that social withdrawal suggests a prognosis of internalizing problems — anxiety, and feelings of loneliness and depression.

To examine the veracity of this hypothesis, we used our earlier observations and peer assessments of non-social play as continuous variables to predict later "outcomes." These outcomes were derived from our developmental model in which it was suggested that internalizing problems should be the consequence of early insecurity/anxiety and social isolation; consequently, measures of depression, anxiety, loneliness, and negative self-worth were chosen as logical outcomes. The predictor variables chosen were those that best mirrored for us, the construct of insecurity/anxiety/social isolation at age 5 and 7 years.

From the outset, it is important to note that we distinguished between different forms of social withdrawal for these predictive analyses. Our kindergarten and grade 2 data indicated that approximately 80% of all solitary activity consisted of quiescent, constructive, or exploratory behavior. This quiescent form of solitary behavior was labeled "passive isolation." The second form of solitary activity was that which included solitary-pretense and solitary-sensorimotor activities, two forms of immature and rambunctious solitary play. We labeled this type of behavior "active isolation." At age 7, passive isolation was significantly correlated with peer nominations of social isolation and sensitivity and not with any derived indices of hostility or aggression. Active isolation, on the other hand was not related with teacher and peer assessments of withdrawal or fearfulness; rather it related significantly with teacher and/or peer derived indices of aggression (see Rubin & Mills, 1988, for an extended description of these different "faces" of social withdrawal).

Correlational analyses demonstrated that observed passive withdrawal in kindergarten predicted self-reported feelings of depression ($r = .40$, $p <$ .01) and general self-worth ($r = -.27$, $p < .04$), and teacher-rated anxiety ($r = .28$, $p < .04$) *at age eleven.* Similar predictive correlations were found for observed passive withdrawal in the second grade. Thus, passive withdrawal at age seven predicted self-reported feelings of depression ($r = .35$, $p < .01$) and teacher-rated anxiety ($r = .29$, $p < .04$) *at age eleven.*

From the outset, however, it was never assumed that social withdrawal, in and of itself, is the sole potential cause of malevolent outcome. Rather, withdrawal is viewed as a behavioral reflection of contemporaneous problems of an internalizing nature. The aforementioned characteristics associated concurrently with extreme withdrawal provide support for this conjecture. Accordingly, in a series of regression analyses, we have demonstrated that the *constellation* of early passive withdrawal, anxiety, and negative self perceptions of social competence in Grade 2 is significantly associated with measures of depression (multiple $R = .59$), loneliness (multiple $R = .65$), and anxiety (multiple $R = .50$) in Grade 5 (Rubin & Mills, 1988). It appears, then, that anxiety and withdrawal, in concert with negative thoughts about the self, ultimately predict negative affect–most notably internalized feelings of loneliness and depression.

Finally, within the past year, children who participated in earlier phases of the WLP (Cohort 1) were tracked into their first year of high school (ninth grade). Forty children who participated in the WLP in kindergarten completed a number of self report measures concerning externalizing and internalizing difficulties at age 14. In addition, their parents completed the adolescent version of the Child Behavior Checklist (Achenbach & Edelbrock, 1981). It was found that children who displayed a high frequency of passive withdrawal at age 5 were the most likely to report that social interaction and social relationships were *unimportant* to them ($r = -.31$, $p < .03$). Furthermore, passive withdrawal in kindergarten was positively associated with believing that doing well in school is important ($r = .37, p < .01$). It would appear, therefore, that quiet, passive constructive play, when produced in high frequencies at age 5 is associated with an emphasis on academic rather than social preference during the early teen period. Predictions to indices of psychopathology were *not* evident.

Passive withdrawal *in the second grade,* however, carried with it strong predictive value in just the ways that the developmental model outlined earlier had suggested. Approximately 40 seven-year-olds who had been observed during free play and who had completed peer assessments of passive withdrawal were reassessed at age 14. Given that observed withdrawal and peer assessed passive withdrawal were highly correlated at age seven, a composite variable of passive withdrawal was created. This composite measure was significantly associated with assessments of loneliness ($r = .52, p < .001$); negative perceptions of social ($r = -.37, p < .01$) and athletic competence ($r = -.29, p < .05$), and of personal appearance ($r = -.30, p < .05$); and feeling a *lack* of integration and involvement in their family ($r = .30, p < .05$) and peer group ($r = .42, p < .01$). This latter measure was construed as an assessment of felt security within the family and peer group in the teen years.

In contrast, an index composed of observed and peer assessed aggression at seven years predicted self-reported delinquency (in particular drug and alcohol experimentation, $r = .31, p < .05$, and criminal activity, $r = .27$, $p < .05$) at 14 years. This latter index was nonsignificantly associated with measures of loneliness, felt security, or self perceptions of competence at 14 years.

Thus, it would appear that: (a) passive withdrawal is a more severe problem at age seven than at age five; (b) it carries with it more significant predictive meaning at age seven than at age four; and (c) it is not predictive of difficulties of an externalizing nature at age 14. This latter finding is certainly in keeping with the traditional clinical literature on the long-term prognosis for socially withdrawn children; as mentioned earlier, however, had the predictive focus of these earlier studies been on internalizing difficulties, the long-term neglect of social withdrawal may have been avoided.

Finally, composites of social behavior were calculated from *grade five* peer and teacher assessments of passive withdrawal and aggression. The passive withdrawal composite was found to predict *ninth* grade self reports of loneliness ($r = .46$, $p < .01$), felt insecurity in the peer group ($r = .49$, $p < .01$), and negative self perceptions of academic ($r = -.39$, $p < .01$), social ($r = .48$, $p < .01$), and athletic ($r = .48$, $p < .01$) competence. Alternatively, the composite measure of fifth grade aggression predicted self-reported delinquency (in particular drug and alcohol experimentation, $r = .41$, $p < .01$) at 14 years. As with the fifth grade predictive analyses, passive withdrawal was not associated with problems of an externalizing nature during the early teen period. Thus, once again, the data support the earlier described developmental model.

SUMMARY AND CONCLUSIONS

To summarize, the WLP has demonstrated that social withdrawal: (a) is stable; (b) is associated concurrently, from early through late childhood, with measures conceptually reflective of felt insecurity, negative self-perceptions, dependency, and social deference; and (c) in concert with indices of negative self-appraisal, is significantly predictive of internalizing difficulties in early adolescence and the early teen period.

It is extremely important to note, however, that because we sampled a *normal* school population, the data support a predictive relation between withdrawal and *nonclinical* problems; this leaves open the question of whether it will also prove possible to predict clinically assessed internalizing difficulties in early adolescence from earlier passive withdrawal and negative social self perceptions. As a start toward addressing this issue, the corpus of fifth-grade data for both cohorts was reexamined. All early adolescents with a *Child Depression Inventory* score (Kovacs, 1980/81) one standard deviation or more above the mean for their age group were identified. For the eight children so identified, self-reported depression scores were at least one standard deviation above the mean for their cohort group (range = 23 to 28 for subjects in Cohort 1 with an overall $M =$ 10.83, $SD = 7.04$; range = 19–30 for subjects in Cohort 2 with an overall $M = 6.44$, $SD = 7.07$). These children, then, constituted the top eight percent of children in terms of depression scores within each cohort. The eight children targeted were then compared with their non-depressed schoolmates on indices of social and emotional well-being that had been assessed when they were in the second grade. Follow-back discriminant function analyses indicated that these children could *not* be distinguished from their normal counterparts on the basis of their popularity among peers in the second grade. Furthermore, they were neither observed to be more aggressive in their free play, nor rated by their teachers as more hostile and aggressive when in Grade 2. The analyses revealed, however, that the depressed children could be distinguished from their normal counterparts on the basis of observed social withdrawal, peer assessments of social withdrawal, and self-reported negative self perceptions of social competence. Results of the discriminant analyses, then, serve to clarify and extend the previously reported correlational results concerning the predictive correlates of depression in early adolescence. Extremely depressed fifth graders were those who expressed less positive perceptions of their own social competence three years earlier, were observed to play alone, and tended to be viewed by their second grade peers as more socially withdrawn.

In conclusion, data derived from recent research concerning the factors associated with the development of social inhibition in very early childhood, in tandem with data drawn from the WLP, provide initial support for the earlier described model of the correlates and predictive consequences of social withdrawal in childhood. Needless to say, it now behooves other researchers to gather further data that would track the veracity of our developmental model from infancy through to the adolescent years.

ACKNOWLEDGMENTS

The research described herein was supported by grants from Health and Welfare Canada and The Ontario Mental Health Foundation. A Killam Research Fellowship (Canada Council) provided the author with teaching release time to devote to the *Waterloo Longitudinal Project*. I gratefully acknowledge the participation of the children and teachers who made possible the program of research described herein. I would also like to thank my colleagues Shelley Hymel and Rosemary Mills and my students and research assistants Laurie Addis, Lilly Both, Xinyin Chen, Anne Emptage, and Linda Rowden for their generous and productive, collaborative participation.

REFERENCES

Achenbach, T. M., & Edelbrock, C. S. (1981). Behavioral problems and competencies reported by parents of normal and disturbed children aged four through sixteen. *Monographs of the Society for Research in Child Development, 46,* (1, Serial No. 188), 1–82.

Ainsworth, M. D. S., Blehar, M., Waters, E., & Wall, S. (1978). *Patterns of attachment.* Hillsdale, NJ: Lawrence Erlbaum Associates.

Bandura, A., & Walters, R. H. (1963). *Social learning and personality development.* New York: Holt, Rinehart, & Winston.

Belsky, J., & Rovine, M. (1987). Temperament and attachment security in the Strange Situation: An empirical rapprochement. *Child Development, 58,* 787–795.

Bowlby, J. (1973). *Attachment and loss, Vol. 2. Separation.* New York: Basic.

Bronson, W. C. (1966). Central orientations: A study of behavioral organization from childhood to adolescence. *Child Development, 37,* 125–155.

Calkins, S., & Fox, N. (in press). The relations between infant temperament, security of attachment and behavioral inhibition at 24 months. *Child Development.*

Chen, X., Rubin, K. H., & Sun, Y. (in press). Social reputation and peer relationships in Chinese children: A cross-cultural study. *Child Development.*

Cicchetti, D., & Toth, S. L. (1991). *Internalizing and externalizing expressions of dysfunction: Rochester symposium on developmental psychopathology.* Hillsdale, NJ: Lawrence Erlbaum Associates.

Cohen, S., & Wills, T. A. (1985). Stress, social support, and the buffering hypothesis. *Psychological Bulletin, 98,* 310–357.

Coie, J., & Kupersmidt, J. (1983). A behavioral analysis of emerging social status in boys' groups. *Child Development, 54,* 1400–1416.

Conger, J. C., & Keane, S. P. (1981). Social skills intervention in the treatment of isolated or withdrawn children. *Psychological Bulletin, 90,* 478–495.

Crnic, K., & Greenberg, M. T. (1990). Minor parenting stresses with young children. *Child Development, 61,* 1628–1637.

Dodge, K. A. (1983). Behavioral antecedents of peer social status. *Child Development, 54,* 1386–1399.

Doise, W., & Mugny, G. (1981). *Le développement social de l'intelligence.* Paris: Inter Editions.

Elder, G. H., Caspi, A., & Burton, L. M. (1987). Adolescent transitions in developmental perspective: Historical and sociological insights. In M. Gunnar (Ed.), *Minnesota Symposia on Child Psychology* (Vol. 21) (pp. xxx–xxx). Hillsdale, NJ: Lawrence Erlbaum Associates.

Engfer, A., & Gavranidou, M. (1987). Antecedents and consequences of maternal sensitivity: A longitudinal study. In H. Rauh & H. Steinhausen (Eds.), *Psychobiology and early development* (pp. 71–99). North Holland: Elsevier.

Ensminger, M. C., Kellam, S. G., & Rubin, B. R. (1983). School and family origins of delinquency: Comparisons by sex. In K. T. Van Dusen & S. A. Mednick (Eds.), *Prospective studies of crime and delinquency* (pp. 73–97). Hingham, MA: Kluwer-Nijhoff Publishing.

French, D. C. (1988). Heterogeneity of peer rejected boys: Aggressive and nonaggressive subtypes. *Child Development, 59,* 976–985.

Gottman, J. M., & Katz, L. F. (1989). Effects of marital discord on young children's peer interactions and health. *Developmental Psychology, 25,* 373–381.

Grossman, K. E., & Grossman, K. (in press). Attachment quality as an organizer of emotional and behavioral responses. In P. Harris, J. Stevenson-Hinde, & C. Parkes (Eds.), *Attachment across the life cycle* (pp. xxx–xxx). New York: Rutledge.

Hartup, W. W. (1985). Relationships and their significance in cognitive development. In R. A. Hinde, A. Perret-Clermont, & J. Stevenson-Hinde (Eds.), *Social relationships and cognitive development* (pp. 66–82). Oxford, UK: Clarendon Press.

Hartup, W. W. (in press). Peer relations in early and middle childhood. In V. B. van Hasselt & M. Hersen (Eds.), *Handbook of social development: A lifespan perspective*. New York: Plenum.

Hetherington, E. M., & Martin, B. (1986). Family factors and psychopathology in children. In H. C. Quay & J. S. Werry (Eds.), *Psychopathological disorders of childhood*, 3rd ed. (pp. 332–390). New York: Wiley.

Hymel, S., & Rubin, K. H. (1985). Children with peer relationship and social skills problems: Conceptual, methodological, and developmental issues. *Annals of Child Development, 2*, 251–297.

Hymel, S., Rubin, K. H., Rowden, L., & LeMare, L. (1990). Children's peer relationships: Longitudinal predictions of internalizing and externalizing problems from middle to late childhood. *Child Development, 61*, 2004–2021.

Isabella, R. A., Belsky, J., & von Eye, A. (1989). Origins of infant-mother attachment: An examination of interactional synchrony during the infant's first year. *Developmental Psychology, 25*, 12–21.

Janes, C. L., & Hesselbrock, V. M. (1978). Problem children's adult adjustment predicted from teachers' ratings. *American Journal of Orthopsychiatry, 48*, 300–309.

Janes, C. L., Hesselbrock, V. M., Myers, D. G., & Penniman, J. H. (1979). Problem boys in young adulthood: Teachers' ratings and twelve-year follow-up. *Journal of Youth and Adolescence, 8*, 453–472.

John, R. S., Mednick, S. A., & Schulsinger, F. (1982). Teacher reports as a predictor of schizophrenia and borderline schizophrenia: A Bayesian decision analysis. *Journal of Abnormal Psychology, 6*, 399–413.

Kagan, J. (1989). Temperamental contributions to social behavior. *American Psychology, 44*, 668–674.

Kagan, J., & Moss, H. A. (1962). *Birth to maturity: A study of psychological development*. New York: Wiley.

Kagan, J., Reznick, J. S., & Gibbons, J. (1989). Inhibited and uninhibited types of children. *Child Development, 60*, 838–845.

Kagan, J., Reznick, J. S., Clarke, C., Snidman, N., & Garcia-Coll, C. (1984). Behavioral inhibition to the unfamiliar. *Child Development, 55*, 2212–2225.

Kashani, J. H., Husain, A., Shekim, W. O., Hodges, K. K., Cytryn, L., & McKnew, D. H. (1981). Current perspectives on childhood depression: An overview. *American Journal of Psychiatry, 138*, 143–153.

Kohlberg, L., LaCrosse, J., & Ricks, D. (1972). The predictability of adult mental health from childhood behavior. In B. B. Wolman (Ed.), *Manual of child psychopathology* (pp. 1217–1284). New York: McGraw-Hill.

Kovacs, M. (1980/81). Rating scales to assess depression in school-aged children. *Acta Paedopsychiatria, 46*, 305–315.

LeMare, L. J., & Rubin, K. H. (1987). Perspective taking and peer interaction: Structural and developmental analyses. *Child Development, 58*, 306–315.

Lewis, M., & Miller, S. M. (1990). *Handbook of developmental psychopathology*. New York: Plenum.

Mangelsdorf, S., Gunnar, M., Kestenbaum, R., Lang, S., & Andreas, D. (1990). Infant proneness-to-distress temperament, maternal personality and mother-infant attachment: Associations and goodness of fit. *Child Development, 61*, 820–831.

Masten, A. S., Morison, P., & Pellegrini, D. S. (1985). A Revised Class Play method of peer assessment. *Developmental Psychology, 3*, 523–533.

Mead, G. H. (1934). *Mind, self, and society*. Chicago, Ill.: University of Chicago Press.

Michael, C. M., Morris, D. P., & Soroker, E. (1957). Follow-up studies of shy, withdrawn children II: Relative incidence of schizophrenia. *American Journal of Orthopsychiatry, 27*, 331–337.

Moller, L., & Rubin, K. H. (1988). A psychometric assessment of a two factor solution for the Preschool Behavior Questionnaire in mid-childhood. *Journal of Applied Developmental Psychology, 9,* 167–180.

Morris, D. P., Soroker, E., & Burruss, G. (1954). Follow-up studies of shy, withdrawn, children—I: Evaluation of later adjustment. *American Journal of Orthopsychiatry, 24,* 743–754.

Moskowitz, D. S., Schwartzman, A. E., & Ledingham, J. E. (1985). Stability and change in aggression and withdrawal in middle childhood and early adolescence. *Journal of Abnormal Psychology, 94,* 30–41.

Olweus, D. (1984). Stability in aggressive and withdrawn, inhibited behavior patterns. In R. M. Kaplan, V. J. Konecni, & R. W. Novaco (Eds.), *Aggression in children and youth* (pp. 104–136). The Hague: Nijhoff.

Parker, J. G., & Asher, S. R. (1987). Peer acceptance and later personal adjustment: Are low-accepted children "at risk?" *Psychological Bulletin, 102,* 357–389.

Patterson, G. R. (1983). Stress: A change agent for family process. In N. Garmezy & M. Rutter (Eds.), *Stress, coping, and development in children* (pp. 235–264). New York: McGraw Hill.

Piaget, J. (1926). *The language and thought of the child.* London: Routledge and Kegan Paul.

Piaget, J. (1932). *The moral judgment of the child.* Glencoe, Ill: Free Press.

Radke-Yarrow, M., Richters, J., & Wilson, W. E. (1988). Child development in a network of relationships. In R. A. Hinde & J. Stevenson-Hinde (Eds.), *Relationships within families; mutual influences* (pp. 48–67). Oxford: Clarendon Press.

Renken, B., Egeland, B., Marvinney, D., Sroufe, L. A., & Mangelsdorf, S. (1989). Early childhood antecedents of aggression and passive-withdrawal in early elementary school. *Journal of Personality, 57,* 257–281.

Robins, L. N. (1966). *Deviant children grown up.* Baltimore: Williams & Wilkins.

Rubin, K. H. (1982). Non-social play in preschoolers: Necessarily evil? *Child Development, 53,* 651–657.

Rubin, K. H. (1985). Socially withdrawn children: An "at risk" population? In B. H. Schneider, K. H. Rubin, & J. E. Ledingham (Eds.), *Peer relationships and social skills in childhood: Issues in assessment and training* (pp. 125–139). New York: Springer-Verlag.

Rubin, K. H., Bigras, M., & Mills, R. S. L. (May, 1992). *Maternal behavior with aggressive, withdrawn, and average children.* Paper presented at The Seventh Biennial University of Waterloo Conference on Child Development. Waterloo, Ontario.

Rubin, K. H., & Borwick, D. (1984). The communication skills of children who vary with regard to sociability. In H. Sypher & J. Applegates (Eds.), *Social cognition and communication.* Hillsdale, NJ: Lawrence Erlbaum Associates.

Rubin, K. H., Bream, L., & Rose-Krasnor, L. (1991). Social problem solving and aggression in childhood. In D. J. Pepler & K. H. Rubin (Eds.), *The development and treatment of childhood aggression,* (pp. 219–248). Hillsdale, NJ: Lawrence Erlbaum Associates.

Rubin, K. H., Chen, X., & Hymel, S. (in press). The socioemotional characteristics of extremely aggressive and extremely withdrawn children. *Merrill-*Palmer Quarterly.

Rubin, K. H., & Coplan, R. (in press). Peer relationships in childhood. In M. Bornstein & M. Lamb (Eds.), *Developmental psychology: An advanced textbook.* Hillsdale, NJ: Lawrence Erlbaum Associates.

Rubin, K. H., Daniels-Beirness, T., & Bream, L. (1984). Social isolation and social problem solving: A longitudinal study. *Journal of Consulting and Clinical Psychology, 52,* 17–25.

Rubin, K. H., Fein, G., & Vandenberg, B. (1983). Play. In E. M. Hetherington (Ed.), *Handbook of child psychology: Socialization, personality and social development.* New York: Wiley.

Rubin, K. H., Hymel, S., LeMare, L. J., & Rowden, L. (1989). Children experiencing social difficultie: Sociometric neglect reconsidered. *Canadian Journal of Behavioral Science, 21,* 94–111.

Rubin, K. H., Hymel, S., & Mills, R. S. L. (1989). Sociability and social withdrawal in childhood: Stability and outcomes. *Journal of Personality, 57,* 238-255.

Rubin, K. H., Hymel, S., Mills, R. S. L., & Rose-Krasnor, L. (1991). Conceptualizing different pathways to and from social isolation in childhood. In D. Cicchetti & S. Toth (Eds.), *The Rochester Symposium on Developmental Psychopathology, Vol. 2, Internalizing and externalizing expressions of dysfunction* (pp. 91-122). Hillsdale, NJ: Lawrence Erlbaum Associates.

Rubin, K. H., & Krasnor, L. R. (1986). Social-cognitive and social behavioral perspectives on problem solving. In M. Perlmutter (Ed.), Cognitive perspectives on children's social and behavioral development. *The Minnesota Symposia on Child Psychology (Vol. 18)* (pp. 1-68). Hillsdale, NJ: Lawrence Erlbaum Associates.

Rubin, K. H., LeMare, L. J., & Lollis, S. (1990). Social withdrawal in childhood: Developmental pathways to rejection. In S. R. Asher & J. D. Coie (Eds.), *Peer rejection in childhood.* (pp. 217-249), New York: Cambridge University Press.

Rubin, K. H., & Lollis, S. (1988). Peer relationships, social skills and infant attachment: A continuity model. In J. Belsky & T. Nezworski, (Eds.), *Clinical implications of attachment* (pp. 219-252). Hillsdale, NJ: Lawrence Erlbaum Associates.

Rubin, K. H., & Mills, R. S. L. (1988). The many faces of social isolation in childhood. *Journal of Consulting and Clinical Psychology, 56,* 916-924.

Rubin, K. H., & Mills, R. S. L. (1991). Conceptualizing Developmental Pathways to Internalizing Disorders in Childhood. *Canadian Journal of Behavioural Science, 23,* 300-317.

Rubin, K. H., & Rose-Krasnor, L. (in press). Interpersonal problem solving. In V. B. Van Hassett & M. Hersen (Eds.), *Handbook of social development.* New York: Plenum.

Selman, R. L., & Schultz, L. H. (1990). Children's strategies for interpersonal negotiation with peers: An interpretive/empirical approach to the study of social development. In T. J. Berndt & G. W. Ladd (Eds.), *Peer relationships in child development.* New York: Wiley.

Sroufe, L. A. (1983). Infant-caregiver attachment and patterns of adaptation in preschool: Roots of maladaptation and competence. In M. Perlmutter (Ed.), *Minnesota symposia on child psychology, Vol. 16.* Hillsdale, NJ: Lawrence Erlbaum Associates.

Sroufe, L. A., & Rutter, M. (1984). The domain of developmental psychopathology. *Child Development, 55,* 17-29.

Sullivan, H. S. (1953). *The interpersonal theory of psychiatry.* New York: Norton.

Thomas, A., & Chess, S. (1977). *Temperament and development.* New York: Brunner Mazel.

Thompson, R. A., Connell, J., & Bridges, L. J. (1988). Temperament, emotional, and social interactive behavior in the strange situation: An analysis of attachment functioning. *Child Development, 59,* 1102-1110.

Wahler, R. G., & Dumas, J. E. (1987). Family factors in childhood psychology; toward a coercion-neglect model. In T. Jacob (Ed.), *Family interaction and psychopathology; theories, methods, and findings* (pp. 581-627). New York: Plenum.

Wanless, R. L., & Prinz, R. J. (1982). Methodological issues in conceptualizing and treating childhood social isolation. *Psychological Bulletin, 92,* 39-55.

Younger, A. J., & Boyko, K. A. (1987). Aggression and withdrawal as social schemas underlying children's peer perceptions. *Child Development, 58,* 1094-1100.

15 Victimization by Peers: Antecedents and Long-Term Outcomes

Dan Olweus
University of Bergen, Norway

In a number of studies two broad forms of social maladjustment in children and youth have been identified. One generally refers to aggressive, disruptive, acting-out behavior, the other to withdrawn, anxious, and inhibited reaction patterns. Several, more or less synonymous terms have been used to designate these syndromes of disturbance: unsocialized aggression and overinhibited behavior (Hewitt & Jenkins, 1946); conduct problems and personality problems (Peterson, 1961); antisocial and neurotic behavior (Rutter, Tizard, & Whitmore, 1970); hostility and introversion (Schaefer, 1971); anger-defiance and apathy-withdrawal (Kohn, 1977); undercontrol and overcontrol (Block & Block, 1979); externalizing and internalizing syndromes (Achenbach, 1978).

There are probably some real differences between these constructs, due to variation in research purposes and conceptualization, and methodology. Nevertheless, it would seem possible to reach considerable agreement on their localization within a two-dimensional model of social-emotional behavior (see Fig. 15.1). Using activity-passivity (or extroversion-introversion) as one reference axis and emotional stability-instability (or good-poor adjustment) as the other, it is obvious that constructs referring to aggressive, acting-out behavior (and such individuals) would be placed in the unstable-active quadrant (unstable extravert, conduct problem). Similarly, concepts reflecting inhibited, anxious, and withdrawn reaction patterns (and such individuals) would belong in the unstable-passive quadrant (unstable introvert, personality problem).

In a previous publication (Olweus, 1984), I selectively reviewed studies on the stability or continuity of individual differences over time in habitually

315

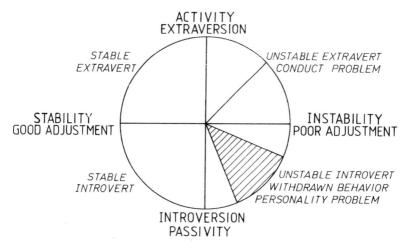

FIG. 15.1. Two-dimensional model of social-emotional behavior.

withdrawn, inhibited reaction patterns (as well as in aggressive, acting-out behavior). On the basis of the empirical findings and conceptual considerations, it was suggested that withdrawn, internalizing individuals and related constructs are somewhat more heterogeneous than individuals and concepts of the aggressive, acting-out type. In agreement with this view, it is natural to represent reaction patterns of the withdrawn, inhibited kind in Fig. 15.1 by a sector rather than by a radius. This view also underscores the desirability of making relatively detailed differentiations among concepts/individuals in the unstable-passive quadrant.

A CLASSIFICATION SCHEME

Such differentiations can of course be made in several different ways. From the perspective of the present volume, with its focus on socially withdrawn and inhibited reaction patterns, it seems natural to use as a starting point what may be seen as the basic characteristic or common denominator of such patterns: habitual lack, or a low level, of social interaction (see Fig. 15.2).

With regard to assumed motivations underlying the relative lack of social interaction, it is possible to distinguish at least three major categories of mechanisms or causes:

1. inhibition, shyness, fearfulness,
2. genuine introvertedness or low sociability, and
3. lack of acceptance by peers.

These three categories can, at least at a conceptual level, be easily separated from each other. The first two categories both refer to charac-

BASIC CHARACTERISTIC   CAUSES/MECHANISMS   FORMS

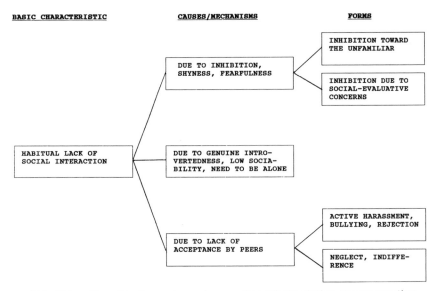

FIG. 15.2. Classification scheme for possible differentiation among reaction patterns characterized by habitually low levels of social interaction.

teristics of the individual, but of a different nature. In the case of inhibition/shyness, the individual has presumably a tendency to approach another individual(s) or a particular situation but this tendency is blocked by an anxiety-based response (Asendorpf, 1990; this volume). However, when lack of social interaction is motivated by genuine introvertedness, there are no grounds for postulating an approach tendency and the individual is characterized by a relative lack of interest in social interaction, a need to be alone. The third category, on the other hand, represents a different situation in that there is an external blocking of social interaction in this case: The individual is not well liked or accepted by peers and this results in a low level of social interaction (e.g., Rubin, LeMare, & Lollis, 1990).

Evidence from the research literature as well as conceptual considerations suggest that it is meaningful to make at least two additional distinctions. Kagan and his coworkers have concentrated on the phenomenon of "behavioral inhibition toward the unfamiliar" or "toward strangers" (e.g., Kagan, Reznick, Clarke, Snidman, & Garcia-Coll, 1984). Authors like Buss (1980) and Asendorpf (1989, 1990) have drawn attention to another important antecedent of inhibition, namely the prospect or presence of (undesired) social evaluation. Taking such considerations and related research evidence into account, it is natural to divide the first major category into the two subclasses of "inhibition toward the unfamiliar" and "inhibition due to social-evaluative concerns."

The second subdivision concerns the third major category, in which a low level of social interaction is a consequence of lack of acceptance by peers. Both conceptual considerations and evidence from the research literature on peer relationships (e.g., Asher & Coie, 1990) suggest that it makes a difference whether the peers' lack of acceptance is expressed in active harassment, bullying, rejection, or in the form of indiffference or neglect. It is certainly reasonable to assume that there are fewer and less serious consequences of being exposed to indifference or neglect by peers than to various forms of active harassment. There is in fact some evidence that children categorized as neglected according to certain criteria (e.g., Asher & Coie, 1990) do not differ markedly from average children (e.g., Rubin, Hymel, LeMare, & Rowden, 1990).

In this context, a few comments about the class of children characterized as "rejected" should also be made. In several studies it has been shown that this group of children is quite heterogeneous (French, 1988; Olweus, 1989; Perry, Kusel, & Perry, 1988), consisting of at least two major subgroups, sometimes called rejected-withdrawn and rejected-aggressive, respectively. In the studies reported in this chapter, I focus mainly on children who are rejected and withdrawn. By limiting the attention to this subgroup, many of the problems involved in focusing on rejected children as a homogeneous group (Olweus, 1989) are avoided.

As shown in Fig. 15.2, I suggest dividing the major category "lack of acceptance by peers" into one subcategory characterized by active harassment, bullying, and rejection and another relating to neglect and indifference.

In closing the presentation of this classification scheme, it should be emphasized, first, that the suggested categories and subcategories are largely derived from conceptual considerations even though several of them are also supported by empirical research. In spite of the fact that the various categories can be easily separated from each other at a conceptual level, it is obvious that there are also links and associations among them. It has been proposed, for instance, that inhibition due to social-evaluative concerns may be in part a consequence of frequent failures and rejection in contact initiations with peers (Asendorpf, 1990), thus suggesting a causal connection between two of the "boxes" in the classification scheme. Furthermore, it is quite possible that children with an introverted predisposition are more likely than other children to be harassed and rejected by their peers, which in turn would increase their probability of developing social-evaluative inhibition. These examples show that it is a major task for future research in this area to determine empirically the linkages between, and the degree of overlap or separateness of, the various categories of the suggested classification scheme.

OVERVIEW

Turning now to the main focus of the rest of my chapter, I am concerned primarily with individuals belonging in the subcategory "habitual lack of social interaction due to active harassment, bullying, and rejection." Using a different starting point and theoretical framework than most researchers in the area of social withdrawal and peer relationships, I have identified, in a large-scale project on bully/victim problems among schoolchildren (e.g., Olweus, 1973, 1978, 1985, 1991, 1992), two kinds of children whose habitual reaction patterns are clearly related to the broad forms of social maladjustment described in the introduction: The aggressive, tough, dominating, and impulsive bully who systematically and repeatedly attacks and bothers other children, and the passive victim, the target of other children's, in particular the bullies' aggression and harassment. This latter group of children is the focus of the present context.

The defining characteristic of a victim is that "he or she is exposed, repeatedly and over time, to negative actions on the part of one or more other persons" (Olweus, 1991, p. 413). Using several different methods, it has been found that typical victims are socially isolated, withdrawn, anxious, and inhibited, with a negative view of themselves and their situation (Olweus, 1978, 1984, 1991, 1992).

My surveys of more than 150,000 students in Norwegian and Swedish comprehensive schools have shown that bully/victim problems are quite prevalent: At a particular point in time, approximately 7-9% of the total school population can be considered as being victimized with some regularity (Olweus, 1985, 1991, 1992). In addition, such problems may persist largely unchanged over long periods of time. For instance, in a follow-up study of 201 Grade-6 boys, a high degree of stability over a 3-year period was found for two peer rating dimensions reflecting being exposed to harassment by peers and relative lack of peer acceptance (average r corrected for attenuation was .81; see Olweus, 1977). In view of the prevalence and relative persistence of victim (and bully) problems, it is important to find out more about factors that are responsible for their development. This is the aim of the first part of this chapter.

Almost nothing is known about the long-term development of children who have been victimized during a sizable period of their school life. Will the reaction patterns associated with their victim status in school be found again if we study them several years later, for example, in young adulthood? Are these individuals still socially withdrawn and isolated, maybe even harassed by their working or student companions? Or, have they recovered in most respects after they have escaped the strait-jacket of companionship forced upon them in comprehensive school, and they can choose more freely their own social environments? Or, does the painful experience of being victimized over long periods of time leave certain scars on their adult personality even if they seem to function well in most respects? These and related issues are explored herein drawing from a follow-up study of young men at age 23, some of whom had been victims of bullying and harassment by peers for a period of at least three years, from Grade 6 through Grade 9. This study is described in the latter part of the chapter.

DEVELOPMENTAL ANTECEDENTS OF VICTIMIZATION PROBLEMS

In a previous publication (Olweus, 1980a), I used path analysis to identify a set of developmental determinants of a habitually aggressive reaction pattern in young adolescents, characteristic of boys who bully and harass other students. A parallel analysis, focusing on developmental determinants of a pattern characterized by systematic victimization and rejection by peers, is reported here. Because the same subject groups, sources of data, and techniques of analysis are used as in the previous study, most of the methodological details can be found in the earlier report (Olweus, 1980a). Accordingly, only a summary description is given in this context.

Briefly about Methodology (First Study)

The *subjects* used in the following analyses were 76 school boys with a modal age of 13 years (Grade 6; Sample I) and 51 boys with modal age 16 (Grade 9; Sample II) as well as their mothers and the majority of their fathers. The subject groups were largely representative of the school population of a suburb of Stockholm, Sweden, from which they were drawn.

Peer ratings (by 4–6 randomly selected boys in each class, see Olweus, 1978) were used to obtain information about the extent to which the boys were systematically bullied or victimized and rejected by their peers. Two rating dimensions (Aggression target and Degree of unpopularity) were combined into a composite measure called *Degree of victimization by peers* (by bullies in particular; X5 in Figs. 15.3 & 15.4): One measuring "how often other boys start fights and are rough with and tease him" and the other tapping degree of unpopularity (from "he is liked by none or almost none of the boys in the class" to "all the boys in the class"). The reliability of this almost continuous composite was .89 in Sample I and .88 in Sample II. Other data (e.g., Olweus, 1978) have shown that the composite as well as its component variables have considerable validity. The composite is the ultimate dependent variable in the analyses to follow.

To provide detailed information about the boys' rearing conditions during childhood and the parents' disciplinary practices and personality qualities, extensive, partly retrospective interviews were carried out with the mothers and fathers, independently. A number of characteristics of the interview procedure were reported in Olweus (1980a), generally suggesting that the information obtained was both reliable and valid. The interrater reliabilities of the particular interview variables to be used in the following path analyses were quite satisfactory and of the same order (.80 to .95) as for those employed in the previous article.

Selection of Antecedent Variables in Causal Model

My own findings concerning the characteristics of typical victims (e.g., Olweus, 1978, 1986, 1992) as well as previous research on parental factors related to withdrawn, inhibited reaction patterns (e.g., Becker, 1964; Hetherington & Martin, 1979; Levy, 1943; Martin, 1975; Rubin & Lollis, 1988) served as general guidelines in the selection of antecedent variables for the causal model.

On the basis of the studies conducted by Levy (1943), in particular, it was natural to include a variable reflecting maternal overprotectiveness. To obtain a relatively broad dimension of overprotectiveness, two variables were combined into a composite: one referred to the extent to which the mother, in different ways, tended to treat the boy as younger than his age and the other referred to the degree to which she was controlling and restrictive in various areas of activity (interactions with peers, spare time activities, etc.). Both variables concerned the current situation as well as earlier time periods. The composite variable is called *Mother's overprotectiveness* (X3). High values on this variable indicate somewhat infantilizing and highly controlling behavior on the part of the boy's mother. The variable is thought to embrace three of the criteria Levy (1943) considered important in identifying maternal overprotection: infantilization, prevention of independent behavior, and excessive maternal control.

Since typical victims can be characterized as sensitive, anxious, withdrawn, and passive (Olweus, 1978, 1992), it was natural to assume that a quiet, calm, and placid temperament could be of importance for the development of status as a victim. To get an estimate of these aspects of the boy's temperament in early years, the same variable used in the previous report (Olweus, 1980a) was selected. This variable was a composite of the boy's general level of activity and the intensity of his temperament (hot-tempered/calm). To facilitate interpretation, the variable was reversed in the present analyses. The variable is called *Weak temperament* (X1) in the causal model.

In addition, the research literature (e.g., Martin, 1975) suggests that fathers of withdrawn, inhibited children are often critical of them and somewhat distant and withdrawn themselves. In view of these findings, a variable designed to reflect the father's basic emotional attitude to the boy during the boy's early childhood was included in the model. This variable, called *Father's negativism* (X2), was a composite of two closely related variables: father's degree of positive attitude (warmth, with reversed scoring) and father's degree of negative attitude. A negative basic attitude could be manifested in (relative) hostility and rejection as well as in coldness and indifference. The variable was rated on the basis of the father interview alone. It should be noted that this variable is a counterpart of the variable "Mother's negativism" found to be important for the development of aggressive reaction patterns (Olweus, 1980a).

Furthermore, it was hypothesized that a boy with poor identification with male adults, in particular his father, might encounter difficulties in asserting himself adequately and in adjusting to the peer group. The variable selected, called *Poor identification with father* (X4), was rated on the basis of information obtained from both the mother and father interviews. It was aimed to assess the extent to which the boy wanted to be like, or identified with, his father (reversed scoring).

Causal Ordering and Analytic Strategy

The causal ordering of the antecedent variables in the path model is fairly straightforward. It is natural that the two variables referring to the first 4–5 years of the boy's life, Weak temperament and Father's negativism, are entered first in the causal sequence (see Figs. 15.3 & 15.4). Although there may be some overlap in time, the variables Mother's overprotectiveness and Poor identification with father both refer to somewhat later periods in the boy's life and are thus given a later location in the model.

The general strategy adopted in conducting the analyses is described in detail in Olweus (1980a). Here I just want to emphasize that the choice was made to retain in the model path coefficients of variables that, in a stepwise regression, explained at least 1% of the variance in the relevant dependent variable.

To examine whether some other potentially important, though less clearly relevant, antecedent variables would significantly increase the amount of variance explained in the ultimate dependent variable, the hierarchical approach described in Olweus (1980a) was adopted. The additional variables used in these analyses included Mother's negativism, Parental divorce, and several indices of the family's socioeconomic status. None of these variables were found to change the basic structure of the causal model.

Main Results

The main results from the path analyses (using standardized path coefficients) are presented in Figs. 15.3 and 15.4 for Samples I and II, respectively. First, it should be emphasized that the pattern of coefficients obtained for the "cross-validation" sample (II) is very similar to that of the

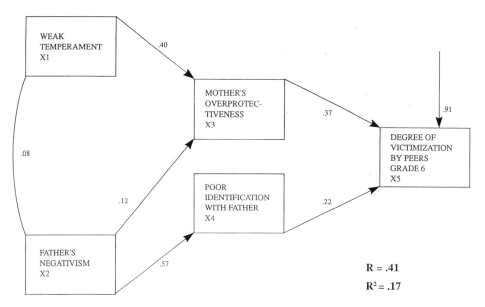

FIG. 15.3.   Path diagram for determinants of Degree of victimization by peers. Sample I ($n = 76$).

"original" sample (I). The basic congruence of the two sets of coefficients certainly increases our confidence in the validity of the model. At the same time, it should be pointed out that the four antecedent variables of the model explain (without correction for measurement error) a moderate 20% of the variance in the ultimate dependent variable (X5), indicating that there are also other important determinants of Degree of victimization by peers (below).

Closer examination of the two figures leads to the following interpretation and comments. The largest direct effect on the ultimate dependent variable comes in both analyses from Mother's overprotectiveness (.37 and .41). A mother who tends to treat her son as younger than his age (some degree of infantilization and prevention of independent behavior) and who is highly controlling is thus likely to increase the probability that her son is victimized by peers. At the same time, the path coefficient from Weak temperament to Mother's overprotectiveness shows that the mother's behavior is, in part, a consequence of the boy's temperament. The implication is that a boy with a quiet, placid, and maybe somewhat passive temperament to some degree will elicit overprotecting behavior from his mother. This is an example of what may be denoted as the boy's "contribution to his own socialization" (Bell, 1968; Olweus, 1980a).

The findings just discussed suggest a fairly close relationship between a boy who is likely to be victimized and his mother. The results in the lower

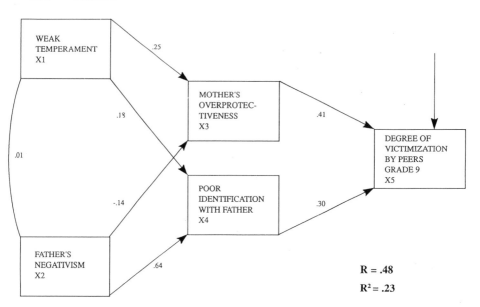

FIG. 15.4.   Path diagram for determinants of Degree of victimization by peers.
Sample II (n = 51).

part of the path diagrams point to the existence in the family of a somewhat
critical and distant father who probably does not regard his son as very
"boyish." This negative attitude will contribute to a poor identification with
the father on the part of the boy. Very likely, the variable Poor identification with father also implies that the boy has some difficulty in asserting
himself in traditionally boyish or masculine ways.

It is worth emphasizing that the ultimate dependent variable as well as the
four causal variables of the model were all essentially uncorrelated with
socioeconomic conditions such as parental income level, occupational
prestige, and length of education. Thus, victimized boys as well as rearing
conditions contributing to victim status can exist in all kinds of families,
independent of their position in the social hierarchy, at least in a society like
that of Sweden. In the previous analyses (Olweus, 1980a), the same
conclusion was drawn with regard to aggressive behavior and its determinants.

Analyses Including Physical Weakness

The focus of the analyses presented in the foregoing has been on relatively
early factors contributing to the development of victim status in a boy. As
was mentioned, the moderate amount of variance explained by these factors

indicates that other, probably later variables in the causal sequence also play an important role. There are grounds for assuming that certain concurrent characteristics of the boy, such as cautiousness, sensitivity, and non-assertiveness (Olweus, 1978, 1991, 1992), *contribute* to his being victimized. At the same time, several related characteristics including anxiousness, inhibition, and poor self-esteem may also be a *consequence* of repeated victimization.

To represent the operation of these and similar concurrent variables may require construction of fairly complex models involving reciprocal relationships. Because the data available don't lend themselves readily to the examination of complex models of this kind, such variables are not considered further in the present context. Instead, I explore the role of another concurrent variable, *Physical weakness,* whose relationship with the victimization variable can be considered primarily unidirectional, from physical weakness to victimization. In a previous study using teacher ratings (Olweus, 1978), physical weakness was found to be clearly more characteristic of victimized boys than of bullies and control boys.

In the present investigation, data on physical weakness-strength were collected through peer ratings, using the same procedure as for the ultimate dependent variable (this chapter; Olweus, 1978). The variable rated was "the number of pull-ups the boy considered is capable of," divided into seven consecutive categories. The average ratings on this scale were quite reliable, .92 in Sample I and .90 in Sample II.

It is noteworthy that physical weakness-strength among boys is clearly related to the boy's level of popularity, even as high as age 16 (Grade 9): The correlation between Physical weakness and Degree of unpopularity in the two larger cohorts (n in Cohort I = 276, and n in Cohort II = 300), from which Samples I and II were drawn, was .39 in both cohorts. Similarly, Physical weakness had sizeable correlations with the ultimate dependent variable in the present analyses, Degree of victimization by peers (which is a composite of Degree of unpopularity and Aggression target, as may be recalled): It was .48 in Cohort I and .45 in Cohort II.

At the same time, it is worth emphasizing that Physical weakness was only weakly related to rating dimensions reflecting aggressive behavior. For instance, the correlation with the variable *Start fights* ("He starts fights with other boys at school"; Olweus, 1977, 1978) was only .14 in Cohort I and .15 in Cohort II. Obviously, the variable physical weakness-strength is largely a measure of something different than a boy's inclination or readiness to initiate aggressive behavior.

Unfortunately, data on physical weakness-strength were collected only in Grade 9 for both Samples (Cohorts) I and II. Accordingly, for Sample I, in which the ultimate dependent variable in the path model referred to grade 6, the physical weakness data were obtained three years later than the data on the victimization variable. This implies that the path coefficient indexing the effect of Physical weakness on Degree of victimization by peers in Sample I will in all probability be considerably underestimated. The best estimate of the effect of Physical weakness will thus be obtained in Sample II in which the victimization and the physical weakness data actually were collected at the same time.

The main result of introducing Physical weakness into the path model for Sample II was a marked direct effect on Degree of victimization by peers (a standardized path coefficient of .43), while the effects from Mother's overprotectiveness and Poor identification with father were somewhat reduced (from .41 to .29 for Mother's overprotectiveness, and from .30 to .23 for the identification variable). The total amount of variance explained by the variables in the model was also markedly increased, from 23% to 40%. Slightly less than half of the variance in Degree of victimization by peers could thus be accounted for by the Physical weakness variable alone!

The results for Sample I were very similar, although the direct effect of Physical weakness was considerably lower (.19) than in Sample II, as expected. The increase in amount of variance explained was also more modest, from 17% to 20%. As pointed out earlier, however, the estimate of the effect of Physical weakness is biased downward in Sample I.

The above analyses clearly indicate that physical strength is a highly valued attribute in a boy, even up to age 16. Physical superiority, however, was not typically used to dominate and harass weaker children: A considerable proportion of the strong boys was obviously non-aggressive. It is the combination of an aggressive reaction pattern and physical strength that makes for a bully (Olweus, 1978, 1986, 1992). On the other hand, *physical strength* in a boy seems to serve as *good protection against victimization* by peers, whereas *physical weakness* appears to *"invite" such behavior,* or rather, to reduce the boy's chances of preventing victimization from occurring to him.

A Summary Picture and Comments

In sum, the preceding analyses suggest the following picture of a boy who is likely to become victimized by peers (the passive victim, cf. Olweus, 1978, Ch. 8). He is a quiet, placid, cautious, and sensitive boy who develops a close relationship with his mother. He is likely to be physically weaker than his peers and has difficulty in asserting himself with other boys his age. His basic temperamental and personality predispositions are strengthened by overprotective behavior on the part of his mother. The father of the boy is critical and somewhat distant, which makes him less suitable or available as a male role model for the boy. This may in turn make the boy even less assertive and "boyish" (though there are no indications that victimized boys are particularly feminine), which will increase his probability of being victimized.

Although the temperamental and family variables represented in the causal model are important as factors predisposing a boy to become victimized by peers, it should also be underscored that the concurrent variable *Physical weakness alone was of almost the same significance for victim status as all of the predisposing factors combined.* This result shows the importance of taking both antecedent and concurrent variables into account for a more complete understanding.

It should be generally underscored that the broad picture outlined in the preceding is a summary of the main trends in the analyses. In individual cases of victimized boys, other factors in the boy or the family may have played a central role, and the pattern of probable causal links may be partly different.

Finally, it must be emphasized that causal models like the one presented here represent a rough, static approximation of the dynamic interplay of events and processes taking place in real life. Accordingly, an empirical estimate of the causal influence of one variable upon another must not be taken too literally, but rather as a tentative indication, given the correctness of the basic causal structure. And there is always the possibility that the causal model has been misspecified in one or more respects, for instance, by assuming a unidirectional rather than bidirectional influence between two variables. Also, there are some problems associated with use of retrospective data (as in the present mother and father interviews, see Olweus, 1980a). Although, in my view, such problems are not likely to have largely affected the present causal analyses, they suggest the desirability of regarding the results of these analyses as somewhat tentative and in need of replication with other data sets.

LONG-TERM OUTCOMES OF VICTIMIZATION IN SCHOOL

As mentioned in the overview section, little is known about the long-term development of children who have been regularly victimized by peers in school. Several questions of possible relevance from that perspective were raised in the overview, and these and related issues are addressed in the latter part of this chapter.

Briefly about Methodology (Second Study)

The *subjects* of this study were 87 men who were approximately 23 years at follow-up in the winter of 1982/83. All of them had participated in an assessment in Grade 9 when they were 16, and for the overwhelming majority, data were also available from Grade 6. Further, a special study of hormone-behavior relationships was conducted in Grade 9 (Olweus, Mattsson, Schalling, & Löw, 1980, 1988), and 67 of the 79 subjects (85%) in this investigation were included in the follow-up sample.

The 87 subjects of the follow-up sample consisted of the following three groups:

1. A largely representative sample of 64 subjects that included six former victims and five former bullies (see Olweus et al., 1980, and Olweus, 1980a, for additional information);
2. A selection of 11 additional former victims. The total number of former victims in the study was thus 17. These boys can be considered to be among the most severely victimized boys in the cohort of 276 boys to which they belonged (Cohort I);
3. A selection of 12 additional former bullies. Accordingly, the total number of former bullies was also 17. These boys were among the most pronounced bullies in the cohort (representing about 6% of the total *n* of 276).[1]

For the purposes of the present analyses, only the following two groups are used: The group of 17 former victims and the representative sample of 58 subjects (64 minus the six former victims). Due to missing data on some of the variables, the actual number of subjects in the present analyses were 15 and 56, respectively.

To be defined as a victim in Grade 6 or 9, a subject had to fulfill the following two criteria:

a. He had to have been nominated by at least one of the main class teachers as a victim (according to the definition: "A boy who for a fairly long time has been and still is exposed to aggression from others: that is, boys and possibly girls from his own class or maybe from other classes often pick fights and are rough with him or tease and ridicule him," Olweus, 1978, p. 34); and

b. He had to have received an average peer rating of one standard deviation or more above the mean of the total distribution (for approximately 275 boys) on at least one of the two variables Aggression target and Degree of unpopularity discussed in the first part of the chapter.

When victims were selected for participation in the special study of hormone-behavior relationships, the intent was to include primarily

---

[1]For the majority of subjects in the three groups, data on early child rearing conditions, as discussed in the first part of the chapter, were also available. Most of the follow-up subjects were included in Sample I.

Grade–9 victims who had been victimized also in Grade 6. This proved to be a simple task since the stability of victimization status over time was quite high. In actual fact, 16 of the total group of 17 victims in the present study qualified as victims in both Grade 6 and Grade 9. Assuming continuity over the interval covered, they had thus been exposed to fairly severe bullying and harassment for a very long period of time.

In addition to having the typical characteristics described above, the habitual victims were also found to have elevated levels of the stress hormone adrenaline at age 16 in comparison with the control boys. However, they did not display an aggressive or teasing behavior pattern and accordingly, the harassment the victims were exposed to cannot be explained as a consequence of active provocation on their own part. As documented in the first half of this chapter, the victims as a group were physically weaker than their peers.

At follow-up, the subjects of this study completed a number of questionnaires designed to tap various dimensions of assumed relevance: Scales for being directly harassed (e.g., "Others are fairly often mean and nasty to me"), for being indirectly harassed (social isolation, loneliness), for social anxiety (shyness, social-evaluative concerns), emotionality-worrying in achievement-related situations, involvement in antisocial activities, several dimensions of aggression (assertiveness) and aggression inhibition, frustration tolerance, neuroticism and extraversion (slightly abbreviated versions of the Eysenck scales; Eysenck & Eysenck, 1968), global self-esteem (7 items from Rosenberg's scale; Rosenberg, 1979) and depression (9 items from Beck's scale; Beck, Ward, Mendelsohn, Mock, & Erbaugh, 1961). Most of the items had a six-point Likert format. The internal-consistency (α) reliabilities of the scales were generally quite satisfactory, in most cases lying in the .80 to .95 range.

In one of the questionnaires, the subjects were asked to look back to the year they were in Grade 9 and to assess (retrospectively), among other things, the degree to which they had been exposed to direct and indirect bullying and harassment by peers. The five items covering these domains were combined into one scale.

Several samples of blood and urine were also collected from the subjects at two different points in time separated by an interval of about eight weeks. These samples were used for the assessment of several hormones including adrenaline, noreadrenaline, testosterone, and cortisol.

In agreement with the recent general trend as regards statistical treatment of psychological data, it was considered appropriate to focus the present analyses not only on significance testing but also on effect sizes (in this context I used the standardized mean difference measure d defined as the difference between the means of the two groups divided by the standard deviation of the non-victim or "control" group; Cohen, 1977). One reason for this strategy is that we are here mainly concerned with exploring possible causal relationships and mechanisms, and from this perspective effect size measures give better information about the relationships of interest than tests of significance. Correlation (Pearson) and regression analyses were also used.

Results and Discussion

A. Lack of Continuity in Victimization.   The first important result to report is a Lack of relationship between indicators of victimization in school and data on both direct and indirect harassment in young adulthood. The point-biserial correlation between Being directly harassed in young adulthood ($\alpha = .91$) and victim/non-victim status in Grades 6–9 (group membership) was only .06 (n.s.). The corresponding correlation for Being indirectly harassed ($\alpha = .84$) was .15 (n.s.). Similarly, the product-moment correlations of these two adult harassment variables with the peer rating variable Degree of victimization by peers, averaged across Grades 6 and 9, were .07 and .18 (both n.s.). The fact that a boy had been regularly victimized by his peers in school for a long period of time was thus basically unrelated to (self-reported) later harassment and social isolation. Obviously, the experience of victimization in school did not seem to increase the boy's probability of being victimized in young adulthood.

Considering this finding, one might wonder if the experience of being bullied and victimized in school had been so painful to many former victims that they had simply come to deny or repress any indications that they were being victimized as young adults. This hypothesis, however, could be safely ruled out by means of the retrospective data. Here we found substantial correlations between the retrospective estimates of degree of direct/indirect harassment in Grade 9 and victim/non-victim status ($r = .42$) as well as degree of victimization in Grade 9 as measured by the peer ratings ($r = .58$). These findings show that a considerable proportion of the subjects had a fairly realistic view of their peer relationships in school seven years earlier. *The "denial/repression hypotheses" was thus not a viable explanation* of the lack of association between degree of harassment in school and in young adulthood.

One might also wonder if the lack of association was a consequence of the fact that different methods of assessment were used at the two time points: The categorization of the subjects as victims and non-victims in school was based on a combination of teacher nominations and peer ratings, whereas the adult measure of harassment was derived from self reports. Accordingly, one could argue that use of "non-congruent" assessment techniques, which sample partly different aspects of the phenomena under consideration, might lead to a substantial underestimate of the "true relationship."

Fortunately, this possibility could be checked within the present study since self-report data on degree of victimization/harassment in school were also available. Four 6–point questionnaire items (such as "Other boys are nasty to me," and "I feel lonely and abandoned at school"), which were part of the assessment battery in both Grade 6 and Grade 9, were combined into a composite averaged across grades ($\alpha = .84$). This composite correlated .42 with concurrent victim/non-victim status and .61 with the peer rating variable Degree of victimization by peers (the correlation within the victim group was even higher, .73). Accordingly, the composite must be considered a valid and meaningful self-report indicator of victimization/harassment in school.

When this scale of self-reported victimization in school was correlated with the adult measures of harassment, the results were very much the same as those obtained with the "other-based" measure of victimization in school: The correlation with Being directly harassed in young adulthood was .05 (the corresponding value for victim/non-victim status in school was .06), whereas the correlation with Being indirectly harassed was .16 (and the corresponding value for victim/non-victim status was .15). Obviously, use of "congruent" methods of assessment would not lead to a different conclusion.

Summing up, the lack of association between victim/non-victim status in school and degree of harassment in young adulthood could not be explained as a consequence of denial/repression or of "non-congruence" of methods of assessment. In all probability, then, the lack of a relation was a reflection of reality (I am also basing this judgment on the substantial correlation of degree of adult harassment with concurrent levels of depression and self esteem, reported in the following).

B. Long-Term Effect of Victimization. In spite of the fact that the former victims were no more harassed or socially isolated than the control boys as young adults, they had clearly higher levels of depression, or maybe depressive tendencies, and a more negative view of themselves (poorer self esteem) at age 23. On the somewhat abbreviated, but highly reliable Beck scale of depression ($\alpha = .87$), the t-value for the mean difference between the victim and non-victim groups was 2.77 ($p < .01$ on a two-tailed test), and the effect size d, a substantial .87 (a "large" effect size according to Cohen, 1977). The point-biserial correlation between group membership and the depression scale was .32. For the equally reliable Rosenberg scale of global self esteem (also somewhat abbreviated; $\alpha = .89$) the t-value was 2.28 ($p = .03$ on a two-tailed test) and the value of d .70. The corresponding point-biserial correlation amounted to .26.

To get a better understanding of how to interpret the results, a more elaborate analysis of the data is required. The key variables and relationships in terms of correlation coefficients are shown in Fig. 15.5 with the Beck scale of depression as the "ultimate" dependent variable.

Three of the variables in the figure have already been discussed and we note the approximately zero correlation between victim/non-victim status during the school period and later degree of direct harassment. The fourth variable in the graph is a scale that was derived through factor analysis of a Q–sort inventory used in both Grade 6 and Grade 9. The factorially derived scale consists of 12 items and was interpreted to reflect feelings of maladjustment, anxiety, and personal inadequacy (Olweus, 1978). The reaction patterns covered by this dimension can be assumed to be precursors of later depressive tendencies and this assumption was supported by the fairly substantial correlation of .48 between this scale (averaged over Grade 6 and Grade 9) and the Beck scale 7–10 years later. The reliability of the scale can be estimated at .92.

The basic starting point for interpretation of the results is the finding that the former victims had higher levels of depressive tendencies than non-victims in young adulthood (alternatively, the correlation of .32 in Fig. 15.5 of victim/non-victim status with later depressive tendencies).

This difference or correlation is clearly not a consequence of different levels of concurrent harassment, since the former victims and non-victims did not differ in that respect at age 23, as discussed under point A (and as evidenced in the .06 correlation in Fig. 15.5). So, even though there is a substantial correlation between level of contemporaneous harassment and depressive tendencies ($r = .49$), this relation is not linked to former victim/non-victim status.

Accordingly, one has to look more closely at the relation with the variables in the right-hand part of the figure. Generally, it seems reasonable to assume that there should be *no direct effect* (in a causal-analytic sense) of former victim/non-victim status on depressive tendencies that were mea-

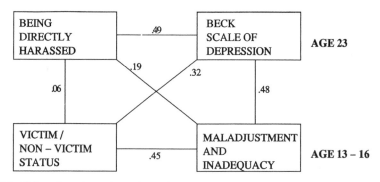

FIG. 15.5. Overview of relations (Pearson correlations) among key variables at age 13–16 and age 23 (n = 71).

sured at a much later point in time (7–10 years later). If there was an effect, it would much more likely be *an indirect one,* with marked, relatively immediate (direct) effects that were in some way "internalized" and manifested (also) later in life as a predisposition to react with depressive tendencies.

Applying this reasoning to the data in Fig. 15.5, one would expect that most of the effect of victim/non-victim status on depressive tendencies was mediated via the concurrent variable Maladjustment and inadequacy. Such a mechanism would also largely account for the cross-lagged correlation of .32, making it close to zero in a path-analytic framework. This is actually what happens if the Beck scale is regressed on Maladjustment and inadequacy and victim/non-victim status: The cross-lagged standardized path coefficient becomes almost zero ($\beta = .13$, n.s.) whereas the path from Maladjustment and inadequacy is .42 (and highly significant).

The pattern of relations discussed thus far is certainly consistent with an assumption of an indirect causal effect of victimization in school on later depressive tendencies. Before drawing conclusions along these lines, however, one should also consider the possibility of a causal relationship in the opposite direction, from feelings of maladjustment and depression to victimization/harassment.

Although there are indications (as discussed earlier) that early psychological characteristics of a boy (in addition to physical weakness and child rearing variables) affect his probability of being victimized, the present data covering somewhat later periods and more anxiety/depression-related characteristics do not seem to support the idea of a causal relationship in this direction. In particular, since the Maladjustment and inadequacy variable (a proxy for depressive tendencies) shows considerable continuity with later depressive tendencies, it would seem intuitively reasonable to expect some degree of continuity also for the victimization/harassment variable (rather than the obtained zero-correlation), *if* there was a causal relation as postulated.

In contrast, the substantial continuity of the depression-related variables can be partly accounted for by an "indirect-effect" mechanism, as discussed in the foregoing, if we assume that victimization/harassment exerts a causal influence on the depression-related variables. It should be added that part of the continuity of the depression-related variables is probably explained by the continuing influence of other factors not included in the model.

All in all, the above results support the view *that the major causal influence is from victimization to depression-related variables, and not the other way around.* This interpretation is strengthened by a consideration of the nature of the peer relationships concerned. As mentioned, the victims tend to be physically weaker than their peers and are typically non-aggressive and non-provocative. Accordingly, it is very reasonable to

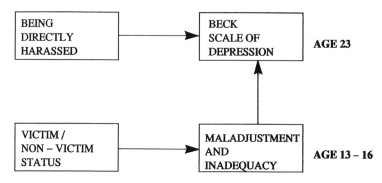

FIG. 15.6.   Major causal relations among key variables at age 13-16 and age 23.

assume that they simply fall prey to harassment and dominance on the part of other, more aggressive students (bullies, in particular). And naturally, the humiliating and hostile treatment they are exposed to is likely to affect their self-evaluations and levels of anxiety/depression.

Further support of this reasoning is gained through examination of the relation between degree of victimization in Grades 6–9 and level of depressive tendencies at age 23 *within the victim group.* In this group, there was a substantial .54 ($p<.02$) correlation of degree of victimization with later depressive tendencies. Although it is possible that chance has played some role in producing the amazingly high correlation in the relatively homogeneous victim group, it should be emphasized that the results was not due to one or two extreme outliers; the scatterplot displayed an essentially linear and fairly regular pattern. This within-group correlation becomes even more impressive when one considers the fact that the two variables involved were derived from completely different sources of data—peer ratings and self-reports, respectively—thereby precluding the possibility that the correlation was inflated due to potentially shared method variance.

Taken together, all of this evidence indicates a pattern of causal relations among the variables as portrayed in Fig. 15.6. Victimization in school (victim status) leads concurrently to heightened depression-related tendencies that continue to be elevated 7–10 years later, even though the former victims are no more harassed than their controls at that point in time.[2] Depressive tendencies at age 23 are also affected by concurrent (adult) harassment but the degree of such harassment is not related to earlier victim status. It is worth noting that the correlation between the two adult measures may be somewhat inflated due to shared method variance, since they were both derived from self reports.

---

[2]The relations among the variables in the figure remained essentially the same also when the temperamental and child rearing variables in Fig. 15.3 and 15.4 were included in the analyses.

It should be added that an analysis parallel to that presented above was conducted with Beck's depression scale replaced by Rosenberg's scale of global self esteem and the Maladjustment and inadequacy scale exchanged with a scale of poor self esteem in Grades 6-9. The latter a priori defined scale consisted of nine items, five of which were included in the factorially derived Maladjustment and inadequacy scale (see Appendix in Olweus, 1978). The correlation of this scale with scores on the Rosenberg scale collected 7-10 years later was .56, whereas its correlation with concurrent victim/non-victim status was .36 (and the cross-lagged correlation of victim/non-victim status with the Rosenberg scale was .26, as previously reported). The relations among these variables were thus very similar to those displayed in Fig. 15.5 and were given a very similar interpretation.

C. *Non-Deviant Development on Several Dimensions.* On several adult dimensions on which it would be natural to expect differences between former victims and non-victims, considering their situation and characteristics in Grades 6-9, there were basically no differences. These dimensions included social anxiety (shyness, social-evaluative concerns), emotionality-worrying, different forms of aggression/assertiveness and aggression inhibition, and neuroticism (several of these dimensions correlated .40 to .50 with similar dimensions assessed in Grades 6-9). In contrast to the findings from Grade 9, the victims also did not have elevated levels of the stress hormone adrenaline (in spite of a correlation around .70 for the group as a whole between adrenaline levels at age 16 and 23, respectively), nor were they more introverted than the controls at 23. In agreement with expectations, however, the former victims had been somewhat less involved in criminal activities, both according to self reports and official records.

Summary of Study 2 and Major Implications

Methodological Adequacy. Before summarizing the findings of this study and pointing out major implications, I emphasize that the results were based on a relatively limited number of subjects. This fact should make us regard the conclusions to be drawn as somewhat tentative and in need of replication. At the same time, it should be underscored that the findings obtained presented a conceptually very meaningful and coherent pattern, in addition to being quite consistent across two distinct but theoretically and empirically related "ultimate" dependent variables, depressive tendencies and global self esteem. Also, the victim group was well delineated and its members had no doubt been exposed to fairly severe bullying and harassment for several years. Finally, the quality of the data was quite good according to standard psychometric criteria. These aspects of the study should lead to an increased confidence in the conclusions arrived at.

I want to add that the present analyses comprise a large proportion but not all of the data collected on this sample at age 23. Accordingly, it is possible that the "final" picture of the victims as young adults may deviate somewhat from that presented herein.

Lack of Continuity in Victimization.   A major finding was the absence of a relation between victim/non-victim status in Grades 6–9 and the highly reliable measure of harassment at age 23. The retrospective data showed the lack of correlation not to be an effect of denial/repression. In all probability, this *lack of continuity is an indication that the subjects,* after having left school, *had considerably greater freedom to choose their own social and physical environments.* In this way, the former victims had succeeded in escaping later harassment and victimization to approximately the same degree as their peers. This finding is, of course, encouraging, though our reactions should be mitigated by the lasting negative effects of earlier victimization, discussed in the following.

It should be added that the lack of continuity with victimization as measured at age 23 does not preclude the possibility that a former school victim could have an increased probability of being victimized under more circumscribed conditions, for example, in a marital relationship.

Situation-Related Strain rather than Personality Disturbance.   Another finding was that the former victims had "recovered" or scored in the normal range (like the controls) on several "internalizing" dimensions at age 23: They were no longer particularly anxious, inhibited, introverted, or nonassertive in interactions with others, nor were there indications that they had elevated stress levels. This pattern of results implies that *a good deal of the anxiety-related/internalizing characteristics of the victims* as measured during the school years *were situationally determined,* that is, relatively transient effects of the harsh treatment they were exposed to from aggressive peers.

A related implication is that a considerable proportion of the school victims cannot be characterized as having a "disturbed" or pathological personality. As already discussed, boys who get victimized are likely to have certain pre-victim characteristics, but many of them would probably function reasonably well if they were not exposed to repeated bullying and harassment over long periods of time. The elevated levels of anxiety and stress that we could register in the school years, were thus more a reflection of situation-related strain than of a relatively permanent personality disturbance.

In a similar vein, the "normal" adult outcome with regard to peer relationships and social interaction (according to self-reports) would seem to suggest that *the victims were not lacking in "social skills"* (e.g., Asher &

Coie, 1990; Ladd, 1985). Or, if they were deficient in such skills in the school period, these problems were not serious enough to prevent normal development in the area of social interaction in young adulthood.

Implications for Intervention. All of this evidence supports the view that *intervention efforts* in this domain should not be primarily *focused on changing* the reactions and characteristics of the victims but rather on changing *the behavior and attitudes of the social environment,* in particular the aggressive bullies. This orientation has guided the development of the successful intervention program against bully/victim problems in Norway, the effects of which have been evaluated in 42 schools in Bergen (Olweus, 1991, 1992, in press). Such a view does not preclude installment of intervention measures specifically designed for the victims: Such measures may help the victims make the harassment stop more quickly and may have good effects on their self perceptions.

A further implication of the preceding analyses is that the *high stability of individual differences in victimization over the junior high school years* is largely *a reflection of the stability of the social environment* (Olweus, 1977, 1979, 1980b), in particular the continuing influence of aggressive bullies and their followers. Although it has been shown that it is possible to achieve dramatic reductions in bully/victim problems with a suitable intervention program[3] (Olweus, 1991, 1992), and it is my conviction that such problems should largely be solved through a "restructuring of the social environment" (Olweus, 1991), the results obtained suggest that *a well-planned change of environment may sometimes be helpful to victims.* Among other things, victims might benefit from interacting with peer groups other than their own class, for example, in connection with sports or musical activities. Also, if an identified bully/victim problem in a class does not seem to be solvable, in spite of serious efforts, it may be useful as a last resort to move the victim to a different class or even school. It must be stressed, however, that such changes of environment should be carefully planned to be successful (Olweus, 1986, 1992).

The Negative Long-Term Effects. Even though the former victims seemed to function well in a number of respects as young adults, there were two dimensions on which they clearly differed from their peers, depressive tendencies and poor self esteem. The elevated levels on these dimensions can

---

[3]The "package" related to the intervention program against bully/victim problems consists of a questionnaire for the measurement of bully/victim problems, a copy of a small book *Bullying at school — what we know and what we can do* (Olweus, 1986, 1992) aimed at teachers and parents, and a 20-minute video (with English subtitles). These copyrighted materials have certain restrictions on their use. For more information, please write to the author at the University of Bergen, Oysteinsgate 3, N-5007 Bergen, Norway.

be interpreted as a consequence of earlier persistent victimization that had marked effects on the self system or personality of some proportion of the young victims; in all probability, they had gradually come to *take over the social environment's* (the dominant peers') *negative evaluations* of themselves as worthless and inadequate individuals (cf. Olweus, 1991, p. 423). These negative self perceptions, which also imply an *increased vulnerability to depressive reactions,* tended to become internalized and "cemented" within the individuals. From a different perspective, one can say that these perceptions and reaction tendencies had gradually become "functionally autonomous" (Allport, 1937), "living a life of their own," independent of their original, immediate causes.

We do not have data available to assess accurately how serious the depression-related problems of the victim group were from a clinical point of view. It is reasonable to believe, however, that they were serious enough to deprive some proportion of the victims of considerable joy and satisfaction with their lives, and generally, to worsen the quality of their existence. In addition, it is quite possible that the full consequences of the increased vulnerability of the victims will become evident only at a somewhat later age. These results make it *urgent* for school authorities and parents *to intervene* against bully/victim problems not only to stop current suffering of the victims (Olweus, 1991, 1992) but *also because of the long-term sequelae* for these individuals (as well as for the bullies; see Olweus, 1991).

Peer Rejection as a Predictor of Later Outcomes.   It is also natural to connect the findings of the present study with some of the results and research issues from the peer relationships literature. In this area, much attention has been directed to the phenomenon of peer rejection, in part on the assumption that peer rejection may have a causal effect on later adjustment, for example, by making rejected-aggressive children more delinquent or criminal than peers who are aggressive but not rejected (Asher & Coie, 1990; Parker & Asher, 1987).

There have been conducted very few longitudinal studies in which it has been possible to test this assumption adequately (see Kupersmidt, Coie, & Dodge, 1990; Olweus, 1989). The empirical evidence obtained so far, however, has produced mixed or negative results (Kupersmidt et al., 1990). My own study (Olweus, 1989), for example, failed to show that aggressive-rejected (unpopular) Grade 6–9 boys had a worse long-term outcome than their nonrejected aggressive peers. In one of the two samples analyzed ($n_1 = 276$ and $n_2 = 195$), there were even indications that aggressive-rejected boys were better off than their nonrejected counterparts. In this study, the long-term outcome was indexed by number of officially registered criminal offenses up to age 23.

Whereas much attention has been directed to the connection between rejection and aggression, recent peer relationships research has shown very little interest in the combination of rejection and social withdrawal — with a few notable exceptions, such as Rubin and his colleagues (e.g., Rubin & Lollis, 1988; Rubin et al., 1989; Rubin et al., 1990). In part, this may stem from the fact that it is only quite recently that the heterogeneity of the rejected group has been documented within this research tradition (e.g., French, 1988). Considering the present data from this perspective, our results clearly indicate that rejection in the form of victimization combined with social withdrawal and passivity has negative long-term effects on depressive tendencies and self esteem. It would seem that the victimization/rejection-withdrawal complex is a promising area for future research.

The Causal Role of Victimization in Depression/Suicide. It can be added that victimization/harassment by peers in school appears to be a factor whose causal role in the development of depressive reaction patterns in adolescents and young adults has been much neglected. Since it is known that a considerable proportion of young people who actually commit or attempt to commit suicide are depressed (e.g., Sudak, Ford, & Rosforth, 1984), it is by extension likely that *victimization/harassment may also be an important casual factor in suicidal behavior.* Incidentally, it is worth noting that the nationwide campaign against bully/victim problems in Norwegian schools, launched by the Ministry of Education, was initiated after it had been discovered that three 10- to 14-year-old boys had committed suicide as a consequence of severe bullying and harassment by peers (Olweus, 1991).

ACKNOWLEDGMENTS

The research reported was supported in various periods by grants from the William T. Grant Foundation, the Swedish Delegation for Social Research (DSF), and the Norwegian Council for Social Research for which the author is grateful.

REFERENCES

Achenbach, I.M. (1978). The child behavior profile: I. Boys Aged 6–11. *Journal of Consulting and Clinical Psychology, 46,* 478–488.

Allport, G.W. (1937). The functional autonomy of motives. *American Journal of Psychology, 50,* 141–156.

Asendorf, J.B. (1989). Shyness as a final common pathway for two different kinds of inhibition. *Journal of Personality and Social Psychology, 57,* 481–492.

Asendorf, J.B. (1990). The development of inhibition during childhood: Evidence for situational specificity and a two-factor model. *Developmental Psychology, 26,* 721–730.

Asher, S.R., & Coie, J.D. (Eds.) (1990). *Peer rejection in childhood.* New York: Cambridge University Press.

Beck, A.T., Ward, C.H., Mendelson, M., Mock, J., & Erbaugh, J. (1961). An inventory for measuring depression. *Archives of General Psychiatry, 4,* 561–571.

Becker, W.C. (1964). Consequences of different kinds of parental discipline. In M.L. Hoffman & L.W. Hoffman (Eds.), *Review of child development research* (Vol. 1). New York: Russell Sage Foundation.

Bell, R.Q. (1968). A reinterpretation of the direction of effects in studies of socialization. *Psychological Review, 75,* 81–95.

Block, J.H., & Block, J. (1979). The role of ego-control and ego resiliency in the organization of behavior. In W.A. Collins (Ed.), *Minnesota Symposia on Child Psychology* (Vol. 13, pp. 39–101). New York: Lawrence Erlbaum Associates.

Buss, A.H. (1980). *Self-consciousness and social anxiety.* San Francisco: Freeman.

Cohen, J. (1977). *Statistical power analysis for the behavioral sciences.* New York: Academic Press.

Eysenck, H.J., & Eysenck, S.B.G. (1968). *The manual to the Eysenck personality inventory,* San Diego, CA: Educational and Industrial Testing Service.

French, D.C. (1988). Heterogeneity of peer-rejected boys: Aggressive and nonaggressive subtypes. *Child Development, 59,* 976–985.

Hetherington, E.M., & Martin, B. (1979). Family interaction. In H.C. Quay & J.S. Werry (Eds.), *Psychopathological disorders of childhood.* New York: Wiley.

Hewitt, L.E., & Jenkins, R.L. (1946). *Fundamental patterns of maladjustment: The dynamics of their origin.* Illinois: D.H. Green.

Kagan, J., Reznick, S.J., Clarke, C., Snidman, N., & Garcia-Coll, C. (1984). Behavioral inhibition to the unfamiliar. *Child Development, 55,* 2212–2225.

Kohn, M. (1977). *Social competence, symptoms and underachievement in childhood. A longitudinal perspective.* Washington, DC: Winston & Sons.

Kupersmidt, J.B., Coie, J.D., & Dodge, K.A. (1990). The role of poor peer relationships in the development of disorder. In S.R. Asher & J.D. Coie (Eds.), *Peer rejection in childhood* (pp. 217–249). New York: Cambridge University Press.

Ladd, G.W. (1985). Documenting the effect of social skill training with children: Process and outcome assessment. In B.H. Schneider, K.H. Rubin, & J.E. Ledigham (Eds.), *Children's peer relations: Issues in assessment and intervention* (pp. 243–269). New York: Springer.

Levy, D.H. (1943). *Maternal overprotection.* New York: Columbia University Press.

Martin, B. (1975). Parent-child relations. In F.D. Horowitz, E.M., Hetherington, S. Scarr-Salapatek, & G.M. Siegel (Eds.), *Review of child development research* (Vol. 4). Chicago: Chicago University Press.

Olweus, D. (1973). *Hackkycklingar och översittare: Forskning om skolmobbning.* Stockholm: Almqvist & Wiksell.

Olweus, D. (1977). Aggression and peer acceptance in adolescent boys: Two short-term longitudinal studies of ratings. *Child Development, 48,* 1301–1313.

Olweus, D. (1978). *Aggression in the schools: Bullies and whipping boys.* Washington, DC: Hemisphere (Wiley).

Olweus, D. (1979). Stability of aggressive reaction patterns in males: A review. *Psychological Bulletin, 86,* 852–875.

Olweus, D. (1980a). Familial and temperamental determinants of aggressive behavior in adolescent boys: A causal analysis. *Developmental Psychology, 16,* 644–660.

Olweus, D. (1980b). The consistency issue in personality psychology revisited—with special reference to aggression. *British Journal of Social and Clinical Psychology, 19,* 377–390.

Olweus, D. (1984). Stability in aggressive and withdrawn, inhibited behavior patterns. In R.M. Kaplan, V.J. Konecni, & R.W. Novaco (Eds.), *Aggression in children and youth* (pp. 104–137). The Hague, The Netherlands: Nijhoff.

Olweus, D. (1985). 80 000 barn er innblandet i mobbing. *Norsk Skoleblad* (Olso, Norway), *35*, 18–23.

Olweus, D. (1986). *Mobbning — vad vi vet och vad vi kan göra.* Stockholm: Liber.

Olweus, D. (April, 1989). *Peer relationship problems: Conceptual issues and a successful intervention program against bully/victim problems.* Paper presented at the biannial meeting of the Society for Research in Child Development, Kansas City, USA.

Olweus, D. (1991). Bully/victim problems among schoolchildren: Basic facts and effects of a schoolbased intervention program. In D. Pepler & K.H. Rubin (Eds.), *The development and treatment of childhood aggression* (pp. 411–448). Hillsdale, NJ: Lawrence Erlbaum Associates.

Olweus, D. (1992). *Bullying at school — what we know and what we can do.* Book manuscript.

Olweus, D. (in press). Bullying among schoolchildren: Intervention and prevention. In R.D. Peters, R.J. McMahon, & V.L. Quincy (Eds.), *Aggression and violence throughout the life span.*

Olweus, D., Mattsson, 'A., Schalling, D., & Löw, H. (1980). Testosterone, aggression, physical, and personality dimensions in normal adolescent males. *Psychosomatic Medicine, 42,* 253–269.

Olweus, D., Mattsson, 'A, Schalling, D., & Löw, H. (1988). Circulating testosterone levels and aggression in adolescent males: A causal analysis. *Psychosomatic Medicine, 50,* 261–272.

Parker, J.G., & Asher, S.R. (1987). Peer relations and later personal adjustment: Are low-accepted children at risk? *Psychological Bulletin, 102,* 357–389.

Perry, D.G., Kusel, S.J., & Perry, L.C. (1988). Victims of peer aggression. *Development Psychology, 24,* 807–814.

Peterson, D.R. (1961). Behavior problems of middle childhood. *Journal of Consulting Psychology, 25,* 205–209.

Rosenberg, M. (1979). *Conceiving the self.* New York: Basic Books.

Rubin, K.H., & Lollis, S. (1988). Peer relationships, social skills, and infant attachment: A continuity model. In J. Belsky & T. Nezworski (Eds.), *Clinical implications of attachment* (pp. 219–252). Hillsdale, NJ: Lawrence Erlbaum Associates.

Rubin, K.H., Hymel, S., LeMare, L.J., & Rowden, L. (1989). Children experiencing social difficulties: Sociometric neglect reconsidered. *Canadian Journal of Behavioral Science, 21,* 94–111.

Rubin, K.H., LeMare, L.J., & Lollis, S. (1990). Social withdrawal in childhood: Developmental pathways to peer rejection. In S.R. Asher & J.D. Coie (Eds.), *Peer rejection in childhood* (pp. 217–249). New York: Cambridge University Press.

Rutter, M., Tizard, J., & Whitmore, K. (1970). *Education, health, and behavior.* London: Longman.

Schaefer, E.S. (1971). Development of hierarchical, configurational models for parent and child behavior. In J.P. Hill (Ed.), *Minnesota symposium on child psychology* (Vol. 5). Minneapolis: University of Minnesota Press.

Sudak, H.S., Ford, A.B., & Rosforth, N.B. (1984). *Suicide in the young.* Boston: John Wright.

Author Index

Subject Index

S

Scaffolding: 123, 124
Security-Insecurity: 54, 65, 77, 109, 110,
    111, 112, 113, 118, 295, 307, 309
Self: 7, 12, 55, 58, 173, 291, 2922, 293, 306,
    338
  concept: 53, 56, 58, 59, 60, 65, 240,
    242, 243, 246, 248, 249, 250,
    251, 252
  esteem: 8, 240, 242, 244, 255, 283, 307,
    325, 331, 335, 337
  evaluations: 237, 239, 249, 298, 334
  perceptions: 56, 58, 59, 60, 61, 117, 170,
    190, 205, 238, 240, 242, 244, 245,
    247, 249, 253, 255, 257, 308, 309,
    310
Sensitivity: 54, 61, 62, 135, 294, 295
Separation: 90, 94, 104
Sex Differences: 154, 166, 170, 231
Shyness: 3, 4, 9, 12, 13, 14, 21, 45, 49, 50,
    51, 52, 53, 54, 55, 56, 61, 62, 68, 69,
    71, 72, 73, 74, 75, 76, 77, 81, 82,
    106, 136, 151, 152, 157, 172, 177,
    178, 186, 189, 190, 191, 192, 193,
    196, 199, 200, 202, 203, 204, 205,
    206, 207, 215, 224, 229, 230, 242,
    246, 265, 305, 316, 317, 319, 329,
    335
  sex differences in: 49, 51, 56, 57, 58, 59,
    60, 61, 62, 63, 64, 65, 66, 67, 68, 69,
    72, 77, 107
Smiles: 36, 37, 38, 91, 92, 104
Social Support: 125, 126, 131, 133, 138,
    139, 14, 141, 243, 245, 296, 297
Social Withdrawal: 3, 4, 5, 7, 8, 9, 10, 11,
    12, 14, 15, 81, 107, 117, 118, 119,
    120, 121, 122, 123, 124, 126, 128,
    129, 130, 131, 132, 133, 134, 135,
    136, 137, 138, 139, 140, 141, 142,
    152, 157, 170, 171, 172, 199, 201,
    215, 216, 217, 218, 219, 220, 221,
    222, 223, 224, 225, 226, 227, 228,
    229, 230, 231, 232, 237, 238, 239,
    240, 241, 242, 243, 244, 245, 246,
    247, 248, 249, 250, 251, 252, 253,
    254, 255, 256, 257, 265, 278, 279,
    291, 292, 293, 294, 297, 298, 299,
    300, 302, 303, 304, 305, 306, 309,
    310, 317, 319, 339

Social:
  acceptance: 59, 60
  cognition: 5, 6, 7, 195, 201, 202, 203,
    222
  competence and skills: 12, 14, 50,
    55, 56, 58, 59, 60, 64, 65, 72,
    74, 75, 118, 119, 124, 127,
    130, 133, 134, 137, 140, 195,
    201, 202, 204, 205, 206, 238,
    250, 251, 252, 277, 287, 291,
    292, 295, 298, 306, 336, 337
  interaction: 6, 7, 14, 189, 265,
    274, 286, 287, 293, 317, 318,
    319, 336
  isolation: 9, 10, 11, 14, 81, 82, 83,
    84, 97, 238, 241, 274, 275,
    297, 301, 302, 307, 329,
    330
  perceptions: 215, 216
  relationships: 76, 190, 191, 206, 243,
    279, 284, 287, 292, 308
  schemas: 222, 223, 224, 225, 226, 227,
    231
Sociability: 21, 50, 102, 109, 123, 152,
    153, 154, 155, 156, 158, 160,
    170, 194, 195, 199, 201, 279,
    280, 300, 317
Sociometry: 10, 11, 81, 82, 111, 135,
    206
Solitude: 4, 7, 12, 13, 14
Speech: 177, 178, 183, 185, 186, 206, 207,
    271, 272
Stress: 125, 126, 130, 131, 133, 138, 139,
    140, 141, 170, 193, 256, 257, 296,
    297, 299, 336

T

Temperament: 14, 19, 20, 21, 26, 27,
    31, 33, 34, 38, 39, 40, 41, 46,
    47, 66, 81, 82, 83, 84, 85, 87,
    88, 90, 91, 92, 93, 94, 103, 117,
    118, 120, 152, 155, 156, 157,
    169, 172, 173, 177, 178, 179,
    181, 183, 265, 266, 274, 279,
    282, 288, 295, 297, 298, 321,
    322, 323, 324, 326, 327
Timidity: 21, 55, 170, 191
Traits: 31, 50, 81, 229